3/13/20

D1153928

IN GOOD FAITH

OSPREY
PUBLISHING

DEDICATION

To a good school friend
Frank de Planta

IN GOOD FAITH

A History of the Vietnam War
Volume 1: 1945–65

SERGIO MILLER

OSPREY PUBLISHING
Bloomsbury Publishing Plc
PO Box 883, Oxford, OX1 9PL, UK
1385 Broadway, 5th Floor, New York, NY 10018, USA
E-mail: info@ospreypublishing.com
www.ospreypublishing.com

OSPREY is a trademark of Osprey Publishing Ltd

First published in Great Britain in 2020

© Sergio Miller, 2020

Sergio Miller has asserted his right under the Copyright, Designs and Patents Act, 1988,
to be identified as Author of this work.

All rights reserved. No part of this publication may be reproduced or transmitted in any form
or by any means, electronic or mechanical, including photocopying, recording, or any information
storage or retrieval system, without prior permission in writing from the publishers.

A catalog record for this book is available from the British Library.

ISBN: HB 9781472838469; PB 9781472838476; eBook 9781472838452;
ePDF 9781472838438; XML 9781472838445

20 21 22 23 24   10 9 8 7 6 5 4 3 2 1

Maps by Bounford.com
Index by Zoe Ross

Typeset by Deanta Global Publishing Services, Chennai, India
Printed and bound in Great Britain by CPI (Group) UK Ltd, Croydon CR0 4YY

Front cover: An American H-21 helicopter hovers above Army of the Republic of Vietnam soldiers
in a combat zone, 1962. (Photo by Larry Burrows/The LIFE Picture Collection via Getty Images)

Back cover: US helicopters carry South Vietnamese troops into action against Viet Cong positions,
1964. (Larry Burrows/The LIFE Picture Collection via Getty Images)

Osprey Publishing supports the Woodland Trust, the UK's leading woodland conservation charity.

To find out more about our authors and books visit www.ospreypublishing.com. Here you will
find extracts, author interviews, details of forthcoming events and the option to sign up for our
newsletter.

CONTENTS

LIST OF MAPS

Chapter 1

THE SERPENT IN EDEN, 1945–60

Yoshijiro Umezu, Chief of the Army General Staff, bowed very low, as well he might. Three weeks previously his country had twice been visited by a divine, destructive wind beyond the imagination of man. It blew in from the east and was released from the bellies of two silver aircraft flying high above the clouds, barely visible except to an attentive observer. Imperial Japan had vowed that the flower of her youth would stop the relentless advance of the American foe. Even on the verge of defeat and faced with the imminent invasion of the home islands, the Imperial Japanese Headquarters plotted insane, fantastic attacks involving 6,500 kamikaze pilots and 5,000 suicide boats to halt the invaders. If it came to it, the generals concluded, 100 million Japanese should sacrifice their lives and charge the enemy with swords and bayonets.

America gave her answer with the thunderclap of two atomic bombs. Metro-Goldwyn-Mayer celebrated this novel way of annihilating entire populations by publishing a full page advertisement of a bikini-clad model called Blanca Welter – Miss Anatomic Bomb – enjoying "solar energy" in an "unexplosive moment," possibly the most vulgar documented response to the sudden, violent deaths of 150,000 human beings.[1] Faced with annihilation, Emperor Hirohito made his "jeweled voice" capitulation speech to the nation, in fact a broadcast of a barely intelligible pre-recorded statement spoken in archaic Japanese. The previous day, Japan had been attacked by the biggest air raid of the Pacific War involving over 1,000 aircraft dropping conventional but no less destructive bombs. An earlier mass leaflet drop revealing the Emperor's secret decision to surrender had raised fears of civil unrest. This last psychological operation, coupled with the unstoppable Soviet advance through Manchuria, sealed the capitulation. Later detractors of the use of atomic weapons would ignore that, even in the very last hours of the war, Japan had to be pummeled into surrendering. The biggest shock of the atomic bomb was just how un-shocked contemporaries were by its use.

An 11-strong Japanese surrender delegation boarded the USS *Missouri* anchored in Tokyo Bay on September 2, 1945. They were led by the bespectacled Foreign Minister, Mamoru Shigemitsu, dressed incongruously in tails, white gloves, and a top hat. His left hand gripped a walking stick, a curiously emaciated symbol of state propping his missing leg. General Umezu, with downturned mouth, wore his customary peaked cap, three rows of medals, and riding boots with spurs. He looked, like the rest of the party, drawn and beaten.

The surrender ceremony lasted less than half an hour, watched in silence by the entire ship's company and 300 journalists and photographers. MacArthur led the proceedings but Fleet Admiral Nimitz made sure his name was also on the instrument of surrender (with the distinction that he was signing on behalf of the American nation, whereas MacArthur was signing in his capacity as Supreme Commander Allied Forces). Immediately behind the table on which the surrender documents would be signed, in single rank, were representatives of all the other countries with a stake in the brief and now vanquished Japanese empire: the old colonial powers, Britain, France, and the Netherlands, as well as the awakened giants, China and the Soviet Union. Under the terms of the surrender, only four of the eight nations ranged against Japan were legally counted as an Allied Power; the remainder were parties to the surrender. The French representative found himself relegated to the second rank of powers, along with minnows like New Zealand.[2]

Following the short ceremony there could be no doubt that the emperor god had been brought back down to earth, and a new deity resided on the summit of Mount Fuji. America now found herself the de jure ruler of an Asian country, her western border stretched across five thousand miles of ocean and now lying on the rim of the most populous continent in the world. Five years later and using a football metaphor, Secretary of State Dean Acheson would call this America's new "defense line" against a fresh enemy – communism. The line snaked all the way from northern Japan to the southernmost islands of the Philippines, bypassing Korea with unintended consequences, and stopping short of the remaining European colonies of Southeast Asia, including French Indochina. Like great military irruptions of the past it left the conquerors both bewildered and fascinated by their new possessions. This was the first important consequence of the war in the Pacific.

For the next four decades, facing down the Soviet Union became the monolithic, unifying theme of American foreign policy, and its abiding metaphor was the race: in the development of new weapons, in space, in industrial output, and on sports tracks. Its constant fear was nuclear Armageddon. The better world that millions had fought for – if not a postwar Eden then at least a place rid of the manifest evils of nationalist and totalitarian governments – had proved a child's fancy. A serpent had entered Eden and its name was communism.

The speed with which this happened forced a complete reversal of policy: if Moscow was going to play the discordant note to Washington's fiddle, then it was time to summon the marching bands. This hyperinflation of communism had profound consequences on American culture and self-image. Americans fought the Japanese to avenge a heinous wrong, trading war crime for war crime, but no American would have defined the essential character of "Americaness" as "anti-Japanese." Despite the horrors perpetrated by the Nazi regime, the average GI held no strong feelings against the average German soldier. The "lousy Kraut" was a figure from the movies, and Patton's crude characterization of Germans was not shared by his Third Army, which just wanted to get the job done and come home. But communism, invariably spelled with a foreboding capital "C," was absolutely different. The dreary ruminations of Karl Marx, read nowhere outside university campuses, became the words of the devil. Communism grew the horns of religious evil, not just political wrong or economic stupidity, threatening the very beacon on the hill the Puritans had first lit.

The immediate postwar tension was and would remain in Europe. This was where vast armies still faced each other across Churchill's iron curtain. But a second front also opened in Asia, where the end of hostilities brought to the surface the many intractable problems exposed by the receding tide of Japanese imperialism. And it was here that America faced in MacArthur's colorful phrase, "a hard, monolithic block of China and Russia with no crevices in it."[3]

All the principal actors viewed the postwar settlement through the lens of their own ambitions and ideologies and the outcome was always going to be more wars. For the French and Dutch, a return to the status quo ante was the logical resolution and they were at first surprised and then resistant when they discovered that the newly liberated peoples of their former colonies no longer welcomed them. "Better to the hell than to be colonized again," ran the slogan on the sides of buses in Java, where British tanks and Thunderbolt aircraft were used to suppress rebellion against the war-exhausted Dutch. The British themselves were divided, but the more reasonable voices foresaw the end of empire and sought to manage Britain's disengagement from her Far Eastern colonies with equity and dignity. Australia and New Zealand had no imperial designs (although both administered a handful of colonial possessions), but eyed developments to the north with wariness. The long indefensible coastline of Australia had been exposed by the Japanese. Could it happen again with the threat of now communist-inspired liberation movements? From Moscow's onion-domed towers, Stalin saw the opportunity to gobble former disputed territories, tidy borders, and spread Soviet influence across the Far East. Nationalist China, exhausted by civil war, parleyed with the Red Army, but the relation was strained and would eventually break down. For America, the undisputed victor, the war had been fought to replace totalitarianism with democracy and especially to champion self-determination, an ideal incompatible with the ambitions of the former colonial powers. Exhausted by this epic war, Washington first settled for Japan and then looked beyond to China, surrendering the complicated ethnic tangle of Southeast Asia to the Europeans. For the myriad native peoples who had witnessed the humiliation of European masters at the hands of an Asian army, the moment was ripe for revolt.

With historical hindsight, the war against Japan proved to be only one of several wars that would ravage East Asia over the subsequent decades. The vacuum of retreating colonialism, swiftly sucking in superpower competition, was one agent. But nationalism and sectarianism, internal power struggles and land-grabbing – much of which masqueraded as liberation movements – also played important roles. This sparking of general, region-wide conflagration was the second great consequence of the war.

For postwar generations of Western Europeans brought up to celebrate the Normandy landings, the sheer scale of America's Pacific struggle was as difficult to comprehend as it was remote. The armed forces of the United States conducted 78 amphibious landing operations over the course of the Pacific War, with the last launched at Sarangani Bay on July 12, 1945. By that summer, US forces had occupied the Ryukyu and Ret To island archipelagos just south of Japan and were within 200 miles of the mainland. It had been a supreme effort. For the average GI or marine who lived through the experience, vengeance was all that counted – and the ticket home. It took almost four years to defeat Japan because of the geographical scale of the war and the necessity to fight on a second European front. But mostly the war was prolonged because Japan opposed Western military competence with ideological fanaticism. This feature of the war would be repeated in every subsequent conflict in Southeast Asia where Western and Asian soldiers clashed.

America suffered 106,207 war dead in the Pacific War. Her main ally, the British, suffered 52,000 fatalities including 12,000 deaths in captivity. A further 86,838 British Indians added to this toll. By contrast, Japan suffered 2,133,915 military deaths (from 1937 to 1945). As a very rough measure, American forces were perhaps inflicting 20 times as many fatalities on their enemy. The "American way of war," at the very least, was a lethally effective way.

The Pacific War not only proved an industrially murderous business. It was also an especially dehumanizing experience for the front-line soldier. A popular wartime poster urged US servicemen to "Stay on the job until every murdering Jap is wiped out!" This invocation was observed with a bloodlust that matched the abhorrent ideology of the Japanese imperial forces. By the end of the war, soldiers returning from the Pacific theater had to make a customs declaration that they were not carrying body parts in their luggage. Never mind wiping out the Japanese: chop them to pieces and pickle them. When the remains of Japanese soldiers were repatriated from the Mariana Islands in the mid-1980s, it was discovered that six out of ten were missing their heads. The same phenomenon of headless (as well as toothless or earless) Japanese corpses was repeated across the Pacific islands.[4] Directives condemning and prohibiting the practice of collecting body parts as souvenirs were widely ignored.

When *Life* magazine, in May 1944, notoriously published the image of a young woman posing with the skull of a Japanese soldier sent to her by her naval officer boyfriend, there was pious public condemnation. But this censure missed the mood of a nation that viewed trophy skulls as legitimate spoils of war: "This is a good Jap – a dead one picked up on the New Guinea beach." Miss Nickerson, unfazed by the macabre gift, named the skull Tojo, after the Japanese general who ordered the attack on Pearl Harbor. The real Tojo kept his head long enough for it to be hung for war crimes in December 1948 (but not his teeth – a 22-year-old Navy dentist called Jack Mallory rectified this by providing him with a set of dentures, with the words "Remember Pearl Harbor" inscribed in Morse code, as a prank). The War Department objected to the *Life* magazine cover, not because it was morally repellent but because it endangered the lives of US servicemen who might themselves be turned into Japanese body-part trophies. The naval officer who sent the skull got away with a reprimand. As far as the *Life* editor was concerned, there was no wrongdoing. Did not the government's own propaganda describe the Japanese as rats, vermin, reptiles, apes, monkeys, bats, and insects? A Japanese skull was just one more animal trophy.

This sense of racial superiority over the yellow, Asiatic enemy, engendered in the Pacific and fortified in the Korean War, would multiply with frightful results in the Vietnam War. The tragic paradox of America as idealistic guarantor of liberty, but acting as out-of-control mobster, was the third great consequence of the Pacific War. Americans wanted to remember the war by the heroic, if staged, image of marines hoisting the Stars and Stripes on Mount Suribachi, not by film of American soldiers shooting prone Japanese prisoners and hacking them with bayonets, footage that would only emerge 50 years after the conclusion of the Pacific War.[5]

—————————

The country least willing to accept the new political order was France – not so much a nation as an idea that emerged from the Second World War in a mess, bankrupted, but with undimmed imperial ambitions. Restoring *la gloire française*, "French glory," quickened the pulse of every Frenchman, communists as much as Gaullists. Even as other European countries were preparing to unwind their colonial histories, France's soon-to-be Fourth Republic embarked on a suicidal project to retain her overseas possessions and the first colony to challenge this vision was French Indochina. When traveler Pierre Barrelon visited Indochina in 1893, for the benefit of readers of the popular weekly journal *Le Tour Du Monde*, he wrote: "*Le cap Saint-Jacques est en vue, c'est la terre française* ... [Cape Saint Jacques is in view, this is French land ...]" Half a century later any Frenchman would have agreed with him.

As early as September 1943, under the leadership of General Charles de Gaulle, a Committee of National Defense had been tasked with planning the recapture of Indochina.[6] For administrative purposes, modern Vietnam was then a colony divided along the lines of its three historic regions: northern Tonkin (*Bac Bo*), with Hanoi as capital; central Annam (*Trung Bo*), administered by Hue the imperial capital; and Cochin China (*Nam Bo*), served by cosmopolitan Saigon. The name "Viet-Nam" was a modern coinage. Vietnam's late imperial dynasties had governed a kingdom named "Nam-Viet," or "South Viet." Chinese invaders reversed the name to "Viet-Nam." The imperial court in Hue used the title "Dai Nam" or "Great South" up to the end of 1945. It was Northern nationalists, led by the communists, who revived the title "Viet-Nam," claiming it for their Democratic Republic of Vietnam. The French, of course, denied any such identity. When future Central Committee member Hoang Quoc Viet worked his passage on a French ship he proudly declared himself "a Vietnamese." But his fellow French sailors shot back "there was no such thing as Vietnam."[7]

Vietnamese history and identity had been defined by rivalry between these various ethnic blocs. Over a period of centuries, northern Vietnamese rulers had extended their rule over Annam and later Cochin China. This became the historic mission inherited by Vietnam's communist leaders. In their way stood the flotsam of a century of French colonialism that had four profound effects on Vietnamese society. In the political sphere, the imperial elite and mandarin classes had been demoralized and eventually dismantled. Economically, traditional land ownership had given way to industrial estates and a rapacious rentier culture. It was said that the workers were fertilizer for the rubber trees because they died in droves and were buried in the plantations. This was an inevitable consequence of Paris designating the Indochinese possessions a *colonie d'exploitation* (colony of economic exploitation). The corollary to this deracination was social upheaval with an urban working class and a growing and educated middle class, fed on a staple of French culture. Incongruously, Vietnamese were taught that their

MAP 1: FRENCH INDOCHINA BEFORE 1945

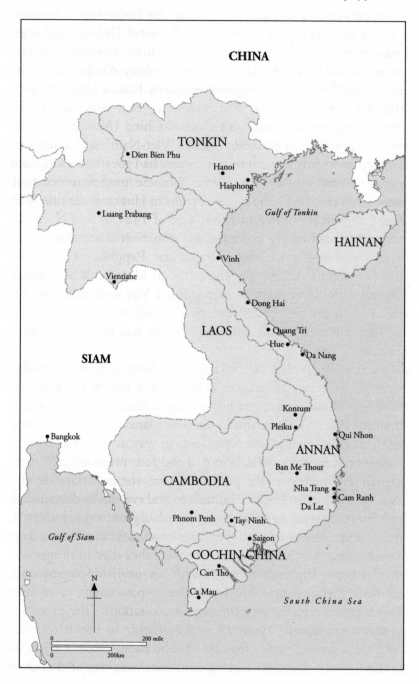

CHINA

TONKIN

• Dien Bien Phu

Hanoi
•

Haiphong
•

• Luang Prabang

Gulf of Tonkin

HAINAN

•Vinh

Vientiane
•

•Dong Hai

LAOS

•Quang Tri

Hue •

•Da Nang

SIAM

•Bangkok

Kontum
•

Pleiku •

•Qui Nhon

ANNAN

Ban Me Thout
•

CAMBODIA

Nha Trang
•

•Cam Ranh

Da Lat
•

Phnom Penh
•

•Tay Ninh

Gulf of Siam

•Saigon

COCHIN CHINA

Can Tho•

Ca Mau
•

South China Sea

N

| 0 | 200 mile |
| 0 | 200km |

ancestors were Gauls. Lastly, the division between north and south was reinforced by policies that favored local French caciques (party bosses) over national unity. Roosevelt was absolutely right when he observed "France has milked it [Vietnam] for 100 years."[8] Ho Chi Minh would quip that the French built more prisons than schools. A legacy of belle époque public buildings barely compensated for these pernicious outcomes. This was Graham Greene's Vietnam of urine and injustices, *Tabu* and *Illusion* "dirty magazines," and restaurants with grill entrances to ward off grenade attacks. *Life* correspondent Theodore H. White, with his deep knowledge of Indochina, sketched it best: "The splendid French boulevards ran like causeways over a basin of hate."[9]

France's humiliation in Indochina began in June 1940 when Japan demanded the closure of the Haiphong-Yunnan railway, used to supply nationalist forces in China. General George Catroux, the Governor-General and an officer steeped in the French colonial experience, had no option but to accede to the demand. For many months he had conducted a skillful diplomatic game with Tokyo in an effort to preserve the unity of the French colony, cognizant that his 90,000-strong Indochina Army was a paper force (just 14,500 were reliable Europeans).[10] Trapped by the feebleness of the French position, Catroux concocted the notion of a face-saving "defensive alliance" with Japan. His interlocutor, the Francophobe General Nishihara, an officer who had served as defense attaché in Paris, readily agreed to this proposal.[11] Two months later, on September 22, his Vichy government replacement, Vice Admiral Jean Decoux, endured greater humiliation. Faced with the ultimatum of an invasion, France agreed to the stationing of 6,000 Japanese troops on Vietnamese soil. A fiction of Japanese-French amity was preserved but the reality was that the Japanese 5th Division had effectively ousted Decoux as the supreme authority in the country. To sustain this false narrative, a neutered French garrison was allowed to remain in territories now forcibly co-opted into Japan's "Greater East Asian Prosperity Sphere."

Decoux proved an energetic governor-general, as keen at hunting down the "Bolshevist" common enemy, as building roads. But in making common cause with the Japanese he had manifested a supreme hypocrisy that infected every subsequent French colonial government. A façade of greater Vietnamese participation in government masked an iron determination to resist the twin threats of a total Japanese takeover, and Vietnamese nationalism. His government's policy, he explained at a secret meeting of *résidents supérieurs*, "the French ruling class," in Dalat, in July 1942, was to play all sides against each other: maintaining "as friendly relations with Japan as possible," while keeping lines of communication open with nationalist China and the Allies.[12] The Japanese similarly played a double-game, in public supporting the French authorities, but in private supporting subversive groups like the Hoa Hao Buddhists and the Cao Dai sect.

From the Japanese perspective, Vietnam's sects were little more than peculiar minority movements but they served the purpose of destabilizing French authority. The latter's full title was *Dai Dao Tam Ky Pho Do*, or The Great Religion of the Third Amnesty. Founded by the probably mad Ngo Van Chieu, the Cao Dai was an occult, syncretic movement borrowing from Christianity, Buddhism, and Taoism. Its saints included such diverse figures as Joan of Arc, the Chinese revolutionary Sun Yat-sen, and French author Victor Hugo. There were as many as two million Cao Daists, mainly in Tay Ninh Province northwest of Saigon, and they owed allegiance to a self-proclaimed pope, Pham Cong Tac, not the government. The Hoa Haos were formed by another religious fanatic, a Buddhist faith healer called Huynh Phu So who would be executed by the Viet Minh, turning the two movements into implacable enemies. There were perhaps one and a half million Hoa Haos, mostly settled in the Mekong Delta.

As the Pacific War expanded, tensions within Indochina multiplied. Gaullists and Vichy supporters schemed against each other, fomented by British intelligence. In the background, an austere wartime economy began to spiral out of control: the cost of a chicken jumped from just over half a piaster in 1939, to 18 piasters by 1945. The cost of a kilo of rice multiplied twentyfold.[13] In May 1941, across the Chinese border in Guangxi Province, Vietnamese exiles anticipating the end of French rule formed the *Viet Nam Doc Lap Dong Minh Hoy* (the "League for the Independence of Viet Nam"). This movement embraced a coalition of the veteran Indochinese Communist Party (*Viet Nam Cong San Dang* (ICP)); the rival Vietnamese Nationalist Party (*Viet Nam Quoc Dan Dang* (VNQDD)); and two smaller parties, the New Vietnam Party, and the Revolutionary Youth League. Nationalist Chinese attempts to manipulate the last three parties led to their loss of credibility and elevated the communists as the only genuine and independent Vietnamese nationalist cause. Internecine struggles then led to the dissolution of the ICP, leaving political leadership in the hands of a handful of armed men. Among the founding members of this resistance was the bone-thin, itinerant political activist later known to the world as Ho Chi Minh. His deputy was a former teacher and newspaper man with an interest in military history called Vo Nguyen Giap. The two had first met as students at the prestigious Lycée Quoc Hoc in Hue, the incubator of many of Vietnam's future leaders. Since those days both had suffered hardship, imprisonment, and in the case of Giap the loss of his wife, tortured in Hao Lo prison where American pilots would later be incarcerated. Giap was entrusted with establishing the first fighting cadres of a rudimentary guerrilla force, the Viet Minh (meaning "Light of the Land"). "Vo" meant "force" and "Giap" "shield," apt names for the future commander of Vietnam's communist forces.[14] With an insurgent war churning around him, he was not short of inspiration.

For the first four years, the Viet Minh achieved little militarily, partly because of the success of repressive measures introduced by Decoux. The Bureau de Statistique Militaires, the army's intelligence service, proved especially effective in this regard. The first formal Viet Minh units were not raised until December 1944 and no significant actions were taken before March 1945. All the while, however, a covert, rural-based infrastructure was being painstakingly built which would provide the foundation for future success.[15] This seeming inactivity was also driven by Ho's painful experience of the failed November 22, 1940 uprising against the

French: a half-cooked revolution, he concluded, was worse than no revolution at all.

The Viet Minh were not isolated during this period of gestation. Nationalist China provided some material support and sanctuary. American support – which marked the beginning of direct American involvement in Vietnam, and hence has a founding quality about it – started with the Roosevelt government through the Office of Strategic Services (OSS). The first mention of Ho Chi Minh was made in OSS files dating to 1940.[16] Secret arms shipments to the Viet Minh were made in 1942 and 1943, although there is some suggestion that the American suppliers were unclear who was actually receiving the weapons.[17]

The OSS was followed by bombers. In a foretaste of future raids, a sortie was conducted by 14th Air Force against Hanoi on April 12, 1943 that resulted in nearly 500 Vietnamese deaths, but only a handful of Japanese casualties. A raid on the docks of Saigon, on May 5, 1944, produced similar results.[18] It was not until 1945 that B-29 and Third Carrier Fleet raids began to inflict worthwhile damage on the Japanese war effort in Indochina, but these attacks also witnessed high numbers of civilian casualties, including Europeans. Pitching French Indochina into the hands of "Wild Bill" Donovan's OSS – rather than subsuming it within MacArthur's military command – had other important consequences. Donovan was strongly opposed to the French regime in Indochina, viewing Vichy colonialism as little better than Japanese imperialism. Anti-French sentiment imbued the Indochinese mission from the beginning, and would continue to complicate Franco-American relations for the next decade.

A Viet Minh irruption in northern Vietnam was finally precipitated by the unannounced Japanese attack on a weakened French garrison, code-named Operation *Meigo Sakusen*, on March 9, 1945. The coup was launched at precisely the same moment that Roosevelt was privately advising the French government there would be no Allied military action in French Indochina. De Gaulle had warned Roosevelt that the collapse of the Vichy government would encourage the Japanese government to "at least subjugate the French administration in the Union [of Indochina]," and so it came to pass.[19] By now, 5th Division had been replaced by 38th Army, commanded by Lieutenant General Yuitsu Tsuchihashi. The French were not entirely caught by surprise. Secret Japanese plans to seize control of French Indochina had been known to the French authorities for quite some time, thanks to American code-breaking.[20] Ever suspicious of Washington's motives, some had discounted this valuable intelligence.

Command of the colonial army in Hanoi fell under Lieutenant General Eugène Mordant. This old-fashioned general with an exuberant walrus moustache took the warnings seriously and prepared a contingency known as "Plan A 835/3." This would see French forces withdrawing to the hills of the Red River Delta to await reinforcement – a forlorn hope. Operation *Meigo Sakusen* unrolled irresistibly and ruthlessly. Despite spirited local French resistance, "Plan A" became a retreat. One of the more encouraging aspects of this otherwise desperate action was the manner in which the French and Viet Minh briefly found common cause against the Japanese enemy. But by May 2 the last soldiers of the demoralized French Indochina Army had crossed the Chinese border, leaving behind only scattered bands of partisans. There they found an "American ill will" and a refusal by General Albert Wedemeyer, Chief of Staff of the South East Asia Command, to treat the French soldiers as anything other than refugees.

This contrary position with the French was the handiwork of the now-deceased Roosevelt. To the end of his life and presidency, Roosevelt clung to the policy that America should not allow France, or any other European power, to bank the lives of US servicemen to save Asian empires, a policy he personally conveyed to Wedemeyer in March 1945.[21] This conflicted with directives issued by the Joint Chiefs to assist the French, as long as the assistance met American war aims and could not be construed as offering political support for the Vichy colonial authorities. In practice, the two aims could not be easily separated. A bombing run served the purpose both of giving the Japanese "hell" and succour to the French. Even as a chorus of French officers led by de Gaulle complained that 14th Air

Force was not doing enough, US State Department officials fretted that they were doing too much. The two principal outcomes that fell out of this unhappy alliance were a reinforced French mistrust of Washington's intentions, and an opportunity for the anti-Gallic OSS to fill the vacuum left by the departing French, an opportunity Donovan did not pass by.

Even as the Allies squabbled, Japanese hopes of Vietnamese compliance were quickly dashed. Abrogation of the 1884 Patenôtre Treaty and a declaration of independence failed to satisfy Vietnamese nationalism. Among those who felt thwarted was a future president of South Vietnam who would so perplex and frustrate American policymakers, the Catholic Ngo Dinh Diem. A haltingly efficient government was established under a progressive politician named Tran Trong Kim, but it was evident that French Indochina, without the French, was no more pacified. Within the month, Ho convened a conference of armed groups in northern Vietnam (the six provinces that constituted the self-proclaimed "Free Zone of the Viet Bac") and announced the formation of a 5,000-strong Vietnam Liberation Army. Confusingly, the now puppet Emperor Bao Dai simultaneously raised an army with the same title.

It was at this juncture that the newly arrived and exotically named OSS Captain, Archimedes Leonidas Attilio Patti, crossed paths with Ho Chi Minh. Chain-smoking Chesterfields, Patti later recalled:

> I first met Ho on the China border between China and Indochina in the last days of April of 1945. He was an interesting individual. Very sensitive, very gentle, rather a frail type. We spoke quite at length about the general situation, not only in Indochina, but the world at large.[22]

In Patti's later, fascinating 600-page account, *Why Vietnam?: Prelude to America's Albatross*, he explained that he actually knew very little about the man. He first noticed the name in a cable to the US ambassador in China dated December 31, 1942, describing the arrest by Chinese authorities of one "Ho Chih-chi (?)" in Kunming.[23]

A year later there was a request for his release. On August 28, 1944, there was a visa request to travel to the United States for a "Ho Ting-ching," an intriguing suggestion that Ho intended to make his advocacy directly to Roosevelt (he didn't, in the end, travel because the Chinese would not issue him with a passport). When Patti asked about this individual, fellow Americans described him as "a friendly Annamite."

Ho impressed on Patti the dire situation of the Vietnamese in Tonkin, at the time facing famine, because the French were selling rice stocks to the Japanese, as well as using them to supply the lucrative rice wine business. In turn, the Japanese had exacerbated the plight of farmers by forcing them to grow hemp to support the war effort.[24] Patti later recalled that Ho showed him a collection of photographs of famine victims: "we look at the Cambodian pictures today and compare them with those, well, there's no comparison. Really, those were sad."[25] Hanoi medical student Tran Duy Hung remembered:

> Hanoi was full of agonizing sights at the time. People dug into the garbage dumps in order to find any edible thing at all: banana peels, tangerine peels, discarded greens and vegetable, and so on. They also ate rats ... Every morning when we opened our door, we saw five to seven corpses of people who had died the night before.[26]

Villager Duong Van Thang, like hundreds of his fellow peasants, joined the Viet Minh to escape the ravages provoked by the French and Japanese: "We simply died in droves because of starvation ... Simply dried up and died."[27]

To Patti's surprise, Ho asked for nothing, except an open line to the OSS. Not only was Patti surprised, but when he reported back to the OSS stations in Kunming and Chongqing, "they wouldn't believe me." The Viet Minh duly supplied the intelligence which was judged "fantastic" and "so accurate" intelligence staffs in Chongqing and Kunming changed their orders of battle and targeting.

However, OSS agents did provide support for America's future nemesis. When Ho fell seriously ill with malaria and dysentery it was an American doctor, Paul Hoagland, who saved him. Following the abdication of Emperor Bao Dai in September 1945 it was Patti who gave the unauthorized imprimatur to Ho's unilateral declaration of independence in Ba Dinh Square (actually a roundabout on the corner of the Jardin Botanique in Hanoi), and it was an American aircraft that provided an unintended fly past. For Patti, it was always clear that Ho's men were fighting for "the cause of independence against the French." Ho reciprocated by professing undying friendship with the new, powerful ally. Patti later confessed, "I just couldn't believe my own ears."[28]

In fact, by the time Patti assumed responsibility for "FIC" (French Indochina) operations, a narrative of undercover missions had been underway for some time. An AGAS (Air Ground Aid Station – China) operator, Lieutenant Charles Fenn (later an author), had made separate contact with Ho in March 1945 following the downing of an American pilot. A second AGAS operator – Lieutenant Dan Phelan – sent "glowing reports" of the Viet Minh in May.[29] Later, a Major Allison Thomas joined Patti's team, brimming with confidence after working in occupied France with the French resistance. Under an existing "nebulous mysterious" GBT (after the initials of the surnames of the three men who took part, Laurence Gordon, Harry Bernard, and Frank Tan) covert operations were being undertaken in Tonkin in support of the Allied bombing. These missions also involved intermittent liaison with Ho's Viet Minh who were keen to help the Americans. GBT had all the hallmarks of freewheeling wartime espionage operations: Gordon was a Canadian expatriate who had managed Texaco's operations in Haiphong before the war; Bernard was a British tobacco dealer; and Tan a Chinese-American businessman.[30] The ring had in fact been set up by the British secret service, which caused some friction with the arriviste OSS. The newly arrived Major Thomas, who was only partly aware of GBT, judged that one of the operators – never identified – offered the best intelligence, although OSS controllers treated his reports "with a pinch of salt."[31]

It was this mysterious individual who presciently warned Thomas that "it would be impossible to work with the French in FIC."

Over May and June 1945, the main effort was the mounting of a Franco-American operation from Taingai, on the Sino-Tonkin border. For a combination of reasons, not least a growing realization that collaboration with the French would not be welcomed, this scheme fell apart. During this period, after some deliberations, it was decided the Viet Minh constituted a potentially useful ally against the Japanese. The deciding factor was the loss of French intelligence contacts within Tonkin. As far as anyone knew, the only organized group capable of filling the gap was precisely the guerrilla movement generally known as the Viet Minh League. Much like Patti, Thomas later confessed that he had barely heard of the Viet Minh, and that the first mention of this group was in conversation with French officers.[32] Fenn may have played a key role in offering to make contact with the Viet Minh as he had quizzed "Hoe" on his communist affiliations – the main concern of the American backers – and concluded that he was basically a nationalist. This line was reinforced by Patti. French contacts insisted that the Vietnamese were "stupid," "infantile," and "communist," but Patti dismissed this jaundiced advice.[33]

The OSS subsequently organized a covert operation – the six-man Deer Mission led by Allison Thomas. The team comprised Lieutenant Montfort, a French Army officer; Sergeant Logos, a French Annamite; Sergeant Phac, also an Annamite; a third Sergeant Zeilski; and the French and Vietnamese-speaking Private Prunier.[34] The group parachuted into Tonkin on July 16, near a village called Kim Lung, 75 miles northwest of Hanoi, where contact was made with Ho's guerrillas. Among the welcoming committee was "Van," the nom de guerre of Vo Nguyen Giap, incongruously and impeccably dressed in a white suit and fedora. Their task, according to Thomas, was "to interdict Japanese lines of communication in the Hanoi-Ningmai area, gather intelligence on the Japanese, including targets of opportunity for the Air Force, and train a group of 100 guerrillas in small arms."[35] In return, the guerrillas offered assistance to downed Allied pilots, under the scheme earlier organized by Fenn. Ho acquired the code name "Lucius," as well as the more prosaic label "OSS Agent 19." Incongruously, Prunier noticed that Ho used stationery from the Parker House Hotel in Boston, a city he had visited as a young man.[36] In addition to Ho and Giap, this core group gave rise to at least two general officers, including Major General Quang Trung, who would first vex the French and then the Americans during the Vietnam War. "This particular group was a select group from all over Vietnam," said Prunier. "They weren't a ragtag bunch of farmers."

The OSS men and Viet Minh quickly established a good rapport, facilitated by a welcoming supper of "beer (recently captured), rice, bamboo sprouts, and barbecued steak." The Deer Mission was impressed that the guerrillas "freshly slaughtered a cow in our honor."[37] Ho assured his guests that he would welcome "10 million Americans" into Tonkin, "but no French."[38] The Frenchman Montfort, in fact, was lucky to have escaped with his life. As Ho later explained, his guards would have shot him dead on the spot had they known his identity (Montfort was later flown out for his safety; it transpired, to Franco-American mutual embarrassment, that Montfort was in fact an M.5 French secret service agent who had infiltrated the OSS; Logos and Phac were also double-agents in a piece of brazen French chicanery). Thomas's opinion on the Viet Minh was quickly formed. In his preliminary report to the OSS base in Kunming he wrote: "Forget the Communist Bogy. VML [Viet Minh League] is not Communist. Stands for freedom and reform from French harshness."[39] He was wrong on the first point, but right on the second. Ho was both communist and nationalist, a juxtaposition that simplistic American labeling could not reconcile.

In the end, the Deer Mission achieved little: military support was neither substantial nor decisive, and various delays meant the guerrilla force was still in training when the Japanese surrender was announced. The only fighting undertaken by Thomas's trainees was a desultory affair against an isolated Japanese contingent in the town of Thai Nguyen (where the Three-Nation Truce Commission would in fact sit at the end of the First Indochina War). After some negotiations, a truce was called, "and the Japs were allowed to circulate in the town without arms where they were surprised to find equally surprised Americans out strolling the streets on a shopping and picture-taking tour."[40]

It was during this heady period that another OSS operator crossed paths with Ho and Giap: a Franco-American called Lucien Conein. The young captain just wanted "to get the hell out of there" and return home, like so many other servicemen stuck in backwaters. In time, he would return to South Vietnam and play a central role in the final drama of the Kennedy presidency. Thomas's untrammelled support for Ho, in the meantime, caused discord in the Deer Mission camp. Another Franco-American called Defourneaux alleged that "the boys" hated Thomas and his pro-Viet Minh ways. Conein in turn fell out with Patti in Hanoi, whom he judged arrogant. These tensions in the American camp aside, it had always been Ho's policy anyway to avoid confrontation with the Japanese (for fear of being worsted) in the same way that he had avoided conflict with his Chinese hosts. In reality, the Viet Minh undertook just one independent action against the Japanese, in the entire war.[41] Ho's reputation as nationalist leader was based on the blare of propaganda, good organization at village level, but little martial substance. His real enemies were competing Vietnamese political groups maneuvering to seek power following the anticipated collapse of French colonial rule.

Unlike his fellow communists, Ho was well traveled and had seen at first hand the great engine of America when he worked his passage to New York as a young man. He instinctively understood this was the power that counted, not a fracturing China, the traditional enemy of Vietnam anyway. Ho accepted the military assistance and reciprocated with intelligence, but what he really wanted was political recognition: every educated Vietnamese was acutely aware of Roosevelt's promise of independence made in the 1941 Atlantic Charter. In their first meeting, Patti had been taken aback when Ho quoted Wilson's Fourteen Points by rote.[42] These were nationalists steeped in the rhetoric of an American-promised independence.

However, the OSS mission was not in a position to fulfill such promises. Both the OSS and Viet Minh were unaware that Secretary of State Stettinius had secretly promised his French counterpart that Washington would respect the status of French Indochina. Ignorant of this deal, Ho continued to act as if independence was imminent. There followed an exchange of messages with Washington which Ho used to press his case as Vietnam's legitimate future head of state. The Viet Minh was portrayed as a genuinely popular movement backed by Buddhists, Christians, businessmen, and farmers.[43] The possibility of an American naval base at Cam Ranh Bay was mooted. Trade between the two countries was offered. In Hanoi, a gigantic Stars and Stripes was somehow found in the war-ravaged city. On August 26, Giap organized a band to play the American national anthem outside the accommodation of the OSS team, while he saluted the unfurled flag. He could hardly have done more to ingratiate himself with a nation that would go to war against him. Four days later, the Viet Minh League cleverly arranged UP news coverage of an anti-French protest that passed outside the Hotel Métropole. All the placards were in English but none of the Vietnamese, of course, were English-speakers. This trick of playing to American public opinion would be repeated with great effect in the later war.

That Ho, one-time student of communism in Moscow, was courting the capitalists did not go unnoticed. Patti soon made contact with the Soviet spook, a polyglot called Stephane Solosieff, "a pleasant man in his late forties with an open smile and a direct approach." There were around five or six hundred Soviet citizens in Indochina, several hundred serving in the French Foreign Legion (indeed, there was a flourishing communist apparatus within the Legion, a small core actually absconding and fighting for the Viet Minh). Solosieff, like all the other secret agents who had descended on Hanoi, was concerning himself with the welfare of nationals, as well as attending to "many other matters." The pair drank vodka "for several hours." Solosieff proved eminently sensible, and perceptive. Nothing could stop the Vietnamese drive for independence. The French should ease this process and the Americans should provide technical assistance. The Soviet Union, he honestly confided to Patti, had no stake in this corner of Southeast Asia.

American in-country reporting continued to portray Ho as a "symbol of nationalism and the struggle for freedom to the overwhelming majority of the population."[44] It was this perspective that had led Patti to open a temporary OSS office in the Hotel Métropole in Hanoi and to participate, as supportive bystander, in the Viet Minh "August Revolution" and Declaration of Independence. Patti arrived in Hanoi alongside Jean Sainteny, the French head of intelligence, and was impressed by the support for Ho.

> I said, Jean, it doesn't look like it's gonna be very good, is it? And, he shook his head and was absolutely stunned by the display of anti-French sentiment, and also by the display of the red flag with the gold star.[45]

Later, he "fell into a depressed silence."[46] Depression soon turned to dismay when he awoke to read the headline in the local press: "Viet Minh Fighting with U.S. Troops in Tonkin, Will Soon be Here to Oust the French Oppressors Who Last Year Starved 2 Million People."

Sainteny's dismay deepened over the manner in which Hanoi fell into the lap of Ho and his supporters. "Certain myths have sprung up over the years over the 'taking' of Hanoi," Patti later recorded. "There was no coup d'état, no bloodshed, no reprisals, no French resistance, no secret plot or arrangement with the Japanese, not even substantive Vietnamese aid from outside Hanoi."[47] The communists were simply the best-organized group, and Ho Chi Minh the only figure of stature known to the Tonkinese. The Japanese, under General Tsuchihashi, had emptied the Bank of Indochina, but otherwise stood aside. The significance of the act, however, was unmissable and news of Ho Chi Minh's success in Hanoi spread like wildfire.

The Viet Minh primarily sought American "moral support" and were prepared to play a propaganda war to win that support. Patti remained supportive, even if his government was turning a deaf ear to Ho's blandishments. The chances that Washington would respond to this correspondence, in fact, were remote. Vietnam had fallen down the list of concerns in the State Department (Roosevelt died on February 12, before the OSS mission initiated its contacts with the Viet Minh). As far as Patti could discern, there really was no Indochinese policy, except keeping the French out.[48] Accommodating a Vietnamese liberation movement, and only one of several with competing claims in French Indochina, was never going to gain Truman's attention in the first few months of his presidency.

At the time, the Division of Southeast Asian Affairs in the State Department was headed by the bald, bespectacled Abbot Low Moffat, who held the post over the crucial years 1944–47. Indochina's mysterious peoples were judged "relatively small potatoes in world affairs."[49] Roosevelt's policy had been spare and barely articulated. Moffat received one brief memo from Roosevelt on the subject. "That was," he recalled, "the full instructions that we had. Period." At Roosevelt's insistence, no aid was to be furnished to the French, but material assistance continued to arrive in clandestine ways, or later with the complicity of the British. Moffat reported these activities to the White House, receiving the peremptory reply "This must stop!" but they continued anyway. At Yalta, Moffat's Department was outflanked by the European lobby, supporting France, and an older and sicker Roosevelt gave up on the issue of trusteeship (more accurately he agreed to the evasion of trusteeship "with the French as trustee," or an effective return to colonial rule). The European lobby dismissed Moffat's "fussing" over Indochina and as casually dismissed Indochinese nationalism as "just the result of Japanese propaganda." When Roosevelt died, it was the European Department that reacted first, forwarding a memo to Truman: "the department thinks it's time to ... change our policy and begin furnishing military aid to the French." Once again outflanked ("my staff was practically ready to lynch me"), Moffat was forced to compromise. Ironically, Stettinius rejected the compromise paper anyway at the April 1945 San Francisco conference, with the result that "we had no policy officially adopted for the department." In turn, Truman showed no interest, and the British eased the path of the French return. "We silently gnashed our teeth," Moffat recorded, "but there was nothing that we could do about it." Such were the divisions and confusions when Japan finally surrendered in September 1945.

For his part, Ho did everything right. The ICP held an all-party conference on August 13–16 at Tran Toa, inviting delegates from across Indochina. It was at this conference that Ho persuaded rival parties that the ICP alone enjoyed the all-important American imprimatur (this was untrue). This was followed by a National People's Conference in which the Viet Minh played a leading role. The outcome of this conference was the outline of a provisional government, with Ho elected president. In an important symbolic move, the Viet Minh flag that would become so familiar to American soldiers was chosen as the national flag of an independent Vietnam.[50] The presence of OSS agents suggested to the Viet Minh that the United States supported this move. A declaration of independence was made on the same day as the Japanese surrender on September 2. In direct imitation of the American Declaration of Independence, the speech began with the words: "All men are created equal. They are endowed by their creator with certain inalienable rights." With an astuteness characteristic of Ho, the September 2 Declaration of Independence also contained allusions to the French 1793 Declaration of the Rights of Man, to the mortification of the French *colons* (colonists) in Hanoi. When Ho finished speaking, "an airplane, a small one circled over us. We did not know whose plane it was. We thought it was a Vietnamese plane. But when it swooped down over us, we recognized the American flag ... the crowd cheered enthusiastically."[51]

Medical student Tran Duy Hung was one of thousands present at the declaration of independence. He recalled:

> On that day, Hanoi was so animated that I can say that I've not seen another day like that since. There was a forest of red banners all over the city. Beginning early in the morning, workers,

peasants and other segments of the population converged on the Ba Dinh Square.

Several days before the event took place, we built a simple platform above this flower bed. Around this square platform we placed honor guards armed with sticks (there were very few guns) to provide security. On the outer ring we had religious leaders from all the religious organizations: Buddhist monks in brown, Catholic priests in black, and nuns were holding their pennants looking as if they were conducting religious ceremonies in the pagodas.[52]

At the time Hanoi had a population of a quarter of a million inhabitants who thronged to the area. The ceremony was supposed to start at 3pm but was delayed because of the crowds. Eventually Ho and the rest of the provisional government ascended the platform. A national anthem was played and the flag of an independent Vietnam was raised for the first time, described by Hung as "the most moving moment." Ho started to read the declaration then asked, "Compatriots, can you hear me?" because the rickety loudspeaker system was "really, very bad." "Yes, we hear you!" the crowd roared back. Ho then delivered his famous declaration of independence with unassuming dignity. At the end, the excited crowds chanted "Independence or Death!" – a warning the French should have heeded.

The "shouts from the heart" which so impressed the Americans in Hanoi became shouts of revenge across French Indochina, a landscape of chaos and random violence not fully painted by characters like Patti. The Japanese surrender on August 16, rather than ushering in peace, had unleashed a wave of anarchy. Civil authority was handed over to the royal government, which then struggled to impose order. Seizing the moment, the Viet Minh had "taken" Hanoi on August 19, followed by a second, less successful power grab, one week later in Saigon. In reality, the Viet Minh had usurped an independence movement already set in motion by the Japanese-installed Kim government. In historian Arthur Dommen's verdict, many Vietnamese – especially in the South where Ho was not well known – in fact viewed the Viet Minh's actions as a *quop chinh quyen*, or "stealing of authority."[53] Faced with the inevitable, Emperor Bao Dai abdicated, but not before warning de Gaulle "as a friend" that the cause of Vietnamese independence was irreversible and that "no human force" could deflect the destiny of his people, a warning blithely ignored by de Gaulle who was already setting in train the despatch of a French Expeditionary Corps to Indochina.[54]

Patti, who witnessed the events first hand, took a more nuanced view. In a deeply superstitious and illiterate society, Bao Dai's abdication was less a legal affair and more a transference of the "mandate from heaven" to a new incumbent (according to Dommen, Bao Dai actually had no idea to whom he was abdicating, a measure of the confusion that now reigned in French Indochina).[55] That the new intercessor was a communist was irrelevant and not understood anyway outside circles of intelligentsia. The reverence shown to Ho, in the north and south, stemmed from this "heavenly intervention" viewed as "an important article of faith among the Vietnamese peasantry."[56]

Bankrupted by war, de Gaulle's rescue force comprised a *Corps léger d'intervention*, "Light Interventions Corps," a hopelessly undermanned and under-trained body in no position to reassert French authority. A point of acute sensitivity was the ethnic composition of the force. A French report noted that, "As much to preserve French prestige, it was necessary that a strong proportion of the troops that liberated Indochina were white." But this was a problem: the Defense Committee could only make up the numbers by recruiting "*noirs*," "blacks," suspected of being unreliable, and "*indigènes*," "locals," suspected of being disloyal. Allied bombing had destroyed the rail network between Saigon and Hanoi, and few roads were trafficable. Parts of the country, especially in the north, were facing the prospect of mass starvation. French civilians who had endured the Japanese occupation were being hunted down, beaten, and, in the worst cases, raped and killed. Europeanized Vietnamese, perceived as collaborators of the old regime, suffered similar treatment. In an echo of the violence swirling in communist-held

China, powerful landowners were attacked and there was rioting in towns. The violence was exacerbated by severe monsoon flooding in the Delta that resulted in the deaths of between 700,000 and two million Vietnamese peasants.[57]

In the south, the OSS was less welcome. Following the Japanese surrender, an old-style Vietnamese gangster called Tran Van Giau led a group of militias loosely affiliated within a United National Front (UNF) in a shooting spree across Cochin China. He was only halted from becoming the unchallenged ruling warlord by the rivalry of the Hoa Hao and Cao Dai.

The vacuum of power was finally filled by advance elements of the British 20th Indian Division, arriving in Saigon on September 12 under the command of the square-jawed, "very gentlemanly, very calm," Major General Douglas Gracey.[58] For political reasons, a single French company drawn from 5th Colonial Infantry Regiment (5e RIC) in Ceylon accompanied the British. Major Philip Malins, a transport and supply officer who arrived on the first flight, remembered curiosity, some welcoming, "and a slight feeling of apprehension." The Japanese had supplied a collection of "large American automobiles" at Tan Son Nhut airport for the British. Malins appropriated a Cadillac, drove to a hotel in central Saigon, and had some drinks. As he and his soldiers had just emerged from the hellish jungle fighting in Burma, "it was literally like going into a beautiful slice of Paris."[59]

However, the city he arrived in was not a happy place. Saigon was home to a sizeable *colon* population – as many as 15,000 Europeans – now fearful for their lives and enraged by Vietnamese aggression. The arrival of Western troops provoked general jubilation: unused parachutes were handed over to Saigon's couturier-starved women to make dresses, and hidden stashes of Pernod and champagne were shared with the soldiers. In fact, the British arrived "with no real specific orders" and remarkably "with less than a company of troops."[60] It was a typically improvised affair. Ordinary Vietnamese who lined the streets cheering the arrival of British troops imagined an imminent independence.[61] This delusion barely lasted two days.

Madame Nguyen Thi Binh, a daughter of French-educated civil servants who later became the foreign minister of the National Liberation Front, recalled the deflation:

> I myself met some English officers. But those officers did not understand anything of the situation in our country. They were interested in other things, not in helping us. Rather, they were seeking pleasure. We saw that it was not with good intentions that those missions were coming to Saigon. And very soon we saw that the Allies were precisely the people who were helping the French to come back.[62]

It was experiences such as these that pushed moderate "intellectuals" like Madame Binh to the communist flag. Later she would be arrested by the French, tortured at the Sûreté on Catinat Street, and jailed in the notorious Chi Hoa prison for three years. Ironically, many of her National Liberation Front comrades would end up in this same hole after the communist victory in 1975.

Gracey had fought in both world wars, won two Military Crosses, and spent virtually his entire career in the Indian Army. Even in the midst of the chaotic situation in Saigon he insisted on formal Sunday mess dinners complete with turbans, pipes, and regimental colors. He represented a world that most Americans found incomprehensible and his style of command was as archaic as his attitudes to the brown or yellow man. Two and a half million Indians had volunteered to serve the British Crown, a baffling proposition to most Americans. Gracey's innate sense of racial superiority was reinforced by the respect and loyalty of his colonial charges (Field Marshal Slim would remark that no Indian troops carried their tail more vertically than Gracey's). One subordinate observed, "They [the Indian soldiers] loved him. He absolutely loved them."[63] He would eventually retire as Commander-in-Chief of independent Pakistan's first national army.

Gracey had little patience for illegitimate pretensions to power, and none for the Viet Minh-installed Provisional Executive

Committee (PEC) which he promptly kicked out of La Grandière Palace.[64] "Communists," he harrumphed by way of justification. In a typical gesture of British jocularity, the Gurkhas under his command nicknamed the Viet Minh, "the Vitamins."[65] His brigade commander, the avuncular Doidge Estcourt "Ted" Taunton, recollected, "I had to balance three things: the Japanese, who were in charge of ... the key points; the French who, having been released, were getting a little bit out of control; and, the Annamites, who were sitting on the government buildings." His instructions were simple: get the French in, and get the Annamites out.[66] Backed by a Mountbatten who was keen to mollify the French, Gracey then set about re-arming former soldiers of the 11th French Colonial Infantry (11e RIC).

This and subsequent actions led to the portrayal of Gracey as pro-French and anti-Vietnamese. Viscerally he was. Gracey was "heartily sick of the Viet Minh [and] the Annamites causing all this unrest and disturbance in Saigon."[67] His overriding concern was restoring law and order, but he was not a maverick. He perfectly understood Britain's neutrality in French Indochina, as well as the difficulties of maintaining it. Crucially, British administrators were not prepared to legally hand over territory seized from the French ally by a Japanese enemy to an unelected and self-proclaimed government, however much the Viet Minh protested it represented the wishes of the people. A secret memo from General Leclerc captured the good relationship that was quickly struck with Gracey, his abstention from politics, and the essence of his mission, which was re-establishing "law and order":

I have, up to now, the best relations with Major General Gracey and his officers. It is evident that above all he wants to sort out the Japanese question. Then, and only when we have sufficient forces, we will work towards the establishment of French authority. Also, without any doubt, the English are abstaining and will abstain from any political action. They will maintain "law and order" but will step aside to let us order the other questions.[68]

Even so, the decision to re-arm the French provoked a violent local response and the random killing of civilians. A subsequent release of French prisoners on September 23 led to a de facto counter-coup and further violence, led by the French acting High Commissioner of Cochin China, Jean Marie Arsène Cédile, and now directed against Vietnamese. 80th British Brigade actively supported this French action, seizing the Garde Civile barracks, as well as the Yokohama and Indochina Banks. Mobs in the Cité Heyraud district of Saigon duly reacted to this French coup by massacring 150 civilians.[69] Faced with a spiraling rebellion in Saigon, Gracey then struck an unlikely alliance with the "charming" Lieutenant General Takuzo Numata, co-opting the 40,000-strong Japanese garrison to maintain order. This was a highly controversial but forced decision given the lack of white troops (until October, Gracey was allocated just 1,800 soldiers to secure various locations in southern Vietnam and the capital of Cambodia).[70] In Brigadier Taunton's recollection, blame lay with the "rampaging" Gallic ally rather than with the Annamites: "the French, being an excitable nation, started to become trigger happy, and it was then, that it was necessary to put control back in the hands of the Japanese."[71] Indeed, the British seemed to warm to the Japanese who were "well behaved" and "disciplined," unlike almost all other armed groups, including the French, on the streets of Saigon.

Newspapers were closed down and a curfew was imposed. British liaison with the Japanese was somewhat complicated by also having to deal with the Southern Army Commander, a truculent Marshal Terauchi, as well as the "dull-witted" Saigon garrison commander, General Manaki.[72] As the Japanese had deliberately set about arming nationalists in the last days of the war, the irony of this reversal of fortunes escaped no one, not least the elderly Numata who rode about the streets of Saigon on a splendid white charger, enjoying a certain *Schadenfreude* over the difficulties the British were now facing. French civilians with minimal military training also joined in the running street battles. When the Viet Minh broke a truce on October 10, Gracey lost all forbearance, and any hopes of parleying with communists ended.

If Gracey showed little patience with the troublesome Viet Minh and other roaming militias, he displayed even less tolerance for an interfering American called Lieutenant Colonel Peter Dewey. The youthful Dewey, son of a congressman, had ostensibly arrived in Saigon to recover American POWs. But he also appeared to be providing moral support to Vietnamese nationalists fighting for "liberty," a dubious concept to Gracey. In fact, there was no exact translation of the Western concept of "liberty" in Vietnamese. The closest word was "*tu do*," which meant "licence," and which commonly appeared over the bordellos in downtown Saigon.[73] French intelligence also soon picked up on Dewey. It was noted that his presence evidently had "another motive" and that his intervention "had the likelihood of greatly annoying the English."[74]

It wasn't just the English who were annoyed. Dewey, like his fellow OSS officer Patti in Hanoi, seemed to be disliked by his own team.[75] When Gracey discovered the ulterior purpose of Dewey's mission he declared him persona non grata, requested he leave the country, and forbade the flying of an American flag on his jeep.[76] This latter order was later attributed as the cause of Dewey's death on September 26, when he was possibly mistaken for a French officer and shot by "Annamite rebels" near Tan Son Nhut airport, north of Saigon.[77] Another theory suggests that he was actually killed by Cao Dai nationalists, because of his well-known support for the Viet Minh.[78]

The facts were that Dewey decided to drive back to Saigon for lunch, after being notified that his midday flight was delayed, and he took a short cut despite warnings over the safety of the route.[79] When the jeep came across a road block, Dewey "shook his fist and yelled something in French." A burst of machine-gun fire struck him in the back of the head and took away most of his lower jaw. A patrol from 3/1 Gurkhas almost succeeded in recovering the body but arrived too late.[80] For the next two weeks, an intensive search was made of morgues but all that was found was French planters with hands or feet cut off, or with slit throats.[81]

Dewey achieved posthumous fame as America's first combat fatality in Vietnam. This claim ignores the several American

POWs and aviators who died in Vietnam over the course of the war. The first American combat fatality on Vietnamese soil may have been a shot-down aviator, only known as Henry, who was killed by Japanese troops in the Central Highlands, sometime after March 9, 1945.[82] Peter Dewey's last reported message to his controller was remarkably brief, honest and prophetic: "Cochin China is burning, the French and British are finished here, and we ought to clear out of Southeast Asia."

The chaotic events of September 1945 led to the "missed opportunity" fallacy but the reality was that the OSS, charmed by Ho, had run away with the script. Independence for the states of French Indochina had been championed by Roosevelt, but this impulse depended on his survival and the compliance of allies. Neither survived the war. It had been at Roosevelt's insistence that Article Three had been included in the 1941 Atlantic Charter, pledging a postwar settlement in which all peoples would enjoy the right to self-determination. This had stuck in Churchill's craw, a committed colonialist, but a desperate British Commonwealth needed the American giant, and there was plenty of time to manipulate the game. Over the next few years, Churchill chipped away at Washington's postwar proposals and Roosevelt's untimely death then removed the last obstacle to European objections to the Charter. At the April 1945 San Francisco Conference, Indochina was not raised. In May, Secretary of State Stettinius advised his French counterpart that Washington would remain "innocent" over the question of French Indochina. In June, American non-interference was officially endorsed in a State Department paper affirming that "the United States recognizes French sovereignty over Indochina."[83] By the Potsdam Conference in July, Truman had publicly abandoned Roosevelt's Atlantic Charter and bowed to French sensitivities agreeing to divide the country along the 16th parallel with French forces eventually taking over from the British in the south. In the north, Nationalist Chinese forces, under American supervision, would impose order as an interim solution to a final settlement. The temporary arrangement did not sit well with the

French who were not informed of the decision until after it was made.[84] Nevertheless, this was a retreat from what Roosevelt had considered to be the only just solution to Vietnam: trusteeship followed by independence (a position repeated in the Cairo, Tehran, and Yalta Conferences; Ho could have been forgiven for believing American promises).[85] Fearful of the implications to the Commonwealth, British intransigence in the last two years of the war ultimately checkmated an America too preoccupied with Japan. De Gaulle, in his imperial robes, simply ignored all initiatives proposing independence in the colonial territories. In the immediate aftermath of the war, America had few realistic options other than to cede Southeast Asia to former colonial powers. Truman, who did not share Roosevelt's anti-Gallicism, in turn lost all interest in the matter.

Notwithstanding these double-dealings, it is highly unlikely that an American administration would have found a comfortable ally in Vietnamese communists who were beginning to impose a violent totalitarianism on the French colony. Having only just served out his first 100 days in office, Truman hardly had the time or inclination to attend to the missives of an Indochinese nationalist he had never heard of. Over 1945–46, Ho Chi Minh would write eight letters to the US government pleading for help – all were ignored.[86] The sense of betrayal from this cold-shouldering was not forgotten. French prickliness and long memories over Roosevelt's proposal for trusteeships also ran deep: when the last French troops finally withdrew from Vietnam in 1956, France's Foreign Minister bitterly recalled the policy, as if the shambles and tragedy of the last ten years had all been an American plot.[87]

In the immediate aftermath of Ho's "August Revolution" American policy toward Indochina remained broadly if uneasily supportive of France – but there were limits to this tolerance. The Navy stipulated that no US-flagged vessel be permitted to transport French war materiel or soldiers to Vietnam. American troops in Vietnam were authorized to conduct "humanitarian" operations but were forbidden to offer assistance to the beleaguered French.

In a contradictory stance, a growing lobby in the State Department's Far Eastern desk argued strongly for a restoration of French rule, a position supported by other European desks which saw the merits of a strong France in a now tense and divided Europe. In the south, the French were able to re-establish control quickly, thanks to the supportive British and because the Viet Minh overplayed its hand. Led by Nguyen Binh, the Viet Minh had never enjoyed the same level of popularity in the south. Crucially, the French were able to enlist loyalists to their side, notably a former teacher, Nguyen Van Tam, "the Tiger of Cai Lay," who brutally suppressed his own countrymen and was rewarded with the governorship of Tonkin (Tam effectively became the godfather of the nascent South Vietnamese Army).[88] In the north, the presence of Chinese Nationalist troops, rather than the limited French military response, derailed Ho's plans to establish an independent state.

In Hanoi, Patti was replaced by Carleton Swift, a former naval officer. Much like his predecessor, Swift quickly came to the conclusion that the black and white portrayal of Ho Chi Minh as ardent communist was an exaggeration. The reality of Ho's politics and Vietnamese relations with the French was far more mixed than an impatient official in Washington might bother to understand. "Vietnam was the last thing anybody in Washington wanted, [or] would even read." Swift's pen-picture of Ho was remarkably accurate, and ignored. Ho was basically a nationalist "concerned for his people." He was not hateful of the French. He certainly wanted to run things by "Lenin's book," but this only caused problems because the State Department could not see grays, only the black and white of communists versus the "free world."[89]

Swift's personal encounters with the "ascetic, thin intellectual" Ho left him posing the question that many contemporaries asked: "Why is this man a leader? Why is this wisp of a man ... such a significant force?" He was never able to answer the question. Following complaints by Jean Sainteny over American "agitation," a charge which left Swift "outraged," the OSS station was removed from Hanoi in October to soothe French sensibilities. The loss of the station, which included five native speakers, effectively left Washington clueless over the subsequent unfolding events.

These events took a turn for the worse. Historic Sino-Vietnamese antagonism was exacerbated by the fact that the occupying Chinese soldiers received little or no pay and were subsisting at the end of a dreadful logistic chain. Hanoi resident Bui Tin, who later rose to the rank of colonel in the North Vietnamese Army, recalled the Chinese as a "miserable sight," "riff-raff elements dressed in rags." On one occasion he was amused to observe a group of soldiers pierce open some tins of paint and take a drink, thinking them to be cans of condensed milk. "They just poured down the streets of Hanoi and looted, taking everything they could get their hands on."[90]

Thus what started out as an internationally recognized and temporary arrangement degenerated into countrywide vandalism and looting by 150,000 ill-fed troops, commanded by the warlord General Lu Han. Four Chinese columns eventually descended into Tonkin comprising the 52nd, 62nd, 93rd, and 60th Armies. Wedemeyer had planned that only the latter should remain as a garrison force, but the opportunity to make money from the lucrative opium poppy harvest extended their stay. Chinese internal politics also interfered with the plan. As many as two thirds of the Chinese soldiers were ethnic Yunnanese who owed their loyalty to a General Lung Yun, a rival of the nationalist leader Generalissimo Chiang Kai-shek. The latter duly exploited the situation and deposed Yun from the nationalist government.[91] The American general assigned as Lu Han's mentor – Philip Gallagher – found himself caught between the rapacity of the Chinese troops, a restless civilian population inflamed by Viet Minh propaganda, and the growing assertiveness of the French. Gallagher's task was made harder by financial meltdown, exacerbated by a "500 piaster note crisis," a scam fomented by Chinese army officers manipulating currency exchange rates. It was only with the greatest difficulty and tact that Gallagher was able to restore financial stability, and with some relief that the US advisory mission was finally withdrawn from Hanoi on December 12, 1945.[92]

Trapped by this deteriorating situation, Ho's position became untenable. Unable to expel the Chinese who had previously backed him with arms and supplies, he had little choice but to seek settlement with the French authorities. The British looked on and lamented the "unfortunate" developments but did not interfere. By February 1946, Gracey and his Gurkhas were gone. This opened the way for the March 6, 1946 peace deal which appeared to offer hope. The Chinese agreed to withdraw, their place taken by French troops for an unspecified period. In return, France recognized Ho Chi Minh as President of the Republic of Vietnam and promised to negotiate a final solution to the question of Vietnam's status. At the heart of this agreement was the promise of elections, which the communists anticipated they would win. As the Viet Minh had won 60 percent of the vote and 182 of 302 seats in the January National Assembly elections, this was an entirely realistic prospect.

The fate of French Indochina was now in the hands of two men hand-picked by de Gaulle, but perversely at odds with each other. Military command was invested in the high Catholic Philippe François Marie, comte de Hauteclocque, a man with a pinched mouth and pencil moustache, better known by his wartime alias Leclerc. His ancestors had fought in the crusades, and he would add one last and brief chapter to this family history. The post of High Commissioner fell in the lap of Vice Admiral Georges Thierry d'Argenlieu, a former Carmelite monk, described by one critic as having "the most brilliant mind in the 12th century."[93] Leclerc arrived in Saigon with the intention of restoring French authority but came to the conclusion that "the hate of the Yellow for the White" was immovable.[94] The pig-headed d'Argenlieu shot off on an opposite track, tearing up the "free state" promises of March 6, and with chilly hauteur informing the Vietnamese: "France does not intend in the present state of evolution of the Indochinese people to give them unconditional and total independence, which would only be a fiction gravely prejudicial to the interests of the two parties."[95] D'Argenlieu then played a role not dissimilar to that of some American officials in the later war, convinced that military success was not only possible but the necessary precondition to political dialogue.

However, his chief and original sin was the peremptory establishment of a separate *Nam Bo* (South Vietnam), intolerable to the communists and indeed to the majority of southerners. In this decision, d'Argenlieu imperiously conflated France's wishes with the imagined wishes of South Vietnam. "She [Indochina] should have the reassurance that she will be neither abandoned nor betrayed."[96] "France would not abandon her role of 'protectress' of these half-formed yellow men." South Vietnamese did indeed fear "the hungry imperialism of the Tonkinese" but this did not make them willing subjects of the French. The artificial political entity that America would defend at such high cost was all the work of a fevered, foolish man who would retire to die in a monastery, sick and confused.

Given French double-dealing, Ho's perseverance and patience were remarkable. He traveled to France and was feted. Through the summer of 1946 he plodded politely through the doomed Fontainebleu negotiations, all the while observing the spectacle of collapsing French cabinets. Prime Minister Pham Van Dong recalled the chief of the French delegation Max André threatening, "We only need an ordinary police operation in a period of eight days in order to clean all of you out." "With this kind of attitude," he reflected, "there was certainly no need for any negotiation."[97] In a gesture of conspicuous magnanimity, Ho signed "the Golden Book" and laid a wreath at the Tomb of the Unknown Soldier in Paris – honoring the very soldiers killing his fellow Vietnamese.

In the absence of national leadership, Giap instigated a program of annihilation of rival nationalist parties, in some cases assisted by the French who naively hoped to form the fledgling Vietnamese National Army as a joint force, naturally dominated by French officers. As many as 15,000 activists may have been extra-judicially executed by these combined operations.[98] Even as Vietnamese fought among themselves, France's colonial administrators and generals convinced themselves of the inevitable restoration of French prestige. "The peoples of the Far East and our allies," General Juin boasted, "have been stunned by the unexpected and truly surprising return of French power."[99] Giap was much less impressed by French power, hollow and fragile as it was. All through the summer and fall, French military missives filled with reports of "rebel bands" and "terrorist bands." The uneasy "modus vivendi agreements" finally collapsed in November when the French shelled Haiphong, leaving some Vietnamese neighborhoods "completely wiped." The dispute was over customs collection, but the heavy-handedness of the French garrison commander, a Colonel Dèbes, virtually assured conflict. Vu Quoc Uy, mayor of Haiphong, recalled:

> Colonel Dèbes sent us an ultimatum, stating that all armed units of the city had to be withdrawn from the city ... And two hours after this ultimatum was delivered to us, artillery shells came from the French boats. And then the infantry, preceded by tanks, attacked us in continuous waves. The battle lasted for more than two days.[100]

Out-gunned, the Vietnamese withdrew.

Serious fighting then broke out in the week before Christmas. The Tonkin garrison commander, General Jean-Julien Fonde, lectured Giap: "I know war: murders, deaths, destruction ... we have to prevent this," to which Giap retorted that he didn't care if it took one million Vietnamese deaths to expel the French.

What hope did the French have of winning this unnecessary war? In 1946, France was trying to hold on to Vietnam with just two under-strength divisions, 9e DIC in the north and 3e DIC in the south. These were supported by two squadrons of Spitfires. It was a hopeless military task, complicated by the difficult terrain and unhealthy environment. Between October 1945 and the end of 1946, the French recorded 1,376 "European" combat deaths, but also lost 390 soldiers to various illnesses, as well as 339 to accidents. Forty-one French servicemen had committed suicide.[101] The pressed General Valluy found an athletic metaphor to express France's predicament: "I would readily compare us to an athlete who because of an optical error imagines he has to run

Map 2: Viet Minh Held and Contested Areas, November 3, 1950

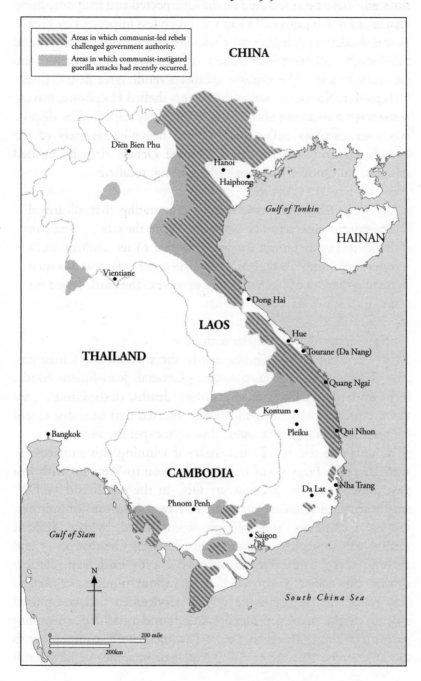

Areas in which communist-led rebels challenged government authority.

Areas in which communist-instigated guerilla attacks had recently occurred.

CHINA

Dien Bien Phu

Hanoi

Haiphong

Gulf of Tonkin

HAINAN

Vientiane

Dong Hai

LAOS

Hue

THAILAND

Tourane (Da Nang)

Quang Ngai

Kontum

Pleiku

Qui Nhon

Bangkok

CAMBODIA

Da Lat

Nha Trang

Phnom Penh

Gulf of Siam

Saigon

N

South China Sea

| 0 | | 200 mile |
| 0 | 200km | |

3000 metress ... and ... realises that the finishing line is not yet in sight ... ."[102] It never would be.

At its height, the French Expeditionary Corps (CEFEO in the French abbreviation) perhaps numbered 115,000, but this was a misleading figure as the numbers could only be made up with colonial or indigenous troops, the inevitable "*jaunissement*," "yellowing," of an army that had run out of European troops. In December 1945, the 32,000-strong French corps had seen fit to recruit just 291 Vietnamese. Within one year, desperate for manpower, 31,000 Vietnamese had been recruited, representing a third of the total French force. However, the French were unwilling to admit the "yellows" into the officer ranks; overwhelmingly the Vietnamese recruits represented hastily trained and not infrequently poorly motivated cannon fodder. The Viet Minh could count on perhaps half a million regulars, regional forces and popular forces. Backing an eventual Viet Minh victory were 22 million Vietnamese, anxious for an end to colonial rule, even if not fully supportive of the communists.

Over the next years, French military command became a revolving door of failures and disappointments. Leclerc gave way to Valluy, who was replaced by Blaizot, who was succeeded by Carpentier, and who lastly handed the reins to Jean de Lattre de Tassigny. By 1952, nine generals' sons had been killed; the war was costing four billion francs per month; and over 600 monthly casualties were being suffered. Every tactical trick was tried: defensive "lines," "hedgehogs," and gallant if futile parachute operations. More darkly, the French resorted to brutality and reaped the reward of a dirty war. As early as 1946, Leclerc was deploring the ill-discipline and "a few bad acts" of individuals, but swiftly dismissed these with a moral myopia that presaged the later degeneration of the US Army. "One must understand the moral and psychological climate under which our soldiers live here and not give it too great importance."[103] Torture, extra-judicial killings, rape – none of these had any importance compared to "the valour and actions of our troops." Doung Van Khang, a Viet Minh guerrilla, remembered this differently. "The French burnt down our village four times," he recalled. "The most painful thing that happened was that the French lobbed artillery shells into this village. One shell hit us right smack in the middle of the house and killed five members of my own family."[104]

Then, de Lattre unexpectedly died, the last best commander in Tonkin. In one of his final diplomatic forays he had attempted to persuade a skeptical Washington to conjoin the Korean and Vietnamese wars, a ploy wisely deflected by the Joint Chiefs. De Lattre would be posthumously promoted to marshal. At his state funeral, his blind 97-year-old father lingeringly ran his fingers over his son's sword lying on the coffin, as if lamenting the passing of French imperial power. The general was laid alongside his son Bernard, also killed in Vietnam. The final chapters of French colonial rule would now be written by the reactionary Raoul Salan and the reckless Henri Navarre, but by then it was obvious that France was embroiled in an unwinnable, unpopular, and futile war.

France's military gambit relied on a strategy learned in North Africa – "*le maroc utile*" or "the useful part of Morocco," meaning the fertile coast and main settlements. The CEFEO would protect the urban centers of population, the useful parts of Vietnam, but cede rural areas where it could not hope to chase down a guerrilla force. Yet it mattered little what strategy commanders pursued or how good the troops were – and they were superb. France had no chance of succeeding in Vietnam because the war was essentially an unwinnable political struggle. France was backing the discredited playboy Bao Dai who had been appointed Emperor at the age of 12, the very antithesis of the ascetic Ho Chi Minh. Her contingent allies were Vietnam's weird and unpredictable sects, as well as the bulwark of Vietnam's two million Catholics. This latter bloc had first supported the "August Revolution," but subsequent Viet Minh abuses swung the Catholics determinedly against Ho. Above all, France was relying on the tiny, educated Mandarin class (85 percent of the population was illiterate), but this intellectual minority feared for its future in the event of a probable French defeat.

The political and economic background to this struggle could hardly have been less promising. Corruption and government mismanagement were rife. The state was bankrupt and reliant on French and later American aid. The offer of autonomy under a French Union was a sham. A full ten percent of France's national budget was being squandered protecting a few thousand wealthy colonial Frenchmen, and buying the uncertain loyalty of Francophile Vietnamese. The French sought to portray themselves as engaged in a vanguard battle of Western civilization against the spread of communism – at least to Americans – but the Vietnamese only saw the French as the cause of all their ills. The hollowness of France's hold on Vietnam was most visibly on display at the elite Cercle Sportif Saigonnais, a club where bikini-clad air hostesses flirted with landowners and businessmen while smart Legionnaires at the gates ensured that local riff-raff steered clear. A saying began to circulate: "Saigon belongs to the French by day and Viet Minh by night." Undeterred, Saigon's French expatriate population partied hard as if the end was near, which everyone with eyes knew it was.

———————————

Given the blood, treasure, and diplomatic effort being expended on the First Indochina War, it is easy to forget that from Washington's perspective Vietnam was just a sideshow, albeit one that was dragging America toward a tentative military commitment. In the Far East, it was China that had traditionally dominated as the great American foreign policy obsession. But as *Time* magazine queried on June 10, 1946: "The most important truth about China is that hardly anybody in China seems to retain any faith in the ability of the present government to run the nation wisely, well or honestly."[105] Washington would only help the nationalists "if the Chinese Government presents satisfactory evidence of effective measures looking toward Chinese recovery," and only if American officials were permitted to administer the aid.[106] Critics called it the greatest foreign policy failure since the end of the war, but an unswerving Truman stepped back, allowing the warring Chinese to settle their differences from Mao's barrel of a gun.

Republicans, ruthlessly capitalizing on a popular consensus that Truman had "lost China," pushed for military aid, but the State Department, now under Marshall, continued to argue for neutrality.

Chiang Kai-shek fled to the island of Formosa in December 1949, where his son had already trained a resistance army, thereby surrendering mainland China to the communists. As if the panorama could darken any more for Washington's Asia policy, communist China and the Soviet Union promptly signed a mutual assistance pact. *Mao Tse-tung wan sui!* – Long Live Mao Tse-tung!

———

These unwelcome developments in French Indochina and China were completely overshadowed by a more alarming turn of events. At 11.02am on September 23, 1949, Truman announced to the world that America had detected an atomic explosion in the Soviet Union – the genie was out.

Even as American policymakers grappled with the novelty of defining a nuclear strategy for the country, they faced the immediate and weekly reality of mapping a credible non-nuclear strategy. Whether there really was "a Truman Doctrine," or whether American foreign policy – at least over Truman's first term in office – was driven by the triumvirate of Byrnes, Marshall, and Forrestal, this question hung unanswered.

The hawks were led by Secretary of Defense James Forrestal. With his sharp hairline like the prow of ship, Forrestal seriously countenanced a military showdown with the Soviet Union while America held the military winning card of an atomic bomb. But he remained the perpetual outsider, the ferocious Wall Street banker who became president of an investment banking firm by the age of 45, and who had no time for the Washington cocktail party circuit. In ordinary times he would not have been called to government service but these were extraordinary times and even his enemies recognized that America's post-wartime rearmament owed much to his disciplined mind and work ethic. Forrestal illustrated the great strength of a meritocracy that readily appointed talent to prominent public positions, but he also exemplified how Washington shunned the outsider. By May 1949 he was dead, mysteriously found on the roof of a walkway with a bathroom sash tied around his neck. The secretive manner in which his death was handled (the full and inconclusive report was only finally released in 2004) only served to convince many that Forrestal had been killed by enemies in the capital. Forrestal had championed the US Navy (where he had started his public career as Navy Secretary) over the Air Force. His successor, Louis Johnson, had links with the Air Force and promptly reversed Forrestal's bias in favor of the younger service. Johnson proved an eccentric if not downright dangerous failure, once confiding to an admiral that he saw no reason for the continued existence of the US Navy or Marines. A grateful Navy made sure that Forrestal lived on in the name of an aircraft carrier.

The leadership of the doves was handed from Byrnes to Secretary of State Marshall, whose foreign policy stance was summed up by the refrain, "Don't point a gun unless you are prepared to fire it." Marshall was forced to retire through exhaustion at the age of 68, and his place was taken by the son of an Episcopalian pastor, Dean Gooderham Acheson, at the beginning of 1949. An instinctive liberal, Acheson over time grew talons as sharp as any hawk's. In a game of Washington musical chairs, Marshall then found himself hauled out of retirement to take over the Defense Department.

There were other protagonists who shaped Truman's thinking and whose shadows would fall over Vietnam. Foremost was W. Averell Harriman, the "last of the New Dealers," a polymath scion of a railroad magnate billionaire who grew up in a 150-room mock-Renaissance castle. Harriman was described as a Gary Cooper type but somewhat withdrawn and melancholy. An ambassadorial posting to Moscow only seemed to increase his sense of sadness.[107] The Russians knew he was warning the State Department of the dangers of appeasing Stalin, which provoked an awkward scene at the lift of the Fairmont Hotel when he and Molotov bumped into each other during the San Francisco conference. The wealthy East Coaster raised his hat and bowed, allowing Molotov and his henchmen to bundle into the elevator first. Then Molotov snapped an order to one of his guards who made just enough room for the American to squeeze in. Harriman accepted the offer but turned his back to the Russian – an impeccable metaphor for the icy collapse of America's wartime alliance with the Soviet Union.[108]

George Kennan, the United States' Ambassador to the Soviet Union, had urgently warned of the dangers of an aggressive Soviet Union in his 1946 "Long Telegram." But it was Joe Kennedy, then a controversial former Ambassador to Britain, who articulated the new paradigm of US foreign policy in an influential article in March 1946.[109] With it, he popularized its capstone idea: "containment." Stalin's goal, he argued, was nothing less than "the worldwide extension of communism" and nothing less than a protective cordon sanitaire would save the free world. An "aggressive, confident and ruthless" Soviet Union need not be confronted in open war, a mutually destructive venture anyway. Rather, communism should be contained by a circumvallation of allies: Great Britain and her Commonwealth; the bloc of free, Western European countries; and nationalist China. The United States, he argued, had no mission to make the world "better," only to avoid war and keep the peace. The notion of spreading liberal democracy was both dangerous and fallacious: "The first defect lies in the fact that by its very nature such a program would involve a nation in minding other people's business on a global scale" and the "most serious defect is that if this policy of minding everyone's business should prove explosive ... then the plan of world betterment will have failed."[110] In short, US foreign policy should be to avoid a Third World War. This was modern expression of the orthodox position driven by Secretary of State John Quincy Adams in the early nineteenth century: America as exemplar of liberty but not the universal headmaster.

These ideas informed the solidifying Truman Doctrine; a peace-waging America, built on alliances and containment of communist expansionism. Concurrently with negotiations leading to the NATO alliance, the National Security Council reviewed all postwar military aid programs, some of which stemmed from Second World War obligations. From 1945 to 1949 the United States had provided military equipment and training assistance to Greece, Turkey, Iran, China, Korea, the Philippines, and several Latin American republics. Based on this examination, Truman proposed combining all existing programs and extending eligibility to any anti-communist government. This became the administration's primary means of containing communism outside Europe. The result was the Mutual Defense Assistance Program of October 1949. The Department of the Army, executive agent for the program, would despatch to each recipient country a military assistance advisory group (MAAG). Composed of Army, Navy, and Air Force teams, each advisory group would assist its host government in determining the amount and type of aid needed and help train the armed forces in the use of materiel received from the United States. The seeds of the future MAAG in Vietnam were sown here.

Out of the broader review, completed in April 1950, came recommendations encapsulated in the top secret NSC 68,[111] which called for a large expansion of US military, diplomatic, and economic efforts to meet the changed world situation. The "fanatic faith" of communism, it implied, was a disease, threatening "the destruction not only of this Republic but of civilization itself." It warned:

> Our free society finds itself mortally challenged by the Soviet Union. No other value system is so totally irreconcilable to ours, so implacable in its purpose to destroy ours, so capable of turning to its own uses the most dangerous and divisive trends in our own society, no other so skilfully and powerfully evokes the elements of irrationality in human nature, and no other has the support of a great and growing military power.

NSC 68 called for much more than Kennan-Kennedy notions of "containment," and indeed it dismantled the latter's isolationism. It argued:

> In a shrinking world, which now faces the threat of atomic warfare it is not an adequate objective, merely to seek to check the Kremlin design, for the absence of order among nations is becoming less and less tolerable. This fact imposes on us, in our own interests, the responsibility of world leadership.

The planning staffs in the Department of Defense answered this clarion call and began at once to translate the military recommendations into enhanced force levels and increased budgets. They somewhat jumped the gun as there remained the question whether the ambitious plans would persuade Truman to lift the ceiling on military appropriations. Events in another corner of East Asia soon resolved this issue.

———

Like Indochina, the overarching question hanging over the Korean peninsula was: did it matter? Before the war, Korea had been a Japanese colony with no strategic significance. The country was promised independence but divided along the 38th parallel, an interim arrangement that would be resolved in time through the auspices of the United Nations. Everybody's attention was fixed on the traditional prizes, Manchuria, Port Arthur, and Shanghai. One of the effects of the Cold War was to inflate the market value of previously ignored real estate and turn it into a battleground. Such was Korea's fate. It became, in the words of a contemporary, "One of those countries that calls forth all the clichés of the political geographers: pivot, buffer, football, dagger-pointed-at-the-heart-of, who-rules-this-rules-that."[112] In the late spring of 1947, the State Department sought half a billion dollars in aid to support Korea, a motion passed without enthusiasm. American missionaries were about the only people who actually wanted to be in Korea, their most successful Asian mission. GIs considered the Koreans "gooks" and their commander Lieutenant General John Hodges described them as "the same cat as the Japs."

On May 10, 1948, nationwide elections were held, sponsored by the UN. Despite widespread violence and intimidation in the campaign, 90 percent of the electorate voted, overwhelmingly backing the veteran campaigner for Korean independence, Syngman Rhee, then heading the National Society for the Rapid Realization for Independence. In his origins, Rhee was a mirror image of Ho Chi Minh; his early life and struggles were every bit as epic as those of his Vietnamese counterpart. But Rhee had thrown his ideological luggage on a capitalist and American train, rather than a Soviet locomotive. The Russians showed their displeasure at the result by cutting off the supply of electricity to the south. Five months later, on October 19, Russia announced the withdrawal of its troops from North Korea. On the same day, a South Korean National Army battalion infiltrated by communist agents mutinied, killed its officers, and seized the towns of Yosu and Sunchon, slaughtering 500 "collaborating" civilians. The mutiny was put down but the irony of Sunchon's name ("Peaceful Heaven") was not missed. North and South Korea were sliding from cold to hot war.

The "day of infamy" was Sunday June 25, 1950. At 4.30am on a drizzly morning, the North Korean Army launched a surprise attack across the 38th parallel, quickly rolling back border posts and inflicting America's first casualties of the war. Air Force Sergeant William Goodwin, a crewman on a B-29 who had survived being shot down in Europe in 1944, had the dubious honor of being the first of 33,686 eventual combat deaths. Suddenly, Secretary Johnson's $13.5 billion defense budget looked completely inadequate for the challenge Washington faced. Nobody doubted Russia's instigation of the war and two days later, Truman, backed by a unanimous UN vote, committed America to reversing the invasion through armed force. Events in Korea, in the meantime, were spiraling out of control. To calm nerves, the old warrior MacArthur arrived from Japan and sniffed the cordite on the battlefield. He duly received the cheers of South Korean peasants – "Victolly Macartar," as if a god had descended from the heavens – but their cries proved premature. "War is not war until the first, miserable, immortal doughfoot has had his guts blown out and his parents have got the word."[113] This happened all too quickly for America's undermanned and out-gunned 24th Infantry Division as it attempted to stem the North Korean advance in what was still euphemistically being called a "police action."

The recriminations started quickly. There were calls for Johnson and Acheson to resign. The soldiers on the front line complained that their bazookas were bouncing off the "Red tanks." The retreating South Korean units were hopelessly disorganized. Nobody seemed capable of coordinating basics like getting rations to the disparate, retreating units. Veteran General Omar Bradley began to appear every morning at 9.30am at the White House carrying an outsized map board under his arm to brief Truman on the status of the war. Vice President Alben Barkley, the first to serve on the newly established National Security Council, seemed to age beyond his 71 years. Only Air Secretary Stuart Symington seemed pleased: he would now receive his promised 70 Air Groups. The US Marine Corps, which some feared Defense Secretary Johnson was secretly preparing to chop, issued draft orders to 47,000 reservists who were given just ten days to get their civilian lives in order and report to their nearest depots. In New Mexico, citizens woke up to hear the local radio station KSIL informing them that all National Guardsmen should report immediately to their armories. In Silver City, a small town of 7,000 people, memories were long. The last time the town received this notice, half the boys never returned home, the majority leaving their bones behind on the Bataan death march.[114] Only in the previous week the town had buried the last repatriated body from that hellish experience, a Sergeant Robert Carpenter. In Japan, the 1st Cavalry Division was loaded on four giant transport ships and serenaded by a band playing the Washington Post March as it prepared to make the 700-mile journey from Japan to Korea (landing in the obscure port of P'ohang-dong because the front line had retreated so far south).

On the battlefield the news seemed all bad. On the left flank of the peninsula, 24th Division was mauled at the town of Taejon, losing its commander, the ruggedly handsome Major General William Dean. He was last seen wounded, handing ammunition to a bazooka team attempting to stop a column of T-34 tanks. Wasn't this how a true American general should fall? Not everyone agreed and some wondered why Dean, captured following a month on the run by the communists, had not busied himself actually commanding his division rather than playing the private soldier. On the right flank, in 25th Infantry Division's sector, there was stout resistance by the Negro Battalion – as it was known – at the town of Yechon, but then the division fell back under the weight of the advancing enemy. The only good news was that Britain, Australia, New Zealand, Thailand, and Turkey all agreed to join battle. America had never started a war so chaotically and so badly on the back foot.

The Korean War then played out in three acts. In the first act, American-led UN forces pushed back the North Korean forces to the 38th parallel. This phase lasted roughly from September 1950 to October 1950. In the second act, the great dramatist of the war, MacArthur, "imprisoned by his own pedestal,"[115] took the war into North Korea, provoked a Chinese reaction, and saw his career end in an ignominious sacking. This lasted from November 1950 to April 1951. The last act was an anticlimax with both sides stalemated on the prewar front line. An armistice but not a peace treaty was finally signed on July 27, 1953.

In August 1950, 8th (US) Army counterattacked from the Pusan perimeter, first with insufficient numbers and limited success. More numbers were needed and, as ever, the loyal if reluctant British showed up first with 27th Brigade joining the fight in Pusan on August 29, followed by 29th Brigade on November 3. The British deployment, like the initial American rush of reinforcements, was a complete shambles but at least another ally was now fighting. A fluid battle of advances and withdrawals followed. Pershing tanks began to arrive in Korea, giving the Red T-34s a run for their money. Then the tide turned, as much as anything as a result of

America's astonishing flair for industrial organization and logistics. The "MATS Airlift" (Military Air Transport Service) involved 236 aircraft making a 70-hour round trip from the West Coast over a sustained 40-day period. It was a stunningly quick response. The pilots knew they were in a war against a covert Russian enemy because as they crossed within 60 miles of Russian positions near Misawa their radios were jammed by electronic warfare detachments. Across the breadth of the Pacific Ocean, the equivalent naval Military Sea Transportation Service (MSTS) re-animated the wartime sea lanes and started pouring supplies into Korea with a 300-strong fleet of transports, cargo ships, and tankers. San Diego, Oakland, and San Francisco hummed again with frenetic activity. Each of the five divisions making up the newly formed 8th (US) Army required 580 tons of daily supplies, a demand satisfied by the relentless MSTS operation.

The decisive blow came with the Inchon landings in mid-September; Operation *Chromite*, staged by X (US) Corps, which unhinged the rear of the communist forces and sent them pell-mell north. It was a bold gamble – the distance between Pusan and Inchon was over 200 miles of enemy-held ground – but the bet paid off. MacArthur the magi, still wearing his world war braided cap, had pulled off a master stroke. Later, on a beach walkabout, he passed the corpse of a dead North Korean soldier and wise-cracked that this was one patient the medics would not have to work on.

Act two should never have happened. The retreating North Koreans left behind over 70,000 dead. American forces suffered around 3,000 fatalities. It had been a whitewash. One American division had swelled into two corps in a matter of weeks. Pusan, far from becoming an American Dunkirk as many predicted, burst like a dam and swept aside the invaders with irresistible force.

The war was prolonged and expanded by a combination of factors: hubris in key US policymakers, gross miscalculation over the possibility of Chinese intervention despite intelligence warnings, and a lack of leadership in the United Nations. When 1st Cavalry supported by the now consolidated 27th British Commonwealth Brigade swept into the North Korean capital

Pyongyang, 95 miles north of the 38th parallel in October, all the talk was about winding up the war. MacArthur clearly thought so. "The war is definitely coming to an end shortly," he confidently told a reporter.[116] The British were so relaxed they stopped wearing helmets and strolled through the empty city wearing regimental headgear.

Five Chinese divisions poured over the Yalu River and knocked out a regiment of 1st Cavalry. Follow-on mass attacks sent the allies retreating all the way back to the 38th parallel and beyond, leaving behind hundreds of dead and trails of abandoned equipment. The spectacle of thousands of civilian refugees fleeing communist reprisals, mingled with desperate troops, filled the news. For the "grunts" of 1st Marine Division retreating from the Changjin (Chosin) Reservoir, an epic march became a tale of remarkable endurance. X (US) Corps did play out an American Dunkirk after all, at the port of Hungnam rather than at Pusan, denying the communist forces an emphatic victory. The entire Corps was evacuated along with 17,500 vehicles, 350,000 tons of supplies, and 91,000 North Korean civilians. Air and naval firepower kept the Chinese at bay who had over-extended themselves anyway. On one day, more soldiers died from experimenting with anti-freeze whiskey than from enemy action, such was the nature of the evacuation by the end. The joke went round that General Almond, the Corps commander, was in fact conducting an amphibious invasion in reverse. Following the evacuation, Hungnam looked like it had been hit by an atomic bomb, so efficient were the demolition teams that were among the last to leave.

Temperatures fell to 20 below zero and the mood in Washington was equally frosty. For a second time, America had been undone by a surprise attack. How had nobody noticed two Chinese army groups, six armies, and 18 divisions, redeploy from the Manchurian interior to the Korean border? Why had no one detected the war preparations, and warning indicators, or predicted the Chinese reaction? In fact, many had, and there was no great surprise. The hubris was all MacArthur's, determined to march to the Yalu, despite overwhelming intelligence evidence that the People's

Liberation Army would not tolerate a US army on its border. When Truman posed the question, "What are the chances for Chinese or Soviet interference?" his chief commander could not have offered a more useless answer:

> Very little ... We are no longer fearful of their intervention ... The Chinese have 300,000 men in Manchuria. Of these, probably not more than 100/125,000 are distributed along the Yalu River. Only 50/60,000 could be gotten across the Yalu River. They have no Air Force ... if the Chinese tried to get down to P'yongyang there would be the greatest slaughter.[117]

There was a slaughter, but it fell on the routed and retreating UN forces, and the tens of thousands of civilians following in their wake.

The military setback in Korea provoked fierce debate in Congress between isolationists and interventionists. Taft, Hoover, and Kennedy led the isolationists; Acheson, Dewey, and Dulles hit back for the interventionists. It was Hoover who best summed up America's dilemma, unchanged for the next half century. The United Nations was a toothless and leaderless institution; it could not guarantee world peace. The United States was being forced to shoulder an unacceptable burden in the fight for freedom: 90 percent of the Western forces in Korea and 90 percent of the casualties were American. The Allies were indulging in "military tokenism," as they would do in succeeding years. On the other Cold War front line, European nations were simply not doing enough. The seduction of trusting in American military strength had already infected the newly formed North Atlantic Treaty Organization. Not "another man or another dollar on their shores," Hoover argued, until the Europeans demonstrate the "spiritual strength and unity to avail themselves of their own resources."

The significance of Hoover's widely publicized words, counter-intuitively, was that they were received with near total rejection. Distinguished historian Arthur Schlesinger Jr.,

America's *éminence grise*, dismissively retorted that Hoover "merely demonstrates once again his inability to learn by experience." Polls suggested that most Americans judged Hoover an idiot. The average American was not ready to throw the towel in. An anti-communist rhetoric, whistling from every coffee pot on Main Street USA, demanded a fight back.

For the next two months the front line ebbed and flowed like a dirty tide. Seoul fell and then was recaptured. Lieutenant General Matthew Bunker Ridgway, the old airborne warhorse with trademark hand grenade hanging off his webbing straps, took over and gave the Allies spine, common sense, and a determination to win. Ridgway arrived in Korea on December 26, 1950 and by the following night he had visited every headquarters under his command. He arrived with a catchphrase – "give me your utmost" – and it was with utter seriousness that he called his first major offensive Operation *Killer*.

But all the tactical sparring led nowhere because Washington and the UN lacked a clear strategy. General James Van Fleet would later argue that May 1951 was the great missed opportunity when the communist armies could have been put to the sword. This indecision sowed the seeds for MacArthur's fall from grace, increasingly impatient with the lack of a grand strategy, and supported by a British press led by Lord Beaverbrook who saw in the general the West's best hope. This was a field marshal who witnessed the 1905 Russo-Japanese War as a first lieutenant and who half a century later was still involved in Asian wars – surely his words counted for something. Truman did not think so. MacArthur's sacking solved nothing on the battlefield, or in the debating chambers of the UN, but it did signal that the Truman government was not prepared to escalate Korea into a Third World War. The only way out now was to talk. MacArthur's last act befitted a personality who had spent 52 years serving in the military (in the last 14 years he had not even returned home for leave). New York greeted him with a ticker tape parade and he was afforded the dignity of one last speech to Congress. Seven and a half million Americans lined the streets to bid him farewell and 2,852 tons of confetti were strewn in his path.[118] Truman all the while gamely took the catcalls from a partisan crowd at a Senators-Yankee baseball match in Washington.

The last act of the war was largely dominated by Korea's hilly topography. This is why many of the battles are simply recorded by spot heights – Hill 626, Hill 79, Hill 347 – a nameless landscape of indistinguishable humps turned into cemeteries. This factor favored defense over attack, infiltration over sweeping maneuver, and the raking machine gun over suicidal bayonet charges. Blitzkrieg was replaced by "Sitzkrieg," summer turned to winter, and it was all costing far too many lives. In some sectors of the front, a surprising level of fraternization developed, especially among the pragmatic British. At one disputed hill, the local British commander came to an agreement with his Chinese counterpart that he would hold the point by day, and the Chinese could hold the point by night. The arrangement became so cordial the Chinese would leave a burning brazier for the British to boil their tea, a gesture that was reciprocated.[119] The Americans found this despicable, but then again, they had always suspected the ailing British imperialists lacked "fight."

Nobody was making any progress on the ground and the war moved to the air where American pilots flying F-86s found themselves being shot out of the sky at an alarming rate in "MiG alley," reigniting bitter criticism over the manner in which the Air Force had been run down. Unbeknown to the pilots, many of their aerial adversaries were Russians, part of a secret contingent of advisors that may have numbered as many as 5,000 at the height of the conflict. Their participation in the war inspired a leaden, racist Russian joke: Russian pilots were better than American pilots because they flew their aircraft with no hands. How so? Because they had to use their hands to slant their eyes, to trick American pilots into thinking that they were Koreans.[120]

By the spring of 1953 Eisenhower was firmly in charge, and the Department of Defense was accounting for 60 percent of government spending. The former General Motors president, "Engine Charlie" Wilson, led the enlarged Department in pugnacious style, too pugnacious perhaps as he would leave disliked by the Joint Chiefs. But President, Congress, and the American people now wanted out. The armed forces had swollen to 3.5 million strong and the federal government was employing 1.3 million civilians, all to preserve an invisible line across a range of hills in a country nobody really cared about anymore.

The truce talks proved as painful and slow as the subsequent prisoner exchanges. After over 1,000 days of fighting and 575 separate meetings an armistice was finally signed late in the summer of 1953. Even as the ink dried, voices were already sniping from the sidelines: this was a war we could have won, if we had wanted to. The Reds were beaten. We probably killed half a million communist soldiers. We destroyed every major bridge in North Korea, we cut every railway, and we bombed every road. We destroyed the fourth largest hydro-electric plant in the world and plunged North Korea into darkness. If only Washington had shown the same resolve as a bomber pilot or front-line GI. It was not the prisoners of war who were brainwashed; it was all those appeasing liberals. To which the liberals responded: harken the wisdom of Omar Bradley – this was "the wrong war, at the wrong place, at the wrong time." Whatever the rights and wrongs, it was the case that Washington did not so much end the war as liquidate it.

The Korean War passed from public consciousness but the material and cultural junk it left behind made the Vietnam War possible. Ordinary Americans got behind the war. It is easy to forget from the stalemated conclusion that the overwhelming mood of the country, at the beginning of the conflict, was captured by the phrase "At last!" Americans were fed up with being pushed about by an aggressive Soviet Union. Korea had offered the chance to demonstrate Uncle Sam's resolve.

The draft was re-instated for all males aged between 19 and 25, potentially raising a 547,000-strong army, almost exactly the maximal number reached in the later war. In 1955, the emergency wartime draft was formally established under the Reserve Forces Act. Each year, potentially, as many as 1.1 million Americans between the ages of 18½ and 26 were obliged to complete six years' mandatory military service. In practice, there was a legion of ways to draft-dodge and just over half this number ever got called up, adding to the social divisiveness of the draft in the next decade. Clever or well-connected young men could volunteer to serve in the reserve program or National Guard, precluding them from service overseas and limiting their active commitment to just six months, or none at all. Most of the 30-odd schemes by which an 18-year-old could be drafted actually only demanded two years' active service, and for many, enlistment provided an opportunity to learn trades, as well as travel for the first time in their lives. Thousands embraced this opportunity. The Air Force alone offered training in 43 schools, providing a vital first step on the ladder to a career in America's burgeoning aviation industry.

The postwar disarmament was abruptly reversed. When war broke out, Truman straightaway requested an additional $10 billion for defense, which was granted. By the end of the first year of conflict, the defense budget jumped 300 percent. Seventh Fleet took station across Formosa to prevent a communist takeover, and then never left these waters. The shock that America might just lose a war as a result of a communist surprise attack seared Washington. After Korea, the United States would never again neglect her armed forces, but this contained a trap. The Truman Doctrine was dead in the water, replaced by the enticement of military intervention.

Increased defense spending spurred technological innovation, a field in which America excelled. The first examples of fiberglass and plastic body armor, weighing 7lb 12oz, made an appearance. A lighter-caliber bullet was introduced. This eventually became the standard NATO 7.62mm round. Tank shot was revolutionized with the development of extremely tough, long rod penetrators. A computerized range finder was added to the tank gunner's sight greatly improving his first round probability of hit. An atomic artillery howitzer was developed. On the first firing, the recoil system broke and the barrel almost came off its mounting. At the second attempt, a shell was lost and it took two days to find the errant projectile – these were the days when weapon trials truly did have heart-stopping moments. Primitive cruise missiles were launched from carriers, in fact surplus Navy Hellcats loaded with explosives and guided to their targets by remote control. If you took on America, you took on her lust for making things bigger, better, faster, and more explosive.

There were other important military and political consequences. The limited objective of re-establishing the 38th parallel provided a model for the Demilitarized Zone on the 17th parallel in Vietnam. The former demarcation line contributed to a sense that the Korean War had, in the end, been phony and pointless, a "half war" – a thought that became virulent in Vietnam. What was the point of going to war if you were not playing to win? China's intervention in Korea created one of the great uncertainties of the later war; if America pushed too hard would the Chinese sweep south again? Perhaps 70 percent of the People's Liberation Army had deployed to Korea as "Chinese People's Volunteers" (2.97 million soldier in total), supported by 600,000 civil workers. These were sobering numbers. The Soviet Union's gleeful role as proxy warmonger was not forgotten, nor her MiGs. The possibility of direct intervention by either of these communist leviathans encouraged the repetition of the uncertain experiment of limited war in Vietnam.

Washington backed Syngman Rhee, who proved a corrupt authoritarian, just as it would later back South Vietnam's crooked rulers, but the old joke that at least he is "our son of a bitch" was not a serious foundation on which to build a foreign policy. Asian opinion of the Western intervention was neutral at best and commonly hostile. While Washington believed America was defending freedom, most Asians just saw another interfering foreign culture; the oil and water of the Western and Eastern minds never really mixed. America met mass attacks with technological superiority but discovered, like her allies, that she was fighting a fanatical enemy seemingly careless of human lives. The specter of using the atomic bomb was raised, as it would be in Vietnam, but discounted. A runaway general over-stepped the boundary of the civil-military relationship in a democracy and was sacked. In Vietnam, Westmoreland would never go that far, but he became as political as the most hardened congressman. Above all, America relied on her air power to stave off defeat. This reliance on air power carried false lessons which would be transmitted to the next generation of politicians.

These parallels aside, Korea opened the door to Vietnam in the very real sense that Truman ordered a military mission to the country, to assist the French, the weekend following the North Korean invasion. A "monstrous conspiracy to stamp out freedom all over the world" had erupted, and had to be halted, whatever the cost.[121] NATO responded by passing a resolution in support of the French war in Indochina. The US Legation in Saigon jumped from a modest seven-strong staff to over 100, brimming with ideas over how to put the country right. A $23.5 million civilian aid package was authorized by Congress, the first hand-out of the multi-billion-dollar effort that would stretch over the next 23 years. Freedom was coming to Vietnam, if only the French could be persuaded to stop using "*tu*" with adult Vietnamese, and if the grubby fingers of petty, provincial French officials could be levered from the reins of power.

The coincidence of the Korean War, the "loss" of China, and a Russian bomb was ultimately decisive to Washington compromising American anti-colonial instincts. That these great events all happened within 12 months of each other only magnified the sense of crisis. Washington had to support France and unrealistically hoped a victorious Paris would subsequently withdraw from Indochina with honor (and pockets) satisfied. French politicians of all parties only saw a threat to their prewar colonies, especially in North Africa. The absurdity of 40 million French controlling the destiny of several hundred million foreigners did not seem so absurd in the late 1940s. Ho the Nationalist became Ho the Communist, and therefore beyond the pale. At the same time, French attitudes toward America had hardened to the point of rudeness. In contrast to a Vietnamese press that viewed

America favorably, Saigon's French newspapers routinely accused Washington of imperialism, a breathtaking ingratitude set against subsequent military support offered by the White House.

American support now went further than words, spurred by the collapse of Nationalist China, the key event that turned the First Indochina War. A sham Vietnamese "independence" was formally recognized on February 2, 1950 but this was preempted by the People's Republic of China granting diplomatic recognition to Ho's Democratic Republic of Vietnam (DRV) in January, the first country to do so. "Independence" in the south amounted to a hollow transfer of power to a restored Bao Dai puppet regime, secured under the flawed Elysée Agreements. Ho was not even in the country at the time but conferring with Stalin in Moscow. In their northern redoubts, the Viet Minh continued to govern the DRV, now also recognized by the Soviet Union. The most important consequence of the Maoist victory was a ready supply of arms to the Viet Minh. Faced with this escalation, Washington felt it had little choice but to start arming the wobbling French.

In March 1950, a task force from the Economic Cooperation Administration headed by Robert A. Griffin was despatched to Indochina, and duly reported on the dire situation facing the French. The solution to the conflict, it concluded, was political, not military. But by May, the Truman government had agreed to arm the embattled French using a $75 million emergency fund originally intended for "lost China." Secretary of State Dean Acheson, now girt in anti-communist armor, proved the hawk. The first direct military assistance by the US government to Indochina was an allocation of $10 million made on May 1 (a postwar $160 million economic package had earlier been granted to French Indochina). In June, a second joint mission headed by John F. Melby of the State Department and Iwo Jima veteran, USMC Major General Graves B. Erskine, descended on Saigon. This would be remembered as "the Erksine mission" for good reason: the marine general dominated the group and returned to Washington with a call for military action, sweeping aside the conclusions of the Griffin mission.

Erskine set a pattern that would bedevil every subsequent fact-finding mission to Vietnam, perceptively observed by Southeast Asia CIA analyst George Allen:

> Survey missions sent to determine what might be done seemed always to return with a program for positive action – to propose a solution no matter how intractable the problem might appear to those participating in the mission. More often than not, such study groups seemed to listen selectively, to minimize negative factors, and to find reasons for doing *something*, rather than proposing that *nothing* can be done.[122]

That "something" almost invariably was military action, which added to the illusion that something was being done, rather than political, which everybody agreed was the true nature of the conflict. Much like modern counterinsurgency wars, eight out of every ten dollars spent on Vietnam went on military programs.

The granite-faced Erskine judged the French "a bunch of second-raters," and conspiratorially suggested that French agents had planted three bombs that detonated in the hotel where the US survey mission was staying.[123] In reality, the French, desperate for assistance, could not have been more helpful on this occasion. A 5,000-page stack of reports was dumped on the Americans and Erskine was feted with parades and social engagements. The latter just seemed to annoy him, and it is doubtful the overconfident Erskine so much as glanced at the French intelligence as his team's three translators were totally overwhelmed by the material.[124]

Instead, he fell back on two diagnoses that would become staples of US missions in the First Indochina War: first, the French were not being offensive enough; and second, American equipment, advice, and ideally training were necessary to win the war. Melby's more subtle and key judgment – that "the political interests of France and the Associated States [French Indochina] are not only different, they are mutually exclusive" – was lost in the bugle calls.[125] Through the medium of Erskine and the Defense Department, a compliant but not enthusiastic White House was being propelled toward a fundamentally contradictory foreign policy. France was only interested in continuing the fight in Vietnam if its interests were served. Paris had no incentive or desire to squander lives or treasure for the cause of Vietnamese independence, the outcome that Washington sought, but which rendered the French war meaningless. The French, in turn, were caught in the irresolvable dilemma that if they ceded more political powers to the Vietnamese, they undermined their own case for remaining in Vietnam; yet if they did not, they increased support for the Viet Minh. The only point of agreement was that communism had to be opposed, but for the French this was more a key for pickpocketing American largesse rather than the ideological conviction now swelling the heads of the Joint Chiefs.

Three weeks later, and with the Korean War now irrupted, Truman announced the establishment of a permanent aid mission to Indochina and accelerated military assistance. The MAAG, or Military Assistance Advisory Group, was born. In a parallel move, Peking established a CMAG (Chinese Military Advisory Group) in the north.[126] The initially 70-strong MAAG complement was assigned to Saigon on August 3, amidst grave French suspicions over its purpose and terms of employment. The MAAG's first commander was a Brigadier General Francis Brink, a veteran of the Burma campaign, who took post on October 10. His tenure was short: in June 1952 he apparently committed suicide in mysterious circumstances. On December 23, 1950, a Pentalateral Mutual Defense Assistance Pact was signed by France, the United States, and the Associated States.[127] This paved the way for the official establishment of the MAAG on January 8 in 1951, by now with an authorized strength of 128. By 1954, it had swelled to a 342-strong force. None of these pioneers could have possibly imagined they would be the historic advance guard of half a million US servicemen.

It was over this period that the great drone note of Vietnam's wars first sounded its dismal tone. It was called a theory, which it was not, and it was based on a bar room game, which was unwise. Paul Warnke, Secretary of Defense for International Affairs under Johnson, later observed that "one of the difficulties is that in foreign policy, you always tend to reason by analogy," and he was right.[128] There have been fewer less appropriate analogies than falling dominoes.

The domino theory had its origins in the testimony given by Major General Claire Chennault to the House Foreign Affairs Committee in the spring of 1948. Chennault had made his name as commander of the volunteer Flying Tigers during the war. It was in his capacity as Commander 14th Air Force in China and unrivalled expert on the country that he was quizzed by the Senate. Without using the term "domino," Chennault predicted that if America allowed China to fall into communist hands then it would only be a matter of time before Indochina followed, imperilling all the neighboring countries in turn: Burma, Thailand, Malaya, and Indonesia. Like many American Sinophiles, Chennault would lament the loss of China to the communists (his second wife was a Chinese reporter), but what really angered him was America failing through passivity. For a man whose entire life had been decisive action, this was the original sin. Future state secretaries would find themselves haunted by Chennault's second law of communist entropy: only the application of equal and greater energy could reverse the collapse.

But why did Indochina matter, a French colony in which the State Department had little interest or even understanding? Why Tonkin, Annam, or Cochin China? If few Americans could place any of these on a map, they could place Pearl Harbor. And it was the Japanese de facto annexation of the French colony in 1940 that had proved the falling domino that preceded the perfidious surprise attack on the American Pacific fleet. Vietnam had an unimpeachable historical precedent as domino: with the French cowed, Indochina had provided the springboard for the invasions of the Philippines and British-held Malaya. Anyone seeking "proof" of the domino theory did not have to look too far.

What emerged was a "Munich mentality" in State Department analyst James Thomson's later verdict – not one "further square foot of territory to communism."[129] This canon infiltrated government with an alacrity that communism was manifestly failing to display.

When in the early 1960s Thomson was asked to draft a speech for Defense Secretary McNamara, his boss instructed: "I want you, finally and most importantly, to destroy forever in this speech the myth that Vietnam is a civil war." When Thomson – an expert who had grown up in the region – protested that it was precisely a civil war, rather than a canonical fault line with the communist evil, he was brusquely told, "Don't bandy words with me, young man." Thomson's misgivings went unheeded: the mistake with "the line-drawing itch" over Vietnam was that the country was a swamp, and "you do not draw lines in swamps."[130]

The domino theory became American foreign policy orthodoxy through the Truman-era NSC 64, approved on March 27, 1950. Again without using the word, the memorandum spoke of "anticipated communist plans to seize all of Southeast Asia," without furnishing any intelligence evidence or convincing arguments to support the charge. By NSC 142/2 (June 1952), the domino theory was implicit and unquestioned: "In the absence of effective and timely counteraction, the loss of any single country would probably lead to relatively swift submission to or an alignment with communism by the remaining countries." In a hysterical judgment, this memorandum suggested that communism would then spread like the Black Death across India and the Middle East, and enter Europe by its soft underbelly (a domino theory proselyter like Walt Rostow would say that Burma was the Ardennes of India, an indefensibly ridiculous assertion, but a measure of just how exaggerated the concept had become).[131] This apocalyptic vision was framed in the context of an America now locked in a Korean War, facing a nuclear and aggressive Soviet Union, and uncertain of communist China's intentions. But it also illustrated how swiftly minds became dizzied by the locomotive of events. In NSC 162/2 (October 1953) – by which time Eisenhower's New Look nuclear defense policy had been endorsed – defense chiefs were being directed to plan for the use of atomic weapons to defend Vietnam against an imagined Chinese invasion.[132]

NSC 162/2 revealed a basic contradiction in the administration's position, revealed starkly in NSC 177, submitted just two months later. A smaller New Look armed forces backed by the club of atomic bombs could not reasonably hope to intervene successfully in Vietnam, except by lobbing "the Bomb," and who in their right mind wanted to do that? What if the French quit anyway, or if US air power failed to turn the tide? What if the Bao Dai regime crumbled? "When we start putting our men into Indochina," Treasury Secretary George Humphrey warned, "how long will it be before we get into the war?"[133]

Eisenhower first publicly invoked the analogy of falling dominoes at an April 7, 1954 press conference in the Indian Treaty Room of the Old Executive Office Building. In Vietnam, he argued:

> ... you have broader considerations that might follow, what you would call the "falling domino" principle. You have a row of dominoes set up, you knock over the first one, and what will happen to the last one is the certainty that it will go over very quickly.[134]

The day before he had contrarily instructed the National Security Council, "there was no possibility whatever of U.S. unilateral intervention in Indochina." He has now been lumped with the historical millstone. But the flawed, confused, and exaggerated notion was already well embedded in institutional thinking by the time he used the phrase.

––––––

In Vietnam, meanwhile, the war seemed to be picking up. After suffering several reverses, including a traumatic ambush on Route Coloniale 4 north of Hanoi that resulted in over 4,000 French dead and missing, it seemed by 1952 that the military campaign was back on track. The martyred de Lattre was heralded as a savior but his victories, in truth, had been hollow. The crucial business of "Vietnamizing" the war was a story of broken promises – just three percent of the officer class were native Vietnamese. In this respect, the management of the war was a mirror image of the hollow political transfer of power to the renamed Associated States. Crucially, the entire effort rested on US aid, which de Lattre had ungratefully railed against, accusing the American head of the economic mission of being "the most dangerous man in Indochina."[135]

Blind to French ingratitude (and duplicity), aid to Vietnam was further promoted by Anzio veteran, Lieutenant General John "Iron Mike" O'Daniel, a short, belligerent man who never gave "a god-damned inch" to the enemy. "Iron Mike" conducted three missions to the region. And on each occasion he presaged the false optimism of the later war, consistently reporting imminent French victory, but for a few more guns and planes – a view hardly any independent observer, or even the French, agreed with. Truman explicitly sent O'Daniel to Vietnam to evaluate "the chances of ultimate victory" – the most insistent question for his administration underwriting the French war – but a question which the unreliable general deflected with the bluster of "a new aggressive psychology" that Navarre had brought to the battlefield.[136] It was true that Navarre re-inflated punctured French pride in Tonkin, but it was O'Daniel who created the myth of "the Navarre Plan" to open purse strings in the corridors of Washington. He then went further, kick-starting the first US training mission in South Vietnam without Washington's approval, buoyed by an invincible optimism that US trainers would succeed where French trainers had so miserably failed.[137] In doing so, he went against the recommendations of the Joint Chiefs who unanimously and sensibly judged that such a training program had "virtually no chance of success."[138] Not for the first time in the Vietnam story, voices forewarning likely failure were ignored in favor of the false advocates of success – a characteristic that has remained true to present-day wars. The promotion and rewards, then as now, went to the individual promising victory.

The unstoppable "Iron Mike" has claim to being the first general to embroil America in Vietnam. His was a generation that won wars – a characteristic of all the Vietnam-era generals – losing just seemed unconscionable. With his unswerving convictions he became the first of a succession of military chiefs justifying intervention in this corner of Southeast Asia. Without the military aid, France's expeditionary corps would certainly have foundered sooner: 361,522 small arms and machine guns, 30,887 jeeps and trucks, 1,800 combat vehicles of all types, 500 aircraft, and 438 naval craft were donated by the summer of 1954.[139] It was a massive effort, and by the end America was financing 78 percent of France's lost war at a cost of just over $1 billion per annum.[140] The total cost of the war to America ran to $2.6 billion – an extravagant price for a lost cause.

American blindness over French Indochina was arresting. As early as 1947, France had given up hope of "winning" militarily in Indochina. Successive and unstable French governments gradually came to the conclusion that an "honorable" withdrawal that protected France's commercial interests was the best and only realistic hope. Military victory developed as an American obsession, encouraged disingenuously by the French who needed the aid to secure their more limited aims. A monolithic communism drugged Washington, unable or unwilling to grapple with the political complexities of a colonial legacy fractured by a world war. Battalions had to be matched by battalions, warplanes by warplanes. Vietnam became the necessary bulwark against communist expansionism, not because it actually was, but because Washington believed the credo with religious fervour, even as the French supplicant was tip-toeing out of the church.

Then Navarre led his government and army into the almighty trap of Dien Bien Phu, a move which Washington had no small part in fomenting. At last the French pupil was demonstrating aggression. But why did anyone believe that Operation *Castor* – a madcap scheme – would ever work? The misbegotten spot was 175 miles from Hanoi, at the very limits of the CEFEO's very limited air support. Just six battalions were dropped into a valley that would become a byword for folly and astonishing endurance. Everything rested on the air bridge but nobody paid close attention to the arithmetic that always threw up the same answer. If the Viet

Minh were to succeed in shutting down the airstrip, the operation would end in failure.

The garrison's over-confident, one-armed artillery chief Colonel Charles Piroth boasted that the communists would never be able to shut down the air bridge. When the Viet Minh's well-concealed guns did just that, he committed suicide by holding a grenade to his chest and pulling the pin. The French gave their strongpoints female names – Béatrice, Gabrielle, Anne-Marie – rumoured to be former mistresses of Colonel Christian de Castries, the overall commander. This only added pathos to the grimness as each of the strongpoints fell in bloody, hand-to-hand fighting. Later there was criticism that the aristocratic de Castries was the wrong officer to command the gutter fighting at Dien Bien Phu. This was excuse-making for an impossible mission. The leadership in the trenches was superb. The garrison's legionnaires, Algerians and Moroccans (the last to surrender) fought valiantly. But the position was hopeless.

When the end came six months later, it felt like relief that the agony was over, for both sides. It was, as General René Cogny later remarked, "Too many deaths for nothing." One month after the fall of Dien Bien Phu the war claimed the life of André Friedmann, better known to the world as Robert Capa, a Hungarian immigrant who made America his home and the camera lens his judgment on a world at war. This was his fifth conflict when a land mine took off his left leg near a village south of Hanoi. His body was temporarily laid to rest at the military cemetery in the city. Among the wreaths was one from his favorite restaurant, La Bonne Casserole, which simply read, "A notre ami."[141] Capa was the first American journalist killed in Indochina.

Dien Bien Phu raised the possibility of direct American intervention which Eisenhower wisely turned down, not least because the Joint Chiefs advised that this would require 7–12 US divisions and 500 daily fighter-bomber sorties to thwart an assumed Chinese intervention, or as Vice Admiral Davis colorfully put it, "One cannot go over Niagara Falls in a barrel only slightly."[142] As importantly, Eisenhower held the strong belief that "we should not be involved unilaterally in activities in that area and that a collective approach was desirable."[143] After the sourness of the Korean War, a collective response was impossible. As long as he remained President, Eisenhower advised a breakfast gathering, the United States was not going to "go in alone."[144] At subsequent meetings, the level-headed Matt Ridgway was instrumental in arguing against American engagement – deflecting intense lobbying by Admiral Radford and Secretary of State Dulles – but Eisenhower in the end needed little persuasion. In a foretaste of later disagreements, the Air Force argued for assisting the French with B-29 strikes, but the Joint Chiefs soberly warned that even the use of an atomic weapon was unlikely to guarantee victory, which somewhat placed the folly of Dien Bien Phu in perspective.[145] French pleas to bomb the Viet Minh anyway with conventional weapons (the aborted Operation *Vulture*) were also ignored. The possible employment of atomic weapons, however, did not go away. As late as the mid-1960s, this card was kept up the sleeve as a last resort, although it is highly implausible that a US president would have sanctioned their use.[146] Hanoi, it appears, genuinely feared this eventuality. Following the ceasefire, a North Vietnamese refugee was later found in possession of a map depicting the likely outcomes of such an atomic strike. It showed a series of concentric circles drawn over the epicentre of Hanoi.[147]

Bullets and bombs failed so words took over, but the Geneva Conference of June 1954 was unsatisfactory from start to finish. Every party sought different outcomes. The Viet Minh wanted legitimacy under a united, independent Vietnam, which a roused Emperor Bao Dai refused to offer, dismissing Ho and his gang as mere rebels. His attitude to the upstart northerners was summed up in one utterance: "There is only one Vietnamese state. It is I."[148] The Laniel government balked at full independence for the Associated States but then fell. The newly installed Mendès-France government reversed this position and could not get out quick enough. In a move that caught everyone by surprise, the outsider Mendès-France – a sleek-haired Portuguese-Jew who had flown for the Free French Air Force – promised to resign if he did not achieve a settlement within the month, an eventuality he only just managed to avoid. This was the 19th French government since the end of the war and weariness was beginning to tell. Catholic opinion, however, was outraged at the betrayal of Vietnamese co-religionists, and a defeated colonial army simmered with discontent. Washington, burned by the experience of Korean negotiations, urged France to get tough – fight on if necessary – and not to concede to communists. Faced with the probability that France would capitulate, and to avoid being seen to acquiesce to a possible communist triumph at the peace talks, the US representative, Under Secretary of State Walter Bedell Smith, only participated as an observer (Foster Dulles deliberately did not attend, despite French pleas). When the signatories finally paraded for the press, Washington's representative refused to join them, unwilling to recognize "participants who were basically communist revolutionaries and subversionists."[149]

Bedell Smith was nobody's fool. A man whose military career began as a private in the Indiana National Guard in 1911 and culminated as Chief of Staff to Eisenhower, he had witnessed more than his fair share of political chicanery. When it became clear that French will had indeed collapsed, Washington settled for containment in a seven-point plan hatched with British support. In a most subtle way, the First Indochina War ended as America's war, or as Kennedy put it, America became the "godparents" of "little Vietnam."[150] Privately, US diplomats viewed the whole shoddy business as a "disaster." Nobody really believed the newly created South Vietnam would last very long anyway.

The Geneva Conference was ultimately flawed because two countries refused to sign (South Vietnam and the United States), and because the French quit. Worse than flawed, it was not even ratified: the only document that was actually signed was the ceasefire agreement between French and Viet Minh forces ("Agreement on the Cessation of Hostilities in Viet-Nam"). Under Article 7 France became the guarantor of Vietnamese sovereignty, unity, and territorial integrity, with the People's Army of Vietnam (PAVN) as the guarantor of armistice agreements under Articles 22 and 23. National elections were also agreed under Article 7 and France agreed to withdraw the French Expeditionary Corps at the request of local governments under Article 10.

All the other documents, including the Final Declaration, remained unsigned. Faced with this impasse, it came down to two bargains: where to draw a temporary demarcation line and when to hold nationwide elections (as the demarcation line was expressly not recognized as "constituting a political or territorial boundary"). Neither satisfied: the line was drawn on the 17th parallel, a totally arbitrary line that had origins in a wartime boundary dispute between Mountbatten and Wedemeyer, and which left the Viet Minh cheated of hard-won gains, notwithstanding the promise of elections in two years. In fact, the division was not wholly without historical precedent. Almost certainly unknown to Mountbatten and Wedemeyer, Tonkin had been separated from Annam by two fortification walls, roughly on the 17th parallel, from 1640 until 1790.

The real significance of this Demilitarized Zone (DMZ) was that Hanoi had no intention of respecting it, or the neutrality of neighboring countries. As Nixon later lamented, North Vietnam's violations of national borders "lengthened the front that Saigon had to defend from 40 to 640 miles."[151] It would prove an impossible task. And why did the DMZ matter anyway, as everyone expected the Viet Minh to win in a free election? Ironically, it was in the end Russian and Chinese pressure that forced Ho to compromise, fearing a wider confrontation with an ambiguous Washington whose policy of "innocence by disassociation," as it was dubbed, spooked the communist powers into believing that a clever plot was being warmed. For the Soviet leadership the absolute priority lay in Europe anyway. The Politburo was desperate to avoid a humiliation of the Radical Mendès-France government which had advertised that it would not join a proposed European Defense Community – EDC (the precursor to NATO). Indochina could not stand in the way of the greater prize of dividing the Western European allies. Molotov, of course, achieved this objective and France duly turned its nose up at the EDC.

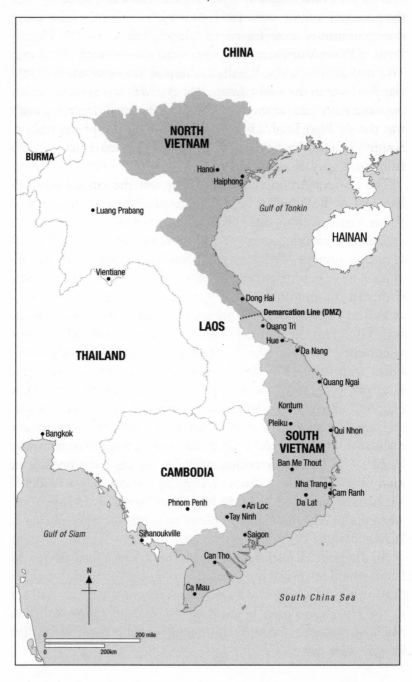

Map 3: The 1954 Division of Vietnam Along the 17th Parallel

CHINA

NORTH VIETNAM

BURMA

Hanoi

Haiphong

Luang Prabang

Gulf of Tonkin

HAINAN

Vientiane

Dong Hai

Demarcation Line (DMZ)

LAOS

Quang Tri

Hue

Da Nang

THAILAND

Quang Ngai

Kontum

Pleiku

Qui Nhon

Bangkok

SOUTH VIETNAM

Ban Me Thuot

CAMBODIA

Nha Trang

Cam Ranh

Phnom Penh

An Loc

Da Lat

Tay Ninh

Gulf of Siam

Sihanoukville

Saigon

Can Tho

N

Ca Mau

South China Sea

0   200 mile

0   200km

So, after a bitter eight-year war which Hanoi emphatically won, the prize was a rump state. In U. Alexis Johnson's colorful analogy, the communists were forced to accept "half a loaf."[152] Deputy Premier Pham Van Dong defiantly closed Geneva with the pledge: "We shall achieve unity. We shall achieve it just as we have won the war. No force in the world, internal or external, can make us deviate from our path." But at the time it was just defiance. The real winner was the sly Ngo Dinh Diem. After assuming the premiership of South Vietnam, he held on to it for another ten years – before falling to a gory assassination.

The Geneva Accords unsatisfactorily left the emperor-in-exile Bao Dai as the nominal head of state, and the French in situ in South Vietnam (now officially known as the State of Vietnam in anticipation of unification). Where Bao Dai was viewed as France's tarnished protégé, Diem was publicly celebrated by Americans as an honest patriot and nationalist. This made him the natural enemy of communists – which garnered Washington's approval – as well as of rival religious groups and criminal interests, which boded ill. In private, however, more skeptical officials judged Diem an incomprehensible "nut."[153] The French relentlessly undermined Diem with Prime Minister Faure holding that he was "not only incapable but mad." He spoke in a "funny central-Vietnamese dialect," which other Vietnamese found hard to understand, and seemed an odd mix of religious fanatic and bureaucratic mandarin. Described as "a physically short, pudgy little man who hated to be viewed or photographed from the back because he kind of waddled like a duck," Diem did not embody a model of Vietnamese manhood.[154] At the Mary Knoll seminary in Lakewood, where he briefly studied as a young man, he was remembered as "Chaplinesque."[155]

All this political jostling created another raft of difficulties for the latest American special representative to South Vietnam, J. Lawton "Lightnin' Joe" Collins, who may well have wished he was back in the Huertgen Forest fighting the Germans. Collins took over from Ambassador Donald Heath and quickly appreciated "the French were not too enthusiastic about my coming."[156] Indeed,

Franco-American relations had hit a nadir. More widely, the entire Western alliance seemed under threat with the French government retaliating to perceived Anglo-Saxon perfidy by refusing to join a proposed European Defense Community in August 1954. John Foster Dulles was sufficiently concerned – judging Vietnam "not worth a quarrel with France" – to propose an American withdrawal from Vietnam the following year.

Like many visitors to Saigon, Collins found President Diem unimpressive. He also soon realized that his brother, Nhu, and "vixenous wife" "really were the powers behind the throne."[157] Stung by the hesitancy over saving the French at Dien Bien Phu, Eisenhower sanctioned the modest deployment of a 200-strong training and advisory contingent to work alongside the now-departing French, a decision subsequently described by the far-seeing Senator Russell of the Armed Services Committee as "the greatest mistake this country's ever made."[158] James Gavin rightly viewed Eisenhower's commitment as a shoddy political compromise, but "we in the Army were so relieved that we had blocked the decision to commit ground troops to Vietnam that we were in no mood to quibble over the compromise."[159] The decision was taken against the Joint Chiefs who did not wish to assume responsibility for training the rag-bag of Vietnamese armed forces and remained doubtful over the success of the project (the original plan would have seen US trainers ironically training the North Vietnamese Army). With impeccable good sense, the Joint Chiefs made an argument ignored to the present day in conflicts such as Iraq and Afghanistan:

> It is absolutely essential that there be a reasonably strong, stable civil government in control. It is hopeless to expect a US military training mission to achieve success unless the nation concerned is able effectively to perform those governmental functions essential to the successful raising and maintenance of armed forces.[160]

At first Collins also advised a US withdrawal then reversed his position when it became apparent that Congress would only sanction aid to a Diem-led government. On January 22, 1955 he submitted a report to the White House not only endorsing Diem but also articulating an early version of the domino theory and predicting the collapse of all Southeast Asia were South Vietnam to fall to communism. In this stance he was echoing the Joint Chiefs now advising "against a 'static' defense for this area [Southeast Asia]" and recommending "adoption of a concept of offensive actions against the military power of the aggressor." Dulles himself, whose support for Diem waxed and waned under French pressure, was now bombastically arguing the "US must not permit Diem to become another Karensky." "Repeated honks on the domino klaxon" were beginning to haul Washington's wagon.[161]

The US Training Relations and Instruction Mission (TRIM) officially assumed its training responsibilities, but only for a southern Vietnam National Army (VNA), on February 12, 1955. The ignorance of this first cohort was deep. As one pioneer later recalled, "A 1952 National Geographic article on the dragon in Indochina was the best thing in English that I could find at the time."[162]

US support for the fledgling South Vietnamese state quickly became bogged in the mire of last-ditch French interference, and Saigon's petty power politics, a harbinger of things to come. The anarchy and institutional chaos was complete. The Treasury was broke. Much-needed land reform, which American interlocutors shrewdly recognized was imperative to achieve an equitable postwar settlement, was deflected. The opinion on the street was that the communists would march straight into Saigon. The commander of the South Vietnam Army, General Nguyen Van Hinh, was in open rebellion against his own government. Diem took to sarcastically calling the French High Commissioner General Paul Ely and Collins "The Good Sisters," dispensing unwanted good advice like nuns.[163] French confusion was such that Ely actually sided with Collins, demanding assurances from Paris and threatening to resign over suspected political double-games being played by special envoy Jean Sainteny, despatched to Hanoi to cobble together a cooperation agreement with Ho Chi Minh.

Diem's authority was directly challenged by a mixed army, made up from an alliance of the criminal Binh Xuyen sect which joined forces with the Cao Dai and Hoa Hao to form a United Front of Nationalist Forces. The former camp, led by a thuggish General Le Van Vien, amounted to little more than a confederation of gangsters, covertly supported by the spoiling French, and mostly based in the Mekong Delta. The Binh Xuyen descended from the "Black Flag" pirates, and by the mid-1950s they virtually controlled downtown Saigon. The thuggish Vien "would have made his way very nicely in the Chicago underworld" in Collins' estimation.[164] In February, the French peremptorily announced they would no longer pay subsidies to the militias, and that only a small number of militiamen would be incorporated into the new Vietnamese National Army. The United Front responded by firing back an ultimatum at Diem. By March 1955, street brawls turned into street fighting.

The catalyst for outright confrontation was Diem's sacking of the corrupt Binh Xuyen-backed police commissioner Sang, while Collins was away in Washington conferring with Dulles (the sect was heavily in cahoots with the police and involved in several rackets). Determined to impose his authority, Diem then appointed a new police chief and established a headquarters outside French control. The French had little sympathy for Diem whom they viewed as one of the architects of the erosion of their authority in South Vietnam, so for once they found themselves in the agreeable position of watching a former enemy attempt to contain insurrection. A half-hearted effort to broker a ceasefire was abandoned and then the French stepped to one side, allowing the two sides to slug it out. Most of the fighting took place in a two-square-mile block around the elegant, tree-lined Boulevard Gallieni where Diem had set up his new police headquarters. Scores of shanty houses were set alight and as many as 500 civilians were killed in crossfires.[165] Strong winds fanned the flames, creating apocalyptic towers of smoke that blew across the city. A group of American servicemen relaxing in a café got caught up in the fighting and had to dodge the bullets to save themselves.

The crisis came to a head in the inaptly named Doc Lap (Freedom) Palace. Bao Dai, who was heavily funded by the Binh Xuyen sect and who held Diem in low regard, stirred in his luxury villa in Cannes and plotted to replace Diem with someone more compliant to his own and France's visions for the new political entity. The man he used to carry out the palace coup was the army's inspector general, Nguyen Van Vy, a sworn enemy of Diem. In a transparent ploy, Bao Dai ordered Diem to fly to Cannes to attend an emergency "conference," which he wisely refused to do. He simultaneously informed the Premier that General Vy would take over as head of the army, an instruction which Diem also ignored. Vy, in the meantime, decided to take matters into his own hands and appointed himself Army Chief.

At first the amateurish coup seemed to pass without reaction. Vy strode into the palace with his supporters, informed Diem's chief of staff General Ty that he was sacked, and sank into a comfortable armchair in the opulent office. Word of the coup, however, spread fast and a crowd led by a hard-smoking paratrooper, Colonel Cao Van Tri, threatened to rain artillery shells on the palace at the stroke of midnight unless the rebels surrendered. Vy proved feeble and capitulated without a fight. There was one moment of high drama when an elegantly attired anti-Bao Dai activist called Nhi Lang suddenly pulled an automatic pistol from his briefcase and threatened to shoot Vy, sending aides running for cover behind the furniture, but Diem's men intervened to save the general.

In the aftermath of the attempted coup Diem displayed clemency and ordered Vy's release. The would-be putschist promptly took the hint and fled. Behind these shenanigans was the Saigon CIA station which celebrated the victory of the man who would prove a terrible millstone around America's neck. For Washington policymakers, these "sexy" operations, over which other government departments were kept in the dark, held a certain allure. A growing consensus in intelligence circles that Diem represented a potential liability was squashed by CIA primacy and an attitude of winning the short-term game, without considering the long-term consequences.[166]

But misgivings were growing, especially in the mind of an enterprising officer making his name in counter-revolutionary warfare – Colonel Edward Geary Lansdale. Lansdale's reputation had been forged orchestrating the defeat of the Huk Rebellion in the Philippines. With complete disregard for whether the two countries were comparable, Dulles despatched Lansdale to South Vietnam with the cover of assistant attaché to the Air Force and with the simple instruction, "I would like you to do the same thing you did in the Philippines."[167] As Lansdale quickly realized, once in-country, the differences were sharp. What he found in Saigon was gangsterism, prostitution, and gambling. The war may have been far from the opium-scented streets, but its rumblings were audible. His first meeting with Diem was hardly auspicious. Bluffing his way to the Prime Minister's office he found a "roly-poly" man, "and the first thing I noticed was that his feet weren't touching the floor when he was sitting."[168] Over time, the relationship blossomed and Lansdale became that rarity – an American invited into the confidences of the Ngo family. But these were honeymoon days when Washington's emissaries were viewed as counterfoils to the departing French. The two men continued to meet in a "tiny alcove" off Diem's bedroom, surrounded by stacks of books and papers. During the Binh Xuyen crisis the pair met almost every night such was the American's success in cultivating the embattled South Vietnamese president. Lansdale was left with the abiding impression that Diem's real calling in life was that of a "student-monk." Propelled into the limelight, he ultimately seemed ill-suited and even unhappy in his role. This was the private Diem, with a "gleam" in his eyes, a persona that was quickly supplanted by the caricature autocrat of later years.

For the communists, the in-fighting of their southern neighbors was solid confirmation that the pretenders and rivals did not deserve to govern Vietnam. What mattered now was the promised 1956 election to reunify the country. But what followed was brazen larceny of the democratic process by Washington's man, Diem. The doubtful Collins departed in May and was replaced by Ambassador G. Frederick Reinhart – under "marching orders ... to fully support Ngo Dinh Diem" – who would serve until March 1957.[169]

In July 1955, a now emboldened Diem made the surprise announcement that he would not honor the agreement to hold nationwide elections. The State of Vietnam had not signed the Geneva Accords, and communist bullying would surely invalidate a popular vote, or so he argued.

In Washington, Dulles supported Diem's betrayal of the Geneva Accords. Paul Kattenberg, then a junior officer in State, remembered the tense meeting in which Dulles dismissed the counsel of his own officials:

> A meeting took place [in July 1955] which I recalled very clearly in Secretary Dulles' office where he sat and read our distillation of over about four pages of a much longer previous paper. He sat very quietly. We all sat very quietly. I can recall distinctly the clock ticking away on his wall and his breathing heavily as he read through the paper turning to us ... and saying "I don't believe Diem wants to hold elections. I believe we should support him in this."

All the hard work undertaken by Kattenberg and his colleagues that involved collaboration with British and Soviet representatives was "totally discarded."[170]

Diem had good reason to fear fraudulent voting because this is exactly what he set about manufacturing. A referendum on the future of the South was held on October 23. This sham exercise was subverted. Diem polled a laughable 98.2 percent of the vote. To ensure that illiterate peasants voted for Diem, a rhyme was coined: "*Xanh thi bo gio, do thi bo bi.*" It meant: stuff the red ballot in the envelope (a vote for Diem), and throw the green ballot in the waste paper basket (a vote for Bao Dai). Secret police were on hand at the polling stations to ensure that the green ballots ended up in the rubbish. Three days later, he appointed himself President of the newly declared Republic of Vietnam (*Viet Nam Cong Hoa*). Even his most ardent American supporters could not have helped notice that "Democratic" was missing from the nation's title; it was already claimed by the northern neighbor, *Viet Nam Dan Chu Cong Hoa*, or Ho's Democratic Republic of Vietnam. The French, with just a few months left in-country, shrugged their shoulders.

"*A vous Américains*," "Over to you, Americans." The hard fact was that Diem had played his crooked hand at the moment of greatest advantage. The North was too economically enfeebled to challenge the de facto coup, France no longer cared, American influence was constrained, and the Kremlin was engrossed in power struggles that would see the elevation of a peasant's son from Tsarist Russia, Nikita Sergeyevich Khrushchev, to the post of Premier of the Union of Soviet Socialist Republics. After 15 years of virtually uninterrupted conflict, Vietnam, for the moment, passed from the high tables of international conferences.

The immediate fallout from the First Indochina and Korean wars was the creation of the Southeast Asia Treaty Organization (SEATO). Even as the lights were switched off at Geneva, Bedell Smith was urging, "We must get that pact!" An inaugural meeting was held in January 1955 in the throne room of the Ananda Smakom Palace in Bangkok. The problem with SEATO, apparent to the throng of journalists, was that it was a white man's club with no funds and no troops. In British delegate Sir James Cable's memorable phrase, it amounted to a "zoo of paper tigers."[171] Only three of the founding members were Asiatic: the Philippines, still effectively an American protectorate; Pakistan, also under British protection; and Thailand. The remainder, France, Britain, Australia, and New Zealand, were part of the old order. If SEATO told John Foster Dulles anything, it was that East Asian countries were very reluctant to squat under an American military umbrella. It mattered little that he wore a white suit, unlike the colonial representatives in their grays and blacks; Asian leaders were not seeing a white knight riding to save them from communism.

The rabidly anti-communist Dulles followed the foundation meeting of SEATO with a whirlwind tour of Southeast Asia, in turn meeting Prime Minister U Nu of Burma, Crown Prince Savang of Laos, King Norodom Sihanouk of Cambodia, and Premier Ngo Dinh Diem in South Vietnam. Each received the

American salesman of democracy with the polite rejection expected from a clique of corrupt satraps. To Washington's disappointment, the hosts rejected offers of military training, universally viewed as a secret American ploy to gain toeholds on their estates. This rejection undermined one of the central pillars of the strategy of containment: the deployment of small military assistance teams to shore up vulnerable Southeast Asian states. The strategy presumed that these states felt vulnerable, which they did not especially, except from the usual internal enemies. Communism at close range did not seem so terrible to some Asians. It was Washington 12,000 miles away that was raising the specter of the Red bogeyman. Ultimately, no Asian ruler wanted to preside over the next Korea for the sake of "liberty." The Western SEATO partners themselves may have demurred had they known that Washington's confidence in its allies was so low that the use of atomic weaponry was included in secret contingency planning in the event of a major communist attack on the SEATO alliance.[172] This pointed to another problem with SEATO which has dogged Washington's relations with allies to the present day. On the one hand, Washington sought the political fig leaf and token military forces of allies; on the other, it reserved the right of US freedom of action. In the 1950s, this included the possibility of lobbing the bomb.

"Non-aligned" Asia answered SEATO with the first Africa-Asian Conference held at Bandung in Indonesia on April 18. Twenty-nine quarrelsome countries attended this staged jamboree, the brainchild of Indonesia's Prime Minister Ali Sastroamidjojo, and it became a naked excuse for stabbing pins into the Voodoo doll of a caricature, imperialist West. Whatever ideologies inflected the prose, Bandung did not speak for ordinary Asians.

Where did Washington stand in this changing landscape? The alarums of war seemed to become fainter as the decade reached its end but the momentum created by the Korean War for defense spending had become unstoppable. Despite Eisenhower's pledge to constrain defense spending, the budget continued to increase through the 1950s. Appropriations in 1957 were $7.7 million for the Army, $10 billion for the Navy, and $15.4 billion for the

Air Force, a 238 percent increase on defense spending compared to a decade previously. The following year the budget exceeded $40 billion, and it was widely expected to hit $50 billion by the beginning of the 1960s. The Pentagon alone now employed over 26,000 people of which 1,500 civilians and over 700 military officers were assigned directly to the OSD – the Office of the Secretary of Defense. Washington's military bureaucracy was now only rivalled by the counterpart apparatus in Moscow, but this was an illegitimate comparison as a democracy in peacetime was not meant to be a militarized state, which the numbers suggested America had become.

In 1956, the fabulously wealthy Nelson Rockefeller established the Rockefeller Brothers Fund to promote the philanthropic study of global issues. With his charm and wallet (grants totaling $3.8 million were awarded that year), he was able to attract some of the best minds to his project including Henry Kissinger, Dean Rusk, Henry Luce, and Edward Teller. In December 1957, the Fund published a report on defense, *International Security: The Military Aspect*, which sold 400,000 copies and which was heavily promoted by the *New York Times*. Eisenhower felt obliged to acknowledge it in his State of the Union address in January the following year, and he appointed Nelson Rockefeller as a personal consultant to the defense secretary. Freedom was in a race against totalitarianism and America, it concluded, risked defeat "by instalments." Truman and then Eisenhower had staved off this possibility in Korea, Iran, the Middle East, Formosa, Berlin, as well as a dozen other places where Russian expansionism had seemed to threaten the delicate Cold War balance. Now, as the century entered a fresh decade and America prepared to vote for a new president, the first of the "instalments" was about to mature.

Chapter 2

KENNEDY'S FINGER IN THE DYKE, 1960–62

Kennedy inherited an America at peace, but a world simmering with conflicts stoked by nationalists, revolutionaries, and not a few crooks. With some justification, the out-going Eisenhower had described the first year of the new decade as "a treasure chest for the communists." Sitting in the grandstands of this coliseum of violence, like rival Caesars, were the two nuclear superpowers, raising or lowering their thumbs to the gladiators below. Nothing seemed to be learned from this contest, except that it had to go on.

In total, over 1960–61, there were just under 20 hot wars (interstate and intrastate), accounting for around 100,000 battle deaths, a relative trough compared to the previous decade, and a respite compared to the spike in battlefield mortality that would be experienced in subsequent years. Just two weeks before Kennedy's inauguration, Khrushchev delivered a speech (in fact a re-hash of a speech he had delivered the previous November at a meeting of communist parties in Moscow) in which he appeared to threaten the Western world with a campaign of "wars of liberation." The January 6 Khrushchev speech provoked great shock. Roger Hilsman recalled, "Kennedy's reaction was to take it very, very seriously."[1] He ordered his staff to read the speech and it influenced his own inauguration address. Subsequently, Congress held a subcommittee hearing analyzing the speech (the transcript runs to 105 pages)[2] – possibly the only instance in history where the discourse of a foreign leader has been so scrutinized by the American legislature.

Faced with this agitated panorama, the 43-year-old Kennedy needed the best by his side. Eisenhower had been associated with the old guard. Kennedy by contrast selected a youthful first cabinet – the "new Frontiersmen" – but were they up to the mark? The average age of Kennedy's appointees, it was calculated, came to precisely 47.3 years; one of the youngest administrations since the times of Washington. Their collective IQs, it was claimed, put them in the genius category. Across the spectrum of political partisanship, there was broad consensus that "the great talent hunt" had indeed resulted in a fresh, dynamic, and exciting government well equipped to lead America into the new decade.

The second-most powerful office in the land – Secretary of State – went to Dean Rusk, a former Rhodes scholar with previous service in the State and War Departments. This nomination was unanimously viewed as a good choice. There was confidence he would represent America with strength and firmness, as well as display the necessary stamina the office demanded. In his first year, the new secretary would rack up 145,000 air miles visiting 17 countries.[3] He eventually served for eight years as Secretary of State (1961–69), the second-longest stretch in US history. There are around 2,100,000 State Department cables with Rusk's name signed to them – a warning to any historian who believes the man, so devoted in his service, may be readily summarized.

If Rusk seemed destined for high office it was illusion. The son of a Georgia Calvinist preacher, Rusk was an academic made by the war. In 1942, the anonymous professor of political science in California found himself posted, as a lowly captain, to Stilwell's headquarters in Burma. His sharp intelligence and serious demeanour led to accelerated promotion and he was elevated to the post of deputy chief of staff with full colonel rank (in which post he was responsible for authorizing air drops of arms and cigarettes to Ho Chi Minh).[4] This pattern would be repeated throughout his career. After the war he was poached from the Pentagon by Marshall, to serve as an assistant secretary in the State Department. Both Acheson and Dulles recognized his obvious intelligence and he completed a distinguished stint at the Department, from which he gained a reputation as the Far East expert, before returning to academia under the auspices of the Rockefeller Foundation. It was from here that he was poached again. Kennedy, in fact, never actually met Rusk; the appointment was the result of glowing references from previous bosses. In this regard he was the earnest, clever outsider, trusting in his ability rather than in politicking. Financially poor, Rusk gave the impression that life was not something to be enjoyed, but rather endured, dutifully.

The Second World War was the transformational experience in Rusk's life. His memory of the disaster of appeasement haunted the remainder of his public service career. We are all, he confessed, to some extent a prisoner of our experiences. As a senior in college he recalled the Japanese seizure of Manchuria. He was present at the infamous 1933 Oxford Union debate.[5]

> One cannot live through those years and not have some pretty strong feelings about the idea of collective security … it was the failure of the governments of the world to prevent those aggressions which made the catastrophe of World War Two inevitable.[6]

The war also had a transformational effect on the department he inherited, which had been trivially small in isolationist America. Rusk took over a bureaucratic empire: the State Department swelled to 23,000 strong; with a further 11,000 employees in the United States Information Agency (USIA); and 15,000 in the Agency for International Development. The country was beholden to 43 separate international treaties, dismissing any notions that somehow Washington could retreat to a better, uncommitted, and isolationist past. Rusk felt this responsibility viscerally: "My generation of students was led down the chute … in the catastrophe of a WWII which could have been prevented." It was now America's mission to maintain and if necessary enforce a postwar peace:

> I have no doubt that there have been times when peace has been maintained [in the postwar period] because people in certain other capitals would say to themselves, now look comrades, we'd better be a little careful here because those damn fool Americans just might do something about it.[7]

That Kennedy did not choose Rusk but rather accepted the recommendations of others was typical, but so was his habit, repeated by Johnson, of unintentionally undermining his own secretary of state by appointing special task forces to deal with specific foreign policy issues. Nixon would reinforce the trend by investing foreign policy in the hands of a colossus national security advisor. The relationship with Kennedy was never close. Jacqueline Kennedy later confided to him that he was the only member of the cabinet that the president called "Mr. Secretary" rather than using a first name. His relationship with Johnson was warmer notwithstanding the frustrations of serving this complex president.

In parallel with State, a foreign affairs Crisis Center was established, staffed in a nepotistic appointment by a brother-in-law, Stephen Smith. The growing Cuban problem was passed to a Pentagon man, Paul Nitze, and then to White House insider Richard Goodwin. The Far East – surely Rusk's forte – was assigned to another Pentagon man, the corporate attorney Roswell Gilpatric. An ambitious Boston Brahmin, McGeorge Bundy, was appointed Special Assistant to the President for National Security Affairs and quickly set about expanding an empire of influence at the expense of the State Department. Acheson was given the tricky job of handling the Berlin crisis, but Averell Harriman and Adlai Stevenson, two heavyweight rivals, were both given appointments as Rusk's deputies, hardly a vote of confidence.

There were irresolvable tensions between these grandees of US foreign policy. Kennedy had wanted to get away from the confrontational posture of the Foster Dulles years, but simultaneously be seen as tough on communism. The appointments reflected these contradictions, as well as Democrat in-fighting: Stevenson was viewed as soft by the Acheson camp who openly derided the veteran diplomat; Acheson was seen by Roosevelt-era survivors as a maverick prone to making peremptory "declarations of war"; and Harriman was perceived as aloof and almost European in his haughty intellectualism.[8] The outcome was a certain institutional anarchy. Taking their cue from the White House, ambassadors began to bypass the divided State Department. Rusk accepted all this with the good grace of someone used to serving difficult masters. "We were in the same foxhole," he later remarked of Johnson, "and as neighbors in a foxhole, you get to know each other pretty well."[9]

In contrast to Rusk, there was very little chance the world would not have taken note of the 44-year-old Robert Strange McNamara, a Ford "whizz kid" who worked his way up to the presidency of the company at envy-inspiring speed, before accepting the post of defense secretary. Opinions were divided on his appointment. Behind the oval glasses was a rapine mind and it was clear that McNamara alarmed many generals and admirals. But few could dispute that he was an organizational genius, "a human IBM machine" with outstanding analytic powers.[10] An intimidated and then awed Johnson thought he was "perfect." This became damaging dependency. "It became very tough on McNamara," McGeorge Bundy remembered, "There was a period in 1964 when the President just didn't feel comfortable without [McNamara] … On the weekends, before church, for a swim, come down to Sunday supper, go for a ride on the boat, it was very tough."[11]

McNamara's capacity for work – and especially his willingness to master technical detail – far exceeded the fading stamina of the tired old war-horses in the Department (who did have the stamina to understand an organization with 7,000 offices and 17½ miles of corridors). In the scores of declassified minutes of meetings which he attended in his seven-year stint as defense secretary, what stands out is the acuity of his mind, so quick to see and get to the point. Like Forrestal, with whom he was compared not least because of his sharp hairline (the guy with "the Sta-Comb hair," as it was joked), McNamara did not enter the clubby world of the top brass and he remained unimpressed if not at odds with the array of medals that sat on the other side of his nine-foot-long General Pershing desk.

His origins were humble. He came from Irish stock, immigrants from the Great Irish Famine and his father was a shoe salesman. He was sent to a school that was literally a wooden shed. In his own words, he worked his "tail off" to succeed academically. Graduating in economics, mathematics, and philosophy, McNamara seemed set for a high-flying career in accounting or academia. The war then intervened – as in Rusk's case – and McNamara entered the Office of Statistical Control. Few draftees found a more perfect fit for their talents. McNamara was statistics, or this was the popular view. What could not be measured, tabulated, or analyzed did not, literally, count. War was a production line and the prize went to the most efficient and productive work force. McNamara set about counting bombers and measuring the effectiveness of their missions, an experience he would carry into the Vietnam War. Like Rusk, he leap-frogged promotion from captain to colonel in a couple of years. "Get the data" was a favorite maxim. It was typical of McNamara that in one of his first acts as secretary he founded a Defense Intelligence Agency (DIA), which grew to rival the established CIA. With his insatiable appetite for facts and trusting in no one, it was entirely natural he should establish his own facts machine. To this day the DIA reflects the character of its founder, such was the force of personality of Robert McNamara.

Without the Vietnam War he would have been remembered for systems analysis, as he was disliked for the same. Systems analysis was management school pseudo-science, but no less powerful for it. The methodology purported to take complex problems, decompose them as components of a meta-system, then recompose them after appropriate analysis to generate a solution. This was "the RAND approach," methodical and analytical, the so-called "whiz kids" that had grown fashionable in American academia.[12] Analyzing the effectiveness of a bombing raid was a legitimate use of statistics. Or working out the most efficient way of churning out production cars, which is where McNamara refined the art of analysis. But extending this approach across the entire breadth of the human activity called war was folly. The chief problem with systems analysis was that you could not expunge the human from the system. This was exactly the point Admiral Anderson made when he angrily quit his post in the Joint Chiefs, attacking "the modern fallacy that theories, or computers, or economics, or numbers of weapons win wars. Alone they do not! ... Man is the key to success or failure." Systems analysis purported to be empirical but it never was or could be. The methodology had the potential to mislead, or be politicized, or in the worst case, to throw up completely the wrong answer.

The Joint Chiefs, however, did not in the main object to McNamara's systematic approach to managing the Department on philosophical grounds. They did so because "he implemented an awful lot of studies which increased work load" (theirs); or because "McNamara got into all kinds of details" (which they found uncomfortable); or because "everything the Army wanted to do had to be evaluated by the DOD cost-effectiveness system." And as Army Chief of Staff George Decker asserted, apparently without embarrassment, "I don't think cost-effectiveness should apply to military weapons."[13] In other words, the Joint Chiefs objected to McNamara because he was trying to reform defense, restore civilian control, and enforce financial discipline. Later, the relationship strained because the hawkish Joint Chiefs consistently sabotaged McNamara's efforts to constrain the war in Vietnam.

For all the quirks, there was a rich vein of genius in this tireless public servant. McNamara did not deserve the opprobrium he later received. The caricature McNamara is just that, a caricature. The cliché of the numbers machine has also been wide of the mark: this was a defense secretary who quoted from T.S. Eliot's *Four Quartets*. Numbers did matter to McNamara but as stepping stones on a broader philosophical quest for truth. In a later interview with Arthur M. Schlesinger Jr. he sentenced the manner precisely. When asked if too much reliance was placed on "computers", he replied that on the contrary, "most of the judgements we make do not depend on computers. But they do depend upon the quantification of the factors affecting the alternatives that we face." "In other words," Schlesinger offered, "a computer is a means of making the alternatives precise?" "Exactly," McNamara replied.[14] In the generous judgment of a colleague, his instincts were all wrong, but his intelligence conquered his instincts.[15]

The capstone irony of his acceptance of the defense secretary post – just weeks after promotion as the youngest-ever head of Ford Motors – was that he was uninterested in war. "McNamara's war" was a coinage of Senator Wayne Morse, repeated by enemies, not fact. His obsessions were efficiency and cutting costs. He accepted the nomination, despite being a registered Republican (who refused to answer the awkward question whether he had actually voted for Kennedy at the nomination press conference – he did), because he had been called "to serve the public."[16] It was as simple as that in his mind, although it took Kennedy two attempts to persuade him to take the job. "Mac the Knife," his first nickname, was more precise and well deserved. Like every American defense secretary of the modern period (acutely in the case of contemporary secretaries presiding over trillion dollar wars), he was conscious that he was taking over an organization squandering billions of tax dollars. He inherited a disastrously mismanaged defense budget and a department determined to thwart his necessary reforms.[17] Cleaning out this Augean Stable was his real mission.

Few if any critics point out that he voluntarily quit a $410,000 job (over $3 million in today's prices) and accepted the $25,000 pittance of a secretary's salary to address this impossible task. Or that he gave up stock options worth roughly $22 million in today's prices. He passed away in 2009, only out-lived by Giap with whom he struck a later friendship. His death was lamentably accompanied by unkind obituaries from a constituency unwilling to give a fair hearing to this remarkable personality.

The other important appointments were nepotistic and nakedly political. Robert "Bobby" Kennedy, the President's brother and confidante, assumed the post of Attorney General. A 32-year-old, bespectacled Theodore Sorensen was plucked from the University of Nebraska to become a speech-writer and policy advisor.

Papering over the cracks in the White House was "the IRA" (Irish Republican Army): Kenneth O'Donnell, Ralph Duggan, and Lawrence O'Brien, all young men who engineered Kennedy's electoral victory and who were rewarded with insider jobs. These would be the backroom boys, seeing, hearing, but speaking no evil.

Notwithstanding the brio of his inauguration speech, Kennedy's foreign policy was at first a continuation of previous policies. Institutional inertia in the State Department made it so. The sales pitch was simple: America stands for freedom, America stands by her friends, and America keeps her word. The main themes were also well worn: collective defense in the face of communist expansionism in Europe and the Far East; robust challenge to the proxy "wars of liberation"; and aid for friendly countries. The great fear was not, in fact, that war might break out, but rather that nations might fall to communism without a shot being fired.

Thanks to his two predecessors, Kennedy inherited unusually strong and well-funded armed forces. Eisenhower's New Look armed forces had been formed in the shadow of an atomic age. This orthodoxy was yielding to the doctrine of "flexible response," championed by the now-retired Maxwell Taylor, in the bestseller *Uncertain Trumpet*. The title came from Theodore Hesburgh's "You can't blow an uncertain trumpet," and there was little doubt and no shortage of blow in Taylor. The case had already been argued in Gavin's *War and Peace in the Space Age*, but Taylor succeeded where Gavin failed by reaching the ear of the President. Communist revolution demanded counter-revolutionary warfare. Flexible response offered "limited war," another fashionable notion circulating in military circles, where New Look sounded too much like Armageddon. These were the "intellectuals with balls," as *New York Times* journalist David Halberstam later damned the new breed of military theorists propelling America toward her Vietnam communion.[18]

Against this panorama, Southeast Asia quickly entered Kennedy's agenda, not through Vietnam, but via the mysterious, peaceful, and poorly understood country of Laos. The day before his investiture, Eisenhower had offered the ill-judged advice that Laos was critical to the security of the region.[19] "Laos is far away but the world is small," Kennedy briefed a press conference within a month of his investiture, and in case nobody knew where or what he was talking about, pointed at a giant map of Southeast Asia showing the progress of a Red tide engulfing the 1.5 million Laotians. Although it is difficult to imagine today, Vietnam at the time was viewed as a peripheral problem. The 1961 *New York Times* index for Laos ran to 26 columns. Just eight were dedicated to Vietnam.[20]

The Kingdom of Laos was a deliberately created buffer state between communist China and North Vietnam and Thailand, a sort of Belgium of the Far East. Most State officials knew next to nothing about Laos. It was Buddhist, addicted to opium smoking, and the last king had maintained 25 wives. The new political entity was granted independence in 1949 and following the 1954 "Little Geneva" Accords it began to receive economic and military aid from America through the International Cooperation Administration ($300 million by the time of Kennedy's inauguration, or three times the country's Gross National Product).

Laos could not absorb this sudden influx of American aid and the Treasury found itself underwriting the Laotian kip by depositing dollars to back the newly printed Laotian currency. One aid official described US policy in Laos as a fairy tale, and was sacked.[21] Fake import licences became a cottage industry. Did Laotians really need 37 tons of toothpaste, four tons of feather dusters, and $1.3 million dollars' worth of cars in a country with a few miles of hard-topped roads? When a consignment of American cheese was imported to Laos, the locals tried to use it as soap. This seemed uncomfortably a case of life imitating art, with Milo Minderbinder and *Catch-22* about to hit the bookstores with a perfect sense of timing.

Throughout the late 1950s, Laos had suffered an intermittent war instigated by Pathet Lao, a communist guerrilla group supported by North Vietnam. In mid-August 1960, a paratrooper captain, Kong Le, marched into the capital Vientiane and announced a *coup d'état*. To give legitimacy to this act, he declared Prince Souvanna

Phouma a member of the new ruling committee. Phouma, a former premier and brother of Souvanaphong, leader of the Pathet Lao, wanted nothing to do with the coup and retired from the field. Caught by surprise, Premier Tiao Somsanith pleaded for Western help (the entire government was in the royal city of Luangprabang paying respects to King Savang Vatthana at the time of the coup). Although Captain Le denied any truck with the communist Pathet Lao, Washington feared the close links between the two groups and saw communism infiltrating Laos through the back door. The more prosaic truth was that a thoroughly corrupted Laos had descended into petty power struggles between various family members of the ruling clans. The coup failed but the fighting went on.

The departing Eisenhower administration had had little appetite for interventions and the problem of Laos had consequently been bandied between two ineffective organizations: the United Nations and SEATO. When SEATO finally met in Bangkok, the language was as pastel-colored as the diplomats' wives, which the press seemed to find more interesting. Admiral Felt's Seventh Fleet was put on standby but this was symbolic. The real dividing line in Laos was the naked contradiction between the reality on the ground, tirelessly argued by honest State Department officials, and the simplistic anti-communist rhetoric drummed up thousands of miles away in Washington. American policy, as Stanley Karnow, *Time Life* bureau chief noted, amounted to colossal, naive waste:

> In Laos, U.S. money has been wasted, squandered and mismanaged by both Americans and Laotians. But the real loss comes from Washington's insistence – often against appraisal of U.S. diplomats on the scene – in trying to fit Laos into a broad strategic military picture, creating and inflexibly following goals and aims which the backward, imponderable little country could not possibly have achieved.[22]

For the Joint Chiefs, charged with coming up with a workable plan, Laos was just a headache. Much of the country was impenetrable mountainous jungle. It shared a 1,000-mile border with North

Vietnam which was impossible to seal. It was landlocked, and the nearest useful bases in Thailand were 400 miles from Vientiane by road and track. During the monsoon season Laos was submerged by rains that turned all land routes into quagmires. With good reason, the best form of transport was the ox and cart, or an elephant. The country had no electricity grid, no radio stations and no telephone system. Just four useable airfields could be found and one of these was in communist hands. The indigenous peoples spoke dozens of obscure languages and practically no English. Worst of all, from the American perspective, Laotians displayed a deep disinterest in fighting. *Bo pen nyan* ("it doesn't matter") seemed to be the national motto. Dean Rusk later recalled: "I remember one report that two Laotian sides on the battlefield left and went off to a water festival together for ten days and then came back to the battlefield."[23] All the military factors pointed to a war conducted by small teams of Green Berets, a Kennedy creation which suited his appetite for covert counter-revolutionary operations. While the Joint Chiefs pondered options, 300 marines were despatched to the Thai-Laos border, just in case.

In Washington, Deputy Defense Secretary Roswell Gilpatric was given the task of finessing military options, but the problem of Laos was then temporarily pushed to the sidelines by another failed coup, again led by a group of paratroopers, but against the Diem government in neighboring South Vietnam. This was led by the three commanding officers of US-trained parachute battalions, legitimized by a lawyer called Hoang Co Thuy. The catalyst for rebellion repeated the story of Laos: rampant corruption and nepotism in a Western-backed government. It little helped Diem's cause that his brother blamed America, a country that from 1955 to 1960 poured over $2 billion in aid into South Vietnam.[24] Diem's loyalist troops dispersed the crowds in Saigon by firing on them, killing and injuring scores. This heavy-handedness did not derail his premiership. In April elections, Diem won an implausible 88 percent of the votes, to the frustration of the communists and relief of the State Department that did not inquire too deeply how the unpopular leader had managed to secure such a swingeing mandate.

The distraction in South Vietnam concluded, events in Laos reached a peaceful if unsatisfactory climax. The fear of communist infiltration in Thailand, which vexed Washington, had been somewhat over-blown. North Vietnamese interest in Laos was based on its usefulness as a transit route south to Cambodia and thence to South Vietnam, or what would eventually become the Ho Chi Minh Trail (the *truong son* in Vietnamese). The general consensus was that Laos had been "lost." A truce and the Geneva Conference only served to confirm that Pathet Lao was now in control of the northern half of the country. At the peace negotiations the rebels demanded the ministries of the interior, rural development, and information, where they could feed off the rich pickings that American aid had provoked. Washington continued to view the situation as communism infiltrating a legitimate "free" government, rather than what it was: unembarrassed nepotism and corruption. Following a ceasefire agreement, a "neutralist" premier was appointed to the temporary satisfaction of the warring parties. This was the portly Prince Boun Oum, bursting in a nuptial-white uniform decorated with ribbons of unearned medals. His appointment made little difference. Outside the capital and a handful of other settlements there was no government authority. Some hill tribes were not even aware they belonged to a political entity called Laos.

The trial now resumed in Vietnam. From the beginnings of the American involvement under the Truman administration, Vietnam had begun to exercise a peculiar fascination on some American minds. David Halberstam described it as a "curiously dangerous romantic assignment."[25] In the popular view, this mysterious "living entity" was a land rich in agriculture, steeped in exotic Buddhist ways but also with a Christian habit, and blessed with beautiful women – a Gauginesque fantasy in danger of being overrun by communist thugs. The fantasy, naturally, was far from the reality. Assistant Secretary of State for Far Eastern Affairs Roger Hilsman, a personality with wartime experience and deep understanding of oriental culture, would later remark that the biggest mistake America made was failing to appreciate that Vietnamese culture was "2,000 years too thick" to be changed by counterinsurgency programs.[26] In June 1956, Kennedy had addressed a meeting of American Friends of Vietnam and colorfully described Vietnam as "the finger in the dyke." As the words tripped off his persuasive tongue, he was unlikely to have imagined it was his finger that would so soon be poked in the metaphorical dyke.[27]

The phrase "the winds of change" may have been coined over Europe's African colonies, but there was a typhoon building up in the South China Sea, for anyone with a barometer and a keen weather eye. The communist leadership in Vietnam was predominantly a generation born in the early half of the twentieth century and as far from the glamour and youth of Camelot as the cardinal points of a compass. It had gained political consciousness and a commitment to nationalist struggle when America's new crop of leaders was dunking basketballs in school playgrounds. The unchanging face of Hanoi's Politburo was mostly composed of wartime and former ICP comrades: Pham Van Dong, Vo Nguyen Giap, Le Duan, Pham Hung, Le Duc Tho, and Troung Chinh whose name translated as "Long March." In a 1960s speech, Ho noted that 31 members of the Central Committee boasted 222 years of imprisonment and deportation between them.[28] Central Committee members Ton Duc Thang, Le Duan, Nguyen Duy Trinh, Le Thanh Nghi, Hoang Quoc Viet, among others, were all caged together at the notorious Con Dao penal island.[29] The latter remembered, "we had no beds and mats. We were forced to sleep on the cold cement floors. And the roofs were leaking, water just poured in."[30] This imprisonment acted as an incubator for the future resistance.

The unchallenged leader of the communists was and would remain Ho Chi Minh. But who was this polite guerrilla who had once charmed OSS Captain Patti with his knowledge of Western liberal traditions? The French had wanted his head on a plate, then reversed course and tried to woo him. Washington ignored him then cast him in the same pit as all the other communists.

Now he was president of a poor country barely five years in existence and supposedly a threat to the freedom of the entire Southeast Asia region.

Ho Chi Minh was born Nguyen Sinh Cung on May 19, 1890, in central Annam. According to French intelligence he was born in the hamlet of An Dan and his real name was Nguyen Van Than. Over a lifetime he would adopt several aliases; Nguyen Ai Quoc, Nguyen Van Thanh, Nguyen Sinh Con, and Ly Thuy.[31] He had three siblings: one became a clerk in the French Army, the second turned to herbalism, and the third died in prison. While still a child, his teacher father was briefly imprisoned. Ho in turn would be imprisoned by the British and Chinese (he adopted the name Ho Chi Minh "the enlightened" following his release from Chinese custody). In Hong Kong he was defended by Sir Stafford Cripps before the Privy Court and was saved from extradition and the death sentence in France on the grounds that he was a political refugee. In a prophetic entry in his prison diary he wrote: "People who come out of prison can build a country."[32]

He attended the Lycée Quoc Hoc in Hue and proved to be an indifferent student, leaving without a diploma. Former alumni included both his enemy Ngo Dinh Diem and his brother-in-arms Vo Nguyen Giap. After schooling, at the age of 19, he went to sea on the liner SS *Latouche-Treville* which heralded the beginning of his long and formative exposure to Western culture in New York, London, and Paris. These were tumultuous years that witnessed a world war, the final collapse of Europe's *anciens régimes*, the Russian Revolution, and female emancipation. When the guns fell silent, a precocious Ho presented demands for Vietnamese autonomy at the Palais de Versailles in a rented suit. The rebuff he received flung him into the arms of sympathetic French socialists.

A 1920 photograph of Ho at a French Socialist Party congress in Paris showed a dapper young man in stiff Edwardian collar with lively eyes. By now he was calling himself Nguyen Ai Quoc, "Nguyen the Patriot." Within two years a receding hairline would rob him of his youthful looks, and a goatee beard would complete the Lenin look. The suits were also discarded, replaced by military-style jackets. He was now in his early thirties and he faced four decades of political and military struggle. It was in Paris, in 1921, that he formed the "Inter-colonial Union," a group of like-minded exiles who would form the nucleus of the Indochinese Communist Party.[33] In one important respect he had become a most un-Asian personality. Where oriental philosophy valued change, impermanence, flux, and subtlety, Ho Chi Minh became as immovable and intractable as a block of granite. This boulder represented a single, unyielding idea that shaped the rest of his life: Vietnam should be a united, independent nation free of colonial interference and guided by a communist philosophy. This vision, enveloped in a blue mist of chain-smoked American cigarettes, became the incarnation of Ho Chi Minh. His implacable negotiating stance owed everything to the shoddy betrayal of the March 1946 Paris Accords that left Ho with little more than the linen shirt he was wearing. From that moment, he lost all faith in Western negotiators. Even his French Communist friends felt embarrassment and despaired at the haughty manner in which he was treated. The 1954 Geneva Agreements only served to reinforce the worthlessness of making treaties with Western governments. When Henry Kissinger heroically took up the portfolio of peace negotiations at the beginning of the 1970s he was joining a long history, all bad.

Ho became the peripatetic ascetic: thin, brooding, and only in his last days softening and becoming avuncular. By 1923 he had drifted to Moscow, and two years later he was editing a nationalist journal *Thanh Nien* in China, the first of many in a long proselytizing career. By now he was becoming a well-known figure in communist international conferences. In a milieu that produced so many prima donnas as leaders, his signature shorts and sandals became an anti-symbol of the corruption wracking Vietnam. Visitors remembered the broad forehead, the high cheekbones, and wrecked teeth. His manner was always polite, even hesitant, but the eyes were steely. He was wily, a supreme survivor and a skillful politician. He courted audiences and crowds. At the Fontainebleau peace talks he presented flowers to female reporters, professed love of children, and invariably encouraged comparisons with Confucius and Buddha. Yet behind the public asceticism was a thoroughly Europeanized indigene who enjoyed a good bottle of wine. He loved French culture and wanted to believe in the ideals of the French Revolution. His favorite author was Victor Hugo. But the mother country had become an exploitative mistress and colonialism abhorrent. "*Nous ne voulons pas vivre esclaves,*" he told General Salan, while sincerely professing "*[mais] nous aimons la France.*"[34] "We do not wish to live as slaves, but we love France." The French – too blinded by cupidity – rashly dismissed Ho as friend and ally. He only turned to America in 1945 after first reluctantly giving up on the French. When America let him down, in his eyes, self-help became the only recourse; but self-help buttressed by military aid from the historic enemy, the People's Republic of China, and a self-interested Moscow. He himself said that "in France he learned how to oppose capitalism, in the Soviet Union he learned how to organize political parties and in China he learned how a semi-feudal semi-colonial country should oppose the ruling class."[35] French intelligence was always right about Ho Chi Minh, but French governors in Indochina did not heed the counsel: "*Hô Chi Minh est sans conteste une figure puissante … Pour les Annamites, le nom Hô Chi Minh incarne une foi, un idéal, une volonté.*"[36] "Ho Chi Minh is uncontestably a powerful figure … For the Annamites, the name Ho Chi Minh incarnates a faith, an ideal, a will."

In later life it seems he became a creature of habits. His personal secretary Tuu Ky recalled that he would wake at 5.30am every morning, "do some calisthenics for about 10 minutes," then go for a walk before breakfast. After a simple fare he would start work at 6.30am by reading the *Nhan Dan* (party newspaper) and other Hanoi newspapers. In the morning "he would sit alone by himself reading documents and reports." In the afternoon, after a short nap in his bungalow, he typically held meetings with cadres or government officials. Ky explained:

> In the evening, after dinner, Comrade Ho Chi Minh went back to work again. During this period I would read the newspapers

out loud for him. By around 9.00pm I asked permission to go home. But he continued to read books until about 11pm or so, or until the Vietnam Radio broadcasts had stopped, before he would turn off the light and go to sleep.

His only entertainment seems to have been gardening, feeding fish, and reading "picture magazines" on Sundays. Such was the life of this companionless and childless revolutionary. On his death bed he said: "Do not organize a big funeral. This is a waste of resources. Let me lie in the hearts of the people … Vietnamese young people and children and young people and children elsewhere in the world."[37]

The question of whether he was communist or nationalist was irrelevant – he was both. The 1946 constitution was a nationalist manifesto worthy of the pen of a European left-wing republican, or indeed Jefferson. War overtook this vision of a liberated Vietnam and the constitution was never institutionalized. By comparison, North Vietnam's second constitution, ratified in 1960, could only have been drafted by a communist (although the word was not used once in the entire document). Such was the corrosive effect of the First Indochina War, which only left the Viet Minh and a re-formed communist Lao Dong (fully, *Dang Lao Dong Viet Nam*, or Vietnamese Workers' Party) standing.

As a matter of semantics, the northerners actually stopped using the title "communist" after the dissolution of the Indochinese Communist Party in the mid-1940s and instead typically referred to themselves as party or front members, or national liberation fighters (Ho joked that anyone wishing to understand communism should go to a library). Nevertheless, the obvious Marxist-Leninist foundations of the Lao Dong, coupled with the unmoveable weight of contemporary labeling, means that Hanoi was always going to be referred to as "the Communists," a convenience repeated by all histories including this one.

What made the Viet Minh different was its popular appeal. It was the single group that could claim support across the three provinces of colonial Vietnam. It was also the only group with a (mythologized) history of armed struggle against the French with roots not in the urban elites but in the rural peasantry. The natural substrate of the Viet Minh was never a smoky, argumentative café on the Rue Maréchal Joffre – it was always the paddy field and jungle. The moralizing zeal of the Viet Minh which urged cadres "to show to the people that you are correct, diligent and disciplined" counted for an awful lot to villagers who cared little for political ideologies, but whose entire lives had been a history of exploitation.[38] Ho borrowed the idea of mobilizing the masses, but these were masses keen on being mobilized. It is a central irony of Vietnam's descent into war that the Viet Minh was a genuinely popular, democratic movement. In any freely held election, it would have run away with the result, yet the two nations with most pretensions to representing democracy and liberty, France and America, became hell-bent on thwarting this outcome. Dulles confidently advised a press conference in June 1955, "We also believe that, if there are conditions of really free elections, there is no serious risk that the Communists would win." However, his more honest boss Eisenhower privately conceded that he did not know a single person not advising him that Ho Chi Minh would win a thumping mandate at the ballot box.

Did America demonize a man who could have been an ally? Ho's Marxism-Leninism certainly had an innocent aspect to it. He quoted communist scripture from rote, like a schoolboy keen to demonstrate that he had learned his lessons well. Ho later professed that he had fallen for Lenin without having bothered to read a single word the Russian uttered or wrote. What counted was the simple narrative of a patriot liberating peasants from cruel enslavement. Later, through the turgid medium of French communism, he learned the argot. There was a comic aspect to this education as Ho struggled to understand the arcane, tedious, and impenetrable debates of his French friends. A borrowed copy of Lenin's *Thesis on the National and Colonial Questions* finally offered him the key, although he had to re-read this slim book several times to make sense of the arguments (and later diligently wrote the first Sino-Annamite dictionary of Marxist terminology).

The sojourn in Moscow, where he was not rated, reinforced his beliefs, but it was probably the example of Mao's China that presented him with the practical example of revolution.

There was a pious earnestness to Ho's world view: he genuinely believed that only a communist system could lift Vietnam from backward peasant economy to modern, progressive society. Thus was fostered the Ho "Tito hypothesis." He might have been the nationalist leader of a communist Vietnam, but a threat to none and a block on (imagined) Chinese expansionism, if only he had received Western support. A barrage of eminent writers made this point, including the war's best historians, Arthur Schlesinger and Bernard Fall. American hyper-sensitivity to communism choked off this possibility. By 1950, Acheson was sneeringly dismissing Ho as an "outright Commie." Acheson then single-handedly doomed any compromise with the Viet Minh by writing a scathing instruction to the US representative in Hanoi foreclosing any possibility of negotiating with Ho Chi Minh.[39] Foster Dulles, Acheson's successor, reinforced the caricature by dogmatically viewing communism as a great monolithic threat answering to Moscow. More than any other American official in the 1950s, this Presbyterian tour de force who viewed communists as "godless terrorists" played the peddler of an apocalyptic vision of communism. Faced with such an apocalypse, inaction seemed fatal. Only Kennedy saw Vietnam's nationalism in its true light, in the same way that he harbored a secret sympathy for his nemesis Castro, recognizing that swimming these powerful currents would only end in a drowning.[40] The young Congressman Kennedy was one of few American legislators who had bothered to visit French Indochina. His verdict was prescient – the Viet Minh would win.

Now President, the Vietnam files landed with a thump on his desk and they were filled with a morass of messy detail, thanks to his predecessor Eisenhower. Along with the files came the burden carried by all Democrat presidents of the period. It had been a

Map 4: Viet Cong Dominated and Contested Areas, Spring 1961

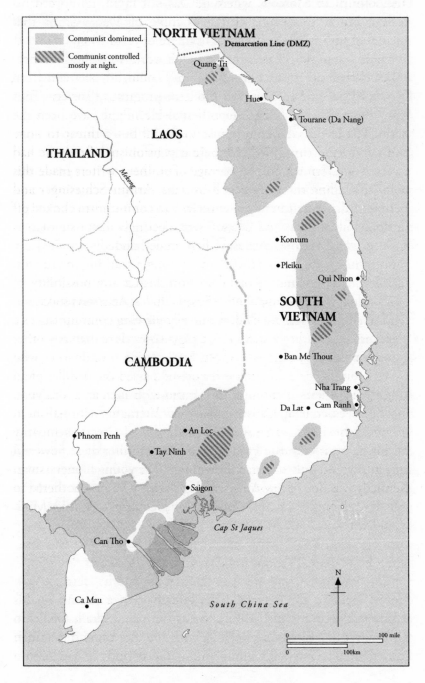

Communist dominated.

Communist controlled mostly at night.

NORTH VIETNAM

Demarcation Line (DMZ)

Quang Tri

Hue

Tourane (Da Nang)

LAOS

THAILAND

Mekong

• Kontum

• Pleiku

Qui Nhon •

SOUTH VIETNAM

• Ban Me Thout

Nha Trang •

Da Lat • Cam Ranh •

CAMBODIA

• An Loc

• Phnom Penh

• Tay Ninh

• Saigon

Cap St Jaques

Can Tho •

South China Sea

Ca Mau •

N

0   100 mile

0   100km

Democrat president who had "lost China." Anything less than a steely, cold warrior struggle with the encroaching Reds was political suicide. Ironically, the very opposite sentiment had emerged in the Pentagon, post the chastening experience of Korea and French withdrawal from Indochina. Maxwell Taylor, then serving as Deputy Chief of Staff, recalled indifference rather than zealotry: "the military interest [was] zero in that area."[41]

The French evacuation from Indochina had amounted to an unsatisfactory transfer of responsibility, garnished with political maneuvering. French troops marched out, in slow time over two years, and US advisors marched in. The decision to establish a training mission had been taken reluctantly and over the heads of the Joint Chiefs skeptical of the chances of Vietnam's survival.[42] With remarkable prescience the Chiefs concluded:

> Unless the Vietnamese themselves show an inclination to make individual and collective sacrifices required to resist communism, which they have not done to date; no amount of external pressure and assistance can long delay complete Communist victory in South Vietnam.

Ridgway especially remained implacably opposed to a Vietnam imbroglio but struggled to control Lieutenant General John O'Daniel in Saigon who had become an ill-disciplined enthusiast for taking over from the French. Eisenhower was also assailed by serious doubts, but the alternative – handing the country over to communists – was unconscionable. The prevailing orthodoxy rested in General J. Lawton Collins' advice to Secretary of Defense Wilson: "I cannot guarantee that Vietnam will remain free, even with our aid. But I know that without our aid Vietnam will surely be lost to Communism."[43] After much "heart wringing" Collins concluded that the US mission in South Vietnam was doomed as long as Diem held the reins of power. This message was unwelcome to the Catholic trio of Senator Mike Mansfield, the young, if secretly realistic Senator Kennedy, and Senator Edna Kelly (Collins was Catholic but set aside his religious biases, faced with the reality of a dominantly Buddhist and frustrated populace).

With the decision taken to support South Vietnam – more properly a gamble – the Defense Department swiftly moved into gear. The country became the seventh-largest recipient of US aid in the world, topping over $2 billion in five years (the top four countries were European: France, Britain, Italy, and West Germany in that order, demonstrating Washington's greater preoccupation with bolstering its NATO partners). Some 80 percent of the aid was poured into security forces incapable of maintaining security.[44] By 1958, South Vietnam was the top recipient in economic aid and hosted the only US military mission commanded by a general.

However, American arrogance over a perceived French failure to properly raise and train indigenous forces soon turned to hubris. The Military Assistance Advisory Group (MAAG) straightaway ran into problems. Under the terms of the Geneva Accords, the United States was limited to providing 342 advisors; far too few to train an entire army (for comparison, the French committed up to 6,000 personnel in this role in the mid-1950s, all of whom, of course, would soon depart). The MAAG, far from inheriting an army, in fact inherited a rag-bag collection of independent battalions, scattered across the country and answering to venal local politicians or strongmen. At Diem's accession to the presidency there were as many as five "armies" in South Vietnam, and none were under his control.[45] At least three separate sects were still maintaining substantial private militias: the 20,000-strong Cao Daists, the 15,000-strong Hoa Haos, and as many as 8,000 Binh Xuyen brigands. Mixed in this stew were the greatly diminished 5,000-strong Viet Minh who had stayed behind in the south, mainly in their traditional stronghold in the Central Highlands. Some estimates put the number lower than 2,000. When General Jacout the last commander of the French Expeditionary Corps left Saigon on April 28, 1956, communist insurgency was not the biggest threat facing the fledgling Diem government, but rather South Vietnamese militias refusing to acknowledge the legitimacy of the government.

In the American camp there were disagreements over the size and funding of the armed forces and militias, as well as inter-agency competition. Last gasp French machinations in courting Ho Chi Minh as a possible future ally, coupled with Diem's compulsive scheming, then conspired against the MAAG fashioning a half-decent Vietnam National Army (VNA). By mid-1957, this bankrupt organization was renamed the Army of the Republic of Vietnam or ARVN, but the name change did not improve its effectiveness or performance. As South Vietnam lacked credible internal security forces, two further bodies were raised: a Civil Guard (CG) and Self Defense Corps (SDC).[46] The training and organization of the latter two organizations was complicated by disputes over their ultimate purpose and who they answered to. For Diem, the Civil Guard was a personal anti-coup force, a hedge against the scheming generals. Overall control was thus batted between the ministries of defense, interior, and the presidency. The Self Defense Corps was treated worse, eventually subordinated to defense but equipped with surplus weapons. Both eventually mutated into the "Ruff-Puffs," or Regional Forces (RF) and Popular Forces (PF).

Most gravely, American trainers, fresh from the experience of the Korean War, were understandably obsessed with fashioning an ARVN capable of defeating the powerful People's Army of Vietnam (PAVN) in the North, in a conventional war. This was seen as the mortal threat to the country, with the consequence that "counterinsurgency" – a novel term at the time – was largely neglected. This went against the advice of South Vietnamese generals like Head of Army Doung Van Minh, "Big Minh," who "argued for the creation of an effective grassroots security organization in the countryside," because, as biographer Denis Warner Harrier wrote, "They knew how the war had been fought and lost."[47] Ironically, a consistent complaint found in MAAG reporting over this period was the manner in which units were being lost to undertake pacification, the very mission US trainers should have been addressing with more seriousness. In the end Diem got an army he neither needed nor wanted, which he mostly used as a patronage machine and internal security force.

There were many other contrasts and contradictions. South Vietnam badly needed half-decent and honest law enforcement officers. But in the summer of 1957, just three New York City policemen were despatched to Saigon to help organize the (thoroughly corrupt) police.[48] At the same time, Diem was requesting $60 million of heavy equipment for his Civil Guard, kit which the paramilitary guards could neither operate nor maintain.

On the American side, at a most basic level, the Joint Chiefs' original assessment that this was a mission unlikely to succeed was undermined by political determination to act, regardless. This compromise was fatal. "The decision to train the South Vietnamese military was based on a compromise between the Departments of State and Defense," an official US author later wrote. "Increasingly a characteristic of U.S. decision making, such compromise maximized the probability of consistently selecting the least desirable course of action."[49] It would be difficult not to argue that "the least desirable course of action" would probably serve as an apt subtitle to every subsequent account of the war.

The mission was further muddied by the artificial division of Vietnam along the 17th parallel which provoked a flight of 600,000 northern Catholics. Helping these refugees acted as a powerful distraction. Columns of desperate civilians fleeing communism attracted evangelical Americans, notably the naval Dr. Tom Dooley, a self-promoting, Catholic homosexual with Ivy League connections. Dooley spared his readers no detail of the emotional anguish suffered by the refugees. His book *Deliver Us From Evil*, serialized in *Reader's Digest*, conflated communism with sin in a way that resonated strongly with American religiosity. Powerful personalities like Cardinal Spellman interlocked with messianic liberals in the International Rescue Committee (IRC) and American Friends of Vietnam (AFV), further perpetuating the myth of "Dr. America" saving the poor northern refugees. A wild priest even called for Dooley's canonization.

Dooley was eventually forced to resign from the Navy when his "tendencies" became too overt to bury (seducing the son of an admiral was impolitic), but with the optimism characteristic of a man with many masks, he set off to Laos with "lots of white sailor hats, baseballs, ball-point pens ... and Sears Roebuck catalogues to show these people a little bit of what America is like."[50] Few Americans better exemplified the contradictions of attitudes toward South Vietnam than the eccentric Dooley; a man awarded the National Order of Vietnam by Diem and a Congressional Gold Medal by Kennedy.

As many as 900,000 refugees (one in 13 of the population) eventually fled the communist regime. Almost eight out of ten were farmers who expected and were promised resettlement. Forty thousand French citizens – administrators, doctors, educators, businessmen – went with them. This contrasted with the fewer than 5,000 South Vietnamese civilians who decided to migrate north (in addition to 90,000-odd Viet Minh who also departed by Soviet and Polish ships, taking with them their one tank).[51] The Navy mounted a massive and biblically named Operation *Exodus*, shifting a third of these internal migrants.[52] Millions of dollars of aid were furnished, each refugee receiving in government-to-government aid the equivalent of $100, or more than the average South Vietnamese worker earned in a year.[53] Diem recruited these co-religionists into the higher echelons of the government and armed forces, reinforcing the anti-communist rhetoric. The Virgin Mary had fled south and become an avenging deity.

However, it was Diem, or *My-Diem* ("American-Diem"), as his enemies started calling him, who proved the biggest threat to the stability and survival of South Vietnam. Hanoi certainly thought so, counting on an implosion of the regime in the years immediately following the Geneva Accords. The French had warned Americans that he was "mad," but Vice President Johnson defended him as Southeast Asia's Winston Churchill in a moment of absurd bombast. Always secretive, he presided over a corrupt and incompetent government filled with family members and Catholic cronies on the make. American efforts to persuade Diem to reform continually foundered against the rock of tedious hour-long monologues on Vietnamese history and culture, told over a cigarette pack. He would start, "When Noah released his first two South Vietnamese," Taylor recalled, and only three hours later "finally reach the present day."[54] The root of the problem was that "we were looking for George Washington under every mango grove in the whole country," but there was none to be found.[55]

Perhaps the best description came from an anonymous US official:

He talked of affairs of state with the extravagant expectations of a Rousseau, and he acted with the zeal of a Spanish Inquisitor. Despite extensive travel and education in the West, and despite his revolutionary mien, he remained what he had been raised: a mandarin of Imperial Hue, steeped in filial piety, devoted to Vietnam's past, modern only to the extent of an intense, conservative Catholicism.[56]

The sympathetic Ambassador Nolting would later assert that Diem had never been a "dictator at heart," but he certainly acted like one.[57] Diem converted the executive office into a family business. His venal brother Ngo Dinh Nhu became Advisor to the President; the wife Madame Nhu, a proto-Imelda Marcos, controlled the presidential office and sat in the National Assembly; a bishop brother Ngo Dinh Can became de facto ruler of Annam; his elder brother and Primate of South Vietnam, Ngo Dinh Thuc, rallied the Catholic vote; and a fourth brother, Ngo Dinh Luyen, was appointed UN Ambassador. Five other family members or in-laws held key cabinet posts including the secretary of state and defense portfolios.

A party was formed – the Personalist Labor Revolutionary Party (*Can Lao Nhan Vi Cach Mang Dang*) – whose philosophy of "personalism" baffled ordinary Vietnamese. Mostly, it amounted to brazen, personal seizure of power. Morale in the armed forces collapsed. A joke circulated that promotion was dependent on the three D's: *Dan* (or "party," meaning Diem's *Can Lao* party), *Dao* ("religion," or Catholicism), and *Du* (a vulgar term for Diem's family home).[58] His mistrust of the generals was such that he gave direct orders to units from a radio caravan parked in his garden, a gift from the MAAG. Provincial chiefs were appointed by patronage in a separate chain of command that bypassed the generals. In many respects, Diem was yet another Vietnamese spiritualist in a country that produced them by the bucket-full, obsessed with strange notions of transcendentalism and justifying his leadership on the grounds that it fitted some "divine law."[59]

Once in office, Diem effectively ruled by decree, bypassing the National Assembly. He reneged on the key pledge of the Geneva Accords and canceled the promised nationwide election, incensing Hanoi. Land reforms stalled and were subsequently abandoned. Around half the land remained concentrated in the hands of two percent of landowners.[60] Madcap schemes inflamed rural opinion and achieved little else. "The people were like a mound of straw," one old Viet Minh cadre remembered, "ready to be ignited." Traditional village power structures were undermined or dismantled. In the view of Dang Duc Khoi, who served as Diem's spokesman before turning against him, the single-biggest error made by Diem, foredooming his rule, was the abolition of the centuries-old tradition of democratic village councils.[61] By 1960, over 80 percent of provinces were being run by Diem-appointed military officers, typically Catholic northerners.

British expert P.J. Honey, who wrote extensively on Vietnam, sketched in 1959:

> Such political parties as existed in Vietnam before the advent of independence were all clandestine so that any political experience acquired from these by the Vietnamese peasants will have been of secret plotting for the overthrow of the Government ... Since 1954, the peasants have been fed on a diet of puerile and frequently offensive slogans by the Ministry of Information. These serve, if indeed they serve any purpose at all, to make the peasant distrust the Government of Ngo Dinh Diem. The peasants, for all their naivete, are far from foolish and they are not deceived by slogans alleging to be true things which they know from their own personal experience, to be untrue.[62]

This was fertile soil indeed for the Viet Cong.

That Diem flouted the spirit of Geneva is undeniable. But it is also true that the North hardly offered fertile soil for free elections. Rather, that soil was being senselessly irrigated with the blood of its own peasents. From 1955 to 1956, as many as 50,000 "peasant landlords" may have been executed in mad Maoist-style agrarian reform programs.[63] This dark episode seems to have been led by Party Secretary Troung Chinh with teams of Chinese advisors. The executions provoked a rare confession from Vo Nguyen Giap in the fall of 1956:

> We made too many deviations and executed too many honest people. We attacked on too large a front and, seeing enemies everywhere, resorted to terror, which became far too widespread. Whilst carrying out our land reform program we failed to respect the principles of freedom of faith and worship in many areas. In regions inhabited by minority tribes we have attacked tribal chiefs too strongly, thus injuring, instead of respecting local customs and manners ... Worse still, torture came to be regarded as a normal practice ...

In the South, the messianic Denunciation of Communists Campaign and the flawed Agroville Project "prosperity and density centres" (*khu tru mat*) were two gross examples of botched programs, but there were many others in the name of resettlement and re-education of the masses, offering a mirror to the equally disastrous but more brutal policies enacted north of the 17th parallel. Villager Nguyen Thi Chiem, whose husband was arbitrarily arrested, tortured, and imprisoned, offered this angry view of Diemist repression:

> They shot and killed people and herded everybody into the agrovilles. They forced people to dismantle their homes and brought them into the agrovilles. The graves were turned over and houses were newly constructed on these grave sites ... Ngo Dinh Diem announced at the time that the life and death of the people were in his hands ... if Ngo Dinh Diem did not repress the population, there would never have been the general uprising.[64]

Mostly, these schemes offered singular opportunities for corruption, particularly for Nhu who took personal charge of the displacement of entire villages to artificial settlements that became shanty towns, or were abandoned. National elections were fixed and opposition parties were banned from taking their seats. Diem's secret police, the *Cong An*, fell in with the Binh Xuyen, running drug and prostitution rackets. Far from a beacon of liberty, South Vietnam was being transformed into a dynastic mafia.

It was the gross abuse of the rural population, more than any other factor, that ultimately doomed South Vietnam in its very infancy. Military Intelligence Officer Orrin DeForest, who had the later distinction of interrogating some 4,000 Viet Cong prisoners, over the course of multiple Vietnam deployments, reflected that he was "quite surprised to learn that they basically were fighting for not a Communist philosophy, but for land reform."[65] This inescapably obvious fact of Vietnamese rural life passed over the heads of a US military advisory mission obsessed with the communist bogey. Desire for an equitable rural settlement was inflamed by chronic corruption that sapped South Vietnamese society. "They [the South Vietnamese security forces] did not have the motivation to fight the Viet Cong," observed DeForest. "They were hustling second jobs. They were involved in owning bars. They were involved in seeking money from the United States government. They were involved in selling United States military supplies ... Hundreds were caught doing that."

Every checkpoint was an opportunity to fleece the farmers. Every government document – and no individual could travel or access even the most basic services without presenting documents – was an excuse to solicit a bribe. Even Orrin DeForest found himself the victim of corrupt officials when he attempted to register his locally bought Honda motorcycle.

The same surprise would later be experienced by nineteen-year-old Second Lieutenant David Morrell. Just one year out of graduate school he found himself running RAND's Viet Cong Motivation and Morale Project, a program that involved interviewing Viet Cong prisoners. He later mused, "The remarkable phenomenon we were probing was why did they keep slugging it out so incredibly?"[66] In his mind, this represented "classic intelligence in the best sense of knowing your enemy." Over the course of his tour he felt disappointed that the new commander, Westmoreland, and his staff seemed more interested in running than understanding the war.

This recollection was somewhat unfair because RAND in fact presented its findings to an interested Westmoreland in December 1964. The Viet Cong, or VC, the analysts argued, were basically nationalists fighting against injustice, the same message the OSS mission had reported in 1945. But "Do they believe in God?" Westmoreland asked oddly. When the same briefing was extended across the mission, "the senior officers were unhappy, unbelieving, and critical."[67] The notion that the Viet Cong may be fighting for a just cause – that the communists were "the good guys" – did not sit well with a military establishment that believed it held the moral high ground. Eventually, the RAND team presented at the Pentagon. Harry Rowen recalled turning to John McNaughton and remarking, "John, I think we're signed up with the wrong side – the side that's going to lose this war."[68]

At the MAAG, another development was undermining the Vietnam mission: compulsive and self-deceiving reporting. O'Daniel had given way to Collins, who ceded to Lieutenant General "Hanging Sam" Williams, another bull-like personality, who enjoyed no more success building a credible South Vietnamese army than his predecessors. But this was not what was portrayed. Williams, fresh from commanding a division in Korea, was absorbed with the threat of an invasion from the North, and dismissed the remnants of the Viet Minh as mere saboteurs and subversives who posed no long-term threat to the country. He enjoyed good relations with Diem, notwithstanding that the president was not only disregarding his advice but countermanding American initiatives behind his back. All this Williams forgave, or pretended to be blind to. There was only one message he wished to hear – that the training mission was succeeding – and this was the positive message his up-country advisors duly fed him at quarterly meetings, even though it was clear that most Vietnamese "candy ass" generals would not have qualified as sergeants in the US Army, as one disenchanted officer put it. In contrast, Williams' relations with his own Embassy were awful, particularly with Ambassador Elbridge Durbrow with whom he was barely on speaking terms. Washington could hardly have deployed a more unbalanced and divisive team in a more intractably difficult country.

Actually, this clichéd view of Williams (much like the later disparagement of Harkins) may have been exaggerated. Lansdale recalled that it was Williams who instigated a policy of inviting General Tran Van Don to MAAG meetings and encouraged him to criticize the American advisors, a measure that ensured "everybody would stop dozing off or thinking of something else and would pay attention because they were the subject of the talk." And like Harkins, Williams was anything but a Saigon corridor polisher. He was tireless in visiting outlying units and seeking the views of the Vietnamese soldiers his advisors were training.[69]

The Francophone Durbrow arrived in a Saigon that had left behind the street violence of the early 1950s: "[it] reminded me very much of a Southern French provincial town ... it was rather calm and nice."[70] At first, he accepted Diem as a pro-American "great Vietnamese patriot," even as it was obvious that the scheming brother Nhu was the *deus ex machina* in the government. Over the next four years the relationship hardened and Diem "didn't particularly like it." However, it was with Williams that Durbrow "raised particular hell," in particular over the manner in which the guerrilla war was being neglected, a view shared by the CIA station chiefs. The relationship with Washington also strained as it became apparent to Durbrow that his masters were not taking the deteriorating situation "seriously enough." As early as November 1960, the worried ambassador was cabling, "conditions here are by no means normal. Diem government is in quite serious danger," a warning that would come to realization exactly three years later. He repeated his warnings in December using words that would be echoed by anti-Diem voices plotting his demise in the summer of 1963: "We should help and encourage him [Diem] to take effective action. Should he not do so, we may well be forced in not too distant future, to undertake difficult task of identifying and supporting alternate leadership."[71] As early as the winter of 1961, John Kenneth Galbraith was secretly advising Kennedy to stage a coup. The Ngo brothers always had good reasons to suspect that their American friends were out to get them. Indeed Lansdale, now promoted to Brigadier General and serving as Assistant to the Secretary of Defense for Special Operations, would report just one month later: "President Diem feels that Americans have attacked him almost as viciously as the Communists."

The economy worsened, though not as dramatically as in North Vietnam where the Mao-style social revolution was wreaking havoc with traditional social structures. Nobody truly believed in Diem – least of all Washington in the beginning – which is why his unexpected survival and fortitude provoked the "miracle of Vietnam" sobriquet. It was not undeserved. When Diem assumed power he was king of a few blocks in downtown Saigon. Within 300 days, this unprepossessing man who seems to have spent most of his life in cloisters had smashed all rivals.

What mattered to Americans, of course, was his implacable anti-communist stance. From no-hoper he thus became South Vietnam's best hope, at least in public pronouncements. National Intelligence Estimates consistently expressed skepticism in the regime's long-term chances of survival, demonstrating without hindsight a notable accuracy in their forecasts of an eventual communist victory. These were unheeded. It was a measure of Washington's blinding preoccupation with containing communism that, throughout this period, Diem's dysfunctional totalitarian state continued to be described in official documents as "Free Viet Nam," as if waving the wand of this magic word could somehow make it so.

From 1955 to 1960 the country edged toward the brink of war, without the intervention of North Vietnam and with little nudging from a still weak Viet Minh traversing what would later be described as "the darkest days in Party history." Throughout, Hanoi continued to engage in political dialogue: from 1957 to 1960, Prime Minister Pham Van Dong made five attempts to persuade Diem to hold national elections (July 1957, March 1958, September 1958, July 1959, and July 1959). On each occasion Diem turned a cold shoulder, well aware that he would be thrashed in a popular vote. In international forums, there was disinterest in the problem of Vietnam, now seemingly resolved through partition. Moscow under Khrushchev unexpectedly began to promote a doctrine of "peaceful coexistence" and at first offered little aid (this position was reversed after 1958). Peking was a mess and in no position to help. At the beginning of the period the main instigators of the endemic rural violence in South Vietnam were the sects, and localized opponents to the Diem government, not the surviving Viet Minh. The former were subdued, if not beaten by 1957–58, but at a cost; as many as 12,000 Vietnamese died in the sectarian violence. It was only toward the end of this period that evidence began to mount of Hanoi returning to the fray and directing a rural insurgency in the South.[72]

The slide to all-out war in the countryside had its anniversary dates. In 1956, *The Path of the Revolution in the South* was published in Hanoi, under the auspices of the Lao Dong. This tract was principally the work of the southerner Le Duan, a hard-line former railway worker and founding member of the Indochinese Communist Party. *The Path of the Revolution* was the first major statement of strategy published by the communists post-partition, and the warnings it carried were ominous. Political dialogue should continue, it argued, but popular struggle would also be necessary to "liberate" the South. To the frustration of the impatient Le Duan, and probably at the insistence of a still-enfeebled Politburo, it was acknowledged that the situation in the South was not yet opportune for armed revolution. This admission only served to redouble Le Duan's determination to galvanize his northern compatriots into action.

Le Duan was born into poverty in 1908 to peasant parents. He migrated to Hanoi for work, largely self-educated, and gravitated to the communist cause. The French jailed him for five years and then repeated the sentence during the war. When he was finally released in 1945, he had spent almost half his adult life incarcerated by the French. The experience gave him a steely toughness which would guide the rest of his life. When the former Viet Minh began to reorganize in the South he took control and adopted the code name Anh Ba ("Brother Ba"). Over this period he made friendships with two comrades who would remain lifelong allies: Le Duc Tho and Pham Hung.

A second turning point arrived in November 1957 at the Conference of Communist and Workers' Parties of Socialist Countries, held in Moscow. Lao Dong historians have consistently highlighted this event as "one of the pivotal events in the history of modern Vietnam."[73] At this symposium Le Duan persuaded Ho that armed intervention was necessary to save the movement in the South. Le Duan was subsequently appointed First Secretary of the Lao Dong, a position from which he exercised increasing control over the party. His ascendancy eventually culminated in accession to power on Ho's death, manipulating the old man's final testament, or so it was alleged.[74] "The Lao Dong leaders were possibly the most experienced and dedicated group of professional revolutionaries in the world," a US author opined, "and probably the most cautious."[75] It was Le Duan who overturned the caution.

The third turning point was the 15th Plenum of the Hanoi Central Committee, held in January 1959. This followed a reconnaissance led by Le Duan in the South, from which he returned strident over the urgent need to resume the armed struggle. Le Duan's call to arms, far from heeded, provoked divisive debates. Vo Nguyen Giap and Truong Chinh favored consolidating the revolution in the North. Le Duan, supported by Nguyen Chi Thanh, was impatient for action now.[76] Hanoi did not rush to war – it was southern exasperation, or more exactly Le Duan's impatience, that proved the motor.[77] An official decision to actually initiate armed struggle, covertly supported by the North, was not taken until May 1959, and it probably did not filter down to village level until the end of the year.[78] This took the form of Resolution 10, formally issued at the beginning of October and described by the future deputy supreme commander of the National Liberation Front (NLF), Madame Nguyen Thi Dinh, "like a rainstorm in a drought."[79] The fateful decision was taken coincident with Diem's repressive Law 10/59; a shoddy pretext for widespread, state-sanctioned killings (mere affiliation to communism attracted capital punishment).

The last significant anniversary was the Third National Congress held in September 1960. This was the moment when Hanoi publicly resolved "to liberate South Vietnam from the ruling yolk of the U.S. imperialists and their henchmen."[80] By this moment it was evident the situation in the South was deteriorating. This came about as spontaneous local retaliation from self-organized cadres in response to Diem's oppression. The Viet Minh's *tru gian* or "extermination activities" were a direct counterpart to the secret police's own programs of assassinations. The village self-defense groups were responses to thuggish local government officials. This was self-defense not subversion, but it acted as seed corn for an expanding and better-organized insurgency.

Official statistics, of which there were several from disputed sources, told a story which South Vietnam's peasants knew to be true from their daily experience. In 1958, there were 236 assassinations and abductions. The pattern of these attacks suggested nobody was safe. In July, a widely reported massacre of 17 peasants was perpetrated; in August, as many as 400 guerrillas attacked the Michelin Plantation north of Saigon, routing the security forces; in September a district chief and his family were shockingly gunned down in broad daylight; in October a series of bombs in Saigon left 13 American servicemen injured; and on December 1, Diem's heavy-handedness landed Hanoi a public relations gift with the so-called "Phu Loi Massacre" at a detention camp north of Saigon.[81]

Viet Cong terror tactics were both merciless and barbaric. Southern propaganda amplified and exaggerated this rural misery, but the reality was grim enough anyway. Australian Dr. R.G.

Wylie, who treated many peasant victims of Viet Cong retribution, recalled:

> The pregnant widow of a hamlet chief arrived with both legs dangling by ribbons of flesh. The Viet Cong had strangled her husband before her eyes and then machine-gunned her and their three-year-old child, who died on the way to the hospital. Both of the woman's legs had to be amputated, and she aborted her child four hours after the operation. Ultimately she recovered … a woman without husband, children or legs … Such are the people who survive to be evacuated to us.[82]

According to one study, "The terror program was central to the violence program – it was the hardener in the formula, the steel in the superstructure."[83] If so, the steel needed more beating.

In 1959, the figure jumped to 343, and an increasingly bellicose tone began to be heard from Radio Hanoi. The year began badly for the security forces when a guerrilla force descended on the headquarters of the 32nd ARVN (Army of the Republic of Vietnam) Regiment in the town of Trang Sup in Tay Ninh Province and walked off with over 350 rifles. The shock of this brazen attack "really put the Vietnamese in a tizzy," and even the habitually dismissive Williams was disconcerted.[84] On July 8, communist guerrillas staged an attack against the major military base at Bien Hoa, north of Saigon. Among the dead were two American servicemen – the first combat fatalities suffered by the MAAG. Documents captured at the beginning of the year indicated that Hanoi had begun directing the establishment of guerrilla camps in the South; the first tangible evidence of direct intervention.[85] Premier Pham Van Dong reportedly boasted to the French Consul "we will be in Saigon tomorrow."[86] By the following year the US Embassy was reporting 282 deaths as a result of guerrilla action, just in the first six months.[87] The 1960 National Intelligence Estimate (NIE) would eventually tally 1,400 assassinations and 700 kidnappings. Some independent observers estimated many thousands of murders (13,000 by 1963).[88] The South Vietnamese government's inaptly named "White Book" (July 1964) tallied 17,000 victims and offered revolting gore to readers with strong constitutions.[89]

Then as now, "terrorism" was portrayed as an unspeakable evil. Innumerable reports sought to fit the violence to calculated communist doctrine. But did a VC guerrilla murder a villager from doctrinal belief, or from any range of local reasons unreachable to a Westerner seeking to understand the violence? The problem with the numbers and the lurid atrocity stories is that most emanated from the government. In the economical judgment of a US official, "What relationship GVN [Government of Vietnam] statistics bore to reality is not known."[90] Whatever the true figure, no one disputed that the countryside was aflame again with a growing insurgency. Faced with a deteriorating security situation, Eisenhower authorized a covert augmentation of the MAAG's strength from 327 to 685 personnel by mid-1960.

The year 1960 was critically one when the first large-unit actions were launched across the South: in Tay Ninh, Dong Xoai, Kien Hoa, Ca Mau, and the Mekong Delta. Worryingly, on each occasion the guerrillas clashed with the ARVN, they came out on top. Over this period, Washington almost allowed Hanoi to creep up while looking the other way. Between 1956 and 1959, the production of National Intelligence Estimates on South Vietnam was suspended. The CINCPAC Official History stopped mentioning the VC at all. MAAG reporting filled the vacuum and this was consistently more optimistic (and self-deluding) than the depressing missives from the intelligence community. It was only after it had become manifest that the country was backsliding drastically that intelligence agencies were once again focused on this corner of Southeast Asia in a unified manner, but by then the insurgency had become hydra-headed.

Over-optimistic reporting by the MAAG and successor MACV (Military Assistance Command Vietnam) would become a consistent theme of the war. Yet it is too easy to dismiss the procession of generals that served in South Vietnam as foolish blow-hards blind to the realities outside the air-conditioned walls of their offices. Congressional support for defense and economic aid budgets – the obligations – depended acutely on the public face of the war. Government servants despatched to these countries understood that they *had* to sell the war. Anything less than declaring "progress" – the tired, debased word re-heated from Vietnam and deployed unconvincingly in counterinsurgency wars of the recent period – was suicidal, not just for personal careers. And the facts are that however hard the in-country team tried to sell its war, Congress always cut funds. Total military grants to Vietnam under Truman and Eisenhower had totaled $709 million. By Kennedy's first year in office they had fallen to $65 million. McNamara wanted to cut expenditure further. The argument that truth should have been reported unto power is not as robust as it may appear. When the White House was determined to act anyway, and Congress was determined to snap shut the purse, what good choices did the generals have?

As well as the misleading reporting, another pernicious effect had also manifested itself. Too many of Washington's China and Southeast Asia experts had been "tarred, feathered ... sent to pasture, dismissed, [and been] driven, in a few cases, to suicide," thanks to the McCarthyite purges.[91] This left, as David Halberstam colorfully described them, "a bunch of super cold warriors and a vast amount of ignorance."[92]

What the resumed intelligence reporting uncovered was a far stronger and entrenched communist apparatus than the MAAG had been reporting. The First Indochina War had acted as a catalyst and a great organizing principle for the communists, creating a hierarchy of armed forces that was readily adapted for the second war. The reporting failed to reckon that at the root of Vietnamese communism – certainly in the South – was a deep-seated hatred provoked by the abuses of the Diem regime.

In the South, a paramilitary National Liberation Front (*Mat Tran Dan Toc Giai Phong Mien Nam Viet Nam*) was established by the beginning of 1960 (the full title in English, used consistently by Radio Hanoi was "National Front for the Liberation of South

Vietnam" – NFLSV). Its first chairman was a lawyer named Nguyen Huu Tho who had spent seven years in Diem's prisons. Many of its original members had belonged to the Saigon-Cholon Peace Committee, a political organization pushed underground by Diemist repression. From January 1962, a People's Revolutionary Party (PRP) acted as its political wing, or more correctly as the southern political wing of the Lao Dong. Military operations were coordinated by a Central Office for South Vietnam (COSVN), a dormant organization reactivated from the First Indochina War. The NLF leadership mainly, but not exclusively, recruited from the ranks of disaffected South Vietnamese intellectuals, and not all were communist. Nevertheless, CIA reporting persisted in branding the NLF "crypto-communists."[93]

If the NLF's leadership had roots in Saigon's café culture, the foot soldiers were all drawn from the disaffected peasantry. Three Diemist policies swelled the ranks of the NLF: the "Communist Denunciation Campaign" which in practice targeted many nationalists who had fought against the French; land confiscations which reversed awards to peasants over the course of the First Indochina War; and lastly the "March Against the North" campaign, or forced conscription.[94]

Tran Nhat Bang, who joined the NLF in 1962, offered a classic example of the alienated peasant. Hailing from the village of Hoa Tien, northwest of Saigon, Bang's father was killed by the French in 1947, and his elder brother, a Viet Minh fighter, was forced to regroup to the north in 1954. The younger Bang remained in Hoa Tien to care for his widowed mother. Under Diem's misguided rural reform programs, the family was forcibly removed to a strategic hamlet and he was forced to undertake corvée (forced) labor. Land which the family received as a reward for participating in the independence struggle was confiscated: "All the land that the Resistance gave us was confiscated by the Diem people. All the paddy fields that the revolution gave us in 1945 were taken." Bang the nationalist was now Bang the communist, and suspect. To survive, he had to hire himself out as a buffalo herder and his mother worked as an agricultural laborer. Both had to attend government re-education camps, a counterpart of the same indoctrination foisted by the communists.

However, the interesting aspect of Tran Nhat Bang's story is not that he was an early recruit to the NLF but rather that resistance was local and spontaneous. Hoa Tien was "liberated" on August 1, 1964 but "there were no revolutionary troops and no regular forces coming to the village at that time. The villagers staged a spontaneous uprising."⁹⁵ Only later did the Viet Cong join forces with the self-appointed village defense committee. This pattern was repeated across South Vietnam.

The first NLF manifesto was published to coincide with a somewhat optimistic and premature *Dong Khoi* or General Uprising, staged in an uncoordinated manner on January 17, 1960. The trigger seems to have been anger over the Agrovilles, a catalyst seemingly missed by the American mission in Saigon. Radio Hanoi subsequently broadcast this manifesto on January 29, testifying to the close links between the NLF and Hanoi. Unsure what flag to fly, the rebels created a simple banner with the words *Dong Khoi* against a blue background, "which represented peace."⁹⁶ According to NLF folklore, the honor of the first actions against the Diem government went to an ad hoc company of peasants in Mo Cay District, Ben Tre Province, the same province that liberated itself from French rule through a soldiers' mutiny.⁹⁷ The so-called "Cradle of the General Uprising" was just three villages: Dinh Thuy, Phuoc Hiep, and Binh Khanh.⁹⁸ Le Van Phuc, who participated in this first uprising with just 20 men, remembered preparing "crude weapons which included bayonets, sharpened bamboo stakes, clubs and machetes." Later, rifles were captured: "The spot where the first gunshot was fired was at the military post in Dinh Thuy at exactly 3:00 p.m. on January 17."⁹⁹ The uprising was a local success. Much like Ho's original political charter for the North, the NLF's political manifesto mixed French republicanism with Vietnamese nationalism. The word communism appeared nowhere.

This appeal to the high moral ground (which both sides made) hid an ugly reality. Communist terror tactics were undeniably abhorrent, but Diemist repression was equally bad. When Quaker Jane Barton visited a prison in Quang Ngai she found:

> ... a 67-year-old woman that was lying on a bare bed frame ... they had just put ... cardboard on the top of it, with a hole cut in it through which she was supposed to defecate, and she had no clothes ... just a blanket that the other prisoners had given her.[100]

How could this woman possibly be a threat to the Saigon government, she mused?

Public beheadings became a favored Viet Cong tactic, reported in lurid details by the propaganda arm of the Saigon government. But who reported the same barbaric executions perpetrated by government officials? NLF cadre Nguyen Huu Tho recalled this policy of collective and probably indiscriminate justice with some bitterness:

> Whenever there was some kind of incident in some place, they would take their special court to that place, put on a trial and decapitate their prisoners immediately on the spot in full view of the local inhabitants. Confronted by this situation, we then decided that we had to fight back.[101]

Villager Nguyen Thi Chiem remembered the village guillotining exacted for the most trivial offences:

> When Diem came into power he issued Law Code no. 10/59. According to this law code, if anybody traveled illegally at night – for example, if you went out at night to fish without a lamp or a torch – then they would guillotine you. At that time, whether you participated in revolutionary activities or not, you would get killed anyway. Since it did not matter to them whether you participated in revolutionary activities or not, the population became really outraged. They did not make any distinction between the Viet Cong and the people.[102]

In many instances, it was a case of local bullies using the veneer of state authority to torment villagers. This is Chiem again:

> In 1956 in my village there was the headman named Chac who was the most brutal of all. He would not be pleased if he did not see blood during a certain day. He shot and killed the inhabitants. For this reason, the inhabitants really hated him and wanted to kill him in order to regain their rights to life in the village of Phu Tuc ... And there was a policeman named Tiep who was also most brutal ... In 1960, Mr. Toan, a soldier, shot Policeman Tiep to express his sympathy for the local inhabitants.

Taking revenge came with risks. Nguyen Thi Nguyet Anh was an early recruit to the NLF.

> In 1963 we killed a local despot who was the cruellest in the village of Thanh Son. We rigged a grenade in his motorcycle and it exploded, killing him. The enemy came and surrounded me at the Cho Con marketplace and arrested me there, shackling my hands up right there ... [Following arrest] ... they tortured us extremely barbarously. They had me tortured every night around midnight. They put electrodes on my ears and turned on the electricity. I got a shock and fell down, then they pulled me up to my feet and turned on the electricity again and again I fell down.[103]

These torture techniques, of course, were learned from the French. Three years later she was arrested again and "beaten up for 21 nights in succession" with "an American advisor standing next to them."

Nguyen Thi Dinh, who rose to become Deputy Supreme Commander of the NLF and had the later distinction of being appointed the first female general in the People's Army, recalled, "the comrades who fought side by side with me were decapitated, had their bellies slit, were buried alive, and murdered in many other barbaric ways. Hundreds of my comrades in arm were killed in the most sadistic manner." If husbands and sons evaded capture, the police would torture the wives:

> There were mothers like Mrs. Ke whose husband and children were all revolutionaries. They arrested her and tortured her, telling her to reveal the whereabouts of her husband and children. In spite of all the torturing, she resolutely refused to divulge any information at all. Finally she said to her torturers:

My husband and my children are in my heart. If you ... want to find them, you can slit open my heart. And so the torturers beat her to death.[104]

In the case of the unfortunate Ms. Hanh, who survived the war and later became a provincial official in Ben Tre, "they even rubbed and stuffed milled black pepper and red pepper into her vagina." Another girl "had a broken beer bottle inserted into her vagina during the torturing. Blood spurted out but she remained close mouthed."[105]

The excesses of America's ally went further. The wives of former Viet Minh who had regrouped to the North were forced to divorce their absent husbands. Universal resistance to this decree provoked arrests and the inevitable torture. Pham Thi Xuan Que was forced to flee Hue to save her life. In her words:

> Women who were faithful to their husbands were stuffed into rice sacks along with rocks. Then they tied these sacks up and threw them down into the river. The infamous Vinh Trinh incident involved 40 women who were stuffed into the rice sacks with rocks and thrown down the Vinh Trinh (Forever Faithful) dam. There were many other massacres.[106]

Within two years, the NLF claimed 300,000 members, although it would always prove impossible to verify numbers.[107] Enrolment was not necessarily voluntary and whole communities could be declared "enrolled" without their knowledge. However unpopular the Diem regime, representation in the organization tells a somewhat different story. The first NLF central committee was announced in March 1962 and was supposed to comprise 52 members. Only 31 could be found. None were public figures of stature. Nguyen Huu Tho, who was elected to this first central committee, affirmed that the organization adopted "four urgent policies for national salvation." These were: "One, making the United States stop its war of aggression in the South; two, dismantling all the strategic hamlets; three, establishing a national coalition government in the South; and four, conducting a foreign policy of peace and neutrality."[108] Two years later the central committee comprised 42 members but half the previous delegates had left. This was not an organization built on solid foundations or wide electoral appeal. The sects were hostile and Buddhists indifferent. Catholics viewed communists as satanic.

Nonetheless, it is too easy to be cynical over NLF pronouncements and to view them as communism infiltrating through the back door of moderate policies. This view does not reflect the wide range of political opinion attracted to the NLF – the only avenue for political opposition to the Diemist regime – and nor does it reflect the division that existed between Northern and Southern communists. The relationship between Hanoi and the NLF was never a straightforward one between patron and client; it was riven with tensions. Many moderate NLF, in particular the so-called "neutralist" camp, feared the northerners. War radicalized Vietnamese politics in a manner that always sent hardliners bobbing to the top like a cork in water.

The armed groups that coalesced around the NLF, many of whom were former Viet Minh who had declined to migrate north, were variously known as the "Self Defense Militias," the "Liberation Army," and the "People's Liberation Armed Forces" (PLAF), but these terms were overtaken by the title by which they would be known for the remainder of the war – the Viet Cong or VC. Hanoi would continue to refer to the armed wing as the South Vietnam

People's Liberation Army, or PLA, in its English-translation texts. The full title of the VC, *Viet Nam Cong-San*, meaning "Vietnamese Communist," was a coinage of the Saigon press as early as 1956, possibly at the instigation of a paranoid Diem who was busy passing draconian security laws and labeling any opposition as "communist."

The work of American anthropologist Gerald Hickey[109] – conducted when it was still possible to visit villages and not fear for your life – suggests that villagers dismissed the VC title and continued to use Viet Minh, associating the guerrillas with a nationalist struggle against government oppression, rather than communist subversion as the Diem government would have wished.[110] In fact, the official title of this new front was neither Viet Cong, nor Viet Minh: it was the National Front for the Liberation of Vietnam (*Mat Tran Dan Toc Giai Phong Mien Nam Viet Nam*), a spontaneous revival of the nationalism of the first Indochinese War. In the eyes of the peasantry, the Viet Minh, of course, were national heroes anyway. The fact that Diem's officials were oppressing these veterans only deepened a sense of outrage and resistance. It was unsurprising that VC units began to organize themselves precisely where the Viet Minh-led fighting had ended in 1954: in the Mekong Delta; in the Central Highlands; in the coastal Quang Ngai Province; and in the border regions of Cambodia, later known as War Zones C and D (the old French *Zone Nord*).

It was this spontaneity of rebellion that American intelligence acknowledged when it assessed:

> While prisoners and captured documents have established these links between Hanoi and the South, reports are too few in number and insufficiently comprehensive to warrant the conclusion that Hanoi was always in a position to dictate or even manipulate events in South Vietnam; they do [however] offer persuasive evidence that the Lao Dong Party continued conspiratorial, political, and military activities in South Vietnam throughout the years 1954 to 1969.[111]

This judgment was perhaps over-cautious. Hanoi deliberately underplayed its involvement in the beginning, fearful of provoking a reaction in Washington. When it became clear that the Kennedy administration would pursue its "special war" anyway, the mask was dropped. By the spring of 1964, Ho Chi Minh was speaking of the "sacred duty" to liberate the South. Radio Hanoi, Radio Peking, and *Hoc Tap* (the party journal) were all openly broadcasting the North's support for the Viet Cong. Postwar, General Tran Do explained:

> ... in the South there was an organization of the Central Committee of the Labor Party of Vietnam [Lao Dong] called the Central Office (Trung Uong Cuc) which was responsible for directing the struggle in the South ... this was [the] organization in charge of overall policies and strategies.

In Tran's colorful analogy, the CO and COSVN were "comparable to the Pentagon in the jungle."[112] Without this support, the insurgency would have collapsed.

Notwithstanding that southern outrage ignited the insurgency it was eventual northern domination via the Central Office that introduced a strategy clearly rooted in the Maoist philosophy of guerrilla warfare. Romantically known as "the struggle" (*dau tranh*), the ideology had two pillars: military struggle (*dau tranh vu trang*) and political struggle (*dau tranh chinh thi*). For Vo Nguyen Giap, always a firm believer in orthodox Marxism, the war had to be pure and "born of the people," the thesis of his most important work, *People's War; People's Army* (1961).[113] For embattled guerrilla commanders in the South, the practical defeat of the South Vietnamese security apparatus was the imperative. Both were preempted by the massive American intervention that forced a mixed campaign of conventional warfare and guerrilla tactics. Le Duan was always right when he observed, "the southern people's revolutionary struggle will be long, drawn out, and arduous. It is not a simple process but a complicated one, combining many varied forms of struggle."

It was also the case that the depicted romance of revolutionary struggle hid an uglier reality. Chieu Hoi ("Open Arms") deserters spoke of the onerous taxation, coercion, and endless political indoctrination. Precious rice reserves were impounded by guerrillas. Extortion rates could be severe. A poor farmer producing less than two bushels might be charged at six percent. But farmers producing over 120 bushels could find themselves charged 30 percent – or effectively be compelled to hand over one third of their annual crop.[114] Villagers were forced to buy NLF "war bonds" for 1,500 Vietnamese piasters which they were assured would be redeemable after the war. Rubber plantation workers in Binh Long Province were forced to donate a day's wage to the cause.[115] Some villagers, like Tran Thanh Van, a 24-year-old rice farmer from Kien Phong Province, joined the insurgency voluntarily then regretted the decision and deserted. Others, like Tran Van Liem, also from the Delta, "said he left the village of Xuan Son because the Viet Cong were forcing all young men to join guerrilla units to replace heavy losses."[116] When 17-year-old Pham Van Dau was asked why he joined the communists he replied, "They threatened to kill my father if I refused. That is why I joined them." Hatred of the Saigon government did not necessarily translate into support for the insurgency.

At the core of the Viet Cong strategy was the successful exploitation of a Vietnamese tradition of secret societies; control of the villages; virulent anti-Diemism; and an equally durable anti-Americanism. The constants were a single-minded persistence and a remarkable capacity to work logistic miracles with raw manpower. The prolific John Kenneth Galbraith would display many fine judgments on US foreign policy over the course of his career. But when he scoffed "the amount of ammunition and weaponry a man can carry on his back for several hundred kilometres over jungle was not increased appreciably by Marx," he could not have been more complacent.[117]

For Washington, the old dilemmas and even older refrains remained unchanged. These were succinctly expressed by the now-promoted Brigadier General Lansdale following a flying visit to Vietnam at the beginning of 1961, in his capacity as Assistant to the Secretary of Defense for Special Operations:

> The free Vietnamese, and their government, will probably be able to do no more that postpone eventual defeat ... the U.S. team in Vietnam will be unable to help the Vietnamese with real effectiveness ... if Free Vietnam is won by the communists, the remainder of Southeast Asia will be easy pickings for our enemy ... a Communist victory also would be a major blow to U.S. prestige and influence, not only in Asia but throughout the world.[118]

Lansdale had actually been telephoned by Kennedy, ten days after his inauguration ceremony, with the instruction to post an article the former had written about Vietnam in the *Saturday Evening Post*. In Lansdale's later amused recollection, "I was at the time wondering which joker in the Pentagon was imitating this Harvard, Massachusettes accent and was having me on, so I said 'yes, yes, yes.'"[119] He fortunately checked later and realized to his surprise that the caller had been Kennedy.

Crucially, the two Eisenhower veterans of Vietnam were replaced over this period: Ambassador Elbridge Durbrow ceding to Frederick Nolting, and General Samuel Williams, who handed over to Lionel McGarr. "Stonehead" McGarr was a wartime hero, the man who commanded 30th Infantry Regiment at Anzio and whose motto "Our Country, Not Ourselves" could well have served as his own. Age had not softened this earnest warrior. His bellicosity was strident, sparing no exclamation marks or alliterative flourishes to make his points. Within a month of setting foot in Vietnam he urged immediate action:

> Our objective must be to find, fix, fight and finish the enemy! No half measures will do. Time is our most precious commodity and the urgency of the situation requires that we use every second gainfully ... MAAG cannot afford the luxury of an eight-hour day or a five-day week ... history will not wait.[120]

This fighting talk ran against the prevailing mood in Washington and a cautious Kennedy. The debate instead became focused on a $42 million military aid package, and on increasing the overall strength of the Republic of Vietnam Armed Forces (RVNAF) by 20,000. This latter measure was in fact a recommendation from the Eisenhower administration's last Counter-Insurgency Plan (CIP) for South Vietnam. This was accepted and perfunctorily signed off on January 28. Kennedy seemed to find both proposals unsatisfactory and was "frustrated" that neither the South Vietnamese government nor the MAAG shared his vision of a counter-revolutionary war.[121] A separate proposal floated by Special Military Representative Maxwell Taylor, and Deputy Assistant for National Security Affairs Walt Rostow, to increase US troop levels to 10,000, simply "horrified" him. In fact, Kennedy was so upset by this recommendation he suppressed the relevant section of the report, which "caused a lot of problems" with government departments demanding the White House reverse its censorship. This proposal in fact had originated from the bellicose McGarr in Saigon. Presaging the later demands for more troops, McGarr had originally pitched for 16,000 US combat troops to be deployed in the Central Highlands immediately. This was a reaction to a widely held view that the middle of the country had effectively fallen to the Viet Cong, or was about to fall. If a divisional-sized force were judged politically unacceptable he suggested a compromise 10,000-strong force.

Setting aside these extreme recommendations, the consensus at this point was that more was *not* necessary. Indeed policymakers implied that if the Eisenhower CIP were implemented properly, the situation in South Vietnam would be resolved. In Hilsman's recollection, the frustration from Kennedy's perspective was that it wasn't: "Kennedy saw the insurgency as [an] essentially nationalist movement, feeding on social discontent. So you don't shoot people. You don't bomb villages, you don't shell villages. You try to remove the causes of social discontent."[122] Instead, the very opposite was happening, supported by American advisors.

At the insistence of Ambassador Durbrow, military aid was linked to political reforms which Diem was unwilling to undertake. At one point, Dean Rusk later recollected, "We counted about forty-four different programs that we were pressing the South Vietnamese to put into effect in South Vietnam in order to strengthen the fiber of the country and mobilize the countryside. That was simply beyond their governing capacities to handle and it was indigestible."[123] It was not just a matter of "governing capacities" – the same refrain repeated in modern counterinsurgency conflicts such as the Afghanistan civil war – it was a matter of culture, which was far harder for Westerners to understand. Nguyen Khanh, briefly Chief of State and Prime Minister, remembered: "The American people, you export too much your democracy and your freedom ... you want to impose that in the country like Vietnam, it doesn't, it cannot work."[124]

Negotiations dragged on for months. Washington's misplaced optimism on this matter was such that the desired reforms had still not been implemented at the time of Diem's assassination three years later. Only five days after despatching the CIP, Lansdale's pessimistic memo reached Kennedy. It caused some shock. Turning to Rostow, Kennedy famously remarked: "You know, Ike never briefed me about Vietnam."[125]

As a consequence of Lansdale's alarmist memo, he was tasked in April, along with Deputy Secretary of Defense Roswell Gilpatric, to review Indochinese policy as part of a presidential Vietnam Task Force. The two men were instructed that they had just six days to report their findings. Concurrently, on April 20, Kennedy ordered a review of US policy in Vietnam under "*A Program of Action to Prevent Communist Domination of South Vietnam.*" Even before the two set to work Kennedy had already displayed his appetite for covert operations in the March 9 NSAM (National Security Action Memorandum) 28, in which he instructed McNamara to report on the possibility of launching guerrilla attacks in Viet Cong-held territory. Concurrently, an Office of Special Assistant for Counterinsurgency and Special Activities

(SACSA) was created within the Joint Chiefs of Staff, another typical Kennedy initiative.

For the remainder of 1961, Indochinese policy was dominated by the weighty bookends of two National Security Action Memoranda – NSAMs 52 and 111 – interrupted by another cold war crisis in Berlin. Three cards fell out of the shuffled pack. First, a general consensus emerged that the solution to South Vietnam lay in a strategy of "pacification." This demanded wresting control of the villages from the Viet Cong and winning over the peasants to the government side. The axiomatic truth behind "pacification" belied the difficulty of actually achieving such a strategy. The second consequence was that soldiers and officials in Saigon and Washington opened the debate on increasing US military advisor numbers in South Vietnam, not by hundreds but by thousands. This would never have been countenanced, still less authorized by Eisenhower. The start of a new presidency seemed to give unholy permission to some personalities to consider the impermissible. And last, as a logical outcome of such calculations, some began to ask the more controversial question: how many US soldiers would it take to win a war in Vietnam? The same question had been posed in 1953, at the height of the French crisis in the First Indochina War, and the Joint Chiefs had warned that as many as 12 US divisions would be needed, and even then victory could not be guaranteed.[126] This accurate assessment had long been forgotten by a new generation of generals.

Gilpatric and Lansdale conducted their whirlwind tour of South Vietnam, but given the tight schedule, their report was substantially based on Eisenhower's CIP. The latter's pessimism impregnated the overall picture with gloom. It was assessed that over 60 percent of the country was now in communist hands; there was an average of 650 violent incidents every month; and as many as 12,000 VC were operating in rural areas with impunity.[127] This was far from exaggeration. The Viet Cong effectively controlled broad swathes of South Vietnam, from the Central Highlands to the Mekong Delta, all areas from which the Viet Minh in the First Indochina War had never truly been dislodged. Communist domination in Laos meant that control of three important passes in the Annam Mountains had passed to Hanoi, easing the infiltration of cadres into South Vietnam. Serious concerns were expressed over an autocratic and corrupt government that was unlikely to "succeed in the battle to win men's minds in Vietnam." Little else in the panorama offered hope: the Geneva Accords were inhibiting necessary action and SEATO lacked both unanimity and will.

Given this bleak assessment, it was a surprise that the initial April 27 draft report only recommended a modest increase in the size of the MAAG. The April 28 so-called "Laos Annex" (there were, in fact, three versions such were the swings of opinion), endorsed a 20,000 increase in the ARVN, as well as a 3,600 increase in US trainers, including the despatch of 400 Green Berets to Nha Trang on the coast. The corresponding increase in military aid was also modest: up from $155 million to $161 million (from a total global program of Military Assistance Packages (MAPs) of $1.6 billion).

Kennedy kept his counsel on the first draft, but his speech to a Democratic Party dinner in Chicago, delivered on the same day, was revealing:

> Now our great responsibility is to be the chief defender of freedom, in this time of maximum danger. Only the United States has the power and the resources and the determination. We have committed ourselves to the defense of dozens of countries stretched across the globe who look to us for the defense of their freedoms.[128]

Whether or not influenced by his own rhetoric, the following day Kennedy tentatively agreed to a modest increase in the size of the US advisory mission in South Vietnam, up from the 342 ceiling imposed by Geneva, to 785. As this breached international agreement, both the number and purpose would have to be kept secret. He also gave the impression – no more – that he was open to an increased training commitment in support of a 150,000-strong

ARVN, 40,000 Self Defense Corps, and 68,000 Civil Guard, as well as creating a Junk Force to counter arms smuggling.

However, the Gilpatric-Lansdale report was drafted at the very height of the fluid crisis in Laos. Two departments with quite different views on Indochina, Defense and State, batted the proposals between them. And even as they argued, the situation changed on the ground, with the Royal Laotian Army and Pathet Lao unexpectedly agreeing a ceasefire. This provoked more divisions of opinion. In total, the Task Force Report was re-written five times in the space of two weeks, including the original draft on April 27: on May 1 (by Defense); and on May 3, 6, and 11 (by State, under George Ball the Under Secretary of State). By the time the final draft was approved all the contentious proposals had been watered down reflecting the de-escalation of the Laos crisis. This was a rare triumph for State that would not be repeated again in the Vietnam story. Unilateral military action became the vague possibility of a bilateral defense treaty (the model was Lebanon's 1958 request for American assistance). The proposal to despatch Lansdale to Saigon as a counterinsurgency guru was scotched, despite Diem making four personal requests for this American whom he trusted. The final draft of the report relegated to annexes all three material military recommendations: the deployment of US Battle Groups and an Engineer Battalion for training purposes to the Central Highlands; the assignment of coastal patrol missions to CINCPACFLT (Commander-in-Chief Pacific Fleet), and an air surveillance and close-support role to CINCPACAF (Commander-in-Chief Pacific Air Force). Over two weeks, Kennedy had blown cold over ramping up the military commitment and instead fell back on the safe recommendations of State. These included a vice-presidential trip and letter to Diem from Kennedy; a modestly increased MAP; and a general commitment to support Diem.

In the wry judgment of a US official commenting later on the apparent wild swings in policy and recommendations:

The lesson in this, which will not come as a surprise to anyone who has ever had contact with the policy-making process, is that the rationales given in such pieces of paper (intended for fairly wide circulation among the bureaucracy, as opposed to tightly held memoranda limited to those closest to the decision-maker) do not reliably indicate why recommendations were made the way they were.[129]

This is certainly true of much Vietnam documentation where what appears to be at stake is at odds with what the administration then decides to do. But it is also the case that some rationales – the domino theory, American prestige – recurred with a dogmatic insistence that did influence policy, and in deleterious ways.

The Pentagon was deflected, but only briefly. As Walt Rostow the Deputy Assistant for National Security Affairs described it, "The 1961 relationship between President Kennedy and General [Lyman] Lemnitzer and the whole JCS [Joint Chiefs of Staff] position of 1961 was a nightmare."[130] Notwithstanding the presidential chill, the Joint Chiefs saw it incumbent upon themselves to at least prepare for unexpected contingencies. On May 1, coincident with the second draft of the report and not even waiting for State's reply, the Joint Chiefs transmitted a top secret memo to the abrasive Admiral Felt (CINCPAC, Commander-in-Chief Pacific), instructing him to prepare a 5,000-strong marine intervention force to despatch to Udorn, Thailand and Da Nang, South Vietnam.[131] Air strikes against North Vietnam and China were also proposed. Simultaneously, at 10pm on April 26, a "general advisory" alert was issued to all US combat commands around the world, in case of a Soviet reaction. This marked the first official statement of a willingness to engage in combat operations in Vietnam – and potentially provoked confrontation with the Soviet Union – taken without Congressional debate or knowledge.

Perversely, the individual behind this change of mind appears to have been Kennedy himself, reasoning, "We [can't] afford to turn over South East Asia to the communists." Alarmed by an unexpected communist advance on the Plaine des Jarres toward the Mekong, Rostow recalled that Kennedy "began to load those marines," an action he judged "a hell of a gamble."[132] Soviet espionage quickly detected the preparations (probably the signals bouncing around the world) "and they came rushing around to the British and said, 'Well, let's have a conference.'"[133] A hasty consultation with Congressional leaders, who opposed any suggestion of American troop deployments, was described by Rostow as, "the worst White House meeting he had ever attended in the entire Kennedy administration."[134] On May 4, the influential Senator Fulbright, Chairman of the Foreign Relations Committee (who had joined his fellow congressmen in opposition to ramping up the stakes), dropped a hint in a press conference that he would in fact support the deployment of US troops to Thailand and Vietnam.

Notwithstanding these military preparations, when policy finally solidified in NSAM 52 (May 11) it proved to be more an excuse not to act rather than to take action. The professorial McGeorge Bundy, as National Security Advisor, fell back on the original April 27 draft, with few substantial additions. This indecision presaged the younger Bundy's subsequent confusion over his entire involvement in the war. As Kissinger later astutely sentenced, this brilliant mathematician was a "hawk on Vietnam," but one "torn between his convictions and his instincts." He would end up supporting a cause for which "he had no passion."[135]

The aims of the memorandum were simply stated, if dauntingly difficult:

To prevent Communist domination of South Vietnam; to create in that country a viable and increasingly democratic society, and to initiate, on an accelerated basis, a series of mutually supporting actions of a military, political, economic, psychological and covert character designed to achieve this objective.

Kennedy's appetite for covert operations was again manifested, with the CIA emerging as one of the real beneficiaries of NSAM 52. The Saigon station gained approval to increase its strength by 40 personnel. A raft of covert actions was either authorized or encouraged: the infiltration of agents into North Vietnam; photographic over-flights; an expanded communications intelligence program supported by the US Army Security Agency (aka Radio Research Unit); and most significantly, an increase in the size of the joint CIA-MAAG First Observation Battalion. This was thin cover for around 400 Green Berets, who were not publicly declared, as they fell under the umbrella of a CIA program. The mission assigned to these soldiers was highly controversial. They were to infiltrate "teams under light civilian cover to Southeast Laos" and attack communist targets of opportunity, "supported by assault units of 100 to 150 Vietnamese for use on targets beyond [the] capability of [the] teams." Clearly, this undeclared war in Laos flagrantly disregarded the Geneva Accords, as flagrantly as Hanoi was ignoring the kingdom's ostensibly "neutralist" status. From the summer of 1960 to the summer of 1962, CIA covert activities were stepped up under the virulently anti-communist leadership of William E. Colby. By the time Johnson deployed the first marines to Da Nang in 1965, the original First Observation Battalion had swelled to a 1,200-strong force.

The second important consequence of NSAM 52 was an authorization to proceed with:

> ... a full examination by the Defense Department, under the guidance of the Director of the continuing Task Force on Vietnam, of the size and composition of forces which would be desirable in the case of a possible commitment of U.S. forces to Vietnam.

Within five months of entering the White House, Kennedy had twice engendered the possibility of a direct military intervention in Diem's Vietnam. Defense had in fact already preempted this directive, but presidential endorsement was more significant than any might have guessed as it sowed the seeds for a sequence of contingency operational plans that ultimately paved the road for America's full entry into the war. NSAM 52 gave birth to OPLAN 34-63, later superseded by Johnson's OPLAN 34-A, which led to the first overt American military actions against North Vietnam.

At the time, an observer would not have necessarily predicted this turn of events. The Director of the Vietnam Task Force was a mid-ranking Foreign Service officer named Sterling Cottrell. In a forgotten footnote of the war, Cottrell advised that no US troops be deployed to South Vietnam. He went further. Like Under Secretary Ball at State, he begged the question whether America should quit now in what to him seemed a hopeless cause. "Since it is an open question whether the GVN [Government of Vietnam] can succeed even with U.S. assistance," he reasoned with impeccable logic, "it would be a mistake for the U.S. to commit itself irrevocably to the defeat of the communists in SVN [South Vietnam]." Cottrell vanished from history because he was mid-ranking. He was one of many such public servants over the course of the war whose good sense passed by over-heated heads in the corridors of power.

There was another problem with personalities like Cottrell. It was precisely that they were Foreign Service and not military officers. Diplomacy seemed weak and cosmetic, illustrating another unfortunate truism of the war. It was always far easier to do something with military forces, the action creating an illusion of progress, than it was to talk about doing things in the halls of foreign ministries, which gave the contrary impression that nothing really was being achieved.

The amiable, broad-faced Ambassador "Fritz" Nolting arrived in Saigon with Rusk's words ringing in his ears: America would be "lucky if we have a mission there for another damned six months."[136] He was tasked to hold discussions on a vague bilateral "arrangement," which neither country wanted; Washington because it feared an open-ended commitment, and Diem, because he feared American pressure to reform. Nolting was closely followed by a Vice President Johnson on a rare overseas trip, despatched deliberately to reassure Southeast Asian leaders following the Bay of Pigs fiasco. Johnson also canvassed the possibility of a bilateral treaty, as well as an increase in US advisors, but no formal or written promises were made. NSAM 52 had authorized an increase of the RVNAF from 170,000 to 200,000, much in line with the April 27 draft. Diem then surprised Washington in a June 9 letter, requesting an increase of 100,000 personnel.[137] Unwilling to make such a commitment, the request was rejected.

Johnson returned from his mission like an Old Testament prophet, predicting that the Pacific would become a "Red Sea" unless battle was joined against communism.[138] In a flight of baroque rhetoric he spoke of "the struggle," "the will to resist," of "free nations," and of "no alternative." It was a stump speech. In the same broad sweep, Johnson also showed his humanitarian face, highlighting that the "greatest danger" was not communism, which would pass, but the four great ills: "hunger, ignorance, poverty and disease." Rostow, who was in the audience, judged it "the best single speech on foreign aid I've ever heard by anyone."[139] Johnson offered no middle way, a malady of thought that was already afflicting many policymakers meditating on the problem of Vietnam. Either America committed to a "strong program," or it was time to "throw in the towel." But much like other voices who raised the temperature that spring, Johnson's proposed actions amounted to no more than what had already been agreed in NSAM 52 garnished with fine words of support for Southeast Asian leaders. In the end, the Johnson mission came across as an exercise in self-promotion, revealing much about the man but not shifting policy any further. Hanoi's response to this sudden burst of American diplomatic activity was peremptory: on May 13, 1961 the Central Committee of Lao Dong made a terse public announcement on Radio Hanoi in which it undiplomatically vowed to "smash" the Diem government.

By the late summer, the Kennedy administration went into overdrive, but it was the crisis provoked by failed talks with Khrushchev in Vienna that generated the frenetic activity. Ask what you can do for your country, Kennedy had posed his countrymen. Now the federal government answered for Americans. Kennedy had warned Khrushchev that if he attempted to strangle Berlin, "there will be a war." In a dramatic 31-minute speech to the country Kennedy announced he would double and if necessary triple the draft.

National Guard and Reserve units would be recalled to active duty. Men needed equipment so mothballed tanks, ships, and planes were reactivated. An extra $3.2 billion was found in the defense budget. A US Army which had become run-down post-Korea, with funds diverted to the missile and nuclear forces, welcomed the financial boost. Airlift capacity was also greatly increased in anticipation of a possible European war. This all accorded with Kennedy's vision of the White House as a sort of fire station headquarters, despatching fire crews around the world to douse communist conflagrations with Green Berets, Peace Corps volunteers, aid dollars, and if necessary, the big battalions. The press cheered from the sides; Kennedy had never seemed so tall or so serious.

The new mood of confidence was buoyed by euphoric economic news. The Democrat government may have made an uncertain start in its foreign policy but at home the news was all good. In July, a bull market set a new record. Industrial output set another record and witnessed its biggest upswing in 20 years. Car sales were expected to exceed 6.5 million and perhaps even challenge the all-time high set in the mid-1950s. More than a million Americans found new jobs (there were now 53 million in full employment) leading *Fortune* magazine to predict that America was heading for a super-boom. Gross National Product was set to hit $600 billion, a fabulous figure. In this context, the increased defense spend was trivial and much less than a growing number of civilian programs started by the government to reward the special interest lobbies that had levered it to power.

This optimism, however, was tempered by the more immediate shadow of imminent nuclear war with the Soviet Union, a possibility which haunted McNamara. On September 7, Kennedy made a second speech to the nation explaining the extraordinary civil defense measures that were being contemplated, including the building of communal fallout shelters, advanced warning systems, and food reserves.

In the spirit of self-help, Americans were urged to build themselves fallout shelters. The "list of materials you will need" challenged any do-it-yourself enthusiast: 500 solid concrete blocks,

12 bags of mortar, nine joists, and one beam (Douglas Fir was considered the sturdiest wood to withstand communist bombs). This was estimated to cost around $200, with $8.95 for a camping toilet, and only bought you the cheapest form of shelter.[140] A pipe shelter was expected to cost $850 and would require the services of a bulldozer. A deluxe bunker, using over 900 concrete blocks, was being offered by a contractor in Florida for $2,195, or more than the cost of a modest house. Kelsey-Hayes, a company based in Detroit, began churning out 5,000 prefabricated shelters per month, with Sears and Roebuck marketing the building in their fall catalog. A grim-looking Carlson family used to showcase the shelter was photographed alongside all the food, equipment, and distractions needed to survive the forthcoming atomic holocaust. Judy, the youngest daughter, had opted for a game of Scrabble. Don't forget to paint your shelter in bright colors was the advice "to add a note of cheerfulness." Would-be shelter-builders were also advised that if a nuclear bomb detonated within a 15-mile radius of their town they should not expect to emerge from the shelter to find their home, which would probably vanish in the blast.

By August, the Berlin crisis subsided. More through a series of misunderstandings than calculation, the two superpowers had pushed each other to the precipice, disliked the view, and pulled back. To the relief of an agitated world, it proved more sound than fury. Unknown at the time, the fact that both sides were riddled with traitors and spies, rendering secrecy of intent impossible, helped keep the peace. American and Russian tanks faced off on *Friedrichstrasse* then returned to barracks. Kennedy grew in stature and Khrushchev opted for building *eine Mauer* ("a wall") rather than trenches. But the real possibility of war hardened American attitudes and confirmed the dogma that the Republic faced an existential enemy. Wherever communism threatened, it had to be confronted.

———

The hot summer in Berlin, meanwhile, had boiled over in South Vietnam, now facing an increasingly emboldened insurgency.

In Washington, it had become clear that the gold star of the North was in the ascendancy.[141] In the first six months of the year, more than 1,500 local officials and civilians had been murdered or kidnapped and guerrilla attacks tripled.[142] There was great public shock at the overrunning of a provincial capital, Phuoc Vinh, north of Saigon, which left the province chief literally without his head, lopped off by the guerrillas in a public execution. Faced with a deteriorating situation, the question was "not whether the Diem government ... could defeat the insurgency, but whether it could save itself."[143]

In the early fall, an embattled Diem made an unexpected volte-face. In a September 29 meeting with Ambassador Nolting and CINCPAC, Admiral Felt, the President surprised his interlocutors by expressing interest in a bilateral treaty with the United States. It was typical of Diem that even as he was demonstrating receptiveness to this earlier American proposal (it is highly doubtful that Congress would have agreed to such a treaty) he was also proving receptive to another suitor.

Several weeks earlier, Robert Thompson, the former Permanent Secretary of Defense in Malaya, had landed in Saigon at the head of the British Advisory Mission (BRIAM). Thompson arrived with all the kudos of an architect of a successful counterinsurgency war, and none of the baggage of the Americans. His manner was courteous, addressing Diem as "Your Excellency," and he clearly seemed tuned to Asian ways. Where the Americans were fretting and pressing, Thompson offered more soothing palliatives. "Using a medical analogy," he wrote in a commissioned report, "the remedy should be clinical rather than surgical."[144] Diem liked this gracious British clinician who turned up with little more than his wit and pen, but feared the tooled-up American surgeon.

Over the next three months, Diem played these two parties against each other, to the consternation of the Americans who worried that Thompson was offering "advice without responsibility." In a wholly forgotten episode the British government in fact sent a police training team to Laos, but not Vietnam. What the Laotians made of the British Bobby appears lost to the historical record.

Diem's interest in a treaty was less about deepening American commitment, and more about deflecting Washington. Fearing both communism and a surreptitious American takeover of his government implicit in MAAG proposals, a bilateral treaty seemed to offer the ultimate insurance policy, without having to pay a great price in lost sovereignty. Most urgently, he sought aid which he reasoned would lead to success, without undertaking political reforms pressed on him by the American in-country team.

Diem's apparent openness provoked a flurry of ideas in Washington. On October 5, Rostow proposed deploying a 25,000-strong SEATO force to the Laotian-Cambodian border. Four days later, the Joint Chiefs countered with a plan to deploy a 20,000-strong force into Laos to halt the communist infiltration, or if this was unacceptable, to Pleiku in the Central Highlands. Both ideas would be revived by Westmoreland in the summer of 1965. U. Alexis Johnson, a future deputy ambassador in Saigon, but then serving as Deputy Under Secretary for Political Affairs, offered that three divisions should be deployed to Vietnam, another idea that would also resurface in later years.

On October 11, Diem's request was discussed at a National Security Council meeting, along with the other proposals, and against the background of yet another gloomy National Intelligence Estimate on South Vietnam. Within the week, the Joint Chiefs' initial modest pitch had been raised: now the generals were arguing that it would take a 40,000-strong US force to defeat the Viet Cong, and a further 128,000 to defeat the North Vietnamese regular forces. This assessment was dramatized by a memo from the elder William Bundy to McNamara – labeled the "now or never" memo – in which the principal deputy to Paul Nitze (then Assistant Secretary of Defense in the Office of International Security Affairs) argued for immediate US military intervention.[145] Illustrating the dangers of government officials resorting to statements of probabilities, Bundy gave a US intervention a 70 percent chance of saving the situation, but even letting a "month go by" would worsen the odds. In the same breathless tone, Bundy repeated the warning canon that the "white men cannot win this kind of fight" and that it could all turn sour quickly.[146] At least the last judgment was prescient. Four years before Johnson made the Vietnam commitment, government officials and senior officers were already sketching its outlines.

The Joint Chiefs' call for more troops might be dismissed as a typical generals' gambit but this would be to discount the fevered mood that existed through 1961. In the same paragraphs, the Chiefs warned that the Soviets might exploit the situation in Vietnam to initiate "multi-prong action" in Berlin, Iran, and Korea. Such speculation was not unusual. In government departments as well as the press, fear of the Reds' next move loomed large in everybody's minds.

However, once again Kennedy stalled. Unimpressed by the dramatics, all the interventionist proposals were shelved. The only tangible outcome from the NSC deliberations was authorization to proceed with the deployment to South Vietnam of 12 aircraft under the newly raised and covert 4400th Combat Crew Training Squadron. Better known as the "Jungle Jim" squadron, this comprised volunteer, deniable pilots – "crazy guys" in the estimation of one volunteer – who would fly combat missions in Laos, under the code name Farm Gate.[147] This was a small victory for LeMay, the brain behind the scheme to add "air commandos" to Kennedy's burgeoning special forces. The squadron was active by Christmas and experienced its first downing in February 1962: an SC-47 lost on a leaflet drop mission near the town of Boa Loc. All six airmen perished – America's first air combat casualties of the war. But the squadron flew on bravado, as well as in vintage aircraft. One pilot laconically noted that he suffered 18 serious failures in just three months, including "bombs fell out of bomb bay when switched battery on."[148]

The second outcome, which proved far more significant, was to task a second fact-finding mission to Saigon. This came against the background of Theodore White's influential reporting that painted a picture of the situation in South Vietnam worsening "almost week by week," particularly in the Delta which had become a sort of obsession with American reporters over this period, probably because it was accessible in a day trip from Saigon. How dispiriting, White wrote, to observe "la jeunesse cowboy" jitterbugging in Saigon night clubs when just 20 miles away their communist contemporaries are living the tough life of a guerrilla fighter.

It was a measure of just how swiftly the situation had changed that Kennedy felt obliged to despatch this second mission, so soon after the Gilpatric-Lansdale task force in the spring, and to appoint two fresh officials: Special Military Representative Maxwell Taylor, and the Deputy Assistant for National Security Affairs Walt Rostow. It was also typical of Kennedy to send his own men and not rely on the in-country team. Belying Kennedy's apparent reluctance to military commitments in Southeast Asia, Taylor and Rostow were set the remit of examining all options, from a limited deployment to a port like Da Nang, to full intervention.

The two men were in many ways ill-matched. Where Taylor offered ballast, Rostow offered buoyancy. Named after the poet Walt Whitman by Russian-Jewish immigrant parents, Rostow was a brilliant academic and economist whose publicly professed anti-communism soon won him high-flying government jobs (in fact, the security services were less sure about his patriotic credentials, and he struggled to get clearances to view top secret material, to Kennedy's frustration). By 1954, at the relatively young age of 38, he was already serving as a political advisor to Eisenhower. His unshakeable confidence in his superior intelligence – he authored one of the seminal books on economic growth in the postwar period – was also his undoing. Rostow's undoubted braininess in the dismal science was not marketable in the arena of war. An "Air Marshal Rostow" proved disastrous.[149] Unshaken by setbacks and curiously insensitive to the mounting casualty bill, Rostow would remain one of the war's great and self-deluded mystics, or "America's Rasputin," in the phrase of Averell Harriman, borrowed by a later critical biographer.[150]

En route to Saigon, Taylor and Rostow made a stop at Hawaii to confer with Felt who had just returned from a SEATO conference in Bangkok. The news he bore was bad, if predictable. SEATO was a paper tiger and the situation in South Vietnam was worsening.

As if to reinforce the seriousness of the situation, in the same week that Taylor and Rostow arrived in Saigon, the body of a South Vietnamese colonel, Hoang Thuy Nam, missing for two weeks, was found. The Viet Cong had cut off his nose, broken all his limbs, and finally killed him off by disembowelling the unfortunate man.

However, the two Americans had been preempted in early October by Thompson who presented his initial "appreciation" of the situation to Diem. An impressed Diem commissioned the Briton to propose a national strategic plan, which was duly delivered after Taylor and Rostow departed, on November 13. Given his experience in Malaya, Thompson gave primacy to civil action programs and the role of the police. The aim was "to win loyalties rather than to kill insurgents."[151] At the core of the plan was an "ink-blot strategy" based on "defended hamlets" in VC-controlled areas, and "strategic hamlets" in government-controlled districts. The latter term became popularized, and misinterpreted, but the hard fact was that Vietnamese hamlets were indefensible. The hamlets would only become "strategic" if a raft of other reforms was undertaken – the familiar American dilemma – which did not appear likely. Without the reforms, the hamlets were simply vulnerable and festering sores, however many palisades were erected.

They were also deeply unpopular. Villager Ama Hoa, forced to relocate to a "strategic hamlet," likened them to prison camps. It was difficult to travel from one hamlet to another, or to find firewood and fish. "Wherever you wanted to go, you had to ask for special papers. Therefore, we did not have freedom."[152] Village gates would open at 8am and close at 4pm. Any person seeking to leave or enter had to endure the humiliation of searches, and bribe-taking. For Vietnam's ethnic minorities, the strategic hamlets were a double disaster, combining land appropriation with affronts to local custom and seemingly petty, Catholic prudery. Villager Y True Nie complained that swimming naked became a banned activity: "When people took a bath or a shower [in a river], they had to wear clothes ... And in wearing the loincloth, people were required to put on a double loincloth otherwise they would be fined from five to ten dong each."[153] Colonel Y Bloc, recruited from a Montagnard minority in the Central Highlands, judged the strategic hamlets "nothing but a giant prison camp."[154] Catholics were favored with so-called "military rice plantations," but ethnic minorities, like Bloc's kinsfolk, were herded into "concentration camps" and prevented from pursuing traditional activities such as hunting and fishing. Resistance came from the French-era FULRO (*Front Uni de Lutte des Races Opprimées* – United Front for the Liberation of Oppressed Races), but there was little the Montagnards could do to stem the encroachment and resettling of ethnic Viets on their traditional lands (or their later oppression by Hanoi). Over time, Bloc observed, "the peoples of the various ethnic minorities created a very large movement to destroy the strategic hamlet program created by Americans and the Diem regime."

Thompson's proposals were not so much innovatory as a reprise of widely held orthodoxies. On September 15, the MAAG had published its own wordy "Geographically Phased National Level Operational Plan for Counterinsurgency," a successor to an earlier draft "Counterinsurgency Plan for South Vietnam." This – like Thompson's national strategic plan – was a blueprint for "pacification," the notion favored among counterinsurgency theorists, who viewed the problem of guerrilla warfare as one of "clearing and securing" rural areas as a precursor to civil action programs aimed at winning over peasants to the government side.

Taylor and Rostow arrived in Saigon on October 18. They found a totally confused situation. The "most startling revelation" was one which Taylor knew existed but had under-estimated: "the complete absence of reliable information on Vietnam."[155] Five days earlier, Diem had indicated his willingness to deploy US troops on the 17th parallel, as a symbolic gesture. On the day they landed and without warning, the President declared a state of national emergency in the National Assembly. Then, in the first meeting with the fact-finding mission, Diem abruptly reversed course and informed Taylor and Rostow that additional US advisors were not required, but that he was open to the bilateral treaty, a reiteration of the position he had conveyed to Nolting and Felt. To complicate matters, the Taylor-Rostow mission coincided with severe flooding in the Delta, the worst since 1937. Over ten million acres of rice were lost, villages were marooned, and more than 320,000 refugees were added to South Vietnam's already dire refugee bill.[156]

On October 24, Diem appeared to change his mind again, probably persuaded by Taylor. Perhaps US troops might be deployed under the cover of providing aid to the civil authorities following the Delta floods (an idea apparently mooted by McGarr, seeking to inveigle Washington into adding more troops to his command). Taylor offered this option – a "straddle" as he termed it – as a compromise between a full US military commitment and the lesser option of small numbers of advisors. He was well aware of the risks and viewed his own proposal as a testing of the waters, literally in this case. There is no evidence that Diem actually agreed to the proposed Delta force, as Taylor later implied, only to helicopter assistance.[157] As Diem consistently argued that the presence of US troops would be "a bonanza for the Viet Cong," this position seems plausible. Nolting broadly agreed with the Taylor-Rostow recommendations but not with the deployment of additional US troops, a proposal only added once Taylor and Rostow were on their way home.

Taylor and Rostow returned on November 2 and the report was issued the following day, but leaks had already made some of the contents known. The White House reacted by briefing against the deployment of combat troops, and Taylor's aides untruthfully denied making any such recommendations. Taylor wisely maintained an enigmatic silence. The press, in fact, paid little attention to the mission, distracted by the more dramatic story of American and Russian tanks confronting each other in Berlin.

At the heart of the Taylor-Rostow report was a proposal for a "limited partnership" to "force the Vietnamese to get their house in order in one area after another."[158] This was a signal triumph of hope over experience. No initiative since the Eisenhower years had succeeded in nudging Saigon toward the path of reform. Sensitive to the political temperature in Washington, the proposed troop increases were modest and strictly couched as engineer aid in the

Delta. Taylor had proposed a reinforcement of 8,000 soldiers as far back as May (he would maintain that the "8,000" number in fact came from the Pentagon).[159] McGarr had made his argument for 16,000 troops, and the Joint Chiefs, as we have seen, were already quoting prodigious numbers. Taylor's proposed modest deployment would include more intelligence personnel, as well as advisors to reform the command and control of the ARVN. Critical of French-style static warfare, Taylor made a strong argument for the deployment of helicopters, seen as the indispensable ingredient for introducing mobility to the battlefield.[160] As the Joint Chiefs had already recommended increased helicopter support on December 6, 1960 in a memorandum to McNamara, Taylor was reinforcing views that had been circulating in the corridors of the Pentagon for many months.

Taylor was not blind to the dilemmas in his report. Washington should expect to take casualties, which could prove unpopular with ordinary Americans (the Indian Foreign Office, deliberating the deployment of Indian and Burmese engineers to the Delta, offered identical warnings).[161] In a separate "Eyes Only for the President" message sent from the Philippines, Taylor then illustrated all the contradictions besetting policymakers. The purpose of the message, Taylor explained in his first sentence, was to present "my reasons for recommending the introduction of a U.S. military force into South Vietnam." The sentence must have made Kennedy despair. He then contrarily went on to give good reasons why the President should probably not follow this course of action at all. If the reinforcement failed to reverse the rot, he argued, there would be "no limit to our possible commitment," unless Washington was prepared to attack "the source in Hanoi." This extreme measure, jokingly referred to as "Walt's Plan Six" (SEATO's ineffectual Plan Five was the standard plan for defending Southeast Asia), was politically unacceptable.[162]

In fact, Taylor had been very crafty in his reporting, cognizant that different actors would react in different ways to a proposal to deploy US troops in South Vietnam. As well as the official report, he also forwarded a separate message to Kennedy copied to Rusk, McNamara, and Lemnitzer, and the "Eyes Only" message to Kennedy. Each was nuanced to address the expectations of the recipients. This "gaming" of the message was a terrible habit that damaged sender and receiver and it permeated the entire American war in Vietnam.

As it happened, the Taylor-Rostow report was met with the same froideur as the Gilpatric-Lansdale effort earlier in the year. On November 8, McNamara forwarded a response memo to Kennedy representing his Department's views and those of the Joint Chiefs. The distinction is crucial. A reading of the memo reveals two voices: the Chiefs raising the stakes and McNamara raising questions. While acknowledging that Vietnam was a vital national security interest, McNamara questioned the proposed recommendations, specifically deploying US troops to the country. Taylor's plan amounted to a gesture; probably 205,000 troops would be needed to defeat Hanoi (the precise number, equivalent to six divisions, had in fact been plucked from an existing contingency plan, CINCPAC Plan 32-59, Phase IV). The proposal so dismayed George Ball in State he made a personal representation to Kennedy on the same day, arguing that deeper involvement would have "tragic consequences."[163] "If we went down that road," he warned, "we might have within five years 300,000 men in the rice paddies and jungles of Vietnam and ... we'd just never be able to find them." "You're just crazier than hell," Kennedy famously riposted. "I always thought you were one of the brightest guys in town but ... you're crazy. This isn't gonna happen."[164] Sketching the inherent contradictions in the options, McNamara argued that if the White House did nothing, and the pessimists were right, then South Vietnam was lost; but if Kennedy acted decisively, a major war was a strong possibility in which there was no guarantee of victory. Either way, Washington faced a probably unsolvable quandary. In careful bureaucratic language the document was "inclined to recommend" a US troop deployment to South Vietnam – typical McNamara phrasing when he was unsure of a course of action – but only on the understanding that more troops would be sent if required, a clear sop to the Joint Chiefs. Bombing the source, Hanoi, should also be considered, an idea that Taylor had floated.

The November 8 memo was not well received. Kennedy recoiled at a message that seemed to be inviting him to make an open-ended military commitment, while simultaneously hedging bets over an ultimate victory. Neither was he comfortable with the portrayal of Vietnam as a vital interest in which he had to act, implicitly doing more and not less.

McNamara then reversed this position in a November 11 memo, co-signed with Rusk. This memo was plainly "more to the President's liking" and there is a suggestion, but no record proof, that Kennedy instructed a re-write, co-signed by his two most important lieutenants, to put an end to the institutional policy drift. In the well-balanced verdict of a Pentagon Papers author:

> The only questions which are in doubt are the extent to which the Rusk/McNamara memorandum simply happened to come to the President in such convenient form, or whether the President arranged it so; and if so, how far this formal paper differed from the real recommendations of the President's senior advisors. The record available gives no basis for even guessing about this. As noted earlier, even McNamara, who is on record with a previous, quite different memorandum [the November 8 memo], cannot be flatly said to have changed his mind (or been overruled). There is too much room for uncertainty about what he was really up to when he signed the memorandum.[165]

The November 11 memo has singular prominence in the Vietnam story because all the conundrums of the later war were nakedly displayed. Reiterating the doomsday scenario that the loss of Vietnam would mean the loss of Southeast Asia, the memo unequivocally stated, "<u>The United States should commit itself to the clear objective of preventing the fall of South Viet-Nam to Communism</u>." [Underlining in the original.] However, this strong statement was not followed by a plan for achieving this "clear objective." Instead, the memo reiterated dilemmas previously expressed in the earlier memo, and added a few more.

South Vietnam had to win its own war, but it could only do this with US support. This support should be given, but the quid pro quo was reform. Yet, even if both these conditions were satisfied it was still probable that South Vietnam would lose the war because the enemy enjoyed sanctuary and the flow of men and materials could not be stopped. To avert this probable South Vietnamese collapse, the United States should be prepared to deploy combat troops and bomb North Vietnam, as Taylor hinted. But if this course were followed, Washington would probably face communist escalation. Worse, "The United States forces could not accomplish their mission in the midst of an apathetic or hostile population." Every step forward seemed to invite a corresponding backward step.

Kennedy, of course, preferred the November 11 memo because it deferred any major decisions and instead made safe, modest recommendations. A quick-witted personality like Galbraith firing over-clever missives from New Delhi may have dismissed all this as Washington experiencing an "intellectual orgasm on the unbeatability of guerrilla war" but history would prove him disastrously mistaken.[166] Washington's orgasm, borrowing Galbraith's metaphor, lay entirely in the entrapping circularity of the domino theory and notions of American prestige. If the first paragraph of the November 11 memo were dropped, with its dramatic judgment that the loss of South Vietnam made any further discussion of a free Southeast Asia "pointless," then the remainder of the edifice collapsed. With the domino theory elevated to religious credo, the argument was shut.

Yet Kennedy avoided the trap. On November 15, the National Security Council sat to deliberate the Taylor-Rostow recommendations. In a repetition of the outcomes of the Gilpatric-Lansdale mission, all the proposals were watered down. Kennedy rejected the full Taylor recommendations but did agree to the deployment of helicopters and a very modest uplift of troops. To accommodate this enhanced commitment, a new command would be established: the Military Assistance Command Vietnam (MACV), under Lieutenant General Paul Harkins. These decisions were endorsed in the November 22 NSAM 111 which essentially restated the arguments of the McNamara-Rusk memo, but crucially deleted the opening statement that the United States should commit to saving South Vietnam (so much for the domino theory). This suited a President who presciently remarked:

> ... the troops will march in; the bands will play; the crowds will cheer; and in four days everyone will have forgotten. Then we will be told we have to send in more troops. It's like taking a drink. The effect wears off, and you have to take another.[167]

To mollify the disgruntled Joint Chiefs, NSAM 111 was entitled "First Phase of Vietnam Program." According to later accounts from Sorenson in the White House and Hilsman in State, this was a deliberate ruse by Kennedy to trick the Chiefs into assuming that further, more expansive military programs would follow. Whether or not this was the case, the Chiefs were always likely to start planning for war anyway, and did.

The MACV is central to the story of the Vietnam War, but it was born amidst tensions and disagreements. Originally, it was intended to be named USFV (United States Forces Vietnam), and McNamara wanted the organization to report directly to him, bypassing PACOM (Pacific Command). The Joint Chiefs were appalled by the proposed arrangement. Moreover, McNamara wanted the head of the new organization to enjoy equal status with the incumbent ambassador, and to assume responsibility for policy areas such as economic aid. This proposal appalled State. Finally, it was intended the organization would supplant the MAAG, which naturally horrified McGarr and his staffs.

The first disagreement was swiftly resolved: the USFV would report through PACOM in the normal way, but McNamara would maintain tight control with frequent face-to-face meetings. The second point of contention was resolved with an acknowledgement that the ambassador would retain primacy over "political and basic policy matters" in return for acknowledging the military commander's enhanced status. In a December 7 response, State also requested the title be changed to MACV, a proposal that was agreed one week later in a Honolulu conference attended by McNamara, Rusk, Nolting, and McGarr. The first MACV would comprise 216 officers and men, over half drawn from the Army, and would be based in a four-story building in central Saigon. Diem's consent was not actually received until the following year, on February 3, 1962. CINCPAC activated the command five days later and Harkins took up post within the week. In a meeting with the ambassador, Diem confirmed his support for the MACV initiative and added that he "hoped our fellows would be on their good behaviour vis-à-vis Vietnamese girls, who are '*en principe, très morales*' ['in principle, very moral']."[168] Nolting did not comment.

The final disagreement – over the new commander's roles and responsibilities – proved harder to resolve. Both Nolting and McGarr strongly protested over the enhanced status of McNamara's new chief. The former was mollified by Rusk, and the latter was sacrificed by the Joint Chiefs, cognizant that McGarr's stock was not high in Washington. Indeed, Taylor had snubbed him during his fact-finding mission, and was unimpressed with a general who had advised him that stopping the communist infiltration would be "an almost impossible thing to do."[169] What McNamara did not do was change the wording of the COMUSMACV (Commander United States Military Assistance Command Vietnam) terms of reference, sent to Kennedy on December 22 and approved at the beginning of the year. This created both ambiguity and tension. Without a clearly stated subordinate status, this ambiguity implied that the personal relations between the ambassador and COMUSMACV, rather than their official stated roles, would determine the success of the endeavor. Nor did tensions with the MAAG disappear. This organization would retain its original advisory role and manage the MAP (Military Assistance Program), straightaway dividing the military effort under two rival commands. The awkwardness of the situation was exacerbated by the fact that the MAAG controlled a small fiefdom, just over 3,000 strong, soldiers who now found themselves re-assigned to MACV, but were still sitting at their old desks, and simultaneously reporting to their old chief.

MACV was thus born amidst organizational wrangles, but it was the choice of its first commander that proved the real difficulty. Paul Donald Harkins, a son of Massachusetts, joined the Boston National Guard in 1922 "just to learn how to ride a horse." After commissioning from West Point he fulfilled this ambition and joined the horse cavalry in Fort Bliss. Following promotion, he then spent six happy years at the cavalry school at Fort Riley, where he mostly served as an equitation instructor. Before the outbreak of war, Harkins appears to have spent the majority of his army career on the back of a horse. Thanks to his convivial personality and good connections with a Colonel Gay, Harkins was elevated to deputy Chief of Staff in Patton's Third Army.[170] This was the pivotal event of his life and he would later write a book on the exploits of "The Third." But Harkins was the eternal deputy and staff officer, rather than commander or original thinker, and his desire to please masters clouded his judgments. In Indochina, this meant pleasing the general who had lobbied for his appointment, Maxwell Taylor. If "Max" thought the war was going well, then it was Harkins' duty to make it so. Subordinate officers who challenged this line – personalities like Lieutenant Colonel John Paul Vann who was gaining a reputation for being outspoken – should be upbraided. But Harkins was not a nasty piece of work who held grudges, rather a puzzled and frustrated general who could not understand why his colonels would not just play along with the game. Vietnam was his last posting before retiring after 44 years' service, not a day too soon for a press corps that quickly came to detest the general. For correspondent Neil Sheehan he would remain the "American General with a swagger stick and cigarette holder ... who would not deign to soil his suntans and street shoes in a rice paddy to find out what was going on ... prattling about having trapped the Viet Cong."[171] Little dented Harkins' rose-tinted view of the war, and he took the attitude that his main function was to serve out optimism, to play "the guy with the goodies," like pinning medals on soldiers' chests.[172]

Focus on Harkins' optimism also underplays that Vietnam attracted all manner of snakeoil salesmen who made their names (and money) promoting "how to win" optimistic ideas. Who now remembers, for example, Australian Colonel F.P. Ted Serong? Serong became a special advisor to Harkins, drafting reports for RAND and peddling the illusory "Clear and Hold" mantra that would bedevil the war. Later it emerged that he had been in the pay of the CIA.

Those who have sought to portray RAND as the truth crusader warning Defense of its myriad follies through a barrage of reports (more than 500 published over the course of the war) bypass that RAND, like the MAAG-MACV, was also vulnerable to its high priests of "rightness." Optimism was also peddled by think-tanks imbued with anti-communism. And it is also the case that US officials – civilian and military – manifested the universal trait of all government bureaucracies, commissioning reports to tell them what they wanted to hear, and selecting findings to suit biased policy recommendations. As an honest analyst later put it, RAND data "could support anybody's perspective on anything."[173] Abuse of operational analysis to "prove" that a failing war is in fact making "progress" was the false cry from Saigon.

The popular view of Harkins was not entirely fair anyway. Unlike many officials who conflated Saigon with South Vietnam, Harkins did actually travel extensively. By his own admission, he was "out every day [and] I don't think there was a place in Vietnam I didn't visit."[174] He may have been selective in what he saw, and even more selective in what he listened to, but he could not be described as a desk-bound general. His relations with Nolting were "absolutely perfect." Diem warmed to him so much they conversed in English, a privilege Diem withheld from other American officials. General Khanh, who later seized the presidency, described him as "the best friend Vietnam has," to a probably sneering press corps.[175] And he was neither blind to the failings of Saigon's generals, nor to the wider weaknesses of the ARVN. General Don, another future conspirator, warned him in his first meeting that, "we're not going to get anyplace until we get rid of Diem," so he was hardly unaware of the scheming either.[176] He arrived in Saigon in time to witness a palace bombing coup attempt against Diem, without, as he recalled, even having had a chance to shave. He quickly appreciated that there was no single war, but that "they had forty-three wars going on," in each of the provinces.[177] In his own estimation, the problem of infiltration from Laos was "bad when I got there, and it got worse and worse."[178] All this did not derail him because he was, in his own words, "born an optimist," which is a useful trait in a general. It was poor timing to exercise this cheerfulness at a time when a band of perceptive American correspondents were beginning to whiff the scent of a debacle.

As damaging, if not more so, was the totally inadequate MACV intelligence set-up commanded by an alcoholic, abusive, and incompetent Air Force colonel, James Winterbottom.[179] Harkins was frequently criticized for doctoring the intelligence – which he did – but the chief spin doctor was Winterbottom who tolerated no assessment that did not portray progress and success. Any dissent, or honesty, was met with hostility. In a most disreputable incident in the spring of 1962, Harkins decided that a briefing map produced for the visiting McNamara displayed too much red (indicating areas under VC control). Winterbottom duly corrected this infelicity by simply removing the red acetates and replacing these with "status unknown" acetates.[180] It was no surprise that McNamara grew to distrust in-country briefings and developed his own back channels. According to CIA analyst George Allen, it was principally due to Winterbottom's interference that MACV's intelligence estimates became a travesty of the truth. That Harkins obliged this dishonesty is highly culpable, but Harkins was far from the only senior American official playing this game. When Taylor, who should have known better, assumed the ambassadorship he continued the practice, simply deleting entire paragraphs from intelligence estimates if he judged they portrayed too negative a picture. Taylor's malfeasance had a certain irony as he complained of the poor quality of intelligence in Vietnam. On occasions, he appeared to also hold a particular view over what constituted "good" intelligence.

US intelligence agencies, military and civil, employed some of the finest minds in government service: at too many key moments they were gagged. It little helped that Winterbottom's successor was another inadequate Air Force colonel who suffered a nervous breakdown, followed by a marine brigadier general with no special interest or flair in intelligence, described as "a jerk."[181]

Notwithstanding these inauspicious foundations, over the next two months, a headquarters and logistics unit, the US Army Support Group Vietnam (USASGV), was established. The first helicopter unit to deploy to Vietnam was 57th Transportation Company (later 120th Aviation Company), arriving on December 11. It was equipped with 33 near-obsolete H-21C Shawnee helicopters. This unit was followed by 8th Transportation Company (later 117th Aviation Company). The handful of American helicopters was soon in action ferrying ARVN troops to trouble spots. America had answered the call.

With Harkins in post and the MACV about to be stood up, it seemed at the beginning of 1962 that all the necessary decisions had been taken. Vietnam fell off the agenda in a White House distracted by many incipient domestic concerns: fears that the boom might be derailed by the balance of payments, a stock market slump, and a "steel crisis" brought on by competition with the European Common Market. In the average home, the main concerns were household expenses and the rising costs of college. By the summer, America would be gripped by the death of the ultimate female icon, Marilyn Monroe. No doubt, Kennedy shared the shock. A second Cuban crisis was in the offing.

The new in-country team soon began to make its presence felt. Harkins banished siestas and five-day weeks. The covert Farm Gate raids were augmented with Mule Train (transport), and Able Mable (reconnaissance) missions flown by 2nd Air Division. Kennedy's Green Berets began to arrive, imbued with the idealism of their president. Advisors began to flood into Saigon: Harkins later recalled that he had to deal with as many as 250 visitors every month. By March 1962, Vietnam had claimed the lives of 13 American servicemen in seven years, in what was not meant to be a combat mission, but this trivial number of casualties was hardly a cause for concern on Capitol Hill. More concerning, at least to the White House, was a hostile press churning out articles emblazoned with depressing and alarmist headlines. "The Last Chance for Vietnam," "The Fading Strength of Vietnam," and "The Agony of Indochina" were just three highlighted to Kennedy by a concerned Schlesinger that month.[182]

However, the press pack was somewhat falling into the trap of repeating its own prejudices. Slowly, a defensive and defeatist mind set was being transformed. In the past, ARVN units had been rooted to their jungle bases, rarely venturing outside. There were around 16,000 such "forts" when Harkins arrived, which he reduced to 6,000. Now, ARVN units were encouraged to patrol and seek out the Viet Cong in ambushes. This "net and spear" tactic, encouraged by American advisors, seem to be paying off. Quick reaction forces, borne in helicopters crewed by the American pilots, responded to guerrilla attacks. The helicopter fleet swelled; by the late spring there were 140 in-theater (one Marine squadron and six Army squadrons). As well as the H-21 transports, the first helicopter gunships made their debut. Some units, emboldened by the flush of new equipment, did become more aggressive, but also more bullying. In the recollection of Viet Cong guerrilla Nguyen Cong Danh:

When the enemy came out with the helicopter tactic he achieved certain successes because this tactic was new to us. They reaped certain results in the battle of Kinh Giua and Trai Lon ... At first we did not think that we would defeat this tactic. However, after we combated the search and destroy operations in Ca Nai, Cau Giong, Boi Tuong, and Cau Van Sap – and especially during the battle of Cau Giong we destroyed three helicopters – we found the solution to our difficulties and we realized that we could use rifles to shoot down the American helicopters and that we did not have to use bigger guns.[183]

Whether the MACV-MAAG was improving a military machine or honing an internal repression force was difficult to tell. All the clichés of the Second Indochina War were already well established before American soldiers and marines joined the fighting. Villages were torched. Peasants suspected of supporting the Viet Cong were abused, tortured, and summarily shot. A dismissive and casual attitude to death was pervasive. America did not export these ills to Vietnam; they were already as rife as the banyan grass.

This apparent "progress" was welcome, but what South Vietnam lacked was an overarching political and military strategy. This was announced on February 3, 1962, typically by presidential decree, with the formation of the Inter-Ministerial Committee for Strategic Hamlets, or IMCSH. Like so many Diemist committees it was toothless and cosmetic but this marked the official start of the Strategic Hamlets Program, the first recognizable counterinsurgency strategy applied to South Vietnam whose origins ultimately lay in the successful experiment of protected villages in Malaya. Beyond this, all comparisons fail. At the heart of the strategy was the catchphrase "Clear and Hold," but there was little agreement on what this meant, and still less on how this might be achieved successfully. For US military advisors "Clear" had the allure of mobile combat operations and "Hold" suggested pedantic defense. For the Embassy, "Hold" opened the doors to a range of civil action programs that would better the Vietnamese patient. For Diem, who was first persuaded of the virtues of the Delta Plan by Thompson in the winter of 1961,[184] Strategic Hamlets was another mechanism for imposing his authority on the provinces. "Clear and Hold" was borrowed from Thompson's four stages of a counterinsurgency, "clearing, holding, winning and won," but the last two concepts fell off the end.[185]

To the MAAG, the Strategic Hamlets proposal felt like a kick in the shin. Thompson had spoken of "clinical rather than surgical" remedies. McGarr retaliated by describing him as "a doctor called in for consultation on a clinical case, actually performing an amputation without consulting the resident physician."[186] The MAAG's dissatisfaction with Thompson was largely based on the fact that his ideas ran counter to a plan US military advisors had been working up for over a year – the Geographically Phased National Plan – which was nothing less than a blueprint for taking the war to the enemy. McGarr wanted aggressive ARVN operations in the tough objective of War Zone D, not police operations in the Delta.

For all McGarr's huffing, Maxwell Taylor's interest in Thompson's ideas created a conduit by which the Strategic Hamlets Program reached Kennedy's receptive ear.[187] The appeal to Kennedy was precisely the reason why McGarr recoiled. Here was an excuse to encourage the South Vietnamese government to engage in civic action and to defer alarmist talk of deploying US combat troops to Indochina. This was Peace Corps operations with soldiers in the background, which chimed exactly with Kennedy's predilections.

In the event, Diem side-stepped all the Western advisors in his customary way, and appointed his corrupt brother Ngo Dinh Nhu to head the program. This was introducing the fox into the chicken coop. Nhu displayed two related talents in his management of the Strategic Hamlets Program: inflating statistics to please Americans, and attracting generous dollops of aid money (the funding for the "Strategic Hamlet Kits"), a proportion of which was siphoned into private bank accounts. The close identification of the brothers with the Strategic Hamlets Program was so deep that when they fell two years later, so did the program.

With typical impetuosity, the first operation was mounted within a month (Operation *Sunrise* in Binh Duong Province) against some skepticism over the chances of its success. Binh Duong was chosen by Diem, over both McGarr's and Thompson's advice, because the ARVN had already started operations in this province where only ten out of 46 villages were under government control. The skepticism proved well founded: only 70 families agreed to move, a $300,000 aid package never reached them, and a large number of the fighting-age males simply disappeared and joined the Viet Cong.[188]

There followed a series of seemingly ad hoc operations across South Vietnam: "Sea Swallow" in Phu Yen, "Let's Go" in Binh Dinh, and "Royal Phoenix" in Quang Ngai. A national strategy was not actually announced until August, by which time Nhu was claiming that 3,225 Strategic Hamlets had been created, with another 8,091 planned on the way.[189] If Nhu was to be believed a third of the population was now living within the protective embrace of the government, or over 4,300,000 peasants. Setting aside the gross exaggeration, it became evident over time that Nhu had completely ignored Thompson's advice and was implementing a continuation of previous, highly unpopular and failed resettlement programs. The ultimate aim of these was to assert his brother's control over the rural population, not pacification as it was understood by Thompson or Taylor. An illusion of progress was created by the prodigious numbers and by the mere fact that a plan now existed, but it was mostly the magic of the illusionist brothers.

Painting success by numbers became compulsive. As the numbers were mostly being provided by the South Vietnamese government the compulsion bordered on the farcical. When US AID advisor Earl Young took up his post in Long An Province he was assured that 219 hamlets were now "secure." The five American military advisors assigned to the province scoffed at his naivety: "don't believe these things ... we'd be lucky if half those are under government control."[190] When another advisor visited a village just 12 miles from Saigon, he left in some haste, after discovering that it was "one hundred percent Viet Cong."[191] Under American pressure, Diem was encouraged to tour rural areas. But his incomprehensible Vietnamese dialect proved a liability. On one occasion, US Information Agency employee Everett Bumgardner recalled: "We had a rather interesting professor from Temple

University, who went through the funny experience of trying to explain to a group of peasants in one particular village what the president was saying in their own language."[192]

In the spring and summer of 1962 the Kennedy administration first became fixated by renewed tensions in Berlin, and was then discombobulated by the Cuban missile crisis. The fevered atmosphere these events created cannot be overstated. This was a period when US government memoranda routinely discussed nuclear war options, as if discussing base interest rates. The construction program of nationwide bunkers was accelerated. Reinforcements were rushed to Europe to face off the possible Soviet threat. Reservists demobilized from the Korean War were again called back into active service. America was a country poised to go on a full war footing.

The crisis came to a head on Tuesday October 16, when General Marshall Carter presented Kennedy with conclusive proof that Soviet nuclear missiles were beyond any doubt deployed in Cuba. This irrefutable evidence led Kennedy to gather his inner cabinet: Robert Kennedy, McNamara, Rusk, Gilpatric, Nitze, Taylor, Admiral George Anderson, and several policy advisors. In total, 14 men deliberated on a decision that could precipitate a world war. Over the next week, meetings were held every day and the circle widened to over 100 staff in various departments working up policy options. Throughout Kennedy maintained his afternoon regime of going for a swim. On Friday October 26 he made time to meet with Foreign Minister Gromyko where the discussion circled the Berlin crisis but barely touched on Cuba. Did Gromyko suspect that Kennedy was holding back or was he lulled by the apparently relaxed attitude of the President? The final decision on how to respond to this provocation was taken late on Saturday night in the Oval Office, following a session of the National Security Council. Sorenson wrote the speech (there were five drafts) but Kennedy had a hand in finessing the phrasing.

Sunday October 21 was a day of perfect autumnal serenity. By now the secrecy had been blown. Both Kennedy and Johnson returned to Washington, cutting short their campaign schedules and citing colds (the former from Seattle and the latter from Hawaii). The implausibility of the coincidence alerted the press. A helicopter was despatched to Gettysburg to retrieve Eisenhower and bring him to Washington – what could this mean? Locals in Florida reported unusual troop movements. Curtis LeMay, cigar butt stuck to his clenched mouth, appeared pensive and not his usual bomb-happy self. By the afternoon, messages were sent to all Congressional leaders summoning them to the capital. In the case of the unhappy Hale Boggs (Louisiana, Republican) who had arranged a fishing excursion in the Gulf of Mexico, a coast guard helicopter was sent to pluck him from his boat.[193] There was a late night meeting in the Executive Office of the White House but by now all the major decisions had been made.

The following day dawned bright again in Washington. The usual crowd turned up for the noon press conference when Pierre Salinger, the White House Press Secretary, strode in and informed the assembly that the President was going to make a speech of grave national importance in the evening. The stampede that followed, as some recalled, rivalled the reaction to Truman's declaration of war over Korea.[194]

The ripple of messages then began to spread from the White House, first to military units, then to ambassadors, and then to world leaders. Harold Macmillan was the first European leader to be informed and he in turn held telephone conferences with Charles de Gaulle and Konrad Adenauer. Other NATO leaders were briefed by Rusk whose department also briefed all the South American ambassadors. The last in line – but perhaps he already suspected by now – was the Russian Ambassador Valerian Sorin who was informed one hour before Kennedy went on air. At 3pm there was a final meeting of the National Security Council followed by a cabinet meeting one hour later. At 5pm the Congressional leaders were invited to the Cabinet Room and a CIA analyst presented the photographic evidence of the Soviet military build-up in Cuba. There was uproar. Kennedy was only able to extricate himself from the indignant congressmen with minutes to spare to deliver his speech.

Khrushchev – at least in public – acted as if he did not know what all the fuss was about. The day after Kennedy's speech he attended a show at the Bolshoi Theater and took time out to congratulate the lead singer Jerome Hines, who happened to be American. The following day he held a long and interesting conversation with William Knox, the President of Westinghouse Electric International. No Soviet preparations for war were detected. The situation in Berlin remained unchanged. But what Khrushchev could not brush aside was the 30,000 feet of film taken by U-2 spy planes, revealing the extent of the Soviet missile sites. A climb down, or confrontation, was inevitable.

In the event, the posturing had rivalled the Bolshoi. On October 26, a conciliatory Khrushchev secretly advised Kennedy, "We and you ought not now to pull on the ends of the rope in which you have tied the knot of war, because the more the two of us pull, the tighter that knot will be tied."[195] The reality was that there were too many reasonable minds in both camps to engage in a mutually destructive tug-of-war. The real danger had always been accident, misunderstanding, and miscalculation, especially on the somewhat chaotic Soviet side. The U-2 shot down over Cuba was fired upon by a Russian officer who took the decision to engage without bothering to consult Moscow. Soviet submarine B-59 only desisted from launching nuclear-armed torpedoes because one of the officers, a Captain Vasily Arkhipof, voted against such an extreme measure.

Against the backdrop of these dramatic events, Southeast Asia again seemed very much a secondary consideration. The mess in Laos appeared to be settled satisfactorily, inasmuch as American negotiators were able to extricate themselves with some honor. On July 23 the protracted 15-month Geneva Conference was closed with a Fourteen Nation declaration affirming the neutrality of Laos. In North Vietnamese eyes the true value of the agreement was that it created breathing space for military rearmament and it flushed away interfering outside powers, content to conspire in the deception that Laos' neutrality would now be respected as a result of a handful of signatures.

On the day of the signing of the Fourteen Nation declaration, McNamara was several thousand miles away in the CINCPAC Headquarters in Honolulu holding a conference on Vietnam. His personal views were well known and echoed the sentiments of Kennedy: "I personally believe that this is a war that the Vietnamese must fight ... I don't believe we can take on that combat task for them. I do believe we can carry out training. We can provide advice and logistical assistance."

When questioned over how long it would take to defeat the VC insurgency with US training and assistance, Felt casually replied, just one year. This reflected the widely held Saigon view that the VC were "raggedy-ass little bastards" and that Harkins' three "Ms" – Men, Money, and Materials – would see them off. Taylor had been offered the same message. "We talked to 174 officers, Vietnamese and US," he explained, "and in the case of the [US] officers, I always asked the question, 'When can you finish this job?'"[196] He was assured the Viet Cong could be defeated by the following year, with the Delta taking a little longer.

McNamara disbelieved this optimistic prediction and Washington was never going to oblige a policy built on dangerously seductive "Ms," the classic cry of generals. Instead he requested that a realistic three-year strategic plan for the withdrawal of American forces from Vietnam be formulated. If successful, it would see US servicemen withdrawn by mid-1965. In the summer 1962, this force now included several sub-commands: a US Marine Corps element; 2nd US Air Division; US Army Support Group Vietnam (USASGV); a Headquarters Support Activity Saigon (HSAS); as well as MACV and the MAAG.

On July 26, this direction was formalized by the Joint Chiefs in a directive to CINCPAC ordering the development of a Comprehensive Plan for South Vietnam (CPSVN). The holiday season appeared to interfere with a quick turnaround of the staff work but on August 14 Felt finally issued his directive to Harkins.[197] The spirit of this directive was entirely in keeping with McNamara's three-year plan, but the detail offered loopholes for increasing, not decreasing the American presence in Vietnam.

Extensive military support would continue to be needed for the duration of the program, it argued. Crucially, previous spending ceilings were judged "not applicable." In a terse statement, Felt instructed, "Program those items essential to do this job." Opening the funding taps was invitation to an escalation of effort, which Harkins was hardly likely to resist.

In effect, this is what happened. On December 7, Harkins submitted a first draft of the Comprehensive Plan for South Vietnam to CINCPAC who promptly rejected it on the grounds of cost. The holiday season again interrupted planning and on January 19, 1963 a second draft was submitted. In the meantime, MACV had actually implemented important reforms without additional funding or personnel commitments. The RVNAF (Republic of Vietnam Armed Forces) had been reorganized and rationalized, command structures and procedures had been improved, and the failing Strategic Hamlets Program had been reinvigorated. All of this had been accomplished with the approval of President Diem who ratified the reforms with a presidential decree.

The second draft unexpectedly went further than the first, extending the program of US assistance to 1968, or three years beyond McNamara's cut-off date. Furthermore, it proposed a total expenditure of nearly a billion dollars over a six-year period. The MACV would reach a peak of 12,200 personnel in 1965, drop to 5,900 in 1966, and only reach the desired target of 1,500 in 1968. The RVNAF strength would be built to just over 450,000 strong, a massive jump on previously agreed force levels.[198]

This was bound to raise eyebrows but CINCPAC passed the draft up the chain of command, now defending Harkins' proposals. Over the Christmas of 1962–63, Honolulu had reversed course and decided to back their man in Vietnam, calling for a bigger program of assistance, against McNamara's July directions.

McNamara, unsurprisingly, rejected the CPSVN. In its place, he ordered a Ford-style assembly line of RVNAF training and US withdrawal, appropriately called the Accelerated Model Plan. This plan would last just 14 months. McNamara's Accelerated Plan involved building up to a total strength of 12,000 by 1964, one

year earlier than Harkins' proposal, followed by a drawdown to
1,500 by 1968, in line with Harkins' original schedule. The MAP
similarly would fall from a peak of $180 million to just over $40
million. Institutional subterfuge would undermine the defense
secretary and ensure that these targets would never be met. By the
time of Kennedy's assassination, the MACV hit 16,732 personnel,
and within one year Johnson would add another 7,000 troops to
the total.[199]

Did McNamara's withdrawal plan stand any chance of success
anyway, without hindsight? Nowhere in the troubled post-
colonial world could anyone point to an insurgency that had been
cleaned up in three years. This was an arbitrary number imposed
by domestic electoral cycles, not by a realistic assessment of the
Viet Cong. Nor did the costs stack up; McNamara's insistence on
reducing the military aid budget ran counter to the stated aim of
building up the RVNAF. In all these calculations, the unraveling
situation in South Vietnam was almost treated as an incidental
consideration. However much buffing and polishing was applied
to intelligence assessments, it was clear the country was descending
into a spiral of violence. With each passing month, McNamara's
direction looked less like a plan and more like denial. In the
unimpeachable judgment of an anonymous author of the Pentagon
Papers, "premises were transformed into conclusions, desiderata
institutionalized as objectives, and wish took on the character of
the force of imperative."[200]

Chapter 3

ANNUS HORRIBILIS, JANUARY–NOVEMBER 1963

Washington entered the New Year, the Vietnamese Year of the Cat, with a growing military commitment to the embattled country. Despite Kennedy's doubts, there were now over 12,000 servicemen in-country: from military advisors in Saigon to Green Berets operating in remote jungle camps. This number would exceed 16,000 by the end of the year.[1] By the same period, 325 Army, 117 Air Force, and 20 Marine aircraft would be operating in South Vietnam, alongside the 219 airplanes and helicopters of the Vietnamese Air Force (VNAF).[2] MACV had helped establish and train two fresh ARVN divisions and three independent regiments. As many as 68,000 militia guards and 62,000 self-defense corps troops would be added to this roll call. The combined strength of the regular Vietnamese forces now exceeded 210,000, with 170,000 new recruits added to the auxiliary forces. In accordance with McNamara's wishes, the effort to build-up South Vietnam's military capability had truly accelerated.

Notwithstanding the higher tempo of operations, just 26 Americans had been killed in combat, and a further 97 had been wounded – still trivial numbers, but at the time they reminded Washington that the policy of supporting the Saigon government would have a human cost. South Vietnamese losses were far worse. Perhaps 10,000 soldiers and militiamen had been killed in the past year. Despite pouring $500 million in aid into the country, worryingly little progress seemed to be made in the countryside where the real fight was taking place. US foreign aid that year passed the symbolic $100 billion threshold. America was now extending aid to 95 countries, or practically every non-Communist developing country in the world.

In public, the official policy in South Vietnam remained Strategic Hamlets, however flawed, imperfect, and corrupted. But MACV knew that more was needed to turn the tide of war. This was provided by the General Offensive Campaign Plan, issued in late February 1963, three weeks after Diem's official announcement of the start of the Strategic Hamlets Program. The guts of the strategy owed everything to McGarr's earlier geographically phased plan which had been deflected by the debates over the fall and winter. In essence it called for three operational stages: a preparatory stage, a period of offensive operations to drive the Viet Cong from its havens, and a consolidation phase. The geographical phasing referred to the logic of the sequencing: Diem's random approach would be replaced by a coherent national scheme.

Yet all this military effort did not address the real issues of the conflict which were well recognized at the time. This was not about piling on more military pressure, as the French had attempted to no avail. It was about winning "hearts and minds." This battle was far from certain, as correspondent Milton Orshefsky, writing for *Life* magazine, observed:

> This is a war for the minds and allegiance of the Vietnamese people. All the military apparatus can do – the choppers, the armored personnel carriers, the T-28s, the troops – is to buy time for the unsteady Diem government to sell itself and its program to its rather indifferent people.[3]

In the same article, Kennedy was quoted remarking that "we don't see the end of the tunnel," and he was right.[4]

Kennedy's private pessimism contrasted with public optimism expressed by his officials. Much of this was led by Harkins in the usual way, but other voices joined the chorus. In early March, McNamara was talking optimistically in terms of cleaning up and terminating the subversion. Crises in communism – starvation in China and a crop failure in the Soviet Union – added a glowing *Schadenfreude* to this assessment. On March 20, the MACV "Summary of Highlights" reported tangible progress in the counterinsurgency war and especially in the Strategic Hamlets Program. On April 17, National Intelligence Estimate 53-63 repeated this message. On May 6, McNamara confidently asserted in a Honolulu Conference that "we are winning," a message he repeated in a July 19 press conference.[5] Two days earlier a DIA assessment reported that Viet Cong activity over the six-month period was lower than the same period in the preceding year. This seemed to accord with Harkins' assessment that helicopters, better tactics, and better leadership were yielding results. An upswing in violence was reported by the DIA on August 4, but this was attributed to the Buddhist crisis, largely contained in Saigon and Hue. This blip was soon corrected by a second SACSA (Office of Special Assistant for Counterinsurgency and Special Activities) assessment ten days later, reporting below average levels of violence. The continuing Buddhist crisis prompted McNamara to issue a memo on August 24 acknowledging the unrest, but the defense secretary could still maintain that the military campaign was not being derailed, but rather was progressing well.

Yet all was not well, and by the end of August it was clear even to optimists that South Vietnam was likely heading toward implosion. On September 6 Kennedy convened the National Security Council and by the evening a most unlikely pair of officials, Major General Victor Krulak and senior Foreign Service Officer Joseph Mendenhall, were on their way to Saigon to reassess the situation. Krulak wryly recalled that the meeting was underway at 11am when Kennedy turned to him and asked whether he was free to travel to Saigon. Krulak replied yes, assuming that a trip would be organized in the near future. To his surprise, Kennedy instructed, "Let's get a jet to take General Krulak – he called me by my first name – out to Vietnam at 1 o'clock."[6] The two were old acquaintances – during the Second World War, an aborted raid led by Lieutenant Colonel Krulak had been rescued by a Lieutenant Kennedy in his PT boat. Krulak had promised the Navy man a bottle of whiskey – "Three Feathers … the most wretched rotgut in the world" – which he was never able to deliver as he was subsequently wounded and evacuated.[7] Now was his opportunity to repay Kennedy.

The two emissaries were not just different in appearance – the diminutive, muscled "Brute" Krulak contrasting with the taller, bookish Mendenhall – they were completely different in outlook. On their return, four days later, Kennedy quipped, "You two did visit the same country, didn't you?" but the joke barely calmed the tension boiling below the surface.[8] Mendenhall, a Southeast Asia veteran, conferred with old acquaintances among the metropolitan elites and was offered a uniformly depressing perspective on South Vietnam's prospects. In Krulak's later sarcastic appreciation, "it was quite obvious that he had been told that the whole town was under water, that everybody was going to abandon ship."[9] Krulak visited the military commands and returned with an upbeat message on the "impressive pace" of battlefield victories. The divergent viewpoints were exacerbated by two officials: Rufus Phillips, the USOM (United States Operations Mission) director for rural programs and advisor to the Strategic Hamlets Program, and John Mecklin, the recently divorced director of USIS (United States Information Service), who at the time was sharing billets with two outspoken Diem critics, journalists David Halberstam and Neil Sheehan. Phillips asserted that the war was plainly being lost, which provoked Krulak into calling him a "damn fool." The volatile Mecklin proposed a radical policy of dumping the Ngo brothers and sending in the marines straightaway. What the meeting revealed was the deep gulf between a Defense Department arguing that "everything's wonderful in Vietnam," and State which was "sore as hell" over this "dirty pool" of false optimism.[10] All sides of the debate agreed the Diem government was awful, but there was no agreement on what should be done about it.

It is to Kennedy's discredit that after Krulak and Mendenhall delivered their contrary judgments, he left the meeting. Krulak was sitting nearest the door. On his way out Kennedy placed his hand on Krulak's shoulder and said, "Come in when the meeting is finished." He obeyed the instruction, accompanied by McNamara. "I just want to tell you," Kennedy confided, "that I believe you."

This expression of confidence was short-lived. One week later, an exasperated Kennedy ordered a second fact-finding mission, led by McNamara and Taylor. The two men arrived in Saigon on September 24, just as America suffered her 112th combat fatality. Hilsman later recalled his and the President's frustration over the visit:

> I was sufficiently upset that I followed Kennedy into the Oval Office and protested again … Kennedy replied, "Look, Roger. I know that. I know that it's costly and bad to send McNamara out there. But the only way that we can keep the JCS on board is to keep McNamara on board, and the only way we can keep McNamara on board is to let him go see for himself. Now that's the price we have to pay."[11]

McNamara and Taylor were accompanied by deputy to Assistant Secretary for International Security Affairs William Bundy, CIA Chief Colby, and aide to the National Security Advisor Michael Forrestal. Years later, the latter would assert that the visit had been a phony exercise in gathering statistical evidence by officials whose minds were already made up and who were determined to prove the success of the mission.[12] This cynical recollection was actually at odds with what happened on the ground. The MACV predictably reported progress but John Richardson, the Saigon CIA Station Chief, warned of collapse. The newly appointed Ambassador Henry Cabot Lodge oscillated between vilifying the Ngo brothers while striving to protect an aid budget that was sustaining the brothers, for fear it might provoke a general breakdown of law and order. The subsequent field trips directly contradicted MACV's prognosis; Vietnamese civilian officials tirelessly criticized the government and McNamara was left with a "lasting skepticism" over the positive assessments he was being offered.[13] At one stage he openly told an optimistic army presenter, "You don't know what you are talking about." A late hospitality call to Diem at the Gia Long Palace proved a disaster.

McNamara and Taylor returned on October 2 with poor information and mixed views. Their report was drafted on the 27-hour flight home (Bundy recalled getting two hours' sleep), and it failed to resolve the contradictions exposed by the previous Krulak-Mendenhall visit, unsurprisingly so because nothing had changed. Taylor seemed to fall for Harkins' assessment and predicted the war would be won by the following year in all provinces except the Delta, which would take a little longer to control. McNamara sensed political implosion but advised reviewing the situation again in the New Year rather than taking precipitous measures now. The orthodoxy of military progress was dishonestly defended and three "goldilocks" policy options were proposed: reconcile with Diem, apply pressure on Diem, or ditch Diem. The former was impossible and the latter unconscionable, so the National Security Council decided on the safe option of "selective pressures." These amounted to the withdrawal of 1,000 US troops, and a partial suspension of aid, notably to the special forces commanded by a Colonel Le Quang Tung, which were being used as an instrument of repression. Repeating a Kennedy mantra, the report re-asserted the policy of Vietnamese primacy:

> The U.S. advisory effort, however, cannot assure ultimate success. This is a Vietnamese war and the country and the war must in the end be run solely by the Vietnamese. It will impair their independence and development of their initiative if we leave our advisors in place beyond the time they are really needed.[14]

These contingent policy recommendations were recognized by the report writers. If no progress was made in the next few months, the report advised, "more drastic action" may be required. What this action might be remained unstated, but the addressees of the report would have been well aware of the developing matter of a cabal of scheming generals in Saigon. On this point, McNamara was clear; Washington should not participate actively in a coup.[15] McNamara's clarity, however, was mud to the Saigon generals who were beginning to interpret the half-hearted response from Washington in a quite different light.

Dealing with Diem was just one problem facing the administration in the summer of 1963. The other was in its own backyard in an increasingly skeptical stream of media reports landing on Washington desks. Young, idealistic correspondents like Peter Arnett (married to a Vietnamese), Neil Sheehan, and especially David Halberstam, working for the influential *New York Times*, turned over the official narratives and found them wanting. In the minds of these reporters, the calculation was plain:

> If you could not win the war on the ground, you could at least win it in public relations and make it look like it was going well. So there was a very calculated and orchestrated policy of people saying how well the war was going.[16]

The reality was very different. As Halberstam, with his characteristic turn of phrase put it, "There was a tunnel at the end of the tunnel and it was filled with VC and NVA."[17]

This was a new breed of "*journaliste engagé*" "committed journalist" and their engagement was critical.[18] When Ambassador Nolting reproached Halberstam for always looking for the hole in the doughnut, he retorted that there was no doughnut, just a hole.[19] Kennedy suggested to his publisher that perhaps the young man should be posted to Paris or London. McGeorge Bundy, who taught Halberstam at Harvard, condescendingly described him as "a very gifted boy," but "who gets all steamed up."[20] This censure and denial only reflected how sensitive the administration had become to its own false reporting.

The growing conflict between MACV and the press corps reached a crescendo over the furore surrounding the battle of Ap Bac (January 3, 1963).[21] Harkins jokingly named it "My Aching Back," and from the perspective of a military officer who had

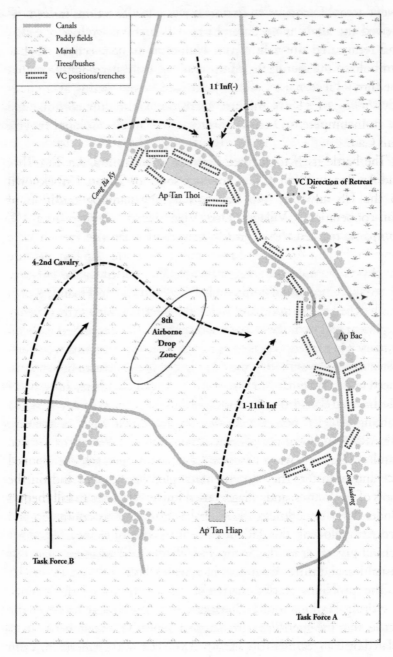

Canals
Paddy fields
Marsh
Trees/bushes
VC positions/trenches

11 Inf(-)

VC Direction of Retreat

Cong Ba Ky

Ap Tan Thoi

4-2nd Cavalry

8th
Airborne
Drop
Zone

Ap Bac

1-11th Inf

Cong luong

Ap Tan Hiap

Task Force B

Task Force A

swept across Europe with Patton it was a trivial action; indeed, he viewed the affair as no different to a French village lost one day, and recaptured the next. From Halberstam's perspective, Ap Bac symbolized the mendacity of the war.[22] A third personality entered the fray – Lieutenant Colonel John Paul Vann – acting as military advisor to 7th ARVN Infantry Division, at the time commanded by an incompetent Diem appointee, the Catholic Colonel Huynh Van Cao.

The battle itself took place between two hamlets, Ap Tan Thoi and Ap Bac, in Dinh Tuong Province south of Saigon. Unbeknown to the US advisors, "Ap Bac had a long-standing tradition of non-cooperation." Villager Dao Vien Trung, serving in a VC company, recalled, "this already happened when the French were here. In the past Ap Bac had been called 'Protesting Ap Bac' because we always opposed the foreign invaders."[23] Alerted to the presence of 261st VC Battalion commanded by Colonel Hai Hoang, a plan was hatched to surround and attack the guerrillas with 11th Infantry Regiment and two Civil Guard battalions.[24] These assaulted early on January 2 but failed to make any headway. Reinforcements were then flown in which resulted in the downing of five American helicopters. Faced with a stalemate and trapped American casualties, 4th ARVN Mechanized Squadron was despatched to the scene in M113 armored fighting vehicles, but also became bogged down. Later in the day, 8th ARVN Airborne Battalion was parachuted to the west of the two hamlets. The drop was a fiasco and the paratroopers fell like "cooked rice and beans."[25] They became entangled in the trees and on the roofs of the houses, and villagers used knives and hoes to kill them.[26] Under cover of darkness, the guerrillas exploited the confusion and fled east, allowing the ARVN to claim a sort of victory. They left behind just 18 dead; the South Vietnamese suffered more than 183 casualties, and three Americans had been killed.

The problems started with the interpretation of the events. A visiting Harkins told Halberstam and Arnett, sent to cover the battle, that the guerrillas were trapped, repeating a version of events related by Cao fearful of appearing to lose face to the American. Vann told a quite different story of a "miserable damn performance."[27]

Vann was telling the truth, but the South Vietnamese units were not so much poor – some fought well – as determined to avoid casualties. Both the ARVN and Civil Guard commander were under strict instructions from Diem to minimize the fatality count. Cao owed his promotion to a scrupulous adherence to this directive. Ironically, at Ap Bac a policy of avoiding confrontation with the Viet Cong backfired and left the ARVN with a heap of bodies. Nor were the Americans entirely blameless: landing troops in half-submerged paddy fields, directly forward of concealed Viet Cong positions, was suicidal. Arguments broke out and orders were countermanded or ignored. For the Viet Cong, of course, the mêlée was a great victory, celebrated in posters. Guerrilla Nguyen Cong Danh recalled:

> This was also the first battle in which we fought all day against the enemy and against all their armed forces: the air force, the navy, the armored units, the artillery and the infantry whose combined strength was ten times larger than ours. But we were able to win nevertheless.[28]

Ap Bac did not deserve its elevation to cause célèbre. The battle certainly marked several firsts: the loss of five helicopters in a single action; the heaviest casualty toll in a Mekong clash; and the repulse of an ARVN battalion by the Viet Cong. But ultimately it was not a significant action for either side. It gained notoriety because conflicting actors sought to use the battle to prove their points: Harkins that the ARVN was winning, and Halberstam that the war was being reported deceitfully. In the meantime the NLF produced a poster celebrating the battle and urging the cadres to shoot down more American helicopters.

The greater irony enveloping Ap Bac was that ground-truth MACV assessments coincided with, rather than contradicted, the reporting of journalists like Halberstam, and had done so for many months. Vann, a statistician by training, was not the only officer attempting to report the situation honestly. There were others similarly frustrated with the charade: Colonel Wilbur Wilson in III Corps, Colonel Dan Porter in IV Corps, and Lieutenant Colonel

Fred Ladd assigned to 21st ARVN Division.[29] All these officers fell foul of Harkins who resorted to undermining their credibility. The runes were not so much being read as buried.

The principal agent of this expurgation was the MACV HQ, filtering negative reporting.[30] A second factor was the paucity of US advisors at ground level. Following the January 1962 Honolulu Conference, it was agreed that just three advisors would be assigned at province-level, in addition to unit trainers. At the time, total US advisory personnel numbered 3,000, including an 805-strong special force contingent run by the CIA, but the overwhelming majority were based in Saigon.[31] This was too few and the problem was recognized (by the end of 1963 there would be 480 advisors and trainers at corps level, 446 at division, 134 at regiment, and 417 at battalion level). But this swelling of the American presence in rural areas did not result in better-quality reporting. Trainers and advisors were as much reporting on their own perceived success in fulfilling their assignments, as reporting on their trainees' competence. Most advisors seldom ventured outside the ARVN bases so they had a very limited sense of what was happening at village level. Language difficulties deepened this ignorance. The US Army had practically no Vietnamese-speakers (this was indeed cited as a good reason for not expanding the mission) and few French speakers. Carl Bernard, a French-speaking world war veteran, witnessed how a cadre of competent Vietnamese officers was displaced:

> The Vietnamese officers who'd been reared in the French army and who spoke French very well, those that didn't acquire English, were pretty well cast aside quite soon. Those who became important to the Americans were those with whom we could speak. Those who spoke English better.[32]

Tom Barnes, a Foreign Service Advisor, was more direct: "For the adviser to speak the language of the country, was as important as the AK-47 was to the Viet Cong."[33] Unfortunately, few could. To compound the problem, language-learning and therefore understanding the culture, were not judged "career-enhancing." Kill counts were.

The ARVN was not so much opaque as incomprehensible, and yet this was the organization on which MACV was chiefly relying for its front-line intelligence. US intelligence personnel were not so naive as to accept Vietnamese reporting at face value – the contrary was true – but in the absence of any other reliable reporting, it was primarily Vietnamese-supplied numbers that were making up the reams of positive statistics, the deliberately named Headway Reports, as if there was no other possibility other than that MACV was making headway. These continued to inform US assessments despite repeated criticisms that South Vietnamese intelligence was poor and commonly distorted for political purposes. Weaknesses on the Vietnamese side were further multiplied by weaknesses in the American set-up. MACV intelligence was not considered a high-flyer's post. Inter-service rivalry meant that some posts were taken simply to deny another service the slot, but appointees had no intelligence backgrounds and little interest in counterinsurgency. The final sandstone grinding away at the truth was a desire for instant gratification. The implausibility that the war could be turned around so quickly was simply not acknowledged. MACV was on a pre-determined timetable of mission success – McNamara's Accelerated Plan – and the numbers, whatever they were, had to fit this schedule.

The collision between reality and the numbers finally came on October 22 with the publication of the seemingly innocuous State Department INR Research Memorandum RFE-90. This document, actually based on data from the DIA and General Krulak's office, examined four sets of statistical measures, "casualties, weapons losses, defectors and Viet Cong incidents," and came to the conclusion that no progress had been made. Rather, "The military situation in Vietnam may have reverted to the condition of six months to one year previous." Forty copies of the document were distributed to various government departments, but the only copy that counted was the one that landed in the Pentagon, which provoked an inter-departmental detonation. A furious Defense responded with a memo itemizing a long list of success statistics which it accused State of willfully ignoring. These counter-statistics were profoundly self-deluding, particularly the claims made for the Strategic Hamlets Program. In a sniffy conclusion, Defense dismissed the study as having "little importance in itself," but warned that "the diffusion of its inaccurate military conclusions could have unfavorable effects, since it contradicts publicly announced Department of Defense estimates on these military matters." This was the heart of the problem: presentation of facts, not their veracity, had become MACV's strategy, which is to say that MACV had no credible strategy at all. State had pulled away the fig leaf of false charts to reveal an embarrassing nudity. In the interests of cabinet unity, a humbled Rusk was forced to apologize to McNamara on behalf of his department.

All these shenanigans and contortions, the fact-finding missions and contradictory reports, the conflicting statistics and intelligence estimates, and the growing sense of an impending crisis – all had their origin in the person of the President of the Republic of Vietnam: Ngo Dinh Diem. By the spring, Washington was no longer talking of communism as the biggest threat to South Vietnam, but rather Diem himself.

Diem's fate was sealed by a most unlikely cast of characters: self-immolating monks, an unsentimental American ambassador, a secret agent, a dentist, and a clique of scheming generals. The trajectory of his downfall began on May 8, in Hue, after government troops led by a Catholic Major, Dang Sy, overreacted to a crowd protesting over anti-Buddhist discrimination laws. The day was auspicious, marking *Phat Dan*, or the birth of the Buddha. Perhaps 3,000 protestors had gathered at the Tu Dam pagoda, before later marching on the government radio station. It was here that Sy gave the order to open fire, an order which he later attributed to Diem's brother, Archbishop Thuc. Nine protestors were killed, including two children. The government blamed the

Viet Cong but this hardly washed as the shootings were captured by an amateur cameraman. Within days the protests had spread across the country, and especially in Saigon where the monks were joined by students. South Vietnam was pitched into "the Buddhist Crisis."

There had been Buddhist unrest in the past but this was different. On June 11, a 73-year-old Buddhist monk called Thich Quang Duc sat in the middle of a Saigon street, surrounded by fellow monks and nuns. Duc adopted the lotus position and was doused in petrol. He then lit a match and set himself alight. The congregation stood back at a respectful distance and held hands in prayer. It took ten minutes for Duc to burn to death. The self-control he displayed was astonishing – not a cry, not a movement. The black and white photograph of Duc with flames licking around his head became one of the iconic images of the war. Eventually, the well-cooked body lost its shape and fell over. His hands had curled like fried pork and Madame Nhu tactlessly dismissed the self-immolation as a "barbeque." When the corpse finally cooled, it was wrapped in a banner and transported to the Xa Loi pagoda, at the center of the protests. One week later Duc's fried heart was removed and mounted as a holy relic on a circular, silver plinth. To this day, Vietnam's communist rulers have not dared interfere with the relic of the Venerable Quang Duc.[34]

The self-immolation of monk Duc horrified a world audience but left the intransigent Diem unmoved. The detested wife Madame Nhu metamorphosed into a megaphone of criticism, yelling at America in rambling paranoid statements and branding all Buddhists as a bunch of crypto-communists who would all die out, if she had her way. For many South Vietnamese, the Ngos were more than just an obstacle to a pacified country. The entire family was a cancer. By the summer, US newspapers were routinely talking of a forced change of government. Diem should have paid heed. The Buddhists were disorganized but they quickly learned to exploit the American press corps. "None of them spoke English," Roger Hilsman remembered, "but all their signs were in English."[35] This had the important effect of reaching the ears of congressmen who in turn began to raise questions with the White House. With only a matter of weeks left in post, Nolting urged Diem to conciliate. In his customary manner, Diem reciprocated by promising reform but then backtracked on the promises. In the last week of May, Nolting left on his end of tour leave. It then fell to the harder-nosed chargé d'affaires, Bill Truehart, to put pressure on Diem to address Buddhist grievances, but his words also fell on deaf ears.

By now Saigon was simmering but the protocols of diplomacy still had to be observed. On July 4, the US Embassy invited the ARVN high command to Independence Day celebrations. Almost all the top generals attended. In the evening, a group retired to the Caravelle Hotel night club on Lam Son Square, one of Saigon's better-known drinking holes (and reputedly a setting in *The Quiet American*; it still exists but is overlooked by the modern 5-star pile with its fleet of Mercedes, luxury suites, and wellness rooms). The Caravelle was a favored haunt for reporters and spooks, sniffing out the war news from behind the smog of cigarette smoke. On this occasion, the generals were accompanied by a stocky embassy official named Lucien "Lou" Conein. In public, he was known as a civilian advisor or CAS Officer. In reality he was a CIA officer.

French-born, Conein had all the ingredients of a successful spy in an age when espionage reached its romantic peak at the height of the Cold War. Forty-nine at the time, ruggedly handsome, and with a deep, gravelly voice, the orphaned Conein had served out the war behind enemy lines helping the French resistance. When Nazi Germany collapsed he was posted to the Pacific Theater where he ran operations against the Japanese in Vietnam. With such a background, Conein thrived in the world of shadows. The fact that he was missing fingers (actually lost in an accident) only added to his aura. He was one of a handful of former-OSS agents who had actually met Ho Chi Minh. In Vietnam, it was his Francophone background that proved important. Conein understood the Vietnamese culturally in a way that non-French-speaking American officers could not. In turn they trusted him. The Conein legend – hard-drinking, swaggering, and bluffing – had some truth in it, but it overshadowed the other Conein, a thoughtful officer who proved a highly able and discreet servant of his government in the delicate art of "liaison."

Conein's instinct to follow the generals was part of the tradecraft. On that evening he was richly rewarded. At some point in the drinking spree, a concerned General Tran Van Don, Chief of the Joint General Staff, took Conein to one side and dropped a bombshell. The generals had endured enough. The country was going to ruin under the corrupt Ngo family; it was time to act. The generals, he confided to an unsurprised Conein, intended to lance the wound and stage a coup.

Don was one of South Vietnam's more impressive generals. French-born, he had attended the *École spéciale militaire de Saint-Cyr* during the Second World War and had a record of genuine military competence as a French Army officer. During the 1950s he variously fought against the Viet Minh and then against South Vietnam's anti-government militias. He helped lever Diem into power but his very competence was his undoing. Feared by the Ngos as a potential rival, he became the emasculated general whose main duty was greeting dignitaries at the airport. Conein listened intently to this general with whom he shared the common bond of a French upbringing. There had been rumors of coups in the past. As Conein later remarked of that summer, "Everyone was cooing around the place like a bunch of pigeons."[36] Roger Hilsman at the State Department similarly remembered, "Not a week went by when there weren't one, two or three coup reports."[37] The US Embassy at any one time was monitoring 11 potential dissident groups.[38] Colonels, government officials, Buddhists, communists – they were all at it. This was hardly news.

However, Don impressed on Conein that this time the army was serious. The plotters were being led by the tall and toothless General Duong Van Minh, respectfully known as "Big Minh" (his teeth had been ripped out by Japanese soldiers). In Taylor's estimation, Big Minh alone "stood for virtue, integrity, and reliability," but the remainder of the conspirators "were ineffective, whether civilians or military." Seduced by Minh's honorable persona, Taylor and other US officials who had lost patience with Diem nevertheless "had a real feeling that he might be the man that should succeed Diem."[39]

General Kim, Don's brother-in-law, and General Khiem were also in the game. The bespectacled and chubby General Tran Thien Khiem, the head of the army, had already been recruited by another disaffected group plotting a so-called "junior officers' coup." This was led by Diem's former head of intelligence, Tran Kim Tuyen, a zealous Catholic dubbed "Vietnam's Goebbels" who then fell out with the Ngos.[40] His secretive career would eventually end with British intelligence resettling him with his family in the university town of Cambridge. The plot itself came to nothing but it did provide a ready supply of foot soldiers for the generals' coup. Many of these recruits came from the key Saigon-based airborne and marine units as well as the tank battalions of 5th Division. Don hinted that the coup might take place in the next ten days but demurred from revealing more.[41] Conein was sufficiently impressed by the general's earnestness to file a report signaling that a credible coup attempt was in the planning stages. Don's candor was naturally self-interested: an open admission that America had become the *deus ex machina* in South Vietnam, an eventuality that Diem had fruitlessly struggled to avert over the course of his presidency. Minh would always insist that there should be no American participation in a coup, but he would be equally firm that Washington should recognize the legitimacy of the act.

Conein's message predictably sent Washington into a spin, already in an effervescent state over the Buddhist crisis.[42] Nolting was recalled from leave and unhesitatingly advised that the US government should not support a coup lest it open a Pandora's Box of disorder. This view was supported by an intelligence assessment that also predicted a potentially chaotic succession.[43] Somehow, rumors of a coup also appeared to reach Nhu who summoned all the generals the following week and railed against their lack of loyalty. This sudden outburst put the wind up Minh and Don but in the long term only served to encourage greater secrecy among the coup plotters. The Ngos were acutely aware of their vulnerability to the generals. The corrupt system of military patronage had been designed expressly to place loyalists in power, although it ultimately failed in its purpose. Chief among these loyalists were the IV Corps commander, General Huynh Van Cao, and the commander of Saigon and surrounding III Corps area, General Ton That Dinh. Cao, already visited in the Ap Bac fracas, was the archetypal Diemist general, a Catholic with ten children, indifferent if not hopeless in battle, and one of the few senior officers who would fail to escape during the fall of Saigon in 1975. Dinh was another Diem protégé, the youngest general in the ARVN better known for his vanity and the hours he kept in Saigon night clubs. His buffoonish boasting later in the summer – following a raid on Buddhist pagodas – would make him the laughing stock of the press corps. The third key loyalist was the diminutive and oddly cherubic Colonel Le Quang Tung, commander of the brothers' Praetorian Guard – the special force battalion – whose winding sheet would become knotted with his master's. Tung, like Dinh, was both feared and ridiculed. Before his death he achieved brief international notoriety over the affair of the miraculous carp: an over-fed fish in a Hue temple pond, revered as a reincarnated monk and grenaded by Tung's men, instantly converting it into the first carp martyr in history.

By mid-July, Nolting had returned to Saigon. Again, he attempted to persuade Diem to change course. It all came to nought. As in his previous relations with Ambassador Durbrow, Diem was confident the Saigon embassy would not, ultimately, abandon him. This canon was so firmly fixed in his mind it would prove his undoing. The two men held a last cordial, if fruitless, meeting on August 14 and Nolting boarded the flight home the following morning. His replacement – Henry Cabot Lodge – planned to arrive before the end of the month.

Lodge was a Republican grandee and opponent of Kennedy who, notwithstanding, willingly served as an ambassador in his administration. Some supporters wished he had thrown his hat into the presidential race, and defeated Kennedy. The Ngos feared him – rightly – but pretended otherwise when his appointment was announced at the end of June. Six months earlier he had offered his services to Rusk, guided by idealism, or as he put it, because young Americans were dying in that far off land and he felt a duty to do something about it.[44] The call up probably surprised him. In the summer he was sent on a counterinsurgency course to prepare him for his post ("a very unhappy phrase" in his view). He then flew to Honolulu for further briefings with CINCPAC.

In the embassy he would prove an aloof and strict disciplinarian, but he was also astute at cultivating unusual and valuable contacts. These included Professor Robert Honey of the University of London, a Vietnamese speaker of some refinement capable of holding philosophical discussions in the language; Apostolic Delegate Archbishop Salvatore Asta who offered valuable insights into the Catholic community; and a Buddhist priest called Xuan Lien who had the distinction of also being a Yale graduate. Conein later recalled that Lodge kept him on a very tight leash, authorizing all meetings and demanding a debriefing as soon as Conein returned to the embassy. He arrived in Saigon in a bad mood, a tall stooping man with slightly too short trousers and white socks. When his tall frame settled in a chair he had a habit of tapping his feet impatiently, as if marking the time to Diem's downfall.

In the interregnum, Nhu, "heavily on opium" and manifesting megalomaniac tendencies, overplayed his hand.[45] Under the pretext of martial law declared the day before, he ordered a midnight raid with his loyal special forces on the Xa Loi Pagoda from where the Buddhist resistance was being orchestrated. Across South Vietnam, more pagodas were raided resulting in hundreds of arrests. Ironically, the imposition of martial law had been proposed to Nhu by two of the coup plotters, Don and Khiem, with Dinh's approval, but their intention had been pacification not aggravation. Nhu's over-clever mind led him down a dangerous path; cynically exploiting the absence of the US ambassador and double-crossing the generals who were blamed for raids they would never have sanctioned. This reckless act provoked Lodge into cutting short his briefings and catching the next flight to Saigon where he arrived late in the evening of August 22. Nhu's deceit was so skillfully executed that the new ambassador arrived with the conviction, shared by the Embassy and Washington, that the events of the last 24 hours amounted to nothing less than an unfolding military coup orchestrated under the pretext of martial law. For Kennedy, "the Pagodas' raid" was the last straw. Hilsman remembered the President turning to him and repeatedly muttering: "Remember Laos – get us out."[46] This exchange, as much as any other, exposed Kennedy's genuine feelings on South Vietnam. He was never the unquestioning devotee of the domino theory and if given a chance he would have settled for a Laos-style "neutralist" compromise. With telephone lines deliberately cut by Nhu and distracted by a barrage of false media stories, it would take the Embassy several days to fully establish that it had been duped. As the truth dawned, so the anger mounted.

What happened next opened the door a little wider to Washington's support for an anti-Diem coup. Disturbed by *Voice of America* broadcasts blaming the army, Don approached Conein to establish on which side Washington stood. To throw off Diem's secret police, Conein arranged to stage the clandestine meetings at the dentist's, or more precisely at the same dentist used by Don. Conein would arrive first, enter the surgery, and pretend to have a dental examination. Don would follow and the meeting would be held in a side room. In case of compromise, the general would escape via a back route and the dentist would continue his innocent examination of Conein's mouth.

When Don arrived, he was in an agitated state. The good name of the army has been slurred – could his American friends not see the only real winners in this situation were the Viet Cong? Surely, it was plain that Nhu had to go. Unbeknown to Conein, this very same message was being conveyed in separate meetings with US officials by General Kim, by Vo Van Hai, Diem's chef de cabinet, and by Nguyen Dinh Thuan, the Secretary of State. This simultaneous and coincident reporting created a powerful impression at the Embassy.

It could only mean that the anti-Diem movement had broadened. However, with bare knowledge of the personalities, Lodge was in a poor position to judge the loyalty of the generals. At best he thought it could all end up as a "shot in the dark."[47] This was the first and last cable in which the normally confident Lodge would express any doubts in the weeks leading to Diem's murder.

The question of Washington's stance was preempted by a cable sent to Lodge from the State Department – the August 24 "Hilsman cable" – which authorized the ambassador to tip off the generals that Washington would not object to Nhu's removal from power. Diem's ultimate fate was left vague and unstated. The language of this cable was forthright and peremptory. "[The] US Government cannot tolerate a situation in which power lies in Nhu's hands," it argued. "If, in spite of all your efforts, Diem remains obdurate and refuses [to get rid of Nhu], then we must face the possibility that Diem himself cannot be preserved."[48] In its dealings with the generals, State's instructions to Saigon were explicit:

> US would find it impossible to continue to support GVN [Government of Vietnam] militarily and economically unless ... steps are taken immediately which we recognize requires removal of Nhus from the scene. We wish [to] give Diem reasonable opportunity ... but if he remains obdurate, then we are prepared to accept the obvious implication that we can no longer support Diem. You may also tell appropriate military commanders we will give them direct support in any interim period of breakdown of central government mechanism.[49]

Lodge's almost certain pleasure at this decisiveness on the part of the State Department was short-lived. The cable had been drafted jointly by the Far East Department's Roger Hilsman with presidential advisor Mike Forrestal, on a Saturday morning. Oversight had been provided by three other officials: Averell Harriman, holding the somewhat toothless post of Under Secretary of State for Political Affairs; George Ball, then Under Secretary of State for Economic and Agricultural Affairs; and Alexis Johnson, Harriman's deputy.

None of these men had authority to formulate government policy over so sensitive a matter. Kennedy and Rusk were "reached … and approved the draft," and concurrence was also obtained from Taylor and Gilpatric, standing in for McNamara.[50]

Ball read the cable to Kennedy over a telephone, on the Saturday night, which would not have given him great opportunity to reflect on its implications.[51] At the time the President was at the family home in Hyannis Port. Was this an appropriate moment to broach such an important matter? Could Ball reasonably have counted on the President paying full attention to the wording relayed down a telephone line? At the time, Ball himself saw no great controversy in the telegram.[52] "I read him the critical paragraphs," he later explained. "I told him that this would certainly be taken as encouragement by the generals to a coup." Kennedy asked him what he thought then "he approved it."[53] Hilsman later laughed that State had simply despatched a "fairly standard cable" which went out "to one country or another in the world almost every week."[54]

However, this was not how it was perceived. When Washington returned to its desks on the Monday morning the hastily drafted cable quickly became contentious. McNamara was concerned that the government was implicitly condoning a coup and objected to the language. Kennedy responded to this objection by asking everyone sitting around the table at the emergency meeting whether the cable should be canceled. "Mr. McNamara, do you wish to cancel that cable? Mr. McCone, do you wish to cancel the cable?" – the same question posed to every member of the National Security Council. No one voted to withdraw the cable.

With hindsight, it is easy to see why the Hilsman cable marks a hinge point in the story, but the voting around the table suggests the conferees did not see it that way, while acknowledging McNamara's concerns. From the perspective of the National Security Council, General Don's words to Conein were taken at face value. A coup was about to be launched, possibly within the week – this was evident in subsequent meetings in which the question "if" was pushed aside by the questions "when" and "how." For this reason, a daily Executive Committee was established, using the precedent of the Cuba crisis. Every cable to Saigon was marked "Emergency." There was a rush to prepare an "E and E" (Escape and Evacuation) plan for the 4,614 US government employees, their dependents, and 840 other American nationals living in South Vietnam (incidentally, Harkins had at his disposal in South Vietnam 296 aircraft, including 90 transports, illustrating the size of the Kennedy commitment by the fall of 1963, and calling into question Lodge's later exculpation that an aircraft could not be arranged to whisk Diem and his brother out of the country).[55] The body of telegrams and cables that bounced between Washington and Saigon over the next five days testify to a febrile atmosphere. Faced with an apparent and imminent inevitability, the Hilsman cable comes across as a not unreasonable response to an anticipated and probably successful coup. Moreover, the telegram had an extremely limited distribution: just "Eyes Only" for Lodge, and "Exclusive" for CINCPAC. Less instigation, the Hilsman cable was more a mechanism for confirming Washington's position to all the principals in a looming event which it believed was about to happen, regardless of how it acted.

In the subsequent telling of the tale Roger Hilsman became the author of the death warrant, drafted over a weekend, sealing the fate of South Vietnam's president. A contemporary like Conein would later argue that it was this cable that proved the turning point and subsequent narratives would reinforce the argument. In this reading, the Hilsman cable represented a sort of Rubicon-crossing: Washington was no longer simply observing events in Saigon but contemplating participation. Kennedy himself rued the telegram and blamed it for encouraging Lodge to follow a line he was always inclined to take. In this judgment he was correct. The real damage in the cable was contained in a phrase in the penultimate paragraph, only added in the second version, but it is unclear by whom (probably Ball, but in his memory he claims he watered down the wording from the first version): "We will back you to the hilt on actions you take to achieve our objectives."

For Lodge, this offered carte blanche to fulfill his personal anti-Diem agenda.

Hilsman was not alone in drafting the cable and the circumstances of the drafting were far from satisfactory. From the perspective of Nolting, the swing against Diem preceded the cable and was instigated by Harriman. The latter's views were so dogmatic on the matter he did not hesitate to tell Nolting to "shut up" at meetings when the latter offered counter-arguments in favor of Diem.[56] George Ball and Alexis Johnson were not at their desks but playing golf when the cable was drafted. In Ball's recollection, "Just as I was finishing up the ninth hole ... Averell Harriman and [Roger] Hilsman appeared in a great sweat. They had a telegram that they wanted me to approve because I was acting secretary." He took the telegram home and "recognized that this was a telegram of considerable importance."[57]

Ball's stamp, not Hilsman's, was thus appended to the cable and it fell to the former to seek the departmental and presidential authorizations.[58] First Rusk was contacted at the UN General Assembly and he agreed on its tenor although the two men avoided discussing details because they were on an insecure line. In a 1969 interview, Hilsman argued, "I, went along with [W. Averell] Harriman and [Dean] Rusk and the others in the State Department," passing responsibility to his superiors.[59] Hilsman knew and liked Diem but was not blind to the terrible liability he represented. He was also well aware of Nhu's madness, on one occasion recalling a dinner in which Nhu urged him to advise his bosses back in Washington to "seize all of Southeast Asia" in a grand military operation.

The point of the cable, in Hilsman's later self-absolving testimony, was not to instigate a coup but to let the generals know that "it's their affair," a stance consistent with Kennedy's view that Vietnam was essentially an internal nationalist struggle in which Washington was prepared to play a supporting role but no more.[60] A more nuanced view suggests that Hilsman fell in with the State Department orthodoxy, promoted by his seniors, which he intellectually supported. In the delicate words of the cable, Diem could no longer be "preserved." Hilsman's complicity is less linked to the cable than to his consistently argued view that, should a coup fail, "we would be on an inevitable road to disaster."[61] This absolutist stance shared by State colleagues like Harriman distorted debates by foreclosing other possibilities. Hilsman's private position – which he argued both in and out of office – was that Vietnam was a political problem that Washington was in danger of militarizing. It is in this context that he must be judged, not by the association of his name with a single, if important, cable.

Words in the end did not kill Diem. It was the changeover of ambassadors that proved decisive. It is inconceivable that US policy in South Vietnam would have followed the same trajectory had Frederick Nolting still been in post (which is not to say, of course, that the generals may not have acted against Diem anyway). As Nolting presciently argued, jumping precipitously was foolish because "there was no place to jump to."[62] Kennedy sent Lodge to Saigon with explicit instructions to engage with Diem, but he refused to talk to the South Vietnamese President and pursued a deliberate policy of "aloofness." Lodge's post-facto denials that the Embassy was not influential and that "we were not major figures in that coup" simply do not match the records, or the number of occasions on which the generals sought Washington's approval.[63] His excuse that he was acting on instructions (principally the Hilsman cable) was disingenuous. Lodge was well aware that the cable had provoked divisions in Washington and he had to contend with differences of opinion in his own embassy, notably from Harkins. In his actions and words, Lodge gave the firm impression that he arrived in Saigon with a pre-judged idea of what should be done, and he followed it. If any American has a claim to be Diem's judge and executioner – and the ultimate responsibility for the demise of the Ngo family lies with the two brothers – it is Henry Cabot Lodge. He himself would later offer this verdict of the coup:

There is no doubt that the coup was a Vietnamese and a popular affair, which we could neither manage nor stop after it got started and which we could only have influenced with great difficulty. But it is equally certain that the ground in which the coup seed grew into a robust plant was prepared by us and that the coup would not have happened with [sic: when] it did without our preparation. General Don as much as said this to me on November 3. Our actions made the people who could do something about it start thinking hard about how to get a change of government.[64]

By "us" Lodge really meant "me."

Whatever misgivings stirred in Washington, events moved apace in Saigon. On the following day, August 26, Conein met with General Khiem. The former was under instruction to inform the general that the "American official hand should not show." In the prudent language set in a top secret telegram to Washington: "We cannot be of any help in an initial action of assuming power of the state, entirely their own action, win or lose, don't expect be bailed out."[65] Concurrently with Conein, a second CIA officer (only known as "Mr. Spera") delivered the same message to General Khanh.

However, Khiem disclosed that the coup plot was at an advanced stage. More generals had pledged their support. They included Nguyen Khanh, the touchy II Corps commander who saved Diem in the 1960 coup; Nguyen Van Thieu, a future president; and Nguyen Ngoc Le, a former police chief. General Minh was confirmed as the coup leader. Khiem warned that Don should not be approached at this time because he feared infiltrators, but a pick-up by jeep would be arranged so that Conein could hold a meeting with Minh. In line with his instructions, Conein reciprocated by hinting that the US government would not stand in the way of a coup. After the general departed, the CIA man briefed Lodge whose enthusiasm for the plot was reflected in a cable to Washington that same afternoon.[66] He dismissed the chances of Diem reforming as "virtually nil" (a judgment made without having met the President), and recommended going straight to the generals.[67]

By now, however, the keenness for a change of government was not unanimously shared in Washington. The question marks over the coup began to focus on one point: would a successful coup help or hinder the war? Nobody could be sure. Nor was Harkins pleased, who countered Lodge's cable with his own advising caution, notwithstanding that Lodge was separately and somewhat disingenuously reporting to State on August 28 that "Both General Harkins and I favor the operation."[68] This seemed to embolden Hilsman who replied:

> We understand that what we have told the Generals is that they will have to proceed at their own risk. While this is sound initial approach, we must surely be ready to play every effective card at decisive moments. Therefore request your report of additional actions you and Harkins expect to take or recommend after coup begins to insure its success.[69]

What actions? Had anyone spoken to Kennedy?

These contradictory messages highlighted the growing division of opinion in Washington, and once again Saigon jumped one step ahead of the game. On August 29 it was General Minh's turn to confide with CIA officers at the Embassy. Give us a sign, he requested, that the US government will support the coup. His interlocutors reservedly suggested the suspension of economic aid, a measure that was already being debated as a result of the Buddhist crisis. Aware that the National Security Council would be meeting later that day, Lodge and Harkins responded to Minh's sudden appearance at the Embassy by firing off near simultaneous messages arguing their case against and for Diem. Lodge wrote in dogmatic terms:

> We are launched on a course from which there is no respectable turning back; the overthrow of the Diem Government. There is no turning back because in part US prestige is already publicly committed to this end and in large measure and will become more so as facts are leaked out. In a more fundamental sense, there is no turning back because there is no possibility, in my view, that the war can be won under a Diem administration ...[70]

This "no turning back" rhetoric traveled all the way to the President while Harkins' words only got as far as Taylor. This seemed to make the difference. At the meeting, Lodge's persuasion won the day – a spectacular result for the tough bargain-driver who had only arrived in Saigon the previous week. It fell to Rusk's State Department to authorize Lodge to suspend aid and to show the coup plotters evidence of Washington's support by revealing that the CIA officer spoke for the US government.[71] By now, National Security Council meetings were already referring to "the operation," a subconscious admission that US officials had been drawn into a coup plot. Kennedy, still hesitating, seemed to fall back on his own better instincts and queried whether whatever happened "we should really pull out of South Viet-Nam."[72]

While Washington held its breath, a reluctant Harkins arranged a meeting with his counterpart, General Khiem, on August 31 to break the news. What a surprise then when Khiem announced that the whole business had been called off. The coup plot was suspended. There was insufficient support in the army, and, in an admission of the paranoid atmosphere swirling in Saigon, he added that the generals could not be sure that Washington had not tipped off the brothers. There may have been some relief in the Defense Department, who all along had backed Harkins' position, but the cat was out of the bag. Regardless that the coup had been aborted, the plotters now knew that Washington was prepared to at least tacitly back a takeover attempt.

Lodge commented in frustration that the last week felt like he had been "pushing a piece of spaghetti" (provoking Hilsman in a later cable to half-jokingly suggest, try pulling). In the ambassador's view, the best chance of success still lay in "the generals taking over the government lock, stock and barrel."

On August 30, he met his French counterpart, the experienced Ambassador Lalouette. On parting, Lalouette advised: "Let me say two things – first, try to calm American opinion," a judicious view of the source of the semi-hysteria that was being generated, "and second, no coups."[73] As if to confirm that all the secrecy over a potential coup was misplaced, on the same day David Halberstam published an article which seemed to recite verbatim Washington's top secret deliberations of the last week, provoking an alarmed Rusk to warn over leaks. The likelihood is that some knowledge or at least suspicion of what had transpired between Washington, Saigon, and the generals was more widespread than the former would have wished and had reached the ears of the Ngo brothers.

The late summer and fall then developed into the great Diem debate. However many memos, cables, and telegrams passed between Saigon and Washington, consensus remained frustratingly out of reach. Every option seemed bad and risky. With Diem, the country was falling apart; without Diem it would probably be lost. The obvious conclusion, suggested by Robert Kennedy – get out – was not pursued. In an interview with Walter Cronkite, his elder brother was equally doubtful, but stopped short of saying that America should withdraw:

> I don't think that unless a greater effort is made by the Government to win popular support that the war can be won out there. In the final analysis, it is their war. They are the ones who have to win it or lose it.[74]

On the ground little changed. The unpopular Madame Nhu was sent away on a world tour. Archbishop Thuc – the President's brother – was recalled by the Vatican. Nhu promised to resign then reneged on the promise. On the streets the protests continued.

The answer, as ever, was to send yet another fact-finding mission to Vietnam – or indeed, two – the Krulak-Mendenhall and McNamara-Taylor missions, described earlier. The compromise solution was a long-threatened suspension of an $18.5 million commercial import program which was duly announced by Lodge on September 14. This had two immediate effects in Vietnam. Within 48 hours Diem responded by lifting martial law. More sinisterly, the generals began plotting again, recalling their August 29 conversations at the Embassy and taking the aid suspension as a green light to proceed. Post the coup, Lodge would report "it was clear throughout that the withholding of commercial imports had a tremendous psychological effect."[75] His continued frosty relations with Diem only served to make the green light blink more furiously.

In Washington, the effect of the aid suspension was to throw the pro- and anti-Diem parties into another round of boisterous arguments. Kennedy's hope that the McNamara-Taylor visit would lead to a reconciliation of views between the Defense and State Departments was misplaced. Too many actors had already made up their minds. Harkins exaggerated military successes, Lodge damned Diem, and the latter chain-smoked and monologued visitors to boredom.

The painful deliberations of the National Security Council were now fast becoming irrelevant ruminations. A reading of Shakespeare might have sufficed: when Caesar falls, squabbling generals and civil war follow. Or a re-reading of Lansdale's prescient report at the start of the Kennedy presidency in which he warned against coups which would leave "a number of highly selfish and mediocre people ... squabbling among themselves for power while the Communists took over." On the same day that the President was conferring with McNamara, Conein held another secret meeting with General Don at Tan Son Nhut airport. His message startled: the coup was back on thanks to the conversion of General Dinh, the vain III Corps commander. Minh needed to speak urgently with Conein – could they meet on October 5? Conein duly kept his appointment and listened carefully to Minh's exposition of three possible coup plans. The first was: "Assassination of Ngo Dinh Nhu and Ngo Dinh Can [the detested younger brother] keeping President Diem in office. Gen. Minh said this option was the easiest to accomplish." (Any assassination was immediately quashed by CIA Director John McCone in a cable to Saigon). The second option was encirclement of Saigon, to force Diem to stand down; and the third option was "a direct confrontation between military units involved in the coup and loyalist military units in Saigon."[76] As they discussed the plans, another Buddhist monk was committing self-immolation on the streets. Although the CIA officer made no promises – he was not expected to in his role as Lodge's secret intermediary – the mere fact that he attended the meeting and was brought into the detail of the plots sent another powerful signal to the generals that Washington was on their side.

This, in reality, was far from the truth. Later that day, Lodge received a message from Washington instructing him that "no initiative should now be taken to give any active covert encouragement to a coup."[77] One version of the events suggests Lodge received and read this message before Conein put a foot outside the Embassy gate, but desisted from telling him.

Following Conein's return and debrief, and indisputably at this stage having read Washington's cable, Lodge brazenly ignored Washington's instruction and replied with a message advising that Conein should be authorized to inform the generals that Washington would not thwart a coup.[78] Kennedy had approved of Lodge's appointment on Rusk's recommendation because he needed a tough negotiator in Saigon. He did not anticipate that he would prove an equally tough negotiator with his own government. In yet another volte-face, Washington acquiesced to Lodge's argument. The US government would not thwart a coup if Diem's removal implied a positive step in the war, a judgment that no one could make with certainty.[79]

The plotting then gathered momentum with all the actors gathered over a single chessboard seemingly moving pieces at will. On October 10, General Minh held another secret meeting with Conein who told him that the US government could not encourage a coup, but neither would it stand in the way of the plotters. This calculated ambiguity seemed to act like a brake, pressed harder by the meddling Harkins who asked General Don not to discuss the proposed coup with US officers, an instruction which he interpreted as an indication that Washington now had cold feet over the whole business.

Unbeknown to the generals, the following day, Kennedy took a decision that would have certainly made them pause for thought. On October 11, the White House issued NSAM 263. This instructed the withdrawal of 1,000 US advisors from South

Vietnam, the first tranche from McNamara's Accelerated Model Plan that would see all American military personnel withdrawn from the country over the next five years. No decision from the Kennedy Vietnam commitment has probably provoked more partisan and ungracious academic sniping.[80] For supporters, this is the proof that Kennedy would have got out of Vietnam. For detractors, it is no such thing. The question is imponderable. We only have the fact of the instruction; a range of views expressed over the previous three years; and Kennedy's untimely death. The person closest to Kennedy on this matter – McNamara – always demurred in later years that he had no idea what Kennedy would have done, an example of humility to copy. Perhaps McGeorge Bundy, with his customary acuity, has made the key observation: Kennedy would have been on his second term, knowing that he did not have to face an electorate again, and therefore "he would have been freer to cut loose." Johnson, until he was done in by Tet, "had himself in his own mind's eye as president for another four years."[81] Not jeopardizing the chance of a second term was probably the difference between the two men.

In Saigon, the ambiguity only lasted a brief two weeks anyway. On October 23, an "agitated" Don called a meeting with Conein at the Joint General Staff. He offered dramatic news. Don explained that the generals' "coup committee" had decided to take advantage of the October 26 national holiday "to stage a coup within the next week."[82] However, there was a hitch. The previous day, Harkins had called on Don and let him know he had advised a Colonel Nguyen Khuong not to mount a coup on October 27. Don was anxious to emphasize to Conein that Khuong had nothing to do with the generals' coup committee. More significantly, as a consequence of these unauthorized conversations, Don feared a leak and sought reassurances from the US government.

Conein adopted a tough bargaining position. He challenged Don "to produce proof that the generals' coup committee existed or that they had any plan whatsoever." Don promised Conein he would provide "the committee's political organization plan" to allay Washington's fears, if they could meet the following evening.

The evening meeting never happened. Instead, Conein received an urgent telephone call at 6.15am from a Don aide asking the CIA man to rush over to Tan Son Nhut airport to meet Don in the VIP lounge within the next half hour. The barely awake Conein made the rendezvous and was informed that following their meeting on the previous day Don had met with Harkins. The latter had clarified he had made an "inadvertent" mistake. He added that he would be meeting with Lodge at 5pm later that day, at which meeting he would confirm the generals' wish to liaise with the US Embassy through Conein "in further discussions on this matter." Critically, he confided that the coup would take place within the next week and no later than November 2. Lastly, he suggested the two should meet again, at 6.30pm, after the Lodge meeting.

This flurry of intelligence raised several problems. First, there was no scheduled meeting with Lodge, which provoked confusion in the Embassy. And second, Lodge was due to fly back to Washington on October 31. If he canceled the trip it might raise suspicions.

Notwithstanding this confusion, Don and Conein met at the dentist's that night. After discussions with his fellow plotters it had been decided that further disclosure would risk a leak. As a gesture of goodwill, the embassy would be given 48 hours' notice and Lodge – but only Lodge – would be initiated into the operational plan. Once again, Conein was skeptical and questioned the strength of the coup. Don assured him, "the coup committee does not expect Diem [redacted in the CIA cable] to stand up under any pressure more than one week."[83] The meeting ended with a lie and an ominous warning. Don assured Conein the new government would be civilian and none of the coup plotters sought a position in the future government. As regards the Ngos, "the generals' committee had come to the conclusion that the entire Ngo family had to be eliminated from the political scene in Vietnam."

Armed with this knowledge, Lodge fired off another cable to Washington the following morning arguing that the US government should now stand back and allow the inevitable to happen.[84] In a side shot, he dismissed Harkins' fears that the coup plotters would fail. The fear of failure, or more properly the fear of being associated with a failed coup, alarmed Washington sufficiently to demand more detail and reassurance.

Over-shadowing this interchange of messages were the celebrations due to take place the following morning to mark Vietnam National Day. Diem was due to attend a parade in Saigon to which foreign dignitaries had been invited. If the coup plotters were genuinely preparing to strike, this was the perfect opportunity. Saigon's fears over a coup attempt on October 26 were well justified. It subsequently transpired that this had been the original date set by the generals, but a number of factors had forced the plotters to abort.

A veneer of normality was maintained the following day, August 27, when Lodge flew to Dalat for talks with Diem, but it was just a veneer – outside, the seventh Buddhist monk had just committed self-immolation. Diem harangued Lodge for several hours, deflecting any questions over reform and confirming in the ambassador's mind that Washington could not possibly do business with this obstinate martinet. The following morning, Lodge, it appears coincidentally bumped into General Don at the airport. The general did not waste the opportunity but took the ambassador to one side and asked whether "Lou" spoke for the US government. Lodge affirmed that he did and unsuccessfully tried to wheedle a coup date out of the evasive Don. The two men then parted. According to Don, it was this meeting with Lodge that convinced the generals to act: "It's the only time I met Cabot Lodge ... and I had the support of the Americans. So we decided to have the coup. That's it."[85]

Reassured with knowledge of this support, Don called another meeting at the dentist's with Conein that night. The timelines were getting tighter. After further consultations between the generals it had been decided that the embassy would only be informed of the coup at the last moment. To allay any suspicions, it was imperative that Lodge should continue to carry out his pre-arranged schedule of meetings, including the planned trip to Washington at the end the week. As it was inconceivable that the generals would embarrass Lodge by striking after he had left for Washington, this was the most explicit signal that the coup would almost certainly be launched within the next 72 hours. Washington's response was immediate. CINCPAC placed air and naval forces on alert in case of a possible evacuation and the National Security Council met for the last time to debate Diem's fate. Kennedy was offered a review of pro- and anti-Diem forces – even at this late stage, he was advised that the balance of forces was even.

The overwhelming question batted between the National Security Council members was: would the coup succeed? The example of the 1960 coup was also discussed at length. There was little debate on what might follow.[86] It fell to Robert Kennedy who had displayed uncommon wisdom throughout the crisis to question the sense of what was about to happen. Taylor and McCone belatedly joined him in a late rally predicting that a coup would sink the war effort, exactly the opposite argument to that offered as orthodoxy at the previous meetings. With a sense of anticipation that the plot was now about to unfold, the vital task was to inform Harkins – who up to this point had been kept in the dark over Conein's secret dealings with the generals – in case a last-minute delay pushed the coup date beyond October 31, by which time Lodge would be en route to Honolulu and Washington.

The National Security Council's concerns over how Commander MACV might react to this novel intelligence proved well founded. On October 30, a furious Harkins drafted three cables to Taylor condemning both the plot and the US government's implicit support for the generals.[87] America had been Diem's "mother superior and father confessor" for "eight long hard years," he argued in a religious metaphor that would have resonated with the Catholic Kennedy – would they now send him to hell? This irate volley put the jitters on Washington. Again, Lodge was asked for assurances that the plot was viable and likely to succeed. Exasperated by the divisions in the Embassy and by Washington's doubts, Lodge effectively shrugged his shoulders and replied that the matter was now out of American hands. This barely satisfied Washington. In what would be the last cable before the coup was initiated, the White House made one final attempt to define America's position *avant le déluge*.[88] If the coup went ahead, Saigon should observe a strict policy of non-involvement (a stricture that was disobeyed as Conein was invited to join the plotters). In the meantime, Washington belatedly requested more detail and further reassurances that the entire affair was not going to collapse and fatally damage American prestige in Indochina.

The stage was now set, or so the plotters thought. Unbeknown to Minh and his fellow conspirators, all their diligence and secrecy had been betrayed. Still fearing the loyal IV Corps Commander General Cao, Dinh had despatched his deputy, a Colonel Co, to make contact with dissident junior officers in IV Corps. The plan to neutralize Cao involved mooring a barrier of boats across the Mekong River to prevent reinforcement. One of the officers cavilled at this betrayal and informed Nhu. The brothers' response to this intelligence lacked all sense of the danger they were in. Dinh was summoned to explain the actions of his deputy whom he disloyally denounced. Rather than arrest Co, which surely would have led to the collapse of the coup, Nhu proposed a bizarre counter-coup which he had apparently been concocting for some weeks. This involved armed gangs attacking Vietnamese and US officials, the brothers fleeing to a safe house, and a subsequent triumphant return to the capital at the head of Cao's 7th Division and Dinh's 5th Division. Dinh's surprise at this plan was only over-matched by his desire for self-preservation. He was now the only general who knew what both sides were plotting. A more committed personality may have pitched for one party but Dinh lacked convictions other than his personal advancement. Instead, he took the decision to play both sides and save his skin.

The last day of October came and went in an atmosphere of high tension. The following morning – the day of the coup – an improbable turn of events threatened to interrupt the plotters. Admiral Felt had made a habit of visiting Saigon unannounced. Displaying a very poor sense of timing, this is exactly what he did. As protocol demanded, a visit by CINCPAC involved a courtesy call to the president. Thus, Lodge found himself accompanying

Felt to the palace for a meeting with Diem at 11am. Neither man knew at this stage that the coup was already underway, although Lodge most certainly knew he was talking to a man whose life could now probably be measured in days, if not hours. The visitors were accompanied by General Don whose nervousness was apparent to all. Diem's last conversation with Lodge was fraught with tension. Both men knew that something was afoot but pretended otherwise. When it was over they shook hands, Lodge returned to the Embassy, and the still unsighted Felt drove to Tan Son Nhut airport where he gave a press conference with a frantic Don still in tow.

The unlikely figure of the dentist then re-entered the story. Even as Diem was hosting Lodge and Felt, the generals had started issuing orders to units to march on Saigon. Although the coup plotters had always been adamant there should be no overt American involvement, Minh did want the imprimatur of covert support. When Don innocently asked Lodge two days earlier in their chance meeting at the airport whether Conein spoke for the US government, Lodge's affirmative reply was accepted. The messenger-dentist was duly despatched to Conein's residence and he was instructed to proceed immediately to the Joint General Staff Headquarters at Tan Son Nhut. Conein grabbed a weapon and radio, said goodbye to his family, and rushed across the city to the headquarters building.

He found a scene of some chaos with "Big Minh" issuing orders and promoting officers on the spot. Every general had been summoned to the JGS (Joint General Staff) with the exceptions of Generals Dinh and Cao. The single officer who protested over the coup, special force commander Colonel Tung, was later executed by Minh's aide, Major Nguyen Van Nhung. Several others who were reluctant to have blood on their hands were arrested including the commander of the airborne brigade, Colonel Cao Van Vien, whose life was spared because his wife played mah-jong with Dinh's wife. General Nguyen Khanh, the marine brigade commander, also refused to take part and he was joined by the air force chief, Do Khac Mai, perhaps recalling the last occasion when pilots had become involved in a coup. As they waited nervously, Minh turned to Conein and told him, "If we fail you are coming with us [to the hills]," an instruction which would hardly have reassured the now-committed CIA man.[89]

It did not take long for the Embassy to learn that a coup was underway. At 1.45pm Don rang Harkins' office (but spoke with a subordinate, General Stilwell). By this stage, the secret was out all across the city as anti-Diem units seized television and radio stations, the post office, the airport, and numerous, key military installations. Other units deployed to the outskirts to block the major highways in case of a counterattack that never materialized. There was a certain degree of confusion as loyalists assumed they were witnessing Nhu's counter-coup plan (Nhu himself, bizarrely, apparently thought so). At 2.15am Eastern Daylight Time, Washington received a Flash CRITIC message from the CIA station in Saigon describing the unfolding coup: "CAS officers report that red neckerchief troops pouring into Saigon from the direction of Bien Hoa. Presumably Marines. Telecommunications center taken by these troops ... additional forces, magnitude unknown continue to enter. As of 13.45hrs local [words redacted] the coup is in progress ..."[90]

Half an hour later, a second Flash CRITIC message was despatched, originating from Conein at the JGS:

Gens [Generals] attempting contact palace by telephone but unable to do so. Their proposition is as follows: if the President will resign immediately, they will guarantee his safety and the safe departure of the President and Ngo Dinh Nhu. If the President refuses these terms, the palace will be attacked by air force and armor.[91]

In fact, across Saigon, there was little resistance and almost no bloodshed. As if wishing the two brothers to escape, two hours elapsed before the coup plotters actually moved against the palace with around 35 armored cars. Conein's CIA colleagues who had drifted to the Gia Long Palace reported "approx 200 troops observed and apparently strong firefight."⁹² This message was almost immediately contradicted by a second message confirming that Colonel Tung had been captured and ordered to issue a ceasefire. Some "insurgents" had entered the palace grounds, "but fighting does not appear intense."⁹³

As loyalist guards held their ground, the trapped Diem vainly tried to ring General Dinh. Soon afterwards, he received the telephone call that confirmed a coup was underway; it was the generals demanding that he and his brother surrender. In Conein's reporting: "Gens [Generals] firmly decided there to be no rpt [repeat] no discussion with the President. He will either say yes or no and that is the end of the matter." This message was received by Washington at 3.40am Eastern Daylight Time. By now, Kennedy had been awoken and advised that the coup was underway.

The response from the palace was defiant refusal. Diem had survived two previous coups as well as an attempt on his life. At this stage he could not be sure if the coup enjoyed widespread support. He also needed to telephone the single person whose intercession could make or break the coup – Ambassador Henry Cabot Lodge. If Diem had had any inkling of the harsh judgments Lodge had penned since his arrival in Saigon on August 22, he would not have bothered to pick up the telephone. In the short conversation that followed, Lodge played the role of demurring executioner perfectly.

> Diem: Some units have made a rebellion and I want to know what is the attitude of the US?
> Lodge: I do not feel well enough informed to be able to tell you. I have heard the shooting, but I am not acquainted with all the facts. Also it is 4.30am in Washington and the US Government cannot possibly have a view.⁹⁴

Graciously, he expressed concern over the President's safety, but with bullets whistling about him, Diem hardly needed the US ambassador to remind him that his life was in danger. One account suggests that Lodge made a genuine offer to escort the Ngos out of the palace and fly them out of the country, a suggestion testily rejected by Diem. Whether or not true, Lodge's later indifference to Diem's fate was undisguised. By habit, he went to bed every evening at 9.30pm. On the night of November 1, Lodge saw no reason to change this custom.

Before retiring, he found time to pen a short and confident Top Secret message to Rusk with Eyes Only for McGeorge Bundy: "Generals will be received at Embassy when coup is over (FYI: I expect to receive them myself.)"[95] Nowhere in this message was an expression of concern over the safety of the brothers.

Realizing that he had been abandoned by Washington, Diem began to telephone his loyalist generals only to discover that they were rarer than an honest general. In turn, 5th, 7th, 9th, 21st, 22nd, and 23rd Divisions had all declared for the coup. The marines, without their general, had also gone over to the rebels. As the fighting intensified outside the Gia Long Palace, Minh asked a succession of generals to attempt to persuade Nhu to surrender (Diem was refusing to speak). These efforts were rejected.[96] In one of many strange episodes over the course of the day, the generals' coup broadcast was accidentally spliced with a selection of cha-cha and twist music, adding a sense of surrealism to the proceedings. At 5.15pm Minh personally attempted to mediate with Diem, but the beleaguered president hung up on him. Shortly afterwards Minh gave the order to bomb the palace.[97]

For the besieged there was another option. It appears that shortly after 8pm, the brothers made an audacious escape accompanied by Diem's aide, an air force lieutenant called Do Tho, and the head of Nhu's Republican Youth, Cao Xuan Vy. The escape was made via a secret tunnel system built under the palace. Another version suggests they simply left by an unguarded back gate near the palace tennis courts. With hindsight, it seems surprising the generals had not anticipated the possibility of an escape route, but perhaps it is in the nature of authoritarian regimes to guard their most intimate secrets well. Whichever means they chose it appears they were then picked up in a park near the French colonial *Cercle Sportif* club. From here they were driven to a second location, switched cars, and were driven to Phung Hung Street and the Cholon home of Ma Tuyen, a Chinese businessman and Nhu confidante who controlled a number of opium syndicates. Nhu's close links with the criminal world had led him to previously install a direct line to Ma's home. This meant that Diem could now ring the generals from the hideaway and give the semblance that he was phoning from the besieged palace.

The timing of this escape and subsequent events at the palace, however, remain confused. The generals informed Conein that the presidential guard had capitulated at 6.30pm.[98] But what seems to have followed is a nine-hour battle for a now vacant palace with tanks and artillery intermittently pummeling the abandoned loyalist troops. The most reliable witness, once again, appears to have been Conein from his vantage point at the JGS. In an umpteenth Flash CRITIC message timed at 14.30hrs Zulu Time (the fixed time used in the military coincident with Greenwich Mean Time), it was explained, "additional air assaults [bombing] not undertaken since Gen Minh desired offer Diem one more chance to surrender. There was great difference of opinion at this point but Gen Minh prevailed."[99] The message related that fighting was still ongoing at 10pm and that rebel troops had moved to the area of the zoo to ensure that Diem did not escape "thru sewer exit" (this may, of course, have been the origin of the rumor that the brothers escaped via a secret tunnel). By now around 1,000 troops supported by 17 tanks had converged on the area of the Gia Long Palace.

Throughout the night, CIA officers monitored and reported troop movements in Saigon's abandoned streets. General Dinh was despatched to the palace to parley with the presidential guards. Several large explosions were heard between 3.15am and 3.25am. Despite the great exchange of firepower, just 11 soldiers would be killed from both sides. All the while, Diem and Nhu remained in the safe house desperately weighing their options. The brothers now had one last chance to save their lives but they failed to take it. With all eyes on the palace they could have made a bid to hand themselves over to the MACV HQ, if not the US Embassy, in the early hours of the morning. In the eventuality that these locations were too well-guarded by Vietnamese security forces, they might have tried the French Embassy (or the Italian Embassy where a number of Diem's ministers had scooted, just in case). Perhaps Lodge's frostiness led them to believe that Washington had abandoned them. More plausibly, the two brothers simply did not appreciate the danger they were in.

Then the critical telephone calls were made. Shortly after 6am, Diem rang General Don from the hideaway "and offered to surrender with honor." His only request was safe escort to the airport so that he and Nhu could leave the country. Conein reported, "Gen Minh has accepted this and is attempting to arrange a ceasefire at the palace where heavy fighting is in progress."[100] At 6.58am Diem made a second call to Don "to surrender unconditionally." At the same time he ordered the presidential guard to stop fighting. What Diem did not tell the generals at this stage was that he was telephoning them from Cholon. The reason seems to be that he wanted to try one more roll of the dice with the US Embassy.

At 7am Diem duly made one last and controversial call to Lodge, which the ambassador never reported to Washington. For the next quarter century this created the impression that Diem's last exchange with the Embassy was on the previous evening and that there was nothing Washington could reasonably have done to save his life. This final telephone call, however, was witnessed by an aide, Colonel Mike Dunn, who, following Lodge's death, offered a quite different version of events. Lodge at first put Diem on hold. What Lodge said or did over this period remains uncertain. What is known with more confidence is that Lodge then informed Diem that it would take at least 24 hours to arrange an aircraft (untrue, the Department of Defense had specifically despatched a special berth-equipped military aircraft to Saigon on the Thursday for Lodge's use).[101] This information was simultaneously passed to Conein who had spent a sleepless night with the generals.[102] Minh reacted with incredulity that the Americans could not conveniently whisk the brothers away, as did probably Diem who must have realized at this point that he was abandoned. Concerned over the safety of the Ngos, Dunn then claimed that he offered to personally escort them from the hideaway, but this suggestion was turned down by Lodge. After the event, the ambassador was heard to remark that the brothers would have been a menace alive.[103]

In the meantime, Minh had driven to the palace to accept the surrender, only to discover to his embarrassment that the quarry had fled. This unexpected development was hinted at in the next CIA cable, timed at 00.15hrs Zulu Time, which reported that the presidential escort was now drawn up outside the palace, but there was no sign of Diem or Nhu. At that moment, by Conein's account, the intention had been to hold the brothers at the JGS, while confirming approval from a host government willing to accept the ousted president. Without saying so in the cable, the likelihood was that the eventual destination would be the United States (where Madame Nhu happened to be touring), probably via Manila.

According to one account, as the defenders in the palace laid down their arms, a Colonel Pham Ngoc Thao learned from a prisoner the location of the brothers' hideaway in Cholon. Thao, a former Catholic Viet Minh fighter, was in fact a communist double-agent who had successfully worked his way up the ranks of the army. So successful was he in maintaining his cover that he became well known among American journalists who rated him one of the best officers in the army. Taking a small force with him, Thao crashed across the city to make an arrest. He arrived at the Cholon safe house 15 minutes later but his loud entrance alerted the brothers who fled to the nearby Church of St Xavier, driven by Lieutenant Tho whose diary and part in the events would not surface until 1970. This appears to have been the first and unofficial attempt to arrest the brothers – that failed. Thao then falls out of the story.

Fittingly, the brothers had sought refuge in the temple on All Souls Day. One version of the story tells that they attended an early morning mass before donning cassocks as a disguise. There appears to have been confusion on all sides as it was not until around mid-morning that the brothers were tracked down by a second party despatched by Minh. The confusion was mirrored in the next CIA cable – oddly without a time stamp – which reported that as of 10am the brothers were at the JGS, but other sources were telling that "Diem and Nhu have escaped." In fact, neither report was accurate.

The arrest was made by General Mai Huu Xuan, promoted later that day to Director of the National Police, thereby ensuring that he would not be investigated. Diem, actually, had never trusted Xuan, remarking that he had served in the French Sûreté, and "once in the Sûreté always in the Sûreté."[104] What happened on the journey from the Church of St Xavier to Tan Son Nhut is disputed. An M113 armored personnel carrier (APC) loaded two live brothers and delivered two cadavers. Diem's bloody head had fallen on a saucepan. Nhu had been stabbed 20 times (three times less than Caeser) and shot. The most plausible explanation seems to be that Major Nguyen Van Nhung, traveling in the back of the APC, fell into an argument with Nhu who apparently had recently ordered the execution of a fellow officer. The argument became heated, Nhung went berserk, he stabbed Nhu multiple times with his bayonet, then shot both brothers in the head.

Nhung was the Minh aide who had earlier executed Colonel Tung and had a reputation for violence. Within two months he too would be dead, following a counter-coup, unfortunately eliminating the perpetrator and key witness. Allegations by Don that Minh ordered the murders with a secret finger signal to Nhung are unproven. This more colorful account has to explain how Minh could have possibly known who in the party – which included five officers, including General Xuan – would actually take physical custody of the brothers, or how they would be held, or how they would be transported back to the JGS. It also has to explain why in the first instance, Minh personally drove to Gia Long Palace to take the brothers into custody, not to murder them. Over the course of the night he made repeated attempts to persuade the brothers to leave and personally mediated with Diem. From the available record, in no conversation with Conein did Minh indicate especial antipathy toward the president. Rather, he held that "the three most dangerous men in South Viet-Nam are Ngo Dinh Nhu, Ngo Dinh Can, and Ngo Trong Hieu."[105] He might have added Madame Nhu to the pot. It was the family, rather than the president, that was viewed as the real cancer.

Don's reliability as a witness is at least open to question. In one of only two known images of the dead brothers, Don unwisely allowed himself to be photographed grinning over Nhu's body. If anyone needed to distance himself from the historical guilt it was Don (interestingly, the photograph often appears with Don cropped out).

The testimony of the single American who was party to the coup, Lou Conein, does not hint of a plan to assassinate the brothers but rather offers a picture of confusion. As described, Minh sought American help to exile the brothers. At the time Minh seemed genuinely surprised, although Conein did later aver that he believed Minh had in fact ordered the brothers' execution. The CIA cable of the following day is a masterpiece of conspiracy theories that blossomed within 24 hours of the brothers' deaths. The reality is that the truth will probably never be established.

Back at the JGS all the necessary preparations had been made for a formal abdication declaration in front of the television cameras. When the news filtered through that the brothers were both dead it caused great shock. The corpses were brought back to the JGS and Conein was offered a viewing, which he declined to accept. The bodies were then offered to a Mrs. Dung, a niece of Diem, who in "near hysteria, refused [to] accept [them]."[106] Saigon heard the jolting news that the president and his brother had "committed suicide by poison" and the nation was now in the hands of a military committee (the news was broadcast on Radio Saigon at 10.45am suggesting that the often-quoted time of the assassination – around 10am – may be right). General celebrations broke out and symbols of the previous regime were attacked. The doubtful Harkins reported:

There is strong public support of the armed forces and the new govt those forces have established. The mood of the population is jubilant, by Vietnamese standards rapport between troops and people is excellent; everywhere, people are bringing food to troops.[107]

The fact that the coup had taken place on a national holiday ensured there were "numerous large, spontaneous and enthusiastic demonstrations." Looting was selective and mainly targeted commercial premises associated with the Ngos.

Lodge found himself elevated to the status of national hero, dismissing any notions that the US government could somehow conceal its role in the coup. In turn, he was elated and took the plaudits of the street mobs, describing the coup as a "masterful performance."[108] As far as ordinary Vietnamese were concerned there could be no other explanation – this was a Washington-inspired coup. In a moment of high delusion, Lodge boasted to State:

Experts who have all along been hostile to the coup and who said "win with Diem" now say that this coup means that the war can be drastically shortened. One observer, watching the performance of the ARVN, said if these men can perform like this when their hearts are in it, why isn't it reasonable to believe that they can do equally well against the Viet Cong?[109]

The disbelieving Viet Cong wondered whether it was all a trick. Ho Chi Minh reportedly commented, "I can scarcely believe that the Americans would be so stupid."[110] If there was a lesson to draw from the violent takeover it was that the White House and National Security Council had been completely out of touch with the word on the street. All the secrecy and touchiness of the preceding months had been for nought. There was no secret to keep. After the Pagoda's raid, General Dinh had openly boasted that he had defeated Lodge's coup attempt. Many Vietnamese thought this was why Lodge had been posted to the country – to orchestrate a coup – an impression reinforced by press stories, some of which may have been planted by Hilsman who had "unfortunate tendencies in this direction."[111] American complicity was assumed by all, if not anticipated. Half a world away, in another time zone, Madame Nhu and her daughter Le Thuy learned of the news in the Beverly Wilshire Hotel, the perfect cinematic setting for her public grief.

It seems it had always been the intention of the coup plotters to capture the two men alive and to exile them. From all accounts, this is the most plausible case. In the heat of the moment, capture became assassination and an unresolved blame game implicating Minh, Xuan, and later Thieu. Their brutal murders stripped away the legitimacy of the coup and left Washington in a deeply embarrassing position. The suicide story was plainly a story. Nobody believed that two devout Catholics, captured in a church, would have contemplated suicide. By November 3, the CIA had already been offered photographs of the bloodied brothers and copies were being offered for sale to the highest bidder in the international press. This was not, as Bundy laconically remarked, a "preferred way of committing suicide."[112] The military committee had to come up with a better story, or the truth, but neither would be forthcoming.

Overturning the chess board was easy. Picking up the pieces and starting again proved much harder. In Washington, the news of the murders was received with dismay. Kennedy especially was deeply shocked and spent the rest of the day in a somber mood. He had been woken at 3am when news of the coup broke. Like the dead brothers, he had attended mass to mark All Souls Day. He consequently arrived late at the National Security Council meeting at which Michael Forrestal later announced that the brothers had been assassinated. It was difficult not to draw the conclusion that a US government had been complicit in a dishonorable act, as Nolting later put it. Johnson would always rue the assassination of Diem as America's biggest mistake in the war, and in one important sense he was right. With Diem, South Vietnam stood as a credible, independent nation. Without Diem, South Vietnam became an artificial political entity held together by a clique of generals and

American firepower. For the communists, the demise of the Ngos was proof of the rottenness of the regime. The National Liberation Front reacted with alacrity, issuing a policy statement with eight demands, the majority of which the new government intended to implement anyway. Across the countryside, Viet Cong attacks spiked, an eventuality predicted by MACV.

The hand-wringing in Washington, however, was short-lived. On November 2, Lodge was instructed to inform "GVN [Government of Vietnam], at your discretion, but not earlier than Monday Washington time that US prepared to resume CIP [Commodity Import Program valued at $25 million] … in order to prevent disruption of war effort and economy and avoid hardships on population."[113] In a follow-on telegram, State remembered, almost as an afterthought, "We have impression generals unfamiliar with it [the economy], and may need some guidance" – an understatement of the unpreparedness of the coup plotters to assume the reins of government. The biggest challenge, addressed two days later at a White House meeting, was a barrage of complaints from Latin American countries protesting hypocrisy over US recognition of a government established by coup. Bundy half-jokingly riposted that Saigon had feted the soldiers with garlands of flowers, and that "Latin American generals" would do well to learn the lesson.[114] Ball was less amused, viewing Saigon's top brass as "a flabby coterie … which didn't constitute a government in any real sense."[115]

The fall of Diem diminished rather than increased support for the National Liberation Front. With "American-Diem" dead, a previously united opposition splintered again, in the traditional Vietnamese way. Hanoi recognized this confusion at the 9th Plenum of the Central Committee of the Lao Dong, held later that year in December. Cautious voices argued for a policy of intensified guerrilla warfare and political agitation in the South. Impatient speakers only saw a protracted and inconclusive struggle in a southern "people's war." The real enemy was the armed forces of South Vietnam, and these could only be beaten by the regular forces of North Vietnam. In a mirror image of debates held in

The advance north: French marine infantry in Tonkin, 1888. The European occupation of Indochina was met with native rebellions from the outset. (Public Domain)

Nguyen Ai Quoc in Moscow (1924). Who could have imagined that this modest young man would lead a successful struggle for national liberation? (AFP/Getty Images)

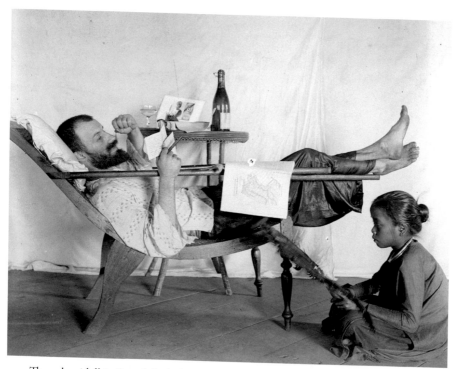

The colon idyll in French Indochina. (Photo by LL/Roger Viollet via Getty Images)

The OSS Deer Mission, 1945: Major Allison Thomas (centre) with his new friends, Ho and Giap. Ho would acquire the codename "Lucius" or, more prosaically, "OSS Agent 19." Thomas dismissed fears of the Viet Minh League: "Forget the Communist Bogey." (Public Domain)

Jean de Lattre de Tassigny drinking with the puppet emperor, Bao Dai. The playboy potentate was more interested in the pleasures of the French Riviera than attending to Indochina's problems. (Bettmann/Getty Images)

Giap and Ho, the improbable double-act that would defeat an American superpower. (Public Domain)

Hanoi, September 2, 1945: an almost invisible Ho Chi Minh declares an independent Vietnamese republic in Ba Dinh Square (actually the roundabout near the Jardin Botanique, opposite the old Citadel). The proclamation was met with "shouts of joy." (Keystone-France/ Gamma-Keystone via Getty Images)

Governor General Georges Thierry D'Argenlieu meeting with General Leclerc (Saigon, 1945). D'Argenlieu did not believe "the yellow man" was ready for self-governance. Leclerc soon realized Vietnamese independence was inevitable. (Keystone-France/Gamma-Keystone via Getty Images)

Head of intelligence and later commissioner Jean Sainteny with Ho Chi Minh (December 1946). The two men are tense after agreeing a ceasefire to end an outbreak of fighting between colonial French troops and the Viet Minh. (Keystone-France/ Gamma-Keystone via Getty Images)

Paris, 1946: Ho Chi Minh is greeted by Georges Bidault. The Vietnamese delegation was cheated at the Fontainebleau negotiations. (Keystone/Hulton Archive/ Getty Images)

It wasn't meant to be this way: the French find themselves in a Vietnam quagmire.
(Public Domain)

"Dien-Bien-Phu Has Fallen" – the headline that stunned the world.
(Bettmann/Getty Images)

La gloire becomes *le grand débâcle*: French prisoners being marched away from Dien Bien Phu, 1954. (Stringer, AFP/Public Domain)

To the victor the spoils: the Vietnam Liberation Army marches into Hanoi, October 1954. (US Army/Public Domain)

General René Cogny bids farewell to French Indochina (1955). "Too many deaths for nothing" he lamented. (STF/AFP/Getty Images)

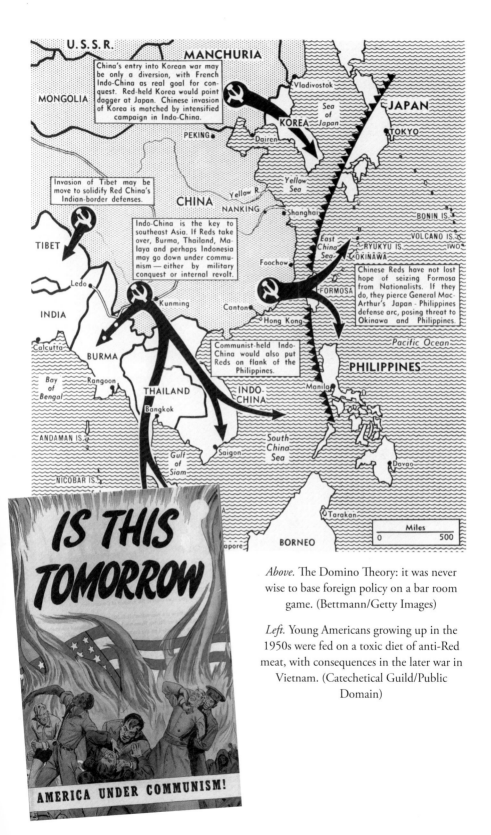

The following text boxes appear on the map:

China's entry into Korean war may be only a diversion, with French Indo-China as real goal for conquest. Red-held Korea would point dagger at Japan. Chinese invasion of Korea is matched by intensified campaign in Indo-China.

Invasion of Tibet may be move to solidify Red China's Indian-border defenses.

Indo-China is the key to southeast Asia. If Reds take over, Burma, Thailand, Malaya and perhaps Indonesia may go down under communism — either by military conquest or internal revolt.

Chinese Reds have not lost hope of seizing Formosa from Nationalists. If they do, they pierce General MacArthur's Japan - Philippines defense arc, posing threat to Okinawa and Philippines.

Communist-held Indo-China would also put Reds on flank of the Philippines.

Above. The Domino Theory: it was never wise to base foreign policy on a bar room game. (Bettmann/Getty Images)

Left. Young Americans growing up in the 1950s were fed on a toxic diet of anti-Red meat, with consequences in the later war in Vietnam. (Catechetical Guild/Public Domain)

The Geneva Conference, 1954, where Vietnam was partitioned.
(ATP/RDB/ullstein bild via Getty Images)

The miracle of Diem: Dwight D. Eisenhower and Secretary of State John Foster Dulles greet
South Vietnam's savior from communism. President Ngo Dinh Diem in Washington, 1957.
(PhotoQuest/Getty Images)

The new president meets the new defense secretary – John F. Kennedy and Robert
McNamara get to know each other. (NARA/Public Domain)

Vienna, 1961 – Nikita Khrushchev and John F. Kennedy agree not to pull
on the rope. (John F. Kennedy Library/Public Domain)

General Graves B. Erskine, the first US general dispatched to Vietnam. A World War I and Iwo Jima veteran, he would also be the first in a long line of American generals urging aggression to defeat the communists. (USMC/Public Domain)

General John "Iron Mike" O'Daniel, commander of the Military Advisory Group Vietnam (MAAG) following the French withdrawal. The Anzio veteran was an enthusiast for the mission, against the more sober assessments of the Joint Chiefs. (US Army/Public Domain)

General J. Lawton "Lightnin' Joe" Collins, shown here in 1944 as the US Army's youngest corps commander in World War II. He advised Eisenhower to get out of South Vietnam, but was forced to reverse position when it became apparent that Washington favored supporting Saigon. (MPI/Getty Images)

Colonel Edward Geary Lansdale was despatched to Saigon as a counter-guerrilla expert with a high reputation. He gained the confidence of Diem, but left believing that the South Vietnamese president was more suited to the life of a monk. (USAF/Public Domain)

Lieutenant General Lionel "Stonehead" McGarr (Commander MAAG, 1960–62). "Our objective must be to find, fix, fight and finish the enemy!" He achieved none of these. (US Army/Public Domain)

Neil Sheehan behind his Underwood typewriter (Saigon, 1963). The war witnessed the emergence of a new breed of *"journaliste engagé"* who questioned the official narrative of a war being won. (Bettmann/Getty Images)

Maxwell Taylor is greeted by Diem on a 1961 fact-finding mission. Ambassador "Fritz" Nolting is to his right. Taylor would return as ambassador after Diem's murder. (Hank Walker/The LIFE Picture Collection via Getty Images)

Smiling for the cameras – Taylor, McNamara and Kennedy discuss the unraveling situation in South Vietnam. (Bettmann/Getty Images)

By the early 1960s Saigon had become the scene of frequent VC terrorist attacks. (Bettmann/Getty Images)

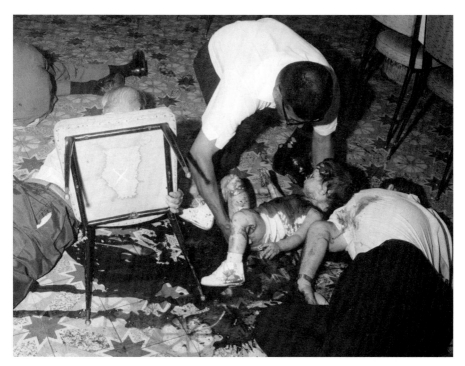

The My Canh restaurant bombing (June 24, 1965). The event caused great public shock. Defiantly, the restaurant opened five days later. (Bettmann/Getty Images)

The MAAG believed that with American advisors and helicopters the tide of the war would turn in South Vietnam's favor. (Larry Burrows/The LIFE Picture Collection via Getty Images)

Not pleased to meet you: Diem and his nemesis Henry Cabot Lodge, Jr. (Larry Burrows/The LIFE Picture Collection via Getty Images)

Roger Hilsman, forever lumbered with the historical millstone of "the Hilsman cable." (Adams/Fairfax Media via Getty Images)

Death of a president: Kennedy lies in state in the White House. (Abbie Rowe. White House Photographs. John F. Kennedy Presidential Library and Museum, Boston)

Lyndon B. Johnson takes the oath of office two hours after Kennedy's assassination. (Public Domain)

DD-731 USS *Maddox*: Johnson reportedly joked "those dumb sailors were just shooting at flying fish." (US Navy/Public Domain)

Viet Cong mortar attack against Bien Hoa Air Base, November 1, 1964. Twenty-seven out of 30 newly arrived B-57s were damaged or destroyed, incensing the Joint Chiefs, who argued for strong retaliation. Johnson demurred so close to an election.
(USAF/Public Domain)

The Brinks BOQ bombing in Saigon, December 24, 1964; a cynical assault on the eve of Christmas. (USAF/Public Domain)

The attack on the US base in Pleiku on February 7, 1965 shocked Washington. A visiting McGeorge Bundy wrote his "time is against us" memo, raising the stakes for intervention. At the same he warned that Americans should know "at its very best the struggle in Vietnam will be long." (Bettmann/Getty Images)

Thanks to the influx of Chinese weapons, the Viet Cong became less local defense groups and more an organized and well-equipped national force.
(Three Lions/Hulton Archive/Getty Images)

Previous Pages. The People's Army on parade (Hanoi, 1964). By the following year many of these soldiers would be marching south. (ADN-Bildarchiv/ullstein bild via Getty Images)

Washington was placing its hopes on the ARVN soldier – but would he fight, and how hard? (David Hume Kennerly/Bettmann/Corbis via Getty Images)

Above. LBJ squares up to Senator Richard Russell, Chairman of the all-powerful Senate Armed Services Committee. Russell told Johnson that Washington's Vietnam commitment was "the damned worst mess I ever saw." (LBJ Library/Public Domain)

Right. Johnson weighs the counsel of Chairman of the Joint Chiefs, General Earle Wheeler. The general was a mathematics graduate but his numbers never stacked up. (LBJ Library/Public Domain)

They're coming down the Ho Chi Minh Trail. McNamara attempts to explain to a skeptical press the administration's strategy of graduated reprisals, April 1965. (Library of Congress)

An awkward triangle: Johnson and McNamara overshadowed by a bust of Kennedy. What would the deceased president have done? (LBJ Library/Public Domain)

Brainy McGeorge Bundy, National Security Advisor to Kennedy and Johnson, and the architect of a gradualist approach that ultimately failed. (LBJ Library/Public Domain)

The patriotically named Walt Whitman Rostow, special assistant to two presidents and a "big bomber man." (Ralph Morse/The LIFE Picture Collection via Getty Images)

Johnson and Rusk: two Southerners swimming with Yankee sharks. (LBJ Library/Public Domain)

Under Secretary of State George Ball. "You're crazier than hell" Kennedy once said. In fact, he was just right and eventually resigned. (LBJ Library/Public Domain)

The guy with the Sta-Comb hair: McNamara in a contemplative mood in an August 1965 cabinet meeting. Three weeks earlier, Johnson had made his fateful decision to commit to the ground war. (LBJ Library/Public Domain)

Rolling Thunder – Johnson sends in the bombers, timidly. (NARA)

Left. McNamara justifies the *Rolling Thunder* bombing targets to a hostile press. (Marion S. Trikosko/ PhotoQuest/Getty Images)

These pages. USS *Ticonderoga* takes underway replenishment from USS *Ashtabula*, the sharp edge of US 7th Fleet (US Navy/Public Domain)

Arc Light: twenty-eight Guam-based B-52s drop 540 tons of bombs on "War Zone D," 30 miles northwest of Saigon (July 29, 1965). This was an equivalent tonnage to the infamous November 14, 1940 Luftwaffe bombing raid against the English city of Coventry. (STF/AFP/Getty Images)

An F-5 Tiger releases its bomb loads on suspected VC positions (Bettmann/Getty Images)

Above. Got it. A McDonnell F-101 Voodoo casts its shadow over the missing spans of the My Dug Highway bridge. The difficulty of destroying bridges in an era without precision bombs should not be underestimated. (Central Press/Getty Images)

Right. Several hundred pilots would eventually suffer a similar unlucky fate to this one. This pilot was Lieutenant Gerald Santo Venanzi. (Bettmann/Getty Images)

Above. What every pilot feared – Hanoi's "flying telegraph poles," the Russian-supplied SA-2 SAMs. (Bettmann/ Getty Images)

Left. Gun camera from an F-105 Thunderchief captures the moment a burst of 20mm cannon fire strikes the left wing of a fleeing MiG-17. The MIGs were more nimble than the "Thuds"; so this scenario would not have been common. (Bettmann/Getty Images)

Lieutenant Everett Alvarez, the first pilot shot down over North Vietnam. He would eventually spend eight years in captivity. This photograph was from a 1967 Soviet propaganda piece. (Bettmann/Getty Images)

The US Army arrived in South Vietnam with a doctrine of air mobility. Was this the ace of spades, or a forlorn hope in a failing war? (Bettman/Getty Images)

The decision to commit boots on the ground inevitably implied a roll call of dead. Here a trooper from 1/7 Cavalry lies dead following fierce fighting in the Plei Me area. He had only been in-country a matter of weeks. (Bettmann/Getty Images)

Westmoreland arrives and Vietnam gets a new general for the new war.
(Co Rentmeester/The LIFE Picture Collection via Getty Images)

Washington over the fear of a Chinese intervention, Hanoi fretted over the possibility of an American intervention. The calculus remained unresolved: it was not until October of the following year that the first northern army unit began the long march down the Ho Chi Minh trail, beating a path for the hundreds of thousands who would later follow.[116] Far from emboldening Hanoi, Diem's death only served to sow dissent.

Following tense negotiations between the generals and former Diemists, an official radio announcement was finally made on November 6 to Saigon's restless citizenry. The 1956 Constitution was suspended. The country would now be governed by a joint Civilian-Military Revolutionary Council. Vice President Tho was appointed Prime Minister but all the key posts went to the coup plotters. Minh assumed the presidency with Don and Dinh taking the key portfolios of Defense and Security respectively. Apart from Tho, not one of the 15 nominated members of the council had any experience of government. This had the important effect of increasing the government's dependency on Washington: Foreign Minister Pham Deng Lam's first act was to seek advice from Lodge on how he should execute his job. As a reward to the officers who had backed the coup, an Executive Committee was established comprising nine generals, chaired by Minh, Don, and Dinh. This inevitably laid the seeds for further power struggles. Who really was in charge: the council, with its handful of inexperienced civilians, or the committee of generals? Minh's patronage was dangerous in other ways. Experienced corps and divisional commanders lost their jobs to novices. Self-important personalities were overlooked – where was General Nguyen Khanh, the II Corps commander, in the new order? – skulking, hurt, and planning a counter-coup. The generals assured Lodge they would serve in a six-month provisional government, but failed to even reach this milestone.

On the American side, a grand conference was scheduled on November 20 in Honolulu, attended by all the significant players: Rusk, McNamara, Bundy, Taylor, and a Saigon delegation led by Lodge. It met in a mixed mood. There was relief that the coup had been successful, notwithstanding the regretful murder of the Ngos.

This was tempered by a growing acceptance that war reporting over the last half year had been significantly inaccurate if not falsified. Far from winning, all the indicators suggested that the Viet Cong were in the ascendancy and had been for many months. This knowledge was somewhat underplayed by Lodge as well as Harkins. The focus of the conference was perversely on South Vietnam's precarious economic situation when it should have been on the generals. Voices that warned of ensuing chaos had been prescient. Washington was placing her trust in a group of men whose entire lives had involved fighting, double-crossing, and the switching of allegiances. The CIA's own secret "Cast of Characters in South Vietnam" was an exhausting 14-page-long roll call of schemers, opportunists, and criminals, as well as the odd idealist.[117] Why did anyone imagine that some good would come from this lot?

All through that frantic summer and fall, events had played out at an accelerated pace. Then, in Dallas, Texas, on the morning of November 22, it seemed the world's clocks were stopped. It took one bullet in the back of Kennedy's head to end the music. The score remained unfinished, ending on a discordant note. He looked so startled in the autopsy photographs, so unprepared to quit. Ted Sorenson lamented, "How could you leave us, how could you die? We are sheep without a shepherd when the snow shuts out the sky."

The 88th Congress had sat longer than almost any other peacetime session, and had stalled virtually all legislation proposed by Kennedy. Taxes and labor reform laws had been high on the agenda but all faced impasses. Much was made at the time of the senior house becoming a clearing house for pork barrel politics; a sour note to end an idealistic presidency. In the summer, America had been shocked by the murder of Mississippi civil rights activist Medgar Evers, a foretaste of battles ahead in the Johnson presidency. Barry Goldwater, son of a Jewish retailer née Goldwasser, had just begun his ambitious ascendancy to the leadership of the Republican Party. Rival Governor Rockefeller reckoned he belonged to the "radical right lunatic fringe" but many were attracted by this individualist from Arizona. Was Goldwater the Grand Old Party's antidote to Camelot? Perhaps he was, but as much as anyone on Capitol Hill, Goldwater was devastated by Kennedy's assassination, an ideological enemy, but a man whom he respected and with whom he had shared some rapport.

Five American climbers reached the top of Everest in the year that Kennedy died, a multi-billion-dollar oceanography program was underway, and an Air Force pilot called Neil Armstrong was practicing simulated landings on a craft designed to land on the moon. Always obsessed with extreme fitness, many Americans were emulating these heroes by adopting the bestselling XBX Royal Canadian Air Force Exercise program, a 12-minute-a-day regime designed to tone your body to a peak of vitality. Kennedy lost his life just as the secret of life – the mysteries of Deoxyribonucleic Acid (DNA) – were being uncovered by a Dr. James Watson at Harvard and Dr. Francis Crick at Cambridge.

There were three funerals: Kennedy's, Police Officer J.D. Tippit's, shot dead by Lee Harvey Oswald, and the assassin's. Perhaps a quarter of a million people filed past Kennedy's catafalque in a queue that stretched eight abreast for 40 blocks. Around 400 mourners attended Tippit's memorial service at the Beckley Hills Baptist Church in Dallas, which took place one hour after Kennedy's casket was lowered into the ground at Arlington Cemetery. Just up the road from Tippit's funeral, Lee Harvey Oswald was also laid to rest in Rose Hill Cemetery at Fort Worth. There were five mourners: his mother, brother, Russian wife, and two children. The FBI had to pay for the $500 funeral costs and seven reporters acted as the pall bearers. No minister could be found to give the last rites, but eventually a Reverend Mr. Saunders who had been retired for eight years volunteered to undertake the duty (on the locally patriotic grounds that no man from Fort Worth should go to his maker without the intercession of a minister). Oswald's plain coffin was laid in a 2,700-pound steel reinforced vault; no chances would be taken with grave diggers. Marina, who barely spoke English, sobbed inconsolably. Voyeurs strained to watch the simple ceremony through the cordon of policemen. In a merciful tone the Reverend Saunders quoted John, Chapter 14: "In my Father's house there are many mansions." When it was all over, a bulldozer piled earth over the grave, a mortuary antithesis to the eternal flame lit over Kennedy's grave.

Kennedy's assassination bequeathed an awful and iconic album of images – dominated by the widow dolorosa, Jacqueline Bouvier Kennedy. Jackie crawling over the boot of the car trying to retrieve a piece of her husband's skull, observed by an out-of-focus family standing on the grassy knoll. Jackie emerging on the hospital steps in Dallas, still dressed in a bloodied navy and pink Chanel suit, her hand held tightly by Bobby. She remained by the side of the hearse all the way to Bethesda Naval Hospital in Washington, unwilling to let go. Jackie, who organized the details of the funeral and requested that a Green Beret be part of the honor guard, remembering her husband's special respect for this unit. Jackie in a black lace mantilla, following Black Jack the horse with reversed boots in the stirrups, all the way to St Matthew's Cathedral, illumed by a blinding, winter sunlight. It was a strangely noisy affair with the lament of the Black Watch pipes, the clatter of horse hooves, and the funeral drums sounding at 100 beats a minute. The reading was from the third chapter of Ecclesiastes: "There is an appointed time for everything ... a time to be born and a time to die ... a time to love and a time to hate; a time of war and a time of peace." "Pie Jesu" was sung – Pious Lord Jesu, Give them everlasting rest. John Kennedy Jr. provided the poignant shot, saluting his father's coffin. More than 220 foreign leaders attended the state funeral; an unprecedented show of international grief. An entire nation stopped for five minutes: pedestrians, cars, boats, and planes. Had Kennedy any idea what he had represented to so many people before he died?

Chapter 4

MOPPING THE FLOOR, NOVEMBER 1963–JULY 1964

Who was Lyndon Baines Johnson? His elevation to the presidency was violent and unplanned, but he was not an accidental president. Johnson was the beaten, rival presidential candidate, a president-in-waiting who then got a second chance, and the distinction is important. He did not assume the executive office as caretaker of the Kennedy flame. He arrived consumed with his own ideas. This is why the transition between the two presidencies was not just violent but absolute. That he privately detested the East Coast Kennedy set, and they in turn looked down on him, only served to stretch the two presidencies further apart. Once on the stage, his persona grew in proportion to the play then outgrew the lines. In his ambitions, appetites, and antagonisms he was Shakespearean. Like a protagonist from the Roman tragedies it seems he was always destined to be with himself at war, and fail the honorable man.

When he assumed the presidency he had already served 32 years in Congress – an exceedingly long stretch. But he was not well known nationally, and most descriptions fell back on the clichés of a folksy, persuasive, and determined senator who was artful in manipulating the business of the House behind the scenes. Before his rise to power he was best known for his emotional nature, the mood swings, temper, and generosity – and only later did he become more controlled and disciplined – but the emotion never went away. Above all, he was ambitious. A confidante who had known the family for decades remarked: "He wants it all ... he doesn't want the history books to say he was as good as Lincoln: he wants them to say he was better."[1]

The sudden succession implied a necessary continuity with Kennedy programs and staffs, but some new faces appeared, including New Dealers who first entered politics with Johnson during the Roosevelt presidency. Johnson would greatly value and depend on the confidences of these insiders: Clark Clifford, a Washington Attorney; Abe Fortas, another lawyer and civil rights activist; the veteran "Tommy the Cork" Corcoran who had worked the Washington circuit for the last three decades; and James Rowe, a law clerk and personal friend. Crucially, both Rusk and McNamara were quickly confirmed as the two pillars of the new cabinet.

Johnson set as his first priorities unlocking the impasses in Congress – Senator Byrd was still holding up the tax bill and Judge Smith a civil rights bill – as well as managing "as frugal as possible" federal government budgets. "LBJ" on the domestic front would be everybody's friend (or so he believed), who would square federal spending with a circle of harmonious relations between business, labor, and the vested interests of Congress.

He also had to tackle the problem of racial discrimination. This was not just a shameful and unresolved domestic wound. The southern states supplied a majority of America's officer class as well as a "Negro" underclass that filled the ranks of private soldiers. Senator Allen Ellender (Democrat, Louisiana), a bespectacled man of Nordic appearance, held that racial apartheid was the biblically ordained, natural order for mankind. His brand of white supremacy was completely unabashed: "I am not against the Negro. But you have got to live among them to know them. They're different. Even the Bible shows that. They're not dependable as a race. They're like a sheep you know."[2] Others like James Eastland (Democrat, Mississippi), could not understand why "Negroes" complained as he employed many of them on his cotton plantation. "I know of no economic discrimination in my state," he asserted. "On our family cotton plantation – we have the biggest compress in the county – I employ all Negroes." If the bill passed, he demanded of the Senate, "Am I gonna have to employ whites? Who ever heard of cotton-pickin' whites?"

Others argued the bill would turn the social order upside down (Russell); that "Negroes" in America earned more than the average Russian (Talmadge); that equal rights would lead to the sexual mingling of the races (a horrified McClellan); and that the bill represented an erosion of liberty and violated the constitution. Johnson squeaked through his Civil Rights Bill, but rather than end protest, it would become the engine of more discord.

Against this panorama of domestic programs, defense was not a priority. Within a week of assuming the presidency, Johnson sent a personal letter to 7,500 defense contractors urging them to constrain costs. If anyone was betting at the start of the Johnson presidency, they would have wagered on a cautious president, keen to support McNamara in his campaign to rationalize and reform an over-bloated military, and even keener to avoid entanglement in a war in Southeast Asia. Nobody at the beginning of 1964 would have predicted increased defense spending, not even the most optimistic staffs in the Pentagon. Johnson entered the Oval Office just as two anti-war films were stirring debate across America, making war seem unfashionable if not risible: *The Victors*, set in the Second World War, that questioned whether there were really any victors in war (it included a memorable scene where an American and Russian soldier pointlessly stab each other to death over the right to walk first over a plank crossing a ditch in Berlin); and *Dr. Strangelove or: How I Learned to Stop Worrying and Love The Bomb*, the ultimate Cold War film that starred Peter Sellers and portrayed a deranged, priapic, trigger-happy Pentagon. Johnson may have laughed at the Stetson-waving Major "King" Kong riding an atomic bomb to its target.

Such conjecture would have been premature. On the domestic front Johnson was a man of absolute and visionary certainties. On matters of war he was a man wracked with crippling doubts, especially over America's commitment to Southeast Asia. At the November 20 Honolulu Conference, William Bundy had detected the stench of a war turning putrid.[3] This malodorous vapour reached the nostrils of the dauphin Johnson, and he was never really able to rid himself of its aftertaste. Within a short period, the whole business of Vietnam would be cast in the language of terminal illness: "a minor irritant" multiplying into a "disease" and "cancer."[4] In the very first days of his presidency Johnson told Lodge that he was not about to be the first president to lose a war.[5] The pledge proved weak.

On November 26, four days after the trauma of Kennedy's assassination, NSAM 273 was promulgated, essentially re-stating a continuation of the deceased President's policy and substantially based on a William Bundy memorandum, but with more emphasis on the Mekong Delta. In Bundy's recollection:

> The keynote of [the] memorandum I drafted, and that was approved by Secretary McNamara and I think by Secretary Rusk, was that, in the face of the much more serious situation as we now perceived it, it was terribly important to pull together the American side of the operation in Saigon and to get the Vietnamese working much more effectively.[6]

The admission of a deteriorating situation in the Delta was a rare mea culpa. At the height of the Buddhist crisis, David Halberstam had penned an article for the *New York Times* describing a Delta in the hands of the Viet Cong and MACV in denial.[7] The article provoked a storm. A pedantic, official refutation took each of the 13 charges made by Halberstam, and "proved" them wrong with a barrage of statistics.[8] Halberstam was of course right. Ap Bac had created the first rift, but it was the Delta reporting that widened the gap between the press corps and MACV which eventually became the irreconcilable "credibility gap."

But something more profound was also happening, beyond a simple conflict between journalistic honesty and government propaganda. Intuition was trumping numbers. Individual human judgment was beating, or at least challenging, an army of systems analysts. This was essentially a philosophical problem. In a passage of arresting wisdom, an anonymous author of the Pentagon Papers later summarized the puzzle facing policymakers:

> Only upon the basis of interpretations (judgments) of the importance, meaning and relevance of things could policy be made. And that judgment or interpretation was seldom or never inescapably inherent in the measurable, sharply definable, completely unarguable concrete detail. It might be derived from or directly reflect such data, but its form would be determined equally, or even more, from the perspective in which it was viewed. And this perspective was comprised of the whole context of incompletely described, not fully identified values, and imperfectly described priorities, that determined the weight and place given to the factual detail in the mysterious calculus of the decision-maker. If this were not the case, any bright college boy given the same set of "facts" would inevitably derive from them the same judgements of what national policy should be, as the canniest, most generally knowledgeable and experienced veteran.[9]

As a rebuke to the Pentagon's obsession with a statistical approach to warfare – evident to this day in recent wars in Iraq and Afghanistan – this was irresistible acumen.

Faced with "the mysterious calculus of the decision-maker," Johnson very quickly reduced the problem of South Vietnam to a binary choice, and convinced himself that whichever option he chose, he would be damned. At dinner with Special Assistant Bill Moyers, Johnson confessed: "I have this terrible feeling of something that's grabbed me around the ankles ... and won't let go."[10] This foredoomed conviction developed many angles, but however many times he played with its edges and lines, Johnson always returned to the same axiom: either he had to get out, or get in. Complicating this geometry were a host of fears, many inflated and self-inflicted, that seemed to cripple the President when he turned his thoughts to Vietnam. Not least was the sense of insecurity that came with the accidental usurpation of the crown.

Long before Nixon's epic paranoia over potential adversaries, a distrustful Johnson "had that goddamned sewer J. Edgar Hoover [the FBI's controversial director for 37 years from 1935 to 1972] flowing across his desk all through those five years" feeding him tidbits of gossip.[11]

Johnson inherited Kennedy's cabinet, Kennedy's Joint Chiefs, and Kennedy's National Security Council. He was the Texas cornpone faced with a battery of East Coast smoothies. This engendered the haunting question: "Do they think I'm as tough? Or as moderate? Or as bright? Or as tenacious? Or as charming? Or as effective? Or as bold? Or as gracious?" How would influential columnists like Joe Kraft, Joe Alsop, and Walter Lippmann portray him?[12] As a "tough" President? Or weakling? When Johnson instructed his staffs, "No man among you should go to bed at night without asking himself whether he had done everything possible to make the policy work," he was really talking to and about himself. Sleeplessness became a feature of the Johnson presidency, and an unhelpful one at that.

Yet why couldn't Johnson "get out" at the beginning of 1964? George Ball recalled, "They [government officials] would only ask one question, which was how? How can we prevail? They would never ask the question why?"[13] But the same George Ball also argued:

> I think it would have been terribly difficult for him to have disengaged immediately, because it would look as though he were repudiating the policy of Kennedy. I think that this is something which would have been almost impossible for him to do. At that time there was no particular opposition to the war amongst the public. I think he would have been subject to all kinds of attack – that the moment he gets in, he turns his back on the policy of President Kennedy and gives something to the communists.[14]

But setting aside the anesthetizing domino theory and arguments over loss of American prestige – two wide obstacles to lucid thought – was there a better period for Washington to liquidate her assets in South Vietnam than when Johnson unexpectedly assumed power? The opportunity for a clear break with the policies of Eisenhower and Kennedy – neither of whom had been enthusiastic over Vietnam anyway – was there. Most senators were disinterested at best and deeply skeptical at worst over America's involvement in an "itty-bitty" country that many could barely place on a map. Rusk, McNamara, and McGeorge Bundy were "all in great despair over what was happening ... in Vietnam."[15] Johnson himself "was seized with an intense intuition that a very dangerous moment had arrived in the history of our relations with Vietnam and our commitments in Southeast Asia."[16] Nobody, not even the Joint Chiefs, really wanted to be there.

A growing suspicion that the war in South Vietnam had been unraveling for many months was thrown into sharp relief by a USOM (United States Operations Mission) report less than one month into the Johnson presidency, describing Long An Province, south of Saigon, as being overrun by Viet Cong.[17] The Strategic Hamlets Program had been intimately linked to Nhu. It was always likely that his death would sound a death knell for the strategy, but its demise was met with frustration and even denial.

USOM at the time had 77 field representatives in 45 districts.[18] This cohort bred idealists like Rob Warne, a bespectacled Princeton graduate with a warm smile and inexhaustible good will. Warne was based in Vinh Binh, in the Mekong Delta, with his dutiful 24-year-old wife Susie and an infant daughter. Susie taught at a school. Once a month they were flown to Saigon (road travel was too dangerous) to escape the primitive conditions of a village where the only other Americans were soldiers. Warne's "patch" was enormous: he was nominally responsible for 1,000 square miles and hundreds of hamlets. In Vinh Binh it was estimated that 375 were on the government side, but this number fell to 274 over the course of his tour. Undaunted by the challenge, he personally oversaw the construction of a school, clinic, and 50 homes in a hamlet called My Long. The intent was to resettle 1,000 refugees, but few if any were voluntary settlers. Gradually, he observed this village wither and his charges slip back into the jungle. By the time he left, two thirds of the houses were abandoned and only 292 refugees remained. Province-wide, Warne used USOM funds to build 18 bridges, eight clinics, six markets, and over 100 classrooms; all to no avail – the province was backsliding, and so he honestly reported it.[19]

Kennedy had inherited Eisenhower's Counter-Insurgency Plan (CIP), the fruit of many months of planning and calculation. Johnson inherited an unraveling plan and many doubts. Faced with this worsening prognosis, typified by the USOM report, Johnson turned to his defense secretary. At the time, McNamara was attending a NATO conference in Europe. On his return to Washington he was diverted via Saigon and tasked to undertake a second fact-finding mission in as many months. The defense secretary spent just two days in-country (compared to ten days in the previous visit) but that was long enough. In a total volte-face to the assessment delivered in October, McNamara flew home four days before Christmas and reported to Johnson that a communist victory appeared likely "within two or three months" unless Washington added more "muscle to the fight."[20]

The detail of his report was disturbing. The Lodge-Harkins relationship was dysfunctional (it would only last another six months). The defunct Strategic Hamlets Program should be replaced by a new pacification plan. The Delta was fast becoming "injun country," a virtual no-go area for security forces with 13 districts rated as "critical." The proposed withdrawal of 1,000 US troops should be reversed; more soldiers and more civilians were needed to support the shaky Revolutionary Military Council.

However, the only decisive outcome of this report was the creation of a separate special force command – the MACSOG (Military Assistance Command Special Operations Group) – formally established on January 24, in the New Year. Krulak, in his capacity as Special Assistant for Counterinsurgency and Special Activities, was offered the command. MACSOG duly gave birth to OPLAN 34-A, the first of a three-phase ramping up of covert operations that would have profound consequences in the fall.

The fecundity of the MACSOG planners was exhausting. In total, some 2,062 possible operations were deliberated, yet in its beginnings OPLAN 34-A remained very modest: just more U-2 flights, more electronic reconnaissance, and 18 sabotage missions, all approved by Johnson. However modest the program, it was evident that "a firebreak had been crossed."[21] Washington was purposefully instigating hostile actions against North Vietnam and the ineffectiveness of these would only serve to reinforce arguments that more should be done. Military chiefs as much as warned of this eventuality: in a covering letter, CINCPAC expressed reservations over the chances of success and argued that only the serious punishment of air attack would force Hanoi's hand.[22] This skepticism was echoed by an inter-agency committee that reviewed OPLAN 34-A and drew the conclusion that "it was far from clear whether even the successful conduct of the operations ... would induce Hanoi's leaders to cease and desist."[23] OPLAN 34-A thus was not born from conviction but doubts. Nobody seemed to believe that a strategy of limited covert operations would work, but equally, nobody was offering a better idea short of what was still judged an unconscionable bombing of the North.

When Washington returned to work after the Yule festivities the cautious optimism of the previous year had been entirely replaced by doom and gloom. On New Year's Day, Lodge sycophantically penned a long missive:

> We are also now just beginning to see the full extent of the dry rot and lassitude in the Government of Viet-Nam and the extent to which we were given inaccurate information. It is also true that praise is due to President Kennedy for his decision to make changes in U.S. policy and personnel without which the trend of last summer and autumn would have rocketed on to certain

catastrophe. I am free to say this because, although I agreed with them, I did not make the policies; I carried them out.

I am happy to read your dismissal of the suggestions that because we belong to different parties, there may be some political tension between us. To me, knowing you, your intelligence, and your broad patriotic outlook so well, and also knowing myself, such a suggestion is fantastic. You are everlastingly right that we are involved in this problem together and I am glad to see it that way.

You can indeed rely on me: to leave no stone unturned; always to keep you thoroughly informed; to make all recommendations to you which I think will lead to victory; and to carry out all your instructions with complete energy and loyalty.

Two events then turned January into a very dark month indeed. On January 22, the Joint Chiefs finally replied to NSAM 273 of the previous November. In a ten-point plan, the military chiefs essentially told the President: take over the war or lose it. Across the road, a belligerent Curtis LeMay was advising a committee of the House of Representatives, "We are swatting flies instead of going after the manure pile." If this counsel was sticking in Johnson's throat, what followed in the succeeding week was indigestible. On January 28, the slighted General Nguyen Khanh confided with his US Army advisor, Colonel Jasper Wilson, that Generals Don, Xuan, and his brother-in-law Kim, were plotting a "neutralist" coup to oust the ineffective Minh. Wilson duly informed MACV and Lodge, who harbored suspicions.

In truth, Khanh was preparing to launch his own coup. Unlike the November coup, Washington was at least spared the ordeal of long hours locked in tense meetings. On January 30, Khanh struck and ousted the Military Revolutionary Committee (on the spurious grounds that Diem's assassins had been conspiring with the French to cut a deal with Hanoi). The coup almost fell at the first hurdle when General Kim forgot to set his alarm clock, but in the event there was no resistance. After recovering from the shock of being wrong-footed, the State Department tacitly approved of this removal of blood-soaked hands from the helm of the nation. Embarrassing questions of CIA complicity might at last go away. It also helped that US Army officers rather warmed to Khanh: in contrast to the soft-handed cabal in Saigon, Khanh was a 36-year-old field officer who chewed cigars, got drunk, and "kicked ass." He was their kind of officer and just the man needed to revitalize the war against the Viet Cong. Not wishing to test McNamara's stamina in another fact-finding mission, Bobby Kennedy was despatched on a Far East tour. Vietnam was avoided. Instead, the Attorney General visited Japan, South Korea, Indonesia, Malaysia, and the Philippines. On American network channels, these events barely raised any interest: The Beatles had just notched the biggest television audience in history on the *Ed Sullivan Show*.

February brought little cheer. A raft of reports landed on Johnson's desk and all were bad.[24] An almost herd-like stampede seemed to overtake the authors. Only two months previously Taylor had judged the war would be largely finished in 1964. Now, Johnson was being advised that South Vietnam would probably be lost. On February 3, in a fit of pessimism, Johnson rang an old friend and newspaper editor, John Knight, a typical recourse when the President needed solace. What options did he have, he complained: "One is run and let the dominoes start falling over, and God almighty, what they said about us leaving China will just be a warming up ... so it really boils down to one of two decisions, getting out or getting in."[25] The "loss" of China had created "a paranoia" in the Democrat Party that no amount of therapy could cure.[26] Already, Johnson felt caught between a Scylla and Charybdis: either hit the rock, "get out" and sink his presidency, or "get in" and enter the whirlpool of an unwinnable war.

In fact, Johnson's self-pitying sense of a hopeless binary choice went back to his visit to Saigon in May 1961, when he was despatched by Kennedy to reassure Southeast Asian leaders following the "neutralization" of Laos. On his return he wrote:

The fundamental decision required of the United States ... is whether we are to attempt to meet the challenge of Communist expansion now in Southeast Asia by a major effort in support of the forces of freedom in the area or throw in the towel.[27]

The problem with this melodrama was that it offered a false choice. A President Johnson, unlike his predecessor who may have taken a more nuanced path, was never going to throw in towels.

The comparison with China had been provoked by the January 6 so-called Mansfield memorandum on Vietnam, agitating against deeper American involvement, much as he had done with Kennedy, and warning, "we are close to the point of no return on Viet Nam." Responding to a disconcerted Johnson, on January 9, McGeorge Bundy professorially wrote:

> On Monday you asked for short comments by Rusk, McNamara, and myself on Senator Mansfield's memorandum on Vietnam … The political damage to Truman and Acheson from the fall of China arose because most Americans came to believe that we could and should have done more than we did to prevent it. This is exactly what would happen now if we should seem to be the first to quit in Saigon.

If Bundy was advising Johnson to stay the course, McNamara's response would not have helped to assuage Johnson's concerns either. While emphasizing the Kennedy-era mantra that "the war is essentially a Vietnamese responsibility" (and reminding that 1,000 troops were being withdrawn), the defense secretary then articulated at length a hyperbolic exposition of the domino theory concluding, "My assessment of our important security interests is that they unquestionably call for holding the line against further Communist gains." With his two brightest counsellors advising Johnson to stand firm, what could he do?

Three weeks after speaking to Knight, on February 24, he telephoned McNamara repeating back the arguments of the domino theory, but highlighting the fear of getting bogged down in a major war: "We could send our Marines in there and we could get tied down in a Third World War, or another Korean action."[28]

The possibility of a third option, a Laos-style "neutralization," seemed totally impractical. He agreed with McNamara that training the South Vietnamese to fight their own war was "the best alternative," but Johnson was too realistic not to appreciate that this policy, Kennedy's exit ticket, to date, had failed, notwithstanding the steady drip of positive reporting from Saigon.

On the same day that he shared these thoughts with McNamara, Johnson secretly telephoned Senator Fulbright, Chairman of the Foreign Affairs Committee, and offered another downbeat appreciation of the situation.[29] If he got out, all of Southeast Asia would be imperilled. If South Vietnam were "neutralized," Hanoi would walk in the very next day. If he got in and sent the marines, America would get bogged down in a long war. Or, he could continue with the present policy of limited military and economic assistance, the policy he intended to pursue. But what if it failed? Then he would be back to the old dilemma: get out or get in. He urged Fulbright to do some "heavy thinking," almost in desperation.

If these were the intractable emotions of the calculus, what were the facts? When Johnson needed the facts, he turned to Robert McNamara. It was a measure of the thrall in which the administration was held by the figure of McNamara that Johnson reacted to the pessimistic intelligence by instructing his defense secretary, now accompanied by Taylor, to undertake a third fact-finding mission. In a March 4 memo of a conversation between the Joint Chiefs and Johnson, Taylor noted astutely, "he [Johnson] does not want to lose South Vietnam before next November nor does he want to get the country into war." The bypassing of Rusk and the State Department was indicative and damaging. South Vietnam was viewed first as a military problem – a war that had to be won – and not a political problem, which was left hanging and without resolution. The militarization which Hilsman feared, and which would lead to his resignation on March 14, 1964, the first casualty of the post-Kennedy era, was established in the first months of the Johnson presidency (according to Ball, he fired Hilsman because he wearied of his "omniscience"; Rusk later joked, "would you do a great favor for me? Would you let me say that I fired him?").[30]

The McNamara-Taylor visit of March 8 took place against the backdrop of the Joint Chiefs openly calling for the bombing of North Vietnam.[31] This would have been unthinkable under Kennedy – how quickly the military chiefs moved to influence the new Commander-in-Chief. McNamara now found himself in the uncomfortable position of being at odds over a major matter of policy with his generals. His instructions from Johnson were brisk: "You want to go out there and you want to tell this fella [General Nguyen Khanh] ... that we're totally in support of him and you want to say this publicly while you're there." At the same time, McNamara and Taylor were to get "an on the spot appraisal of what was really going on."[32]

Dismissing the call for bombing the North, McNamara made a series of incremental recommendations to Johnson on March 16.[33] The Viet Cong now controlled 40 percent of the country and were especially strong in Phuoc Tuy, Binh Duong, Hau Nghia, Long An, Kien Tuong, Dinh Tuong, Kien Hoa, and An Xuyen. The situation was particularly bad in the IV Corps area (Delta) where the Viet Cong were judged to control "virtually all aspects of peasant life in the southern provinces" and where any movement now had to be accompanied by armed escort.

Even as the guerrillas were getting stronger, ARVN desertion rates were climbing. Across the country there had been a collapse of purposeful command. With the Diem patronage overturned, every top military post had changed hands; 35 out of 41 province chiefs had been replaced, 15 provinces were on their third chief, seven on their fourth, and two on their fifth chief since the Diem coup.[34] Hundreds of other officials had lost jobs or voluntarily left. Much of this was the result of corrupt peddling of offices. "Many Vietnamese military officials made fortunes in 1964," CIA analyst George Allen correctly deduced, "When the government changed hands at least five times, even though they may have been in office only a few months."[35] The outcome was a massive and hugely damaging hemorrhage of institutional memory and intelligence: "It was a rarity in 1964 and early 1965 to find a Vietnamese who had been in an assignment for more than three months, and few American military men remained in post for more than half a year." In his travels later in 1964 and 1965, Allen often encountered situations in which no official – American or Vietnamese – was aware of specific incidents of significance a year or so earlier.[36]

That this institutional churn happened as a prelude to Johnson's decision to intervene in Vietnam could hardly have been more untimely. At the very juncture when the President needed the most experienced and knowledgeable counsel on the facts on the ground, that body of understanding had vanished in a drain of Vietnamese greed and American short-termism.

Two days after McNamara briefed Johnson, his visit report, without amendments, became NSAM 288. This was an emphatic endorsement of the defense secretary. The significance of the memo was that, at a stroke, the Kennedy-era overarching policy of an American withdrawal was now replaced with an open-ended commitment. In an effort to take back control but simultaneously satisfy the Joint Chief hawks and allies, McNamara had been forced to compromise. If it could be argued that Henry Cabot Lodge dominated US foreign policy in Vietnam in the events leading up to the Diem coup, the initiative was now back with McNamara, but only contingently.

NSAM 288 introduced itself with a quite exaggerated statement of the domino theory copied almost verbatim from previous missives to Johnson:

> ... almost all of Southeast Asia will probably fall under Communist dominance (all of Vietnam, Laos, Cambodia), accommodate to Communism ... or fall under the domination of forces not now explicitly Communist but likely then to become so ... Thailand might hold for a period with our help, but would be under grave pressure. Even the Philippines would become shaky, and the threat to India to the west, Australia and New Zealand to the south, and Taiwan, Korea, and Japan to the north and east would be greatly increased.[37]

The stakes were raised even higher by the far-fetched claim that "all these consequences would probably have been true" had America not taken up the baton from the French in 1954. This was the worst sort of sloppy, grand strategic thinking now propelling Washington's foreign policy. As this was the first significant, Vietnam-related NSAM of the Johnson presidency, there is a sense that McNamara was attempting to fashion an orchestral entrance for his master by scoring the great themes of US foreign policy in Southeast Asia. If this was the case, what followed seemed at odds with what was purportedly at stake.

Once again, three Goldilocks options were offered to counter the imagined, communist apocalypse: a "neutralist" solution à la Laos, limited military action against Hanoi, and a strengthening of the South Vietnamese war effort. The first would almost certainly have tempted Kennedy. The second was a sop to the Joint Chiefs. And the third was the only option Johnson would realistically accept and which McNamara supported. NSAM 288 thus became the vehicle for several new or reinvigorated programs but it was the second, rejected option that would have the graver consequences. General Earle Wheeler, the Army Chief of Staff, had tried this on with Kennedy in January 1963 but got nowhere. Now the Joint Chiefs were instructed to prepare to take retaliatory actions against North Vietnam in 72 hours and to maintain contingency forces at 30 days' notice to mount "overt military pressure" against Hanoi. The implicit argument that Saigon was hopeless – with the corollary that the war should therefore "go north" – had been introduced into the administration's calculations. An almost overlooked point expressed in NSAM 288 – which was destined to become one of the most-quoted memoranda of the war – was a reiteration of the refrain that this was a Vietnamese war that had to be won by the Vietnamese themselves. With hindsight of what followed, it is remarkable how within a year this orthodoxy was completely overturned.

Military action required public justification. This was presented in an April 7 speech at Johns Hopkins University. "Why are we in South Vietnam?" Johnson begged to an audience of 60 million television viewers.

> We are there because we have a promise to keep. Since 1954 every American President has offered support to the people of South Vietnam. We have helped to build, and we have helped to defend. Thus, over many years, we have made a national pledge to help South Vietnam defend its independence. And I intend to keep that promise. To dishonor that pledge, to abandon this small and brave nation to its enemies, and to the terror that must follow, would be an unforgivable wrong.

But behind the bombast, Johnson sought a deal – the offer of a major infrastructure project in the Mekong Delta that would benefit all Vietnam – to end the war. "Old Ho can't turn that down, Old Ho can't turn that down," he confided to an aide, as if the North Vietnamese Politburo were corrupt and biddable US congressmen. They were not, and Ho was disinterested in dams. There could be no "peace without conquest."

A frustrating feature of what was soon to become Johnson's war was the manner in which officials, civilian and military, willfully disregarded agreed policy positions endorsed in documents like NSC memoranda, and pursued their own agendas. This ill-discipline undercut both broad policy and specific programs and shortened the relevance of both. Coupled with the political instability in South Vietnam, the result was a foreign policy that not only switched horses but direction as well. As long as dust was kicked up, and later bullets cracked, there was an illusion of purpose. Over time, the illusion became the purpose and nobody could remember why the posse had ridden out in the first place. Vietnam became "just one goddamn thing after another that nobody expected."[38]

This happened very quickly under Johnson. Two weeks after NSAM 288 was endorsed, William Bundy, who had replaced Hilsman as Assistant Secretary of State for East Asian and Pacific Affairs, sent a letter to Lodge requesting views on how domestic opinion might be marshalled for a bombing campaign against Hanoi.[39] This would be the first of a series of increasingly influential interventions by the elder Bundy. The letter was followed by a Rusk-Wheeler fact-finding mission to Saigon on April 15, the first by the slighted Rusk since his appointment as Secretary of State under Kennedy. If the intent was to mollify Rusk and reinvigorate political dialogue, it failed. The Army Chief of Staff was soon discussing bombing both with President Khanh and the country team at the Embassy (with unfortunate irony as the justification made by McGeorge Bundy for promoting a Rusk visit was "that our posture is too McNamara-warlike and that it would be helpful to the [State] Department and to the Secretary for him to spend a day with the Ambassador and with Khanh.")

Rusk and Johnson, two Southerners who on occasions imagined themselves encircled in a sea of Yankee sharks, actually got on well. Rusk was too easily overshadowed by McNamara because the latter was more dynamic and the former "incurably reticent." As McGeorge Bundy amusingly recalled, communications with the White House were a disaster. Rusk would not use the telephone, Johnson's favorite means of communicating; and Johnson would not write, Rusk's favorite form of receiving information.

A measure of how far the debate had traveled can be gauged from the detail that the use of nuclear weapons was discussed, echoing deliberations over an atomic strike during the Eisenhower presidency. The double irony is that Rusk deliberated a nuclear option because, as he explained to Khanh:

The United States would never get into another Korea with large conventional forces, and enlargement of the war might mean a high level of military action in which we would have to consider using nuclear weapons. Because of these problems, we should do absolutely all we could to improve the situation here before we started actions against the North.

As in 1954, this cataclysmic option was dismissed.[40] Diem, like Kennedy, would have rejected the idea of bombing the north, but Khanh was enthusiastic and soon a reckless proponent. The fact-finding mission returned little wiser, a coda to the course already set by McNamara.

Khanh was less enthusiastic, or able, to implement an agreed draft and reform of the war effort, and this encouraged an emboldened Lodge to start making up policy. The overarching aim of the US program in South Vietnam, through the two McNamara-Taylor missions and NSAMs 273 and 288 (October 1963–April 1964) was to create conditions for the South Vietnamese government to fight "their war" better, with the long-term view of withdrawing US troops. The overarching effort was pacification, not war-making. This was always McNamara's intent notwithstanding the bombast of domino theories.

Lodge now proposed the opposite. Impatient with Khanh as he was with Diem, Lodge staged a démarche at the end of April in which he persuaded the general that more US advisors were needed. The pliant Khanh, who was fast becoming the puppet to any American suggestion, agreed. Not wasting any time, Lodge fired off a cable to Johnson on the same day telling him so.[41] The ambassador had not faced down Khanh alone. To add some firepower, Lodge had brought along a general, Deputy Commander MACV – William Westmoreland. Five days earlier, Westmoreland had been informed that he would assume command of MACV in the summer. This practically invisible general, whose name hitherto had appeared in no letters, no cables, no memos, was about to become America's most visible general.

The ramrod William Childs Westmoreland – "Westy" to his intimates – was a distinguished wartime artillery officer. From the beginnings of his 36-year military career he demonstrated the drive and ambition of an officer determined to reach high rank. His peers acknowledged him as "gracious and gentlemanly," but he could also seem "distant and difficult," and even "odd." His slow monotone presentation and impassive eyes under beetle eyebrows added to the cold persona. Westmoreland undeniably hauled himself up the army ranks by his own boot straps, but Maxwell Taylor also played an instrumental role in his advancement. In many respects, he was typical of a generation and class of US Army officers, holding old-fashioned views that would soon become intolerable. He opposed the entry of women in West Point. He viewed Asians as different and not sharing in the same feelings over the sanctity of life as Westerners. He never made a statement condemning injustices against Negro soldiers. He lacked academic curiosity and book-learning was never his forte. Westmoreland would be cast as the arch-editor of optimistic statements over the war, but he was no Harkins and indeed warned his staffs to be "realistic" in their reporting. Like any military commander, he judged that his role was to be "a weathervane" to morale. "When I appeared before the press and public," he later confessed, "I had to reflect confidence. It was no act on my part, but I was sharply cognizant of the need to avoid any impression of pessimism or defeatism."[42]

There would be many charges against Westmoreland: the flawed strategy of attrition, an obsession with additional troop requests, and an equal obsession with statistics and their manipulation. But in the spring of 1964 he seemed like a very good choice for a difficult job. Westmoreland plainly demonstrated that he was a modern-thinking officer, embracing the latest fashions in military doctrine: this was a general who had attended Harvard Graduate School of Business to better understand the management of warfare. He also championed the introduction of the novel subject of "counterinsurgency" at West Point. He was diligent, correct, hardworking, and demanded a 60-hour week from his staffs. He visited tirelessly, conferred openly, and listened attentively to subordinates. His administrative and organizational skills were phenomenal. He was supported by probably the best cast of general staff officers the US Army could muster: General Throckmorton, his deputy; Chief of Staff, General Stilwell; and Assistant Chief of Staff for Operations, Brigadier General William E. DePuy. He enjoyed good relations with Lodge, and even better relations with Taylor who took over the Saigon Embassy in July. He understood from the beginning that Vietnam was a political struggle, and that "the real battle here is for the people," but set about trying to win a war anyway, which proved his downfall. In many ways Westmoreland became the victim of a perennial American hunger for hero generals, and a summary disdain for a "loser." When he finally quit, there were no regrets and no apologies. He retired to golf courses and to his loyal wife Kitsy, making a brief, unsuccessful foray into politics. In a final humiliation, in 1975, he was forced to hastily change the title of his book, *The War Nobody Won*, when Hanoi made the title redundant.

Westmoreland's time had not yet come. An increasingly marginalized Harkins remained in post, barely on speaking terms with Lodge. On May 28, Johnson put an end to the charade and summoned COMUSMACV home. Harkins would never return to Vietnam but Westmoreland would only finally be confirmed in post on August 1. This left Lodge still pulling the puppet strings of Khanh who was in danger of becoming an out-of-control warmonger. This was always likely to have been a danger if political power passed to the generals. The Diem-Nhu government had its flaws but the brothers were civilians who understood that the war was rooted in a political and social struggle. The military chiefs had no experience or patience for these aspects and naturally viewed the struggle as a contest that had to be decided on a battlefield. At the beginning of May, Khanh visited the Embassy with all the zeal of a newly promoted cadet. Not only did he now want to put the country on a war footing, he also wanted to "go north" with American support. Give me 10,000 American special force soldiers, he pleaded with Lodge. In a quite mad scheme, Khanh proposed evacuating the entire two million-strong population of Saigon and declaring war on Hanoi.

This was bluster – a month-old, promised mobilization decree had still not been signed – but Lodge reported the war-talk and this panicked Washington, especially Rusk whose discomfort over the April visit now came to the surface.[43] Washington was not going to start a Third World War to please a South Vietnamese general who had just staged a coup. Two days later a frustrated Johnson called a National Security Council meeting. At last Rusk's views were properly heard but these only served to prompt a third McNamara-Taylor fact-finding mission (May 12–14), and McNamara's fourth since the previous October. It little helped to calm minds that the trip was undertaken against the background of a fresh communist offensive in Laos that resulted in the capture of most of the strategically important Plaine des Jarres.

It is difficult to conceive how many more facts the travel-weary McNamara could possibly uncover. The "facts" were not the issue. After the misleading reporting of the previous year, intelligence assessments had become more rigorous thanks to improvements introduced by McCone in the CIA. The issue was certain personalities – particularly Lodge – exploiting the post-coup disorder to push radical policy options, specifically bombing the North. The ultimate responsibility for restoring institutional order lay with the Oval Office but Johnson preferred to let McNamara control the unruly. This was a mistake because there were far too many back channels and mechanisms available to bypass the defense secretary. Johnson would later boast that not a single bomb could be dropped without his authority, but this was an idle claim, not least because as Churchill observed, whoever unleashes the dogs of war no longer becomes a master of events. But more importantly, Johnson did not stamp his authority from the beginning or make it clear that he was intolerant of dissent. His administration had a South Vietnam policy: McNamara's NSAM 288, agreed just eight weeks previously. Nothing had substantially changed to revisit this policy – it had not even been given a chance to work. It was the drumbeat and hurrahs of war lobbyists that had changed the landscape. Lodge at the Embassy was the principal conductor of this orchestra but it is also a matter of historical fact that every memo or paper submitted by the Joint Chiefs to McNamara over this period made arguments for more, never less. It was as if the long-term policy of an American withdrawal which McNamara had painfully wrung out of the Chiefs at the end of the Kennedy presidency had been summarily ditched – which it was.

On May 27, Johnson rang the filibustering Richard Russell, who also served as Chairman of the all-powerful Senate Armed Services Committee. Johnson and Russell may have been at opposite ends of the civil rights debate but they were in unison over Vietnam. The interchange between the two men perfectly condensed the mired dilemma over America's involvement in Vietnam. Neither "get in" nor "get out" would lead to a satisfactory outcome. On the state of Washington's Vietnam policy, the senator was quite blunt: it was "the damned worst mess I ever saw."[44] Questioned over the familiar fears engendered by the domino theory, he was totally dismissive: "It isn't important to us a damn bit." So much for every orthodoxy on communist expansionism espoused in government policy papers since the Truman years. However, rather than offering Johnson options, he argued what Johnson secretly believed and feared. No matter what he did, "It's one of those places where you can't win." The logical conclusion of this exchange was to liquidate the losses and "get out," but typically Johnson raised exaggerated qualms: "Well, they'd impeach a president, though, that would run out, wouldn't they?" he pleaded. Unable to resolve the impasses, the confidential telephone conversation ended at the familiar fork on the road with Johnson unwilling to follow either. "I haven't got the nerve to do it [get in]," he confessed to Russell, but "I don't see any way out of it."

Johnson sought the views of personalities like Russell, because this was the old LBJ, wheeling and dealing in the Senate. But he also did so because it was Congress, or more precisely a hypocritical, warmongering Republican caucus, "raising hell over 35 killed," while simultaneously baiting Johnson to get tough, that was acting as the most effective block to getting out. The Democrats still carried the stigma over "losing China" – how could Johnson add to this toxic political legacy by losing Indochina as well? With elections in November, which president dared appeared weak?

In his heart, Johnson did not give a jot for South Vietnam. The woman Johnson self-confessedly loved was his historic ambition to mold a Great Society, but "that bitch of a war" was threatening to wreck this dream. "Every time we have gotten near the culmination of our dreams," he lamented, "the war bells have rung."[45] If he quit, the recriminations would fatally weaken him in Congress, or so he believed; but if he pitched the country into a full-blown war "all those conservatives in the Congress would use it as a weapon against the Great Society."

In fact, Johnson's arithmetic, if not his politics, was misjudged on this matter. Such was the rapid advance of America's GNP over this period that the economic burden of Vietnam was proportionately much less than Korea, even at the height of the former war when Vietnam expenditures hit an annual peak of $25 billion. At the same time, the proportion of increases in GNP for welfare purposes (Medicare, education, and related programs) continued to increase. The guns or butter quandary was always a myth – Johnson could have had both. Inflation proved the devil in the economic equations rather than federal budgets.[46]

Nixon's later summation of Johnson's fateful choice was exact: he could not afford to lose the war, and he did not do what was necessary to win it. Either way, he believed he stood to lose the Great Society. "He made the worse possible choice: He would fight – not to win, but only not to lose."[47]

Ultimately, the crux was that Johnson feared being a war loser – in Bill Moyers' estimation he simply could not bear being remembered as the president "who tuck his tail and ran."[48] When McNamara warned him at the end of June of "very heavy risk" if Washington were sucked into a ground war, he riposted that "walking out" was the bigger risk.[49] Dovish opponents he branded "a bunch of sissy fellows," an insult that probably drew a manly snort on his ranch, but which was unhelpful at this critical moment in American postwar history. The "get out or get in" dilemma was false from the outset. As early as the spring of 1964, America was never going to "get out" because a self-pitying, insecure Johnson viewed himself as an actor foreordained to follow a path he never really believed in – to "get in." Men didn't "pull down the flag" – and certainly not Texan men. It was not accidental that he viewed criticism from newspapers like the *New York Times* as attempts to unsex, "to castrate me." Five days after the Tonkin Gulf incident, Johnson was on the telephone to clothing company owner Joe Haggar issuing instructions for six pairs of summer pants. "Now another thing," he told Haggar, "the crotch, down where your nuts hang … give me an inch so I can let them out there."[50] This was a president entangling his very manliness in foreign policy. McNamara's efforts to limit and ultimately withdraw the American commitment were always heading for failure.

If McNamara-Taylor fact-finding missions had become a cliché of the administration, so had Honolulu Conferences, and this is where Johnson's wise heads assembled on May 30 against the backdrop of the 227th American serviceman killed in South Vietnam. A stellar cast attended. The conferees included: McNamara; Rusk; Lodge; William Bundy; Taylor as Head of the Joint Chiefs; Westmoreland, still as Commander MACV-designate; Admiral Felt, Pacific Fleet Commander; Philip Chadbourn, the head of the US diplomatic mission in Laos; William Guad, the head of the AID effort; Carl Rowan, Director of USIA; and Graham Martin, the Ambassador in Thailand. Only the Joint Chiefs, now advocating the total destruction of North Vietnam's industrial base, were conspicuously absent.[51] Their views, nonetheless, were well known. In light of the "gradualist" course that the Johnson government would eventually take, they deserve quotation:

> We should not waste critical time and more resources in another protracted series of "messages" but rather we should take positive, prompt, and meaningful military action to underscore our meaning that after two years of tolerating this North Vietnamese support we are now determined that it will stop … the United States should seek through military actions to accomplish destruction of the North Vietnamese will and capabilities as necessary to compel the Democratic Government of Vietnam (DRV) to cease providing support to the insurgencies in South

Vietnam and Laos. Only a course of action geared to this objective can assure that the North Vietnamese support of the subversive efforts in Laos and South Vietnam will terminate.[52]

With supreme confidence, the Joint Chiefs reckoned that America's bombers could finish the job in precisely 46 days. Taylor, representing the Chiefs, left these proposals in his briefcase.

A review of the situation made somber reading. As many as 13 provinces were judged to be "critical," seven of which lay in the Delta. The so-called National Pacification Plan, replacing the Strategic Hamlets Program, amounted to rhetoric. The reasons for the failure of this program were complex: at the most basic level it was not being executed with conviction, confidence, or the necessary funds. The ARVN was reportedly conducting over 60 battalion-sized operations a week to little effect; the Viet Cong was gaining ground. Three times as many weapons were being lost as captured (this was one of several statistics that became elevated as a key metric of success, or failure). The Chieu Hoi program (encouraging ralliers, or deserters) had stalled. There were now over 16,000 US servicemen in South Vietnam with air bases in Saigon, Da Nang, Nha Trang, Bien Hoa, Can Tho, and Soc Trang. Five government departments – State, Defense, AID, the CIA, and US Information Services – were throwing their best minds at the problem, and 14 other countries were now supporting the campaign in various, modest ways. The United States was a country with a $47-billion defense budget – how could the country be failing in this "itsy-bitsy" war?

McNamara had faced these conundrums earlier in the year in a House Armed Services Committee hearing and his answer had been faithful to the assassinated Kennedy:

I don't believe that we as a nation should assume the primary responsibility for the war in South Vietnam. It is a counter-guerrilla war, it is a war that can only be won by the Vietnamese people themselves. Our responsibility is not to substitute ourselves for the Vietnamese.[53]

There was undeniably a Quixotic aspect to McNamara's strict policy of limited engagement because, as he freely admitted at the National Security Council meeting on May 24 in preparation for Honolulu, "where our proposals are being carried out now, the situation is still going to hell. We are continuing to lose. Nothing we are now doing will win." The following day, McGeorge Bundy penned a memo to Johnson advising that "you make a Presidential decision that the U.S. will use selected and carefully graduated military force against North Vietnam," the first such explicit recommendation from an aide. It wasn't just the situation in South Vietnam that was going to hell but the spirit of McNamara's policy of restraint.

The significance of Honolulu was not that any important measures were proposed to address what everyone agreed was a badly deteriorating situation. None were. As Taylor astutely remarked, the conference was in danger of reasoning itself into inaction. Fear and uncertainty over how China and Russia might react, or whether Laos might fall, was turning Washington into hand-wringing Hamlets. In Moyer's memorable phrase, China and the Soviets had become the "hidden persuaders" in the room. A personality like Rusk:

... had been deeply imbued with what happened in Korea [when he was Assistant Secretary of State for Far Eastern affairs]. When MacArthur got too close to the Yalu and the Chinese hordes came pummeling in, Rusk was aware of that, so was Johnson. One of the great weaknesses of the evolving policy in Vietnam was that we never really had a true estimate of what the Chinese and the Soviets would do ... In effect, they became the hidden persuaders of our deliberations about what was going to happen.[54]

This fear was amplified by a Defense memo for the President circulated the week before on May 24 which advised that communist China might invade Southeast Asia including Burma with up to 24 divisions – a quite absurd exaggeration of the threat posed by Mao's crippled country.

Rather, the conference gained a belated significance because the orthodoxy of Vietnamese primacy was chipped away. In what was recognized as a "radical" proposal, the conference was urged to consider a strategy of "encadrement" of US military and civilian personnel, in fact the April Lodge-Khanh proposal for more active US military assistance. This implied a decisive switch from the provision of advisors and trainers to embedding "assistants" within the South Vietnamese chain of command. The difference between an advisor and an assistant was not wordplay: the latter offered temptation if not encouragement to take over the war.[55] Taylor viewed this as a "third coup" which would necessarily raise the question: whose war is this?

McNamara, in the meantime, shaken by the bad news and sensitive to Johnson's need to show resolve, reversed his instinctive dismissal of an expanded US military commitment, made just three months earlier, and asked both CINCPAC and MACV to study "what military actions, in ascending order of gravity, might be taken to impress Hanoi with our intentions to strike North Vietnam."[56] This "integrated political-military plan for graduated action against North Vietnam" was unhelpfully placed under his deputy John McNaughton, a personality secretly tortured over the commitment to Vietnam. Within six months of Kennedy's death, "going north," which he would never have countenanced, had already taken on the character of a policy objective. The sticking point, of course, was that Johnson could not "go north" anyway without a Congressional resolution. This too was already being debated by mid-May and events at the beginning of August would provide the answer.

For want of any major new initiatives – or because the only initiative was to add more US assistants to the pot – much of the discussion was dominated by the question of how many and where. The biggest constraint was the unbridgeable language difficulties. Virtually no US personnel spoke French, Vietnamese was too difficult to learn, and the recruitment of thousands of interpreters was deemed unworkable. In the end, a very modest 434-strong increment was agreed that would provide US military advisors in

113 out of 239 districts. The greatest effort would be focused on the seven critical provinces: Long An, Dinh Tuong, Kien Hoa, Hau Nghia, Tay Ninh, Quang Ngai, and Phu Yen. Other proposals amounted to tinkering at the edges. It fell to Westmoreland to provide the sound bite at the conclusion of this unsatisfactory conference. "It is absolutely inconceivable to me," he told a panel of correspondents, "that the Vietcong could ever militarily defeat the armed forces of South Vietnam."[57]

Changes, in the meantime, were being wrought in Saigon. The arrival of Taylor brought with it a more military-style unified control in the Embassy. A Mission Council was established, meeting weekly and involving the heads of all the government departments, although disagreements still persisted over the detail of policies. The departure of the warmongering Lodge provided some relief, but Taylor too saw virtues in "graduated" military pressures and he was no dove. The MAAG, dispersed across 60 buildings in Saigon, was disbanded on May 15, against last-ditch opposition, and MACV assumed responsibility for the Military Assistance Program (MAP).[58] MACV HQ duly swelled to over 1,000 strong with predictable mutterings from the other services over Army dominance of the billets (four fifths went to the land command).[59] The Air Force reacted by posting the well-regarded Major General Joseph H. Moore as 2nd Air Division Commander, replacing General Anthis. LeMay distrusted Moore, a boyhood friend of Westmoreland, but he was no patsy. Disagreements over the management of the air war soon boiled to the surface and even reached Congress, to the consternation of the Joint Chiefs who tried to keep a lid on these inter-service disputes. In Honolulu, Admiral Ulysses S. Grant Sharp succeeded Felt as CINCPAC on June 30, and in Washington, General Earle G. Wheeler succeeded Taylor as chairman of the Joint Chiefs on July 31. The new team was taking shape.

Even as Washington rearranged its pieces on the board, the enemy team was also taking shape. Under Hanoi's direction, a now reorganized Central Office of South Vietnam (COSVN) was located in Tay Ninh Province, close to the Cambodian border, which acted as the headquarters for the Viet Cong and its political wing.[60] A proto-COSVN had originally been based in Ca Mau peninsula, south of Saigon, and it appears it continued to exist in dormant form post-1954. Captured Viet Cong referred to this shadowy organization as the "PRP Central." Overall command was vested in the deputy chief of staff of the PAVN and member of the Lao Dong Central Committee, a man named Major General Tran Van Tra. He also went by the pseudonym Tran Nam Trung. Senior General Nguyen Chi Thanh also appears to have held a leadership role. Their command was divided along the lines of the old Viet Minh division of the country. In the north, known as Military Region 5 (or in the French *Interzone 5*), command was retained by a North Vietnamese officer, a Major General Nguyen Don. By 1966, he had been replaced by two other PAVN officers: General Hoang Van Thai, another deputy chief of staff of the People's Army, and Major General Chu Huy Man, a member of the Lao Dong Central Committee.

These reorganizations were the consequence of decisions taken at the 9th Plenum of the Central Committee, held in December 1963 in Hanoi. Up to this point, the Giap-Truong Chinh faction had prevailed within the Politburo over the Le Duan faction. The differences ran deep, exposing ideological divisions between supporters of Khrushchev's "Revisionism," and allies of Mao's brand of fanatical communism. After months of deliberations, and one step ahead of Washington, the Party then took the momentous decision to escalate the war in a bid to finally destroy a weakening ARVN. In the words of the Plenum, the primary aim of the armed struggle was now to "attack, destroy, and defeat the army of the lackey administration."[61] This was a triumph for Le Duan and his allies. "It is necessary to be determined," he wrote in the party journal *Hoc Tap*, "to liquidate imperialism and capitalism." Hanoi was no less blind to the possibility of American intervention than Johnson was fearful of Chinese intervention, but the imperative of national liberation gave the war faction in the north the steel which was missing in Washington. Even if Washington pitched another 100,000 men into Vietnam, how could this match the millions of Vietnamese yearning for unification, so they reasoned.

In April, soldiers drawn from the elite 95th Regiment of 325th Division were prepared for the march down the Ho Chi Minh Trail. These were almost all southerners (the other "Southern" divisions were 305th, 324th, 330th, and 338th). Typical of this group was Duong Long Sang. In his words:

> While I was in the north I heard that the inhabitants of the south were killed in droves, among them were members of my family. Therefore, I was very worried and my heart ached terribly. Hence, I went to my superiors and volunteered to go back to the south to fight in any circumstances and with any means.[62]

By October the first group had made the arduous two-month trip to join guerrilla comrades in the south. According to the official North Vietnamese history, this group of pioneers was just 542 strong of which only 27 traveled the length of the virgin trail to "Nam Bo," or the provinces north of Saigon. Remarkably, 18 from this group survived the war.[63] Sang eventually made his way to Saigon then became a "special forces" trainer in the sanctuary of Cu Chi. Using forged papers, Sang and his fellow guerrillas had few problems mixing with the general population. "Sometimes our people even flew into Saigon on passenger airplanes," he later confessed.

The trail had only been officially established in early May 1959. Previously, covert resupply had been undertaken using a network of routes running through the northern provinces of South Vietnam. However, it was appreciated that these historic land routes were both too small and too vulnerable to support a significant reinforcement south. It was for this reason that the entire network was shifted west, over the Annamite Mountains, and into Laos. Here the PAVN already boasted an established transport infrastructure through its support of Pathet Lao.

The task of developing this network of supply routes to the South was assigned to Military Transportation Group 599 under the command of Colonel Vo Bam. The beginnings were extremely modest. Bam had just one battalion – 301 Ground Transportation Battalion – under command. The first resupply comprising just half a ton of weapons was delivered to Viet Cong units in Thua Thien Province on August 20, 1959. To maintain operational security, only Western weapons were included in this first consignment. This secrecy, however, was soon dispensed with. By December, over 1,600 weapons had been delivered including almost 800 swords and machetes. Within four years, more than 165,000 mostly Chinese-supplied weapons would be despatched down the trail, this flood coinciding with the resolutions adopted at the 9th Plenum.

From 1960, the growth of "Group 599" was spectacular. By 1962 it had swollen to a 6,000-strong force of two regiments. A fleet of bicycles augmented by the native Hmong horse and Asian elephants was being used to shift hundreds of tons of foodstuffs and war materials – 317 tons by 1961. Russian pilots maintained a secret airlift to Tchepone in northern Laos. As many as 45 way stations were built roughly every 20 kilometers, or a day's marching distance. Trucks were used sparingly at first to avoid attracting attention. By the summer of 1965, a 25,000-strong military force reinforced by "assault youths," civilian workers, and covert Chinese labor was assigned to the trail. These were protected by as many as eight antiaircraft battalions.

304th Division was the first full division to enter South Vietnam, complete by 1965, and was joined later by 320th Delta Division in 1966.[64] The majority of the early infiltrators were the Southern regroupees, keen to return to their families. Ironically, they also sought escape from the grim existence of the communist North. However, by the time Johnson entered the ground war in the summer of 1965 three out of four were northerners.

Notwithstanding an understandable American concern with infiltration, intelligence estimates show that numbers were not especially high, at least in the early years. In 1959, MACV confirmed 4,556 infiltrators (estimates were based on the testimony of at least two prisoners or captured documentation). At the time of Diem's assassination in 1963 this number had only risen to

4,726 (communist figures are consistently much higher but appear exaggerated). The first spike was recorded in 1965, exactly when Johnson chose to escalate. In this year, 23,770 infiltrators were confirmed, reflecting the deployment of PAVN regiments and later entire divisions.[65]

This was the state of play as Washington entered the summer season in 1964. In public, the administration reported progress and attempted to keep the problem of Vietnam off the front pages of the *Washington Post*. Privately, a very different consensus was developing. In Johnson's tortured mind; in McNamara's impossible balancing acts; in dissenting Congressional voices; in the statistics spewed by MACV, if only the runes had been read with clear-sighted honesty; in the despatches of Halberstam and his colleagues; and probably in the hearts of many South Vietnamese; it was already a doomed and lost war. A glance at a 1950s map of Viet Minh-dominated areas of Vietnam would have revealed that territorial possession had remained essentially unchanged in 15 years of intermittent warfare. From the north, through a swathe of the Central Highlands extending from the Cambodian border to the coast, and all the way south to the Delta, nothing had changed. However much fighting and clearing was undertaken, the enemy seeped back. To borrow the metaphor of a visiting CIA officer, Washington was "trying to mop the floor before turning off the faucet."[66]

Chapter 5

SHOOTING AT FLYING FISH, AUGUST–DECEMBER 1964

It is an axiomatic truth that no president seeks foreign entanglement in an election year. Johnson, obeisant to this iron rule of Capitoline politics, was not rushing to be the first president to squander a handsome advantage in the polls for the sake of a foreign war. Instead, he threw his considerable energy into domestic wars. In a hectic final session of Congress, America's legislators swung from passing no bills to losing their heads. In total, they voted for $11.5 billion in tax cuts; $1 billion for an omnibus bill to wage a "national war on poverty"; $375 million for transport infrastructure projects; $556 million in pay rises for federal employees; and $1 billion in a housing bill – Johnson was practically bribing the country to vote for him.

The Republican Party, in the meantime, was traversing a periodic bout of collective suicide under the leadership of Barry Goldwater. "The Goldwater problem" was reduced to a choice between electability versus ideology: the electorate seemed to prefer him to Rockefeller, but the party establishment found him intolerable, which translated as too liberal. Since 1960, Congressman Goldwater had consistently voted against every cherished Republican cause. God forbid an electorate should plump for this chameleon candidate – it was time to ramp up the "anyone but Goldwater" campaign.

At the beginning of August, Washington slipped into summer languor, or should have. The Beatles had just hit the top of the Billboard 100 with "A Hard Day's Night." *The Spy who Came in from the Cold* was in the bestseller list. The presidential election was just three months away and Johnson's to lose. The capital was overrun with tourists rather than Civil Rights marchers. Anyone with sense was heading off to the nearest beaches. The war news seemed distant, like the war itself. Johnson and Humphrey were running on a non-interventionist ticket, making Goldwater look like the warmonger candidate. The President only had to avoid embroiling himself in controversies to emphatically win a second term. All of which made the events of August 2–4, 1964 the more remarkable. At the center of the imbroglio that was about to overtake Washington was the unlikely and graceful Allen M. Sumner-class destroyer: DD-731, the USS *Maddox.*

Maddox was launched in June 1944. Like the sister destroyers in the same class, she was recognizable by her shallow curving prow and two funnels set at rakish angles. She boasted six 5-inch guns, which were used in the long blockade of Wonsan in the Korean War. During the Pacific War she was fitted with 23 antiaircraft guns to counter the threat of aerial attacks. A kamikaze pilot still managed to get through when *Maddox* was sailing off the coast of Formosa, but the destroyer survived. On the morning of Sunday, August 2, 1964, *Maddox*, commanded by Commander Herbert Ogier, was deployed on a patrol roughly 28 miles from the North Vietnamese coastline in the Gulf of Tonkin. She was sailing in a south-southeasterly direction at 15 knots. Also on board was Captain John J. Herrick, the Commander of Seventh Fleet's Destroyer Division 192. This division fell under overall command of Admiral George Morrison, sailing on the flagship USS *Bon Homme Richard* (CV-31). Sailing conditions were good and the ship's company anticipated nothing out of the ordinary. The destroyer was at Condition Three, meaning that a third of the crew were at their stations. Her mission, as in previous patrols of this nature, was electronic eavesdropping. Anticipating no threat, *Maddox* was undermanned. Her wartime complement was 228 men, but her "Westpac" (West Pacific) allocation was only 193 men.[1]

Seventh Fleet fell under CINCPAC, the newly appointed and patriotically named Admiral Ulysses S. Grant Sharp. CINCPAC's command was imperial; he counted half the surface of the planet as his demesne and he patrolled this territory with over 400 ships and 3,500 aircraft, Zeus and Poseidon rolled into one compact man with a high-pitched voice (he was only five foot seven inches tall). Sharp should never have been a sailor, growing up in landlocked Montana, but the whiff of salt air seemed to convert him and a distinguished 38-year career followed. At the time he was 59 years old and based in Honolulu, exactly halfway between Vietnam and Washington. Sharp would brag to a correspondent, "Sometimes when things are going on in Vietnam we stay in the war room for 22 hours. We don't sleep but we don't get tired. When something tricky and important is happening, you're sustained." But this was an idle boast.[2] Over the course of events that were about to unfold, Sharp proved a confused, contradictory, and unreliable interlocutor.

The origins of *Maddox*'s mission lay in a decision taken under the Kennedy presidency in early 1962, to augment covert signals gathering in support of Navy operations. Initially, the intent was to mount surveillance operations against the broader communist enemy. Only later, DESOTO missions, as they were known (**De**Haven **S**pecial **O**perations off **T**singta**O**), began to be run against the specific North Vietnamese enemy in the Gulf of Tonkin. Rather than employ dedicated, Soviet-style, electronic warfare ships, the Navy came up with the compromise solution of loading a signals intelligence van (essentially a portakabin with room for over a dozen signalers) on board destroyers like *Maddox*. These vans had the capability to intercept voice and Morse communications as well as detect radar emissions. The men who operated in the vans were drawn from the Navy's cryptologic division, known as the Naval Security Group (NSG).[3] The 16-man detachment on board *Maddox* was known by the signal address USN-467N. The ship's call sign was CTG 72.1.

There were two other SIGINT (Signals Intelligence) stations fulfilling an important role in Southeast Asia. In total, over 700 cryptologic personnel were deployed in-theater under the code name Kit Kat.[4] The larger of the two was an NSG site based at San Miguel in the Philippines. This was known as USN-27 and included a marine detachment. The second was a forward SIGINT station based in Phu Bai, on the Vietnamese coast, known as USM-626J. Confusingly, there was an additional marine detachment located at Phu Bai, known as USN-414T.[5] As was the routine for these operations, *Maddox* operated with a SIGINT "guard" – another station that sent it reports of relevance. Although the identity of this station is not clear, it appears not unlikely that this was the Special Support Group (SSG) at Tan Son Nhut. In total, then, there were at least four ground stations in the Southeast Asia theater intercepting and translating principally HF messages transmitted by North Vietnamese stations. "Technical support" was also made available to the ship before she departed allowing her to receive "additional technical information of high relevancy" from other stations.[6] In this respect, *Maddox* was the best-informed USN ship in the western Pacific.

Maddox was not alone in the Gulf of Tonkin. She was joining a much longer history of US maritime covert operations against North Vietnam. In the 1950s, the CIA had run a scheme called Nautilus that involved infiltrating agents using seven junks, as well as conducting hit and run raids and frogmen attacks. Known as the Seaborne Infiltration Force, this had been predominantly manned by specially selected individuals from the Nung ethnic minority. These missions were eventually discontinued when they became easy prey to a better-equipped North Vietnamese Navy (NVN). By 1962, the CIA had handed over to the Department of Defense (Operation *Switchback*) and the junks were replaced by three Swift boats. These were captained by Norwegian mercenaries who predictably became known as "The Vikings." Norway's cameo role in the Vietnam War was short-lived. The contract for their services expired after a year and they were replaced by German crews. These survived an even shorter period because "they were usually inebriated."[7] The CIA eventually paid off the hopeless Germans and the policy of using deniable European crewmen ended.

In September 1963, the Joint Chiefs had approved of a plan to undertake covert raids on North Vietnam, known as OPLAN 34-63. This was cloak-and-dagger stuff dreamt up by staffs keen to satisfy Kennedy's appetite for special operations. OPLAN 34-63 remained stillborn following the Diem coup but was revived the following year as OPLAN 34-A. The strategy was straightforward: make Hanoi pay for its support to the Viet Cong through a strategy of dissuasion and graduated response, without escalating the war or provoking a Chinese response. This was essentially a continuation of policy that had been instigated by Lansdale in the Saigon Military Mission, later carried forward by William Colby in 1959, when he was posted CIA head of station in Saigon. Whereas the former had been a covert operations enthusiast, Colby quit Saigon in 1963 to take a post in Washington, doubtful that the operations were having any significant effects.

On May 25, in preparation for the forthcoming Honolulu conference, the CIA had submitted Top Secret SNIE (Special National Intelligence Estimate) 50-2-64, *Probable Consequences of Certain US Actions with Respect to Vietnam and Laos*. The study informed a meeting attended by McNamara, Rusk, McCone, Ball, Taylor, Goodpaster, and McGeorge and William Bundy, specifically to discuss possible military options against North Vietnam. In response to a "graduated scale" of "GVN (US-assisted) operations against the DRV and Communist-held Laos," the CIA assessed:

Hanoi would probably agitate world opinion against the US, hoping that a new Geneva conference or UN action would result, and bring a cessation of attacks. We think that North Vietnam, while taking various precautionary measures, would order the Viet Cong and Pathet Lao to refrain from dramatic new attacks, and might reduce the level of insurrections for the moment ... the Communists' line would probably be that the outcome of a conference should be to stabilize the situation in South Vietnam and Laos.

SNIE 50-2-64 was concurred by the Intelligence Board: nobody in the summer of 1964 could envisage any other rational outcome to a calculated demonstration of American military muscle, other than Hanoi backing down.

This assumption – on page one of the document – was based on an assessment that regime-preservation would overtake all other considerations. In giving so much weight to this single factor it somewhat clouded many insightful judgments later in the document that a busy reader may have skipped over. In most other respects, the CIA assessment proved strikingly accurate.

There remained a "significant danger," the study warned, that Hanoi might choose to fight and expect to defeat the United States, as it did France. The conundrum in South Vietnam was not Hanoi's interference anyway, but Saigon's "misrule." The United States might hope to influence the "will" of the North Vietnamese leadership, but the measures proposed were unlikely to affect military capability. And if the limited military actions failed, the "difficulties of comprehension might increase on both sides as the scale of action mounted." In other words, Hanoi might fail to read the graduated signals and read total war instead of limited war. What then? In the CIA's estimation: "There is evidence that confidence has been growing in Hanoi that the final phase in the struggle in South Vietnam is approaching." Limited US military engagement might delay this outcome, but not forestall it for ever. Crucially, the CIA correctly deduced that neither China nor the Soviet Union would become directly involved, a false fear that consistently muddied White House deliberations. NATO allies were even less likely to offer support, reasoning that, "prevailing opinion among many observers in much of Western Europe seems to be that any American efforts to expand the war to the North would probably be ineffective and not worth the risk."

SNIE 50-2-64, then, stands as a classic example of an intelligence assessment that drew the wrong conclusion from all the right inferences. This perverse outcome mostly fell out of the question that was pitched at the agency; which was to estimate the consequences of graduated American military action, with a view to forcing Hanoi to respect the 1962 Geneva agreements. SNIE 50-2-64 should have argued that no military action was likely to encourage Hanoi to return to the negotiating table, but this would not have answered the White House's question. Whatever the CIA advised, it is also likely that the protagonists were going to read into it what they wanted, suppressing passages that warned of doubtful outcomes.

SNIE 50-2-64 was drafted against a background of increasing tension over the summer. On June 7, two US armed reconnaissance aircraft flying covert Yankee Team missions were shot down over Laos, provoking a retaliatory air strike. One week later, China threatened unspecified actions over American air incursions into Laos. On June 18, William Bundy confirmed in Congressional testimony that the United States would be prepared to deploy troops to Laos, if necessary, to halt any further advances by Pathet Lao. This matched the strong stance taken by Congressman Richard Nixon who in April had argued that US troops should be used to "hot pursuit" into Laos and North Vietnam. Two days later, Admiral Felt, in his last days as CINCPAC, made a hawkish statement that America should be prepared to risk war against China to halt communist expansionism. On the same day, reinforcements were flown to Thailand and major construction was started on an airbase in Da Nang, half way up the South Vietnamese coastline. Faced with this war-talk, at the beginning of July, UN Secretary General U Thant called for a reconvening of the 1954 Geneva Conference, but was roundly ignored. General de Gaulle had earlier called for a reconvening of the Fourteen Nation Geneva Conference on May 20, but was also ignored. In Saigon, Premier Khanh addressed a rally of 100,000 supporters and called for an invasion of the North (discomfiting the newly arrived Taylor who had just taken over from Lodge). Thus, by the end of July, all sides had been brought to a pitch of war rhetoric. The main consequence of this war of words was that Johnson had already been forced into a position from which it would be difficult to back down, before any shots had been fired.

OPLAN 34-A, agreed in December the previous year, had several elements. In total, over 2,000 missions were proposed, including sabotage, psychological warfare, and raids. To ensure deniability, these would be conducted by South Vietnamese, instructed and equipped by Americans, and augmented by Chinese nationalist mercenaries. Johnson authorized the plan on January 16, 1964, but its implementation was slow. The Special Operations Group (MACV-SOG), later re-titled the Studies and Observation Group, was only formally stood up in March. South Vietnamese agreement to the conduct of covert operations was tardy, and the CIA disputed its primacy over operations in Laos. A small staff of 99 soldiers and 31 civilians made up the first SOG, reporting to MACV, but in practice taking instructions from Washington.[8]

OPLAN 34-A was drafted by Colonel Clyde R. Russell, the first commander of MACV-SOG. It was originally intended as a 12-month campaign, involving commando raids and parachute operations generally on the Laotian and Cambodian borders. The Vietnamese coastline was largely neglected. Special force operations had already been underway under Kennedy, and a secondary aim was to better coordinate these multiple existing covert programs under OPLAN 34-A. Operations in Laos, in fact, were proving a huge disappointment, partly because of objections from the ambassador in Vientiane; and partly because the Vietnamese Special Forces (the VNSF), operating under the code name Leaping Lena, proved unreliable, at one stage mutinying in their base at Nha Trang. A Montagnard rebellion in the Highlands further complicated American efforts.

The omission of a coastal strategy was the catalyst for the MAROPS or Maritime Operations that went by the code name of Timberwork operations. These missions were mounted by South Vietnamese crews, as well as a small number of Chinese and Korean mercenaries, but coordinated and commanded by US special forces personnel. The special force units involved were the *Luong Dac Biet* and *Biet Kich* (Coastal Security Service and Sea Patrol Force).[9] The boats they used to undertake the raids were called "Nasties"; wooden-hulled, ex-Norwegian patrol boats, designated "PTF" with a single numeric suffix (for example, PTF-1). The name "Nasties" was derived from the boat builder "Nast" rather than from their purpose. The inspiration for the design had come from the hugely successful, British wartime Fairmile motor launches (most famously used in the St Nazaire raid). In the early 1960s, the "Nast" was by some margin the king of raiding boats. Armed with twin 20mm cannon, port and aft, and a 40mm cannon on the aft deck, the boat could hit a top speed of 50 knots. Handled well, nothing could touch it. Over the course of eight years, more than 1,000 missions would be launched using "Nasties" and only one was lost to enemy action (a freak incident in which a North Vietnamese biplane managed to drop a homemade bomb on the rear deck of a boat).[10] An important aim of this effort was interdiction of the so-called "maritime Ho Chi Minh Trail." In the first half of 1964 alone, 149,000 junks and 570,000 sailors and fishermen were stopped and searched.[11]

The raids began haltingly in January 1964 with very modest results. Following the McNamara March visit to Saigon, it was proposed to ramp up the raids. The general consensus was that the scale of the raids was insignificant and unlikely to have any measurable impact on the North Vietnamese government. This proposal was accepted by the cabinet and formally endorsed in NSAM 288. McNamara, along with the JCS, continued to exercise tight control over these operations. McNamara, in particular, tended to view these as his operations, provoking later allegations that the defense secretary led Johnson by the nose and provoked an unnecessary escalation of the war.[12] This is an exaggerated claim but there is a suggestion that McNamara, like his former boss Kennedy, believed in and invested too much faith in special operations. The real significance of the machinations that summer, encapsulated in NSAM 288, was that the Johnson government was already seeking ways to deepen the conflict, even before the events of the first week of August.

Frustrated with the lack of results, the JCS, MACV, and the NSC then jointly drafted OPLAN 37-64, in June. This proposed three actions: bombing 94 targets in North Vietnam, attacking

Viet Cong camps in Laos and Cambodia, and ramping up the OPLAN 34-A raids.[13] Johnson could neither bomb North Vietnam nor order significant ground operations in neighboring countries without congressional approval. The only politically viable option in OPLAN 37-64 was to increase the number of coastal raids, which is what happened. In this respect, the Pentagon was placing a loaded gun just out of reach of Johnson's hand and simultaneously creating a confrontational situation that was likely to result in the President snatching the gun anyway, and pulling the trigger. Or as Robert Hanyok, the former NSA (National Security Agency) analyst and cryptologic historian later put it: "What was critical was that the situation along North Vietnam's territorial waters had reached a near boil."[14]

In fact, the North Vietnamese response to these violations of its territorial waters was surprisingly tepid. It was not until June that the Central Committee authorized the Navy to attack any boats violating territorial water and it was not until July 6 that the NVN formally went on a war footing. As most of the raids were taking place between the coastal towns of Dong Hoi and Vinh, a forward HQ was established near Quang Khe, under Nguyen Ba Phat, the deputy commander of the NVN. A second base at Ben Thuy was also made operational. The NVN had no major surface combatants but instead relied on a small fleet of steel-hulled, Swatow-class patrol boats and up to 12, wooden-hulled, P-4 torpedo boats, supplied by China and the Soviet Union respectively. The former was a Shantou Type 55A-class gunboat, based on the Soviet P-6-class torpedo boat. At Quang Khe and Ben Thuy these fell under the command of 135 Torpedo Boat Squadron. The boats were ideal for littoral defense but vulnerable in blue water operations.

The distinction between the two types was important. The slower and larger Chinese Swatows were armed with 37mm medium caliber cannons and machine guns. These boats could only achieve a maximum speed of perhaps 20 knots and they carried no torpedoes. They therefore represented a negligible threat to a major surface combatant like a USN destroyer.

The faster P-4 torpedo boats, as their name suggested, carried 18-inch torpedoes, typically two either side of the bridge, as well as a heavy machine gun. These boats did represent a realistic threat to USN ships by virtue of their torpedoes and their speed (40–50 knots maximum). However, to stand any chance of a successful launch, the torpedo boats had to sail within 1,000 yards of the target, which made them vulnerable. North Vietnamese tactical handling of these craft generally involved using the Swatows as command ships vectoring the zippier P-4s toward "Nasty" intruders. The P-4s invariably came off worse as they lacked the heavy firepower to engage the "Nasties" armed with 40mm cannon. On other occasions, the Swatows would engage the "Nasties" in a fairer fight. One recorded engagement in July involved a 45-nautical-mile chase, the furthest distance any North Vietnamese boat had ventured along the coast.[15] Mostly, however, they remained within territorial waters, an important consideration that was not given due weight when later threat assessments were made. Indeed, clashes between the two navies were extremely rare, mostly it seems because the NVN lacked confidence in its boats and was wary of air attacks. The majority of raiders never saw, let alone fired upon, a North Vietnamese patrol boat in their entire service.

As *Maddox* took station in the Gulf of Tonkin, on July 31, four OPLAN 34-A raiders had shelled two islands, Hon Me and Hon Nieu, just north of Vinh. These in turn were attacked by Swatow T-142 that would play a prominent role in the subsequent sequence of events involving *Maddox*. The attack on the islands came about as a deliberate escalation ordered by McNamara, on July 24, who was concerned that the heightened state of alert of the NVN would make prohibitive – or at least inhibit – shore raids. The raiders actually attempted to land but met stiff resistance. Shelling from a safe distance seemed the better option although, given the inaccuracy of long-range cannon fire from a patrol boat, it is doubtful that such shelling achieved a great deal.

Maddox's separate mission had been requested by Sharp on July 15. The mission received approval and 48 hours later *Maddox* received her orders. In the after-action report prepared by Ogier, he described his task thus:

> The primary purpose of the patrol was to determine the coastal patrol activity furnished by the Democratic Republic of Vietnam (DRV) along the North Vietnam coast. Other intelligence requirements included collecting ELINT (Electronic Intelligence) and hydrographic information, monitoring of junk density and junk traffic patterns, conducting radarscope photography, and photographing landmarks.[16]

Although not stated explicitly in her orders, she would also gather useful intelligence by intercepting North Vietnamese communications during the OPLAN 34-A raid.

Maddox took station on July 30, the day of the attacks on the two islands, but remained in international waters well away from Hon Me and Hon Nieu. The following morning, however, she sailed close to the shoreline, close enough to catch the end of the raid and be spotted. The four boats involved were PTF-2, PTF-3, PTF-5, and PTF-6. The last had been hit by machine-gun fire and had suffered four casualties. From the North Vietnamese perspective there was an obvious connection between the raiding boats and the presence of the destroyer. This was not intended and reflected poor coordination between MACV-SOG and the DESOTO patrol. The listening station at San Miguel was aware of this possible connection being made because on August 1 it intercepted communications between two Swatows tracking the DESOTO patrol in the vicinity of Hon Me.[17] *Maddox*, however, had been completely unaware of the raids and her presence provoked an exchange of signals on the American side questioning why the destroyer had sailed so close to an area marked for covert operations. The confusion was so thorough that DIRNSA (Director NSA) later demanded to know who had informed *Maddox* and through what channels. A request was also made for a copy of *Maddox*'s operating instructions, an indication of just how heated some felt over the incident.[18]

That same day, August 1, intercepts of North Vietnamese communications suggested that an unspecified attack was being planned, possibly led by Swatow T-146.[19] The warning also correctly identified three vessels "from Battalion 135" that were possibly being prepared for the attack. This led San Miguel to issue a report entitled "DRV Navy may attack Desoto Patrol," issued at 19.24 Zulu – or 12 hours and 33 minutes before the ship was indeed attacked (the first intercept of this message was actually timed at 16.00Z or 11pm Saigon time).[20] The message indicated that it had been "decided to attack the enemy tonight," although the recipient of this instruction from Ben Thuy remained unclear. This report was backed up by a second, 30 minutes later, giving the same warning.[21] This alarmed *Maddox* sufficiently to warrant a change of course and the destroyer sailed away from the coast into international waters.

In the words of *Maddox*'s Sitrep 2, transmitted on the same day: "If info received concerning hostile intent by DRV is accurate, and have no reason to believe it is not, consider continuance of patrol present an unacceptable risk." *Maddox* remained about 25 miles offshore and east of Hon Me until the morning of August 2, after which time she then resumed her coastline track in a northerly direction toward a navigation point known as Point Delta, before turning around and heading south again, never less than eight miles from the coast. Again, North Vietnamese intercepts suggested that an attack was being planned now involving P-4 torpedo boats. However, none offered definite evidence of a planned attack against *Maddox*. The interpretation – understandable in the circumstances – was made by the SIGINT stations. A failure to warn of a possible attack would have been disastrous. In fact, the NSA got it absolutely right.[22] Just after 10am Saigon time an urgent message was flashed warning of a possible attack on *Maddox*. This message was copied to CINCPAC, MACV, and Seventh Fleet but did not reach the most important addressee, *Maddox*.[23]

By now, *Maddox* had reached a point four miles east of Hon Me, turned around, and was heading north to Point Delta again. During this part of the track, at 11.30am, a time when many of the crew were eating their Sunday lunch, the radar operator detected three hits at a range of ten nautical miles astern the *Maddox*, in the vicinity of Hon Me. The operator was familiar with these. They were typical of North Vietnamese torpedo boats. The three P-4s were also visually sighted and judged correctly to be "probable Papa-Fours." At 11.44am, Phu Bai then intercepted a message indicating that the NVN intended to mount an attack "with enemy following launched torpedoes" which led to the issuing of a CRITIC warning to all commands and *Maddox*. As *Maddox* reversed track she detected a further two boats at 12.15am, Swatows, also apparently heading for the island. These were also visually sighted. In *Maddox*'s Sitrep 3 all these craft were assessed to be heading south toward Hon Me at slow speed. Three minutes later, San Miguel also intercepted the same message captured by Phu Bai indicating a probable imminent attack. At 12.31am *Maddox* sent a signal recording all the NVN boats ten miles north of Hon Me and reporting that she had arrived at her rendezvous point (Point Delta).[24] It appears that at this stage *Maddox* was unaware that these were in fact the boats identified in signals intercepts preparing for a possible attack on the destroyer. The five boats were T-333, T-336, T-339 (P-4 torpedo boats), and T-142, T-146 (Swatows). Together, if they ganged up on *Maddox*, they stood a chance of causing some damage. Herrick did not order General Quarters and instead continued to sail on the pre-planned bearing.

A confused period of roughly two hours followed. Unbeknown to *Maddox*, the confusion was mostly on the North Vietnamese side with the boats receiving contradictory orders from Haiphong and Port Wallut. According to Vietnamese sources, the final order was a recall order but this was either not received, or it was ignored.[25] At 12.51pm, heading north, *Maddox* altered her course by 35 degrees to starboard to avoid "passing thru junk concentrations" of around 70 boats. At this stage, she was recording "no further evid hostile intent received," indicating that Herrick was aware of the CRITIC message signaling a probable imminent attack. Shortly afterwards, at 1.06pm, San Miguel intercepted another message instructing

NVN boats to "turn back [to the path] of the enemy." This message specifically identified the three P-4s but the import was misread. It appears that roughly 45 minutes later these boats received an order to attack the DESOTO patrol, countermanded by another order (that never reached them, or was ignored, as we have seen).

By 2pm *Maddox* was 12 miles east of Point Delta again when she detected a single blip on her radar 30 miles away. This hit was sailing at 30 knots and apparently toward the destroyer. Two hours after the first SIGINT warning, USM-626J at Phu Bai warned again of an imminent attack and went further, naming the North Vietnamese boats being prepared to take part in the attack. USN-27 in San Miguel confirmed this message with a translation of the North Vietnamese intercepts. The CRITIC message was issued by San Miguel at 2.16pm and advised that enemy boats were closing on the DESOTO patrol and intended to use torpedoes. This message was issued 55 minutes before the actual attack – a fantastic example of an alert warning functioning perfectly. Port Wallut, the North Vietnamese naval station, appeared to have a hand in coordinating the various boats. There is no firm evidence that Le Duan, as has been alleged, was responsible for ordering the attack to provoke Washington. The general commanding the coastal defenses was Phung The Tai. In his account of the events, he conferred with General Van Tien Dung in Hanoi.[26] There is no suggestion of a North Vietnamese provocation but rather paranoia that the American warship was cooking up some surprise attack. Indeed, Tai seems to have believed that *Maddox* attacked some northern junks, and for this reason "our patrol boats were therefore forced to fight back."

At 2.30pm Ogier sent a flash signal to Commander Seventh Fleet and ordered his ship to General Quarters. The destroyer then increased speed from 10 to 25 knots and altered course east, before then heading southeast. At 2.40pm a second signal was sent indicating that three boats were in apparent pursuit and *Maddox* intended to fire in self-defense if threatened. At 2.45pm, her fire control radars locked onto the boats at a range of just over 13 miles. The P-4s either used the junks deliberately for cover or

Map 6: Gulf of Tonkin Incident, August 2, 1964

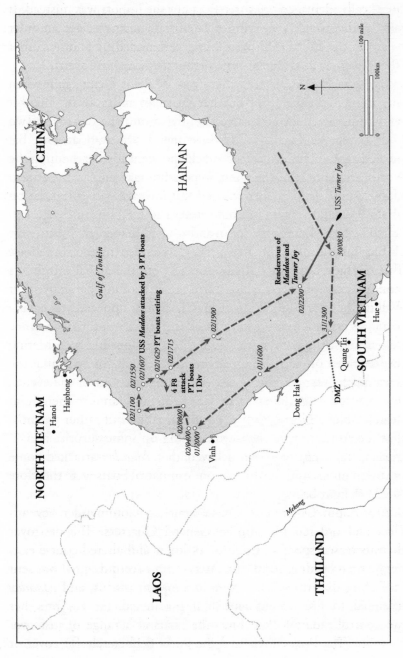

simply careered a track through the fishing fleet as it was evident to *Maddox* that the junks were dispersing. The torpedo boats were also observed to be weaving. By now the destroyer was steaming at 27 knots but the torpedo boats were capable of 40–50 knots so it was only a matter of time before they caught up. At 2.47pm, *Maddox* requested air cover. At 3pm, *Maddox* was 25 miles from the coast, with the three boats eight miles away, visually sighted and positively identified as P-4s bouncing on the sea at high speed. At 3.08pm *Maddox* sent her third signal reporting that she had been attacked. In fact, what had happened was that the destroyer had fired three warning shots – 5-inch shells fired at a range of 9,800 yards. This important opening salvo was never reported in the subsequent version of events described by Johnson.

The three boats were led by T-336, followed by T-339, with T-333 bringing up the stern. They were determined and brave. *Maddox* fired 151 5-inch shells and 132 3-inch shells at her pursuers. The gunnery was too challenging against such elusive targets, but eventually, at 3.16pm, T-339 which had taken the lead was hit at a range of around 3,000 yards. The P-4 swerved wildly, describing a full circle before coming to a halt. She then appeared to restart her engines, retreat north, then broke down again. As well as facing very difficult targets the destroyer experienced a series of technical failures: a net appeared to be jammed; the interlocks on the air search AN/SPS 40 radar tripped; the IFF (Identification Friend or Foe) failed; and many shells were exploding prematurely due to the trajectory proximity to the surface of the water. In fact, not a single 3-inch shell hit its target – all the damage was done by a single 5-inch shell. The two fire control radars (Director 58 aft and Director 37 forward), however, did remain operable throughout the attack.

T-336 had in the meantime peeled to starboard, with T-333 following behind the stricken T-339. *Maddox* believed that at least two torpedoes were launched by T-339 and that the boat was launching a third when hit. At some point after this T-336, the command boat, was also hit, killing a Lieutenant Tu. This boat was assessed to have launched a dud torpedo at a range of around 2,000 yards. T-336 was also the only boat that actually managed to hit *Maddox* with a single machine-gun round, which hit a radar pedestal and then ricocheted down a service magazine. T-333 never launched a torpedo although she did draw close to *Maddox*'s stern at one point during the attack. *Maddox* then turned to starboard at 3.24pm to attack her pursuers but discontinued this maneuver four minutes later because of the risk of unspent torpedoes.

As this action unfolded, four F-8E Crusaders already airborne from USS *Ticonderoga* (CVS-14) appeared on the scene. Armed with 20mm cannon and 5-inch Zuni rockets they gave chase to the torpedo boats. It was all over in eight minutes. T-333 and T-336 received hits and limped home. No rockets were fired but the cannon seemed to do the job. T-339 eventually joined them after restarting her engines. *Maddox*, somewhat over-optimistically, later reported that one boat sank and that the two survivors had been "badly damaged." Four crewmen, it later emerged, had been killed. The North Vietnamese claimed that two aircraft had been shot down when in fact one aircraft had sustained wing damage and the black smoke had been misinterpreted as a hit. The torpedo boats also mistakenly reported the sinking of T-339, an error that took a day to correct. *Maddox* in the meantime had steered south and headed for a rendezvous with her sister destroyer USS *C. Turner Joy* (DD-951). The excitement was over although the crew stayed at General Quarters for some time afterwards in anticipation of a possible second attack. A measure of the nervousness can be gauged by the fact that San Miguel sent a spot report at 7.32pm advising that the DESOTO patrol was under continuous surveillance and that "at least four torpedo boats were in position preparing for an imminent attack" – which was not true.[27] Phu Bai sent a similar alarmist CRITIC message the following day at 4.56pm. Nobody was taking chances.

For the North Vietnamese, it was time to lick wounds. The Swatows were tasked to find and escort home the limping P-4s and two days later, in the early hours of the morning of August 4, Swatow

T-146 transmitted a detailed message to Haiphong describing the damage sustained by the boats. This message was intercepted and was significant because it implied an extreme unlikelihood that any of the casualty boats would become involved in further action for the foreseeable future.[28] It does not appear that the contents or import of this intercept were appreciated.

On the American side, the main repercussion from the August 2 attack was a certain degree of embarrassment. One of the principles of special force operations is that they should not become entangled with conventional operations – a cordon sanitaire should be imposed. This principle had been violated. *Maddox* was unaware of the OPLAN 34-A raids on July 31 but had been allowed to steam so close that she witnessed the latter half of the operation. The destroyer was close enough to observe the withdrawal of the "Nasties" and the subsequent chase by Vietnamese Swatows. It was entirely likely that the North Vietnamese would associate the presence of the USN destroyer with the South Vietnamese patrol boats. In this respect, the mission had been compromised. The embarrassment was especially acute because de-confliction of OPLAN 34-A raids and DESOTO missions had been a point debated by MACV (Westmoreland) and CINCPAC (Sharp) over several months. From Westmoreland's point of view, there was obvious value in exploiting the DESOTO patrols to support the raids. From the Navy's point of view there was concern that the two quite separate tasks might become entangled with political repercussions. By the summer, agreement was reached to use DESOTO patrols to gather intelligence specifically useful to OPLAN 34-A operations, while not compromising the integrity of either. However, to achieve this, close liaison was required between MACV-SOG and the DESOTO patrol. This liaison appears to have been lacking. A subsequent declassified Top Secret message from HQ NSA Pacific revealed that "several days" prior to the DESOTO patrol there had been a flurry of messages between "CINPACFLT, CONSEVENTHFLT, and COMUSMACV concerning liaison to prevent interference between DESOTO and 43A operations."[29] In addition, there had been personal liaison between Rear

Admiral Robert Moorer, Commander of Task Force 77 aboard the *Ticonderoga*, and Westmoreland to ensure that "there would be no difficulties." Clearly, something had gone badly wrong.

In Washington, with the benefit of SIGINT intercepts, there was a sense that the entire episode had been a mistake. It was clear that Haiphong and Port Wallut had transmitted contradictory orders. As McNamara later stated, it was probable that a local commander had become over-excited and acted impetuously. Whether pre-meditated or impulsive, the hostile act demanded a diplomatic démarche, which Johnson duly delivered. Historically, this was the first diplomatic note sent by the United States government to the Politburo in Hanoi in the war.[30] The main concern remained asserting the right to freedom of the seas, which was reinforced by ordering the DESOTO patrol to continue. On the day following the attacks McNamara gave a private briefing to the Senate Foreign Relations Committee in which no mention was made of the link between the OPLAN 34-A raids and the attack on the *Maddox*. This disingenuous brief would later be held against the defense secretary.

On Monday August 3, *Maddox* and *Turner Joy* sailed together for mutual protection but there were no incidents and sea conditions remained calm. A planned OPLAN 34-A night-time raid against a radar site at Vinh Son went ahead, despite the obviously provocative nature of this raid after the events of the previous day. This involved PTF-1, PTF-2, PTF-5, and PTF-6 attacking a radar station at Vinh Son, as well as a Navy post on the Ron River. The Swatows, on the same day, were trying to locate the missing P-4s, which resulted in a rich stream of signals traffic. These communications were intercepted by USM-626J at Phu Bai that mistakenly, as has been noted, interpreted the mustering of boats near Hon Me as a prelude to another attack. This interpretation was significant. A pattern was being set. The nervous signalers were now viewing any concentration of North Vietnamese boats as a possible indicator of an attack.

Shortly after 8pm, an unidentified transmitter sent a message to Swatow T-142 that it had radar hits on two enemy ships on a bearing of 60 degrees, 20 nautical miles away. The ships were heading east, or toward the coast. T-142 subsequently indicated that it had received orders to shadow these ships – *Maddox* and *Turner Joy*. She continued to track the two destroyers at a safe distance using her Skin Head radar until the tracks disappeared late in the evening. There were, however, no incidents involving the DESOTO patrol. Nonetheless, there was some action and North Vietnamese caginess was fully justified. That night, the four "Nasties" sneaked along the coast to Vinh Son and fired off 700 40mm and 57mm rounds at a radar site. A third boat shelled a coastal security post on the Ron River. The Vinh Son raiders escaped but the third boat was subjected to retaliatory fire and was subsequently chased by a Swatow.[31]

On Tuesday August 4, the weather began to deteriorate as a storm front moved across the Gulf of Tonkin. That afternoon, Haiphong had informed T-142 that the US destroyer group was in the vicinity of "106-19-30E, 19-36-23N." Then at 6.40pm it was reported that both T-142 and her sister ship, T-146, had received orders to make preparations for operations for the night of August 4. Torpedo boat T-333 was also ordered to refit but there appeared to be a problem obtaining oil for this boat. This was one of the torpedo boats that had taken part in the August 2 attack, which had sustained damage to an auxiliary engine, possibly from aircraft fire. These two intercepts were linked by the marine SIGINT station at Phu Bai which warned of "immeninent [sic] plans of DRV naval action possibly against Desoto mission." The warning was issued at 6.40pm by USM-626J (USN-414T also co-located at Phu Bai had already transmitted a preliminary warning at 6.15pm).[32] This was the critical message that led Ogier to order *Maddox* to General Quarters. *Maddox* acknowledged this message exactly one hour later – at 7.40pm – and reported that she was heading away from the area at best speed in a southeasterly direction.

A moment's reflection on the possible import of the two intercepts would surely have led to a different conclusion. T-142 and T-146 were Swatows. They were armed with 37mm cannon but no torpedoes. They could not realistically threaten *Maddox* or

Turner Joy, except in some suicidal gesture that would have almost certainly resulted in both boats being sunk. The interpretation made by the Phu Bai SIGINT station was plainly wrong. Was it credible that two Swatows were going to launch in darkness and poor weather, with the mission to find the destroyer group, 80 nautical miles from the coastline, and then to attack the ships? How would they even find the destroyers with their limited Skin Head radars? The P-4s had even less of a chance. Equipped with the rudimentary Type 253 radar, they could only detect targets out to 15 nautical miles, if the radar was erected. It was known that this was not usually the case as the radar suffered damage at high speeds and was usually kept in the folded position (hence the North Vietnamese tactic of using the Swatows to vector the P-4s). Actually, in the August 2 incident, the radars were raised and the Vietnamese later claimed they were functioning but no ELINT was picked up.[33]

The entire scenario was extremely far-fetched, even after the events of August 2. If Phu Bai can be forgiven the overstated interpretation – it was after all their role to warn – there is less room to excuse *Maddox*. Why did *Maddox* not dismiss the warning as implausible? She had noted earlier that the Swatows had lost her track as she sailed further into international waters. Why was the more obvious interpretation not drawn that the two Swatows were probably being prepared for counter operations against OPLAN-34-A raiders, as they had been in previous nights (albeit, even this interpretation would have been wrong, as they were only being prepared to recover the damaged torpedo boats)? The least likely interpretation was that T-142 and T-146, possibly with a repaired T-333 in tow, were about to sail into the night in search of an engagement with the destroyers. The idea was preposterous, without hindsight.

There were other problems with this signal that would be exposed following declassification.[34] The original text – *hanh quan* in Vietnamese – meant "long march," not attack. That is, the Swatows were probably being instructed to prepare for a long task (which proved to be a salvage operation). There were no references to an enemy in the signal. The majority of this transmission, in fact, was lost. Phu Bai only caught a snatch of the message. This alone should have made the station cautious. Lastly, Phu Bai was not the only station to intercept this transmission. San Miguel in the Philippines also overheard the message. But the signalers at San Miguel presented a completely different, and as it turned out accurate, interpretation of the transmission. In their assessment, some sort of refuel operation was being prepared.

Why was San Miguel's interpretation ignored? The answer lay in the level of precedence. Phu Bai issued its signal as "CRITIC" – the highest precedence. San Miguel issued its signal as "PRIORITY" – just one level of precedence above "ROUTINE." As a consequence, the DESOTO mission received Phu Bai's message immediately on transmission, and San Miguel's message was only finally transmitted two hours after the shooting was over.[35] The station crying wolf had shouted the loudest.

By the evening, there was a blanket of low cloud, visibility was poor, and thunder storms were imminent. The latter were significant because they gave spoof readings on radars. That afternoon, *Maddox* had already picked up what it assessed to be possible torpedo boat tracks that were probably just caused by meteorological phenomena.

At 7.40pm, with the crew now at General Quarters as a result of the warning from Phu Bai, *Maddox* sent a message stating that an attack was believed imminent. Placing the crew at this heightened state of alert probably roused imaginations. Even if there was nothing out there, the captains were already looking for a threat to justify this decision. At this time, *Maddox* and *Turner Joy* were 85 nautical miles from the Vietnamese coastline – the chances of an attack, by sea or air, were nearly negligible.[36]

The subsequent reported chain of events of the evening of August 4 was pure invention. The deception involved inviting a *Life* correspondent, Bill Wise, to the Pentagon, where he was personally briefed by naval intelligence, a highly unusual step. One did not have to be a cynical old hack to figure out that Defense was spinning a story, and that Henry Luce's influential magazine was obliging Johnson by printing a desired, official version of events.

This was the tall tale the White House wanted Americans to hear:

> In 20 more minutes the *Joy* and the *Maddox* were under continuous torpedo attack and were engaging in defensive counterfire. There was now plenty for the radar-directed guns to shoot at. The *Maddox* and the *Joy* were throwing everything they had. By 10.15 the *Maddox* had avoided several torpedoes and had sunk one of the attacking craft. For the next half hour the *Maddox* and the *Joy* weaved through the night seas, evading more torpedoes and sinking another of the attackers. By this time a second wave of fighters had arrived from the *Ticonderoga*, but low ceilings prevented them from giving effective help. Despite their losses, the PTs continued to harass the two destroyers – thus making ideal targets for themselves. They also peppered the ships with more 37mm fire, keeping heads on the U.S. craft low but causing no real damage. At midnight a new wave of jets showed up equipped with flares which they dropped and attacked the PT boats, but then the action slowed down. By 1.30am the *Maddox*'s radar showed that the North Vietnamese PTs had broken off contact.[37]

None of this happened. A casual inspection of the two destroyers would have revealed that neither ship had been hit by so much as a passing albatross (other than the single round that struck *Maddox* on August 2). This *Life* account was actually published ten days after the alleged attack – plenty of time for the truth to be established, if the truth had mattered. *Maddox* and *Turner Joy* opened fire on spoof targets. The aircraft hit nothing because they found nothing. The commanding officer of the squadron flew between 700 and 1,500 feet and reported observing many gun flashes and air bursts from *Maddox* but no Vietnamese fire. Commander James Stockdale later confessed to buzzing waves.

He too had been unable to find the enemy boats. In his words, there had been "no boats, no boat wakes, no ricochets off boats, no boat impacts, no torpedo wakes – nothing but black sea and American fire power."[38] In fact, not one pilot in the subsequent debriefs reported seeing a single North Vietnamese boat.

However, by the following week, the invention had become fact. The North Vietnamese had probably attacked *Maddox* to provoke Chinese intervention (Peking obliged by staging a modest anti-American rally in Tiananmen Square, filmed by a French reporter). As many as 25 patrol boats were then reportedly sunk (half the fleet) in a retaliatory raid ordered by Johnson. Defenses were strengthened on the 17th parallel and South Vietnam's premier, General Khanh, visited the front line in a slightly comical jeep camouflaged with ferns, pursued by a press pack, aware that this was a significant turn of events in the war, but unclear what it should be reporting.

McNamara almost to the end of his life stood by the myth, albeit conceding doubts. Johnson played the same game.[39] To be fair to both men, the classified chronology of the Gulf of Tonkin incident, published by the National Security Agency (NSA) in October 1964 and based on the only truly reliable evidence – the signals intercepts – also concluded that an attack had taken place (as did numerous other reviews and reports). This chronology, however, omitted a mass of evidence that would have led to the inescapable conclusion that the events had been misconstrued.[40] Indeed, just six out of 59 relevant SIGINT products were quoted. No officials deliberately, it has been generously argued, set about to fool McNamara or Johnson, although many officials clearly sought to avoid embarrassing the national leadership. Nonetheless, the omissions were vital. It is understandable that the two men would defend their record in subsequent years as the limited top secret information they were presented supported their decision-making. The USN's official history of the Vietnam War would also record the second attack as fact (an historical infelicity uncorrected to this day). In subsequent inquiries, the NSA would refuse to release the pertinent missing material, citing security concerns. The North

Vietnamese, in contrast, would always maintain that there was no second attack.

An accurate version of the events surrounding the Gulf of Tonkin incident would have to wait another 40 years, pieced together from declassified materials. The unassailable version of the truth of events that took place on August 4 reposed in the SECRET KIMBO signals intelligence (SIGINT) intercepts.[41] What they revealed was a certain level of tension in the Tonkin Gulf following the events of August 2, some innocent NVN activities – but, no attack.

Following the August 2 attacks, Vice Admiral Roy Johnson, Commander Seventh Fleet, advised caution and argued that the DESOTO patrol should withdraw on August 4. This recommendation was overruled by Moorer (one rung under Sharp and known by the acronym CINCPACFLT to distinguish him from CINCPAC). Washington had already made a public statement denouncing the attacks. Withdrawal now would send a mixed message to the North Vietnamese and suggest a lack of resolve. Furthermore, the JCS, following consultations with McNamara and Johnson, had already decided to despatch *Turner Joy* to support *Maddox*. The DESOTO mission would continue as planned. While these decisions were being taken, Commander Seventh Fleet was warned by Captain Herrick that SIGINT indicated the North Vietnamese were linking the coincidence of *Maddox* with the special operations raids and a further attack on the destroyer was a distinct possibility.

As we have seen, at 6.40pm, Phu Bai warned *Maddox* that it assessed an attack on the ship as imminent which led to Ogier ordering the ship's company at General Quarters. This message was received by the Defense Intelligence Agency's (DIA) Indications Center in the Pentagon at 8.13am by the watch officer.[42] Another source suggests that the warning arrived in Washington at 7.40am.[43] When the Chairman of the JCS, General Earle

287

Wheeler, arrived at work, he and McNamara were advised of the intelligence warning received by the watch officer. This occurred at around 9am. Wheeler, coincidentally, was about to fly to New York for a meeting with the *New York Times*. Canceling the meeting abruptly would raise suspicions so McNamara suggested that Wheeler continue with his planned schedule. Whether or not intentional, this decision left McNamara as the only captain on the bridge, if a crisis blew up, which suited his temperament. After Wheeler departed, McNamara informed the President of the intelligence warning. This phone call was made at 9.12am.[44] At the time, Johnson was at a breakfast meeting with congressional leaders which had started at 8.45am.

At the Indications Center, all then went quiet and the Pentagon settled down to another day at work. This calm contrasted with what was happening several thousand miles away in the Gulf of Tonkin. *Maddox*, now on full alert, began to detect phantom threats. At 8.36pm (message received in the Pentagon at 10.30am) the destroyer informed *Ticonderoga* that her radar operators had detected two "skunks" (possible enemy boats) and three "bogies" (possible enemy aircraft) near Hainan Island, over 100 miles from the North Vietnamese coastline. *Ticonderoga* retransmitted this message. Air cover was requested and four A1-H Skyraiders were despatched arriving roughly one hour later over *Maddox*. The "bogies" proved to be spoof tracks and the "skunks" were unidentified ships, 40 miles northeast of the destroyer. For reasons that have never been fully established, but were probably technical, *Ticonderoga* was only able to forward *Maddox*'s second message to the Indications Center a full two hours later (hence the receipt of the message at 10.30am).[45] Two more sets of spoof tracks were detected over the next hour and a half and four A-4 Skyhawks investigated the second detections but found nothing.[46] At this stage, it should have been evident that over-heated imaginations were beginning to overtake rational thought.

As this second message was being transmitted, McNamara called an emergency meeting to discuss the events in the Gulf of Tonkin. This was convened at 9.25am and was attended by Lieutenant

General David Burchinal, the Director of the Joint Staffs; Cyrus Vance, McNamara's Deputy Secretary; and their staffs.[47] The meeting had only been running ten minutes when Johnson returned from the breakfast meeting with congressional leaders and contacted McNamara asking for more details on the intelligence warning (at around 9.43am according to the presidential diary). If McNamara could be accused of micro-management it was also entirely in keeping with Johnson's meddling that he should demand more information and become drawn into the meeting only half an hour after receiving the first call from his defense secretary. A more detached president would have continued with his schedule and bided his time – after all, what could possibly have happened in the intervening 30 minutes that demanded his full attention? The original message had only suggested possible preparations for an attack. No ship in the Gulf, at this stage, had detected an actual threat or attack. Had an attack taken place, it would have been reasonable to assume that McNamara would have alerted Johnson, but he had not.

McNamara spoke at length with Johnson. Sharp in Honolulu was in a hawkish mood and was seeking authorization to hunt and sink North Vietnamese patrol boats. He wanted *Maddox* and *Turner Joy* to steam toward, not away from the Vietnamese coastline. McNamara viewed this proposal dimly, mostly it seems, because he feared that events might spiral out of control, or more exactly, his control. The last thing he wanted was a group of admirals getting carried away with a naval action, which it seemed they were quite likely to do unless reined in. Johnson seemed to side with the admirals. Can't we attack? He demanded. Why can't the Air Force drop a bridge? Didn't the Pentagon have three pre-selected targets that could be attacked as immediate retaliation? McNamara bowed to Johnson and promised that a target set would be prepared over the next few hours (in fact, he had already informed McGeorge Bundy, the Special Presidential Advisor, that this planning was underway). The call ended with both men agreeing to meet at lunchtime in the White House. At this stage, *Maddox's* second message had still not reached the Indications Center so neither man knew that the destroyer group only believed that it had detected North Vietnamese boats and aircraft.

What followed, then, was puzzling. Moorer, aboard the *Ticonderoga*, sent a signal reporting that the original "skunks" reported by *Maddox* were detected at 40 miles, but that three new "skunks" had been detected at 13 miles and were closing to 11 miles. This followed a message from *Maddox* at 9.08pm (received in the Pentagon at 11.04am) reporting the disappearance of the "bogies" but the continued presence of unidentified surface ships. He also added that the CAP (Combat Air Patrol) was now overhead the DESOTO ships and control of the aircraft had been passed to Ogier.[48] What boats were detected, if indeed the detections were not spoof, is not established. As it is known that the aircraft did not, in the end, find or attack any Vietnamese patrol boats on the night of August 4, there appears to be a high probability that everyone was now reacting to phantom threats.

Then, at 9.34pm, *Maddox* detected what she assessed to be a single boat east of her position, at a range of roughly 10,000 yards and closing at 40 knots.[49] Some minutes later, this track, now at 6,000 yards, appeared to veer south. This phantom track proved to be the blip that provoked the entire sequence of events that followed. Calmer heads would have reasoned that even if this were a P-4 torpedo boat, it posed no threat. Not only was it now apparently sailing away from *Maddox*, but to stand any chance of a successful launch, the Russian torpedoes she carried had to launch at a range of less than 1,000 yards. *Turner Joy*, meanwhile, had also detected a quite separate false track (which was later conflated with *Maddox*'s detection), adding to the developing sense of paranoia. Around six minutes later, at 9.40pm, *Maddox* flashed a fourth message indicating that she had commenced radar-directed fire against the suspected Vietnamese torpedo boat. *Turner Joy* joined in. The gun flashes from the two destroyers were the flashes later reported by the pilots. The communications difficulties being experienced were evident as *Ticonderoga* reported this engagement in a signal erroneously timed at 04140Z (oddly missing a digit), which was retransmitted by the JCS to the White House, among other recipients, at 041617Z, or 11.17pm Saigon time and 11.17am Eastern Daylight Time.[50] However, according to former NSA cryptologic historian Hanyok, a flash message indicating that the destroyers were under attack did reach the Pentagon at 10am Eastern Daylight Time, or over an hour earlier.[51] What this message was remains unclear because the top secret chronology compiled subsequently by the NSA, which indeed referred to a 10am attack message in the main text, then referenced this warning to an annex (Tab 37), which is the message timed at 11.17am. Clearly, it looked much better if it could be claimed that notice of an attack reached the Pentagon at 10am, but, as we shall see, the actions and conversations of the protagonists in Washington suggest otherwise.

These opening salvos only lasted five minutes after which the guns fell silent because the tracks had disappeared (all the firing was radar-directed and at no time did the destroyers engage by visual detection). For the next nervous quarter of an hour the two destroyers continued to steer a southwesterly course. Then all hell broke loose. *Maddox* reported at 9.52pm that the ships were under continuous torpedo attacks.[52] Just after 10pm, a series of phantom blips provoked *Turner Joy* to open fire. The fact that the blips were detected east of the destroyers (on the seaward side) did not provoke questions. Hundreds of shells were lofted into the sea. The pilots overhead flew from one reported track to the next, failing to find any torpedo boats. Star shells were fired but nothing was seen. At one point *Turner Joy* was reporting an attack by as many as 13 "contacts" – or the entire NVN torpedo boat fleet.[53] This farrago lasted for another hour and a half before the "engagement" was declared closed. *Maddox* conservatively reported that two boats had been sunk and a third damaged, although she did not subsequently open fire because her single operable radar could not detect any of the blips being reported by *Turner Joy*. Given the difficulty *Maddox* had experienced hitting the attacking patrol boats on August 2, in broad daylight and at close range, even if there had been an enemy out there, this was a highly flattering and improbable post-action assessment.

None of this should have happened. At almost the same time that *Maddox* opened fire against the first blip, Phu Bai transmitted a rather interesting spot report.[54] It stated that T-333, along with another boat, was being towed to port, and it added that Swatow T-142 had warned the tug to avoid the American destroyers, if it chanced upon them. In other words, the North Vietnamese had no clue where the DESOTO mission was, and furthermore they mistakenly believed it was sailing somewhere close to the shoreline, not 80-odd miles away. Rather than attacking the American destroyers, the NVN was fully preoccupied with trying to recover its two stricken torpedo boats from the August 2 attack, and was doing everything it could to avoid the American ships while it undertook this vulnerable operation. It subsequently transpired that this is exactly what happened. The tug and Swatows spent the entire August 4–5 involved in a salvage operation. Phu Bai, at the time, was well aware that this was happening because more intercepts over the course of the night added more detail to the salvage attempts.

By now the JCS was receiving situation reports on the developing situation in the Gulf of Tonkin and alternative retaliatory actions were being discussed. At 9.55am, McNamara held a brief conversation with State Secretary Dean Rusk.[55] Rusk supported retaliating against the torpedo boats but was cautious about bombing targets in North Vietnam. McNamara countered that Johnson was in a bullish mood. He had already instructed McNamara to propose options for a bombing raid in North Vietnam.

At 10.19am, McNamara spoke with Sharp in Honolulu (where it was just after 4am, hardly a propitious hour for clear-headed thought).[56] Sharp, in fact, had only just been roused and had not yet read the growing body of signals. The two men concurred that the Navy had the right to self-defense. When Sharp explained that four aircraft were already launched, and in fact by now were on the scene, McNamara told Sharp not to limit the aircraft launches after an attack had taken place, but to launch eight, ten, or even 20 aircraft – an example of McNamara playing the tactical commander. These were events taking place thousands of miles away, about which the JCS only had an incomplete picture, and McNamara was effectively attempting to take over the bridge of *Ticonderoga*. What was significant about this exchange, however, was that both men assumed, at this stage, that *no attack had taken place*. The conversation was about what should happen, *if* an attack were mounted. The point of McNamara's call was to assure Sharp that he had Washington's backing to defend with all available means American warships in the Gulf of Tonkin.

Over two hours after the first message had been received by the Indications Center everyone was discussing theoretical attacks but acting as if actual attacks had taken place. There is some confusion on this point, as we have seen, because Hanyok asserts that a message indicating that the destroyers were under attack did in fact reach the Pentagon at 10am (10.04am precisely), or when *Turner Joy* opened up for a second time.[57] If this is the case – and this author is reluctant to question Hanyok's forensic analysis – then the message did not reach McNamara before his 10.19am conversation with Sharp, as their discussion would otherwise not make sense. It is unambiguous from the audio recording of the 10.19am telephone conversation that both men are discussing how to respond, if an attack takes place.

Fourteen minutes later, at 10.33am, McNamara signaled Sharp, authorizing the carrier aircraft to attack within three nautical miles of the North Vietnamese coastline (the standing rules of engagement stipulated that the aircraft could only attack in daylight and on the seaward side of USN ships).[58] At the same time, a second carrier, USS *Constellation*, received confirmatory orders to join *Ticonderoga*. McNamara had previously indicated this change in the rules of engagement in the 10.19am telephone call.[59]

The confusion and the ramping up of the military stakes continued. At 10.53am McNamara phoned Johnson and advised him of *Maddox*'s first message (the spoof detections of "bogies" and "skunks"), now several hours old, and the launching of *Ticonderoga*'s aircraft. The fact that he was recycling old news seemed to pass everyone by. The old news was being used as a substitute for new news, because there was none to tell. The conversation concluded with McNamara telling Johnson that he would bring along a potential target set for retaliatory action when the two men met in an hour's time. The JCS by now had drawn up a list of potential targets. They included: the torpedo boats and their bases (the only justified target, if an attack took place); a steel mill; some bridges; and some oil installations. At this stage, McNamara was being advised by General Burchinal that any such attacks could probably not be mounted any earlier than first light on August 5.

While these deliberations were taking place, Burchinal was in conversation with Sharp who informed the general at around 10.59am that he had received a message from *Maddox* reporting that the destroyers were under torpedo attack.[60] This appears to be *the first confirmed reporting of a purported attack*, albeit only by telephone, received in Washington (if the earlier reported 10am or 10.04am message times are discounted). As is known, *Turner Joy* was simply engaging phantom targets in the night, as were the pilots. Burchinal told McNamara of the development and he informed Johnson two minutes later, at 11.06am. It was agreed that Rusk and Bundy should straightaway drop what they were doing and rush to the Pentagon to agree on appropriate retaliatory actions. The dice was now rolled.

To be fair to the protagonists in Washington, how could they possibly know that Sharp's report of an attack on the destroyers was erroneous? Shortly after these exchanges, the JCS retransmitted the 11.17am Eastern Daylight Time message describing "PT from west continued attacking run," and *Maddox* opening fire. This made sense in the context of an earlier 10.59am Eastern Daylight Time message from the JCS to the White House (retransmitting a 9.52pm Saigon time message), "Am under continuous torpedoes attack," as well as the telephone call between Sharp and Burchinal.

At this stage, the majority of the protagonists were at a meeting convened in the Pentagon at 11.20am. The attendees included several generals and senior officials: LeMay, McDonald, Johnson, Greene, Goodpaster, Burchinal, and Mustin. Rusk and his Deputy Assistant Secretary of State for Far Eastern Affairs arrived at 11.38am. Bundy arrived two minutes later. The meeting was held in the Pentagon State Dining Room. It is unclear why this venue was chosen (the JCS would normally meet in a room known as "The Tank" which was equipped with appropriate secure communications links). A number of options were discussed and the veteran LeMay, deputizing for Wheeler, was asked to prepare a military plan for the next 48 hours. Burchinal by now had informed Sharp (at 11.18am) that the JCS was taking a hawkish view on the attacks and was preparing a stiff response. This exchange took place over an insecure line in coded language, suggesting that Burchinal had now left "The Tank." As the carrier aircraft lacked a credible night attack capability, it was agreed that a retaliatory response would have to wait until first light.

The meeting in the State Dining Room only lasted 20 minutes. McNamara retired to his office with Vance, Rusk, and Bundy, leaving the military staffs in the JCS to continue working up the military options. At 12.20pm Vance returned to confer with the JCS over conducting strikes at first light. McNamara, Rusk, and Bundy had already left for the White House. The drive took 18 minutes. Five minutes later, Vance joined them.

At the White House, a National Security Council (NSC) meeting was convened in the Cabinet Room at 12.35pm. There were 17 attendees, including all Johnson's principal lieutenants. Scribbled in the presidential diary were the ominous words "On Vietnam." Johnson only sat for around half an hour as he had a prior engagement with 30-odd representatives of the National Medical Association.

While this NSC meeting was underway, the JCS continued working on the military problem for almost another hour and a half before closing the meeting at 1.49pm. Burchinal took responsibility for informing McNamara of the JCS's conclusions. The defense secretary was by now having a working lunch with the President, along with Vance, Rusk, McGeorge Bundy, and John McCone, Director of the CIA, who had joined the group. The lunch started at 1.04pm but the delayed Johnson was only able to join at 1.36pm.[61]

However, the reporting from CINCPAC, by now, had become erratic. Just before Vance wandered back into the JCS (at 12.22pm), Sharp was informing Burchinal that nine torpedoes had been launched and that two Vietnamese torpedo boats had been sunk. Even as they were speaking, the number was bumped up to ten torpedoes and Burchinal was told that *Constellation* had already launched aircraft that were at the scene (now past midnight off the North Vietnamese coast). As would very soon be determined by the two destroyers, these purported torpedo attacks were all false readings caused by the wakes of the ships steering evasive courses. It appears that even before the "attacks" were over *Maddox* was already beginning to suspect that this was the case.[62]

At around 1.30pm, just before the JCS finally concluded its meeting in the Pentagon Dining Room, McNamara pestered Burchinal for an answer, presumably because Johnson had now leaned on McNamara for a definitive option. Burchinal informed McNamara that the JCS had concluded that the most appropriate course of action was to attack the three known torpedo boat bases and oil installations at Vinh and Phuc Loi. Alarmingly, he added that signals intercepts reported a torpedo boat had been hit and an aircraft shot down. According to an intercept, cataloged as Report Number 12, Swatow T-142 signaled the news of a shot down aircraft at 10.54pm (or 041654Z) to My Duc.

Fourteen minutes later, a very similar message was sent, only stating that an aircraft had been damaged and two comrades "sacrificed." The date on this message, Report Number 13, was changed to August 3. The NSA redacted the sender, 40 years later, when the signals were finally declassified. A desire to protect the originating station appears evident. No aircraft were shot down or damaged on August 4. The reported shot down aircraft, it may be assumed, was one of the F-8E Crusaders damaged on August 2 that began to smoke from one of its engines and which flew to Da Nang. The transmission timings of these two SIGINT messages were also significant. The first was forwarded at 10.30pm and the second at 10.44pm. These coincided with the rough times of the "attacks" on the *Maddox* and *Turner Joy*, reinforcing a perception that they had to refer to this purported event. In fact, there was significant debate over what these messages related to among the NSA staff but by then a certain pressure to provide proof of an attack was building, although this was later denied.[63]

The reason why these and a later NSA message were crucial to the whole affair was that they allowed McNamara and Johnson to assert that something had happened, as it became clearer in the succeeding days that the DESOTO mission had probably not been attacked. News that a USN aircraft had been shot down raised the stakes. McNamara retorted that he needed more information from Sharp and he informed Johnson of the unfortunate development. The key later message was issued by the NSA at 2.33pm Eastern Daylight Time and included the "clincher" phrases: "shot down two planes in the battle area," and, "we had sacrificed two ships and all the rest are OK."[64] This unambiguously suggested an action had taken place, at least in the minds of the protagonists in Washington.

Then technical problems appeared to overtake the management of the incident. The saturation of flash messages caused an overloading of the communications system forcing Sharp to issue an instruction to downgrade the precedence level of messages to ease the blockage. This measure also slowed down the passage of signals. For apparently unrelated reasons voice communications between Honolulu and the task force also broke down for about half an hour.

A single crucial message did get through from Captain Herrick which began to raise doubts over the previously reported events. This message was sent at 1.27pm Eastern Daylight Time to Sharp, who passed it on to Burchinal. What is not clear is when exactly Sharp told Burchinal, and when the latter then told McNamara. The timings indicate the interchange between Sharp and Burchinal probably happened at some point between 1.30pm and 2pm, or when McNamara and the others were still at the working lunch with Johnson. McNamara recalled that he was not informed of this message while he was at lunch but first read it back in his office (which would have been roughly after 3.30pm). If it is the case that McNamara only saw this crucial information after he left the White House, then some responsibility may fall on Burchinal because he was relaying messages to McNamara, and he had already relayed the critical Swatow T-142 intercept that was later treated as the "clincher." Reportedly, Burchinal told Sharp that he would pass on the message expressing doubts to McNamara, but this is not to say that he did so immediately, or at all. There is a possibility that in fact he did not pass on the message for the innocent reason that very shortly afterwards, Sharp then offered a contradictory version of events.

Regardless, at an early stage it is evident that some protagonists knew there were doubts over the incident. The crucial message read:

> Review of action makes many reported contacts and torpedoes fired appear doubtful. Freak weather effects on radar and overeager sonarmen may have accounted for many reports. No actual visual sightings by *Maddox*. Suggest complete evaluation before any further action taken.[65]

Maddox also stated that "the entire action leaves many doubts except for attempted apparent ambush at the beginning."[66] Herrick may have been motivated in sending this message, at least in part, because he was aware of the kerfuffle that the purported attack was causing and his reputation was now on the line. The truth was beginning to out.

Whether he was told verbally, over a telephone line by Burchinal while he was still in the White House (judged unlikely as McNamara would not have lied on so important a matter, and if he had, the White House telephone record would have revealed the lie), or whether he first read this message back in his office as he later maintained, McNamara's first duty should have been to inform Johnson that there was a significant question mark hanging over the purported events. New information was beginning to filter through suggesting that there had been no attack. As *Maddox* was candidly suggesting, a "complete evaluation" was required. That McNamara almost certainly did not discuss this message with Johnson has been held against him as evidence that the defense secretary was duping his master. This viewpoint misses important timings.

The working lunch had ended at 2.55pm and Johnson retired to his bedroom from where he typically despatched private business. Over lunch, as we shall shortly see, Johnson had already made up his mind and ordered retaliatory attacks.[67] In characteristic fashion, Johnson then began working the telephone from his bedroom. It was not until 3.44pm that the President rang his secretary of defense (now back at the Pentagon) and McNamara returned the call seven minutes later at 3.51pm. In the interim there had been further developments overtaking the message, casting doubts on the attack.

At 2.08pm, Eastern Daylight Time, Sharp again called Burchinal. Now he offered a contradictory message. Moorer had sent him a message with a 36-minute delay reporting three torpedo boats sunk. How could this possibly fit the 1.27pm message that cast doubts over the attacks? Pressed by Burchinal, Sharp seemed to backtrack. There probably had been some spoof hits, he suggested, but there was also "no doubt" that a torpedo attack had taken place, he thought. Or did he? Sharp, who had now been awake since the early hours of the morning, grappling with frustrating communications systems, may well have become befuddled by the stream of reporting. Burchinal did exchange this information with McNamara while he was still at the White House lunch because the defense secretary then held a conversation with Sharp. Once again Sharp was ambiguous. There had been an attack, but there was "a little doubt on just what exactly went on," he told McNamara.[68] At this stage everyone in the White House believed that an attack had taken place, that at least one Navy aircraft had been shot down, and Johnson was about to give the green light for retaliation.

Johnson's decisiveness was based on a single message. At 2.33pm – still at the White House working lunch – McNamara was passed NSA T10-64, the hugely important and misleading message that summarized the earlier SIGINT reporting of a damaged or shot down Navy aircraft.[69] This message was definitely conveyed to Johnson, as in his recollection he was advised this implied an attack had clearly taken place. It was on the strength of this information, according to Johnson, that he resolved a retaliatory attack should be executed. McNamara then advised the attack could not take place earlier than first light Saigon time (the advice Vance had gleaned from the JCS before joining his boss in the White House) and he now needed to return to the Pentagon to work out the details. It was agreed the National Security Council would re-convene at 6.15pm and Johnson would meet congressional leaders at 6.45pm. As described, lunch was then concluded at 2.55pm, Johnson retired to his bedroom, and McNamara drove back to the Pentagon.

NSA T10-64 has been exhaustively and brilliantly analyzed by cryptologic historian Robert Hanyok. To avoid simply regurgitating Hanyok's arguments and to save the reader more confusion, his conclusions were these. The original Vietnamese signal was almost certainly transmitted more or less when the purported attacks started, which implies that it could not have been an after-action report as later claimed; the original Vietnamese translation has been lost, complicating interpretation; a second San Miguel translation also appears to be missing from the archives; a San Miguel signal that does exist, Report 38 timed at 10.50pm (or 20-odd minutes after the earlier signals conveying the same information), also only talks of two comrades "sacrificed" which later became "boats";[70] the message landed at the White House at the worst possible time when everyone was looking for a smoking gun amidst the growing doubts; and another intercept, possibly reporting the flares and star shells of August 4, was conflated with the falling aircraft intercept.

This was mishandling of SIGINT material. The critical original text of an intercepted North Vietnamese report purportedly on the events of August 4, used as clinching evidence by Johnson, was drawn from two discrepant translations (one drafted by the SIGINT station in the Philippines and the second by the NSA) which were conflated into a single document. The original text, it appears, was then destroyed, effectively only leaving the secondary sources (the translations). Without the original Vietnamese, it would be impossible to determine why two different translators drafted quite different interpretations.[71] Taken together these arguments seriously undermine the credibility of NSA T10-64. The unexplained destruction of the crucial North Vietnamese text – which presumably contained the unvarnished truth, in the sense that it was direct transcript rather than translated interpretation – also undermines the NSA's honesty, although Hanyok stops short of making such an allegation.

By now McNamara had rushed back to the Pentagon, arriving at around 3.30pm, and joined the JCS who were planning the retaliatory strike. Even as the staffs were preparing the orders, the JCS began to receive more and more messages adding fresh doubts to the reported events of the morning. Nobody had seen North Vietnamese boats. The sonar and radar hits were almost certainly spoofs. In fact, by now, clarification of the contradictory SIGINT messages was beginning to emerge, a story too involved to relate. There was also the evidence of the August 2 attack which had provided the SIGINT stations with a priceless record of the transmissions and radar emissions of the NVN actually undertaking an attack. None of these indicators were detected – not one. The single lesson that emerged from the real attack on August 2 was just how difficult it was for the North Vietnamese to coordinate a torpedo attack, in daylight, in visual contact, and with ideal sea conditions. Across the network of protagonists there was now abundant noise to at least call for a pause.

It almost was. By now, it was difficult to ignore the doubts cast on "the attack." To McNamara's credit, he realized that thundering down the taxiway of a retaliatory air strike was wrong before first re-checking the facts. Just after 4pm, following his two conversations with Johnson, he contacted Sharp to clarify what was known of the incident. CINCPAC now quoted *Maddox*'s immediate after-action report (timed at 2.48pm or roughly an hour after the first *Maddox* report expressing doubts). This report stated:

> Certain that original ambush was bonafide. Details of action following present a confusing picture. Have interviewed witnesses who made positive visual sightings of cockpit lights

or similar passing near *Maddox*. Several reported torpedoes were probably boats themselves which were observed to make several close passes on *Maddox*. Own ship screw noises on rudders may have accounted for some. At present cannot even estimate number of boats involved. *Turner Joy* reports two torpedoes passed near her.[72]

Criticism that seeks to portray "McNamara the liar" bypasses this message. Yet its significance is not that it served to convince the defense secretary that something had happened. The opposite happened. McNamara sensibly viewed this report as unsatisfactory. More certainty was necessary. Sharp pleaded for more time but time was now running out. The defense secretary needed to coordinate the NSC meeting, a press release, and an air strike within the next two hours to meet the 7am Saigon time deadline. Sharp believed it was do-able if he were just given one more hour. The fact was McNamara did not have more hours to play with. Just over half an hour later, at 4.47pm, he sat down with the JCS and a judgment was made, it appears collectively, that an attack had taken place. At 5.09pm, McNamara conveyed this determination to Johnson.

Throughout this period, Johnson, who was busy despatching other business, was not kept fully in the loop over the growing doubts. That this has been portrayed as a deliberate attempt by McNamara to withhold information from the President does not take into account the fog of confusion that afternoon. Nor does it weigh Johnson's political calculus, which McNamara and everyone else involved was well aware of. Rusk escapes lightly in this version of events, but he as much as McNamara was convinced that an attack had taken place and urged strong action, as did all the members of the JCS. Nobody was dissenting.

Following the August 2 attack, Johnson's biggest worry was his presidential rival Senator Goldwater "raising so much hell about how he's gonna blow 'em off the moon," and the White House, by contrast, not appearing "firm."[73] In late May, Goldwater had raised the stakes so far as to suggest that America should drop low-yield nuclear bombs on all the North Vietnamese infiltration routes, an irresponsible rabble-rousing suggestion that appealed to a Republican electorate. In April, he had called for the destruction of the Vietnamese rice harvest. For Johnson, the real significance over events in the Gulf of Tonkin lay in domestic politics. He didn't give a flying fish over what had actually happened. Indeed, just before the NSC meeting, held at 6.16pm later that evening, Johnson told his White House operator to get hold of Goldwater, then at the Balboa Bay Club in California. That Johnson should remember Goldwater at this juncture, and attempt to reach him, is terribly revealing of what was actually going on inside his head. As it happened, Goldwater was out in the bay sailing, and could not be reached immediately; he finally returned the call at 10.06pm from Newport Beach. A canny Johnson then instructed his secretary, "Type up these Goldwater notes, just the last part," in case he needed the ammunition for a later moment on the campaign trail.

McNamara knew perfectly well that Johnson wanted to appear "firm" – they had held a conversation on this very issue following the first attack. In this light, McNamara emerges not so much as a deceiver but as a too-loyal servant keen to deliver the President an opportunity to show mettle. It was Johnson, not McNamara, who was urging that the North Vietnamese be hit "damned quick" if a second attack took place.

A secondary consideration is that events in the Gulf of Tonkin were not the only fare on the President's menu that day. The lunchtime NSC meeting had in fact been called to discuss crises in Cyprus and the Congo (which would result in Under Secretary Ball being despatched to the former and Governor Harriman to the latter). This meeting, quite separate to the events in the Gulf of Tonkin, had attracted no lesser a crowd than Robert Kennedy, McCone, McDermott, Ball, Talbot, Dillon, Reedy, Valenti, Clifton, Bromley Smith, and Komer. McNamara had effectively gate-crashed another meeting and added friction to minds already focused on other issues. On the domestic front, Johnson was vexed by the news that three missing civil rights workers had been found buried near a dam at Philadelphia, Mississippi, a story that was receiving international coverage. Tonkin was a distraction in what would have been a busy day anyway.

Five reasons were cited as proof of the attack, which have subsequently been pored over by historians. The first two amounted to "battlefield anecdotal reporting" in operational analysis parlance. In other words, they were uncorroborated witness statements of doubtful credibility. One was the claim that *Turner Joy* was illuminated and fired on by machine guns. The other was that one of the ships saw enemy cockpit lights. The third reason was Sharp's word – an example of buck-passing that should not have been allowed to stand because Sharp was not in the room to agree. If all Sharp's telephone conversations are joined together what comes across is a man who was not expressing himself with conviction, for understandable reasons. It was weak to effectively argue that "Sharp said it happened, so it must have happened" because this was not a true reflection of all that Sharp reported that morning. The last two reasons were the "clinchers," which thanks to Hanyok's meticulous analysis, as we have seen, were anything but proof of an attack. The first was Swatow T-142's message that it had fired on two American aircraft and the second was the NVN's report that two boats had been "sacrificed." These flimsy reasons and especially the SIGINT "evidence" would justify both the retaliatory attack and Johnson's subsequent manipulation of Congress.

Even while these deliberations were taking place, at just after 5pm the news wires began to sing with reports of an attack on American ships, adding to the sense of urgency that the administration had to act fast or appear weak. Now Sharp phoned Burchinal one last time (at 5.23pm) to discuss the message describing the sacrifice of two boats. Burchinal, it appears, was afflicted by self-doubts and wondered, correctly, whether this message actually referred to the August 2 attack.[74] Both men then seemed to talk each other into believing that this referred to an attack that night and the message constituted the best evidence that *Maddox* and *Turner Joy* had been ambushed.

It was time to pull the chocks away. At 5.29pm, the JCS transmitted the execute order to the carrier task force, ordering strikes against five targets by 7am, or more crucially to everyone in the room, at 7pm Washington time.

If only time and space could bend to the wishes of presidents. It straightaway became clear that when Sharp asserted that an attack could be carried out by 7am, what he really meant was, give or take one hour or possibly longer. The President was addressing the nation at 7pm. Before that he was meeting congressional leaders.

The time-on-target (TOT) now slipped to 8am with the off-target time estimated at 9am. Even this estimate was wrong. The harassed Sharp had not calculated that *Ticonderoga* could not simply compress her rota cycles (carriers typically operated on three eight-hour cycles). The carrier was in the middle of a cycle with aircraft in support of the DESOTO mission.

At 6.16pm, the NSC convened anyway. McNamara briefed all the attendees of the attacks and the planned retaliatory strikes. At least one voice (Carl Rowan, Director of the United States Information Agency) questioned whether the attacks had really occurred and he was assured that classified information would be released shortly as proof. McNamara also hinted that a congressional resolution would be sought authorizing further action, if required, after the attacks, now estimated at 9pm Washington time. Half an hour later, at 6.45pm, the same scene was repeated with congressional leaders who gave their support to the presidential decision after listening to Johnson at his persuasive best. "Are we going to tuck our tails and run?" he asked the congressmen. Hell no, hit them.

It was at this latter meeting that McNamara untruthfully assured congressmen the attack had been unprovoked. This has also been held against the defense secretary. But once again, criticism bypasses important points. A personality like Senator Fulbright was cleared and briefed on the Pentagon's special operations and was aware of the OPLAN 34-A raids. Others were not. The defense secretary was procedurally perfectly correct not to reveal either the existence of the raids or the nature of *Maddox*'s mission. McNamara, though, did propose leaking the existence of the OPLAN 34-A raids.

George Ball has explained that he and McNamara discussed this option following the August 2 attack.[75] The measure was not in the end pursued. Had it been, McNamara would not have had to behave evasively with the congressmen.

With 20 minutes to go before Johnson's television address, McNamara telephoned Sharp. Find out when the aircraft took off, he demanded. Sharp scuttled away. Half an hour later, with the 9pm deadline now past, McNamara telephoned Sharp again. Where are the aircraft? When did they take off? Sharp's answer sunk McNamara, the only boat that was sunk that day. Actually, no aircraft had taken off, he told the shocked McNamara. It would probably be another 50 minutes before any aircraft took off and they were unlikely to be on target before 11am, but he couldn't say which target. Clearly, Johnson could not go on national television and tell the North Vietnamese: switch on your radars and man your antiaircraft guns – we are coming for you.

What followed was a comedy of errors, except for two pilots, one of whom lost his life. Johnson did eventually deliver his address to the nation shortly after 11.30pm but out of synchronization with events in the Gulf of Tonkin.[76] What actually happened was that *Ticonderoga* launched a four-ship at 10.30pm Washington time. But these were only A1-H Skyraiders that would take an hour and 50 minutes to reach their targets. Then, at 12.16pm and 12.33pm (on August 5) the jets were launched: A-4 Skyhawks and F-8E Crusaders. *Constellation* then launched at 1am, followed by a second wave at 2.30am. It would be ungenerous to recount the several telephone conversations between McNamara and Sharp that took place over this period as both men attempted to understand what was happening and when. It should also be recalled that both men had now been running for over 16 hours with barely a pause, and in Sharp's case since before dawn. Exhaustion was beginning to take its toll.

At Loc Chau, one of the A1-H Skyraiders was shot down. At Hon Gay, further north, Lieutenant Everett Alvarez Jr., flying an A-4 Skyhawk, met the same fate but parachuted and survived. Alvarez then gained fame as America's first pilot POW and he would eventually spend over eight years in captivity. By the time he was released, the unfortunate Alvarez returned to a quite different America. Both aircraft had launched from *Constellation*. Johnson's broadcast had made no difference. It was *Ticonderoga's* earlier strikes that placed the North Vietnamese on general alert and subsequent intercepts showed the aircraft had been detected anyway. In total, 64 sorties were flown against North Vietnamese naval bases at Hon Gay, Loc Chao, Phuc Loi, and Quang Khe. The pilots rammed home their attacks: eight boats were sunk, 21 were damaged, and an oil facility was burned to the ground. At least the naval aviators had played their part.

It is plain there were many mitigating and ensnared factors in the Gulf of Tonkin incident. A patient reader will have appreciated that the timings were hellishly difficult. All military reporting is in Zulu Time, or Greenwich Mean Time (GMT), which even military personnel can find confusing. There was a seven-hour difference between Zulu Time and local Saigon time (Golf Time), and a further 12-hour difference between Saigon time and Eastern Daylight Time, or Romeo Time (in Washington). Romeo Time itself was GMT minus five hours. To add to the confusion, the USN generally used Hotel Time (GMT plus eight hours) throughout, rather than Saigon local time. *Maddox*, however, was using India Time in her after-action reporting (GMT plus nine hours) because she had sailed from the Philippines. All this required agility in mental arithmetic which was beyond the JCS in the fevered atmosphere that was being generated that morning. But it does not excuse later reflection that would have determined important mismatches in the timings.

A second factor was the communications difficulties. Making sense of an incident taking place literally half way around the world, with strained communications, with some signals arriving out of chronological order, with others being relayed by telephone, and with constant interruptions was a recipe for bad decision-making.

A third was the improbability of an imagined attack. If you were McNamara, arriving at your office in the morning of August 4, could you have even begun to imagine that a Navy patrol was about to fire off several hundred shells into the ocean in the belief that it was being attacked by a dozen non-existent torpedo boats, on a dark, stormy night? Did US Navy commanders really behave in such wild ways? The more probable explanation was that something had happened. The counter was ridiculous.

These factors aside, a judgment must still be made that few emerge from the Gulf of Tonkin incident with intact reputations. Johnson comes out as the arch manipulator of Congress, cynical and joking over the whole affair. Only a few days later he reportedly joked with Ball, "those dumb, stupid sailors were just shooting at flying fish." The worst caricature of McNamara as control freak is on display and his openness with the full facts has been questioned by critics. As we have seen, congressmen were told this was an unprovoked attack, which McNamara knew not to be true – an OPLAN 34-A mission was despatched on August 4 to attack Hon Matt, which was not revealed. Sharp, struggling with communications difficulties in the early hours of the morning, could only offer half-answers and hesitation. When pressured he seems to have decided to simultaneously back his subordinates and please his masters in Washington by supporting the claim of an attack. The JCS was far too unquestioning and trigger happy. Too many officials smelled a rat but elected to say nothing. Congress was too compliant, with the notable exception of Senator Wayne Morse who may have received a tip-off from an informant who has never been identified. It is striking that all the intercepts and messages were forwarded to at least five major US command addressees including COMNAVFORJAPAN (Commander Naval Forces Japan), and COMTAIWANDEFCOM (Commander Taiwan Defense Command), as well as a presumed wider distribution set (listed on the signals as "Golf Eleven/Alpha"). Many senior naval officers, and others within the secret reporting loops, at least had an opportunity to view the same intelligence the White House later used to inflate the Tonkin Gulf incident. Nobody spoke up though some later claimed skepticism. Nobody challenged the version of events offered to the Senate, or sought to retouch, for the sake of historical accuracy if for no other reason, the choppy seascape painted by Johnson. Individuals who later claimed they knew it was "bum dope we were getting from the Seventh Fleet" did not dare challenge Johnson at the time.[77]

The key questions, which it appears will never be answered satisfactorily, are at what point *after* the retaliatory attacks did Johnson and his key lieutenants, acutely McNamara, realize that the version of events related on August 4 may not have happened as portrayed, or at all? Johnson's reported joking aside to Ball has not been accurately dated. Assuming this anecdote is not invention, it suggests that by this point and by an unknown route, Johnson had been warned there were doubts. The double challenge with this much-quoted anecdote is that not only can it not be dated, but it is not certain that it actually happened. Ball is not the author of the story. In an oral history interview granted at the beginning of the 1970s he only stated: "the President always had considerable doubt during at least part of that period and even afterwards in a sort of kidding way, he would say to McNamara, 'Well, those fish [inaudible] were swimming,' or something."[78] Somehow, this half-recollection appears to have become an elusive flying fish shot at by less than sapient sailors.

In the case of McNamara, the privileged access granted to *Life*, ten days after the events, would not have happened had Defense not judged that the official narrative had to be bolstered. It is difficult not to notice that the single lacuna in the otherwise bruisingly honest Pentagon Papers, commissioned by McNamara, is discussion of the Tonkin Gulf incident. It seems the 30-odd anonymous authors were instructed that this event would not be examined.

Notwithstanding these outstanding questions, it would be highly ungenerous to allege – and the detail of the events of that day do not support – a version of the Tonkin Gulf incident in which McNamara and Johnson set about to deceive. They didn't. There are over 50 audio files – the so-called "Gulf of Tonkin Recordings" – available to historians.[79] Listening to the protagonists over half a century later is not only a moving experience – it confirms just how confused everybody was as the events unfolded. At one point Sharp and Burchinal struggled to agree what time of the day it was, let alone what happened. Believing and seeing can both be wrong, as McNamara later put it in the documentary *The Fog of War*. McNamara was still alive when Hanyok drafted his brilliant forensic study of the intercepts and messages exchanged on that day. His verdict was that the study should be declassified, "period."

CIA Deputy Director of Operations Ray Cline later stated the obvious point that condemnation of Johnson and McNamara ignores: "It was impossible, dealing with the first reporting of these events, to sort them out carefully and decide the exact sequence of events. That was the source of the confusion ... The whole policy debate was ... over before the final analysis of the two incidents together had been completed."[80] "The intelligence officers were having trouble getting unconfused," in his words, but the White House could not dwell on the details of the confusion. American destroyers had reported being attacked. A response was demanded. In Cline's generous judgment neither Rusk nor McNamara later duped Congress. They were too savvy not to realize there were questions over the details of the alleged incident, but they put it down to "honest confusion."

Focus on Johnson and McNamara also bypasses that every senior government official and military officer directly involved in the incident believed and maintained that something had happened long after they had retired from public service, when they no longer had any conceivable reason to sustain a lie, if they saw it so. Rusk's view was typical:

I never had any doubts about the facts. Certainly, no one has seriously challenged the first attack. There has been some doubt cast on the second attack. But the commander of the ship and all the intervening commanders had no doubt about it, and I was impressed with the intercept material which we picked up from North Viet Nam because my impression at the time was that North Viet Nam had no doubt about the fact that they were attacking these ships, you see. And they were the ones who would have the best means of knowing.[81]

Belief in a second attack was universal.

The commanders of *Maddox* and *Turner Joy* were flighty at best. Their actions can only be viewed as overreactions to phantom threats. The integrity of the SIGINT community as the events were unfolding is not in question, although some procedural and interpretive aspects of their work may be questioned. What is less excusable is the subsequent official report on the Gulf of Tonkin incident. By August 5 it was abundantly clear there were problems with the official version of events. But by dawn that morning, the retaliatory raids had taken place. Who had the courage to inform the President that he had acted on wrong information? Nobody. Director NSA was not in Washington when the crisis erupted. It appears that an anonymous, mid-ranking official was left to carry the can and mollify the White House. It is difficult then to see the official report that followed in any other light than as a cover-up by the NSA leadership, deciding in camera that an embarrassing challenge to the subsequent Gulf of Tonkin Resolution was politically unacceptable. The wrong version of events would have to stand. No evidence has ever emerged that the Johnson administration leaned on the NSA to back the executive office. It appears more probable that the NSA, perhaps reasonably in its judgment, realized that contradicting the now-official version of events would create a political and international furore. As a consequence, 90 percent of the relevant SIGINT was omitted from the final October report – information that would clearly have revealed the scale of the mistake.[82]

The farcical Gulf of Tonkin incident mattered not only because this marked the first time an American president ordered an air attack against North Vietnam. This alone made it a singular event in the simmering war. It mattered, of course, because it allowed

Johnson to secure from Congress the Gulf of Tonkin Resolution which he subsequently used to escalate the American role in the war in Southeast Asia without further appeal to Congress.

But it is only with hindsight that we can see the Gulf of Tonkin Resolution as the future key to expanding the war. At the time, Johnson continued to act in a measured manner. The Gulf of Tonkin Resolution was only "a resolution in search of an incident" because Johnson was acutely aware of the mistakes of past presidents who had failed to secure congressional support – not because he necessarily intended to cash in his chips.[83] In fact, the just-retired State Department legal advisor Abram Chayes was hauled back to Washington to draft the resolution. With good economical sense he mostly re-warmed the Congressional resolution drafted in September 1962 when conflict seemed a possibility over the deployment of Soviet missiles in Cuba. Ironically, two of the subsequent war's sternest critics – George Ball and Senator Fulbright – undertook much of the drafting legwork on the night of the reprisals (Rusk later joked it should have been called "the Fulbright Resolution" to embarrass the turncoat senator). The intent was *not* to use the resolution, but rather to create freedom of action for a US president to authorize military action if necessary. Nobody was fooled who did not want to be fooled, as an interviewer subsequently put it.[84] In Special Assistant Bill Moyer's colorful analogy, all through 1964, Vietnam had been "a small cloud no bigger than a man's hand ... on the horizon of the administration's agenda."[85] Who in the fall of 1964 could have guessed that within a year America would have deployed almost 200,000 soldiers and marines to Vietnam?

The genius of Johnson was to portray himself as the cautious President, responding proportionately to foreign policy threats, while casting Barry Goldwater as the trigger-happy Republican candidate likely to lead America into a Southeast Asian imbroglio. Johnson always knew "he would whomp Goldwater" in the elections.[86] Tonkin gave him the excuse to appear tough to the electorate without getting drawn into a war. For Johnson, it was "more for political reasons than anything else."[87] It was not an excuse to get into a war he did not believe in. He "wanted to be Franklin Roosevelt, not Ulysses Grant." In this regard he was handsomely rewarded. Just three percent of Americans disapproved of the retaliation; 85 percent cheered Johnson. But Johnson seemed to forget his domestic audience was not paying half as much attention to candidate pledges on Vietnam policy as a thoroughly confused Hanoi. The mixed foreign policy statements, one day hawkish the next dovish, used to appeal to different audiences, made sense in the marathon of a US presidential election, but made little sense to the North Vietnamese government. A conclusion was drawn that Washington was largely bluffing.

There was another important consequence. The whole incident took the bottom out of the so-called "Rostow Thesis," a widely read study circulated within government departments during the fall of 1964. McNamara thought Rostow was "a big bomber man" and he was half-right.[88] Rostow proposed attacking the source of an insurgency – in this case North Vietnam – rather than the insurgency itself. In fact, what he argued was that the United States should deploy troops into northern Laos to choke off the infiltration, occupy North Vietnam as far as Vinh, and force Hanoi to settle.[89] This part of the scheme tends to be forgotten. Instead the thesis is remembered for a call for calculated and precise attacks that would raise the stakes and force the aggressor to desist rather than risk widespread destruction. The theory was compelling and even enticing, even though it had been challenged by RAND SIGMA I/II war games.[90] It chimed with fashionable limited war thinking that the Cold War and the prospect of nuclear war had engendered. This was neither complete withdrawal, nor a full commitment but something in between that offered a chance of success. The fatal flaw lay in an assumption that the aggressor would be intimidated, a defect that without hindsight seems readily forgivable. What country would welcome a fleet of B-52s reducing its factories to rubble?

In fact, without hindsight, smart minds in State unpicked the logic long before a single bomber took off. Invited to conduct an inter-agency critique of the thesis, prescient, accurate and wholly ignored conclusions were drawn:

> Given present attitudes, application of the Rostow approach risks domestic and international opposition ranging from anxiety and protest to condemnation ... currently, then, it is the Rostow approach rather than the measures it counters that would be seen generally as "unstabilizing" changes in the rules of the game, an escalation of conflict ... even in this case [Vietnam and Laos] the degree of U.S. interest, the degree and acceptability of the risks, and the potential effectiveness of this approach are subject to question. In particular, the likelihood and the political costs of failure of the approach, and the pressures for U.S. escalation if the early moves should fail, require serious examination.[91]

This, pretty much, is exactly what followed. The problem with the Rostow thesis was its author – over-clever, impatient, and dismissive. Kissinger later recalled that when he had the temerity to pose a question to Rostow, then Director of Policy Planning Staff at the State Department, he responded as if "teaching the alphabet to an illiterate."[92]

But anonymous analysts were not the only dissenting voices. George Ball was so "deeply alarmed" by the Tonkin Gulf Resolution, "I began late at night to put together a memorandum which turned out to be a document of 70 or 75 pages ... and I sent it to Rusk and McNamara and Bundy."[93] This document "challenged every assumption of our Vietnam policy," and had the predictable effect of resulting in a call for a meeting. Unfortunately, the meeting was held on a Saturday afternoon and it was obvious to Ball that his interlocutors did not have the inclination to address his arguments "point by point." In an oral history interview granted at the beginning of the 1970s, Ball maintained that McNamara was "absolutely horrified" that someone should set down such arguments in a government paper, and "treated it like a poisonous snake" – a teasing remark misconstrued by at least one author.[94] Ball only finally presented the memo to Bill Moyers in January 1965, who then passed it to Johnson. "The President called me very disturbed. He said 'I've read this. Why haven't I seen it before?'"

This episode has been used against McNamara (the insinuation is made that McNamara blocked the memo). The story is untrue. McGeorge Bundy, not McNamara, was Johnson's gatekeeper. Columnist Joe Alsop was tipped off about the existence of the memo and wrote a piece rudely declaring that Ball's knowledge of Southeast Asia would fit in a thimble (to which Ball riposted that it was closer to a soup plate, broader but shallow). Johnson was unamused. Ball chose not to pass the memo to Johnson because he was in the middle of campaigning (which explains why Bundy, who was subsequently quizzed many times on this matter by sundry authors and historians, always answered that he could not honestly remember the memo). Ball finally passed it to Moyers at the beginning of the following year, at a lunch, when it seemed the opportune moment. Ball himself remarked that although "we had very, very hot arguments, that never affected my relations with Dean Rusk or Bob McNamara."[95] There was no McNamara Machiavellism.

The Gulf of Tonkin Resolution became a card that Johnson kept up his sleeve but it also had important implications for America's military posture in the region. MACV's manpower ceiling was raised to 23,308. USS *Ranger* and 12 destroyers were despatched from First Fleet. The USAF opened a 2nd Air Division HQ at Tan Son Nhut and redeployed 80 aircraft closer to Vietnam. In the background, the building blocks of war were being laid. In public, to the frustration of service chiefs, Johnson pulled back temporarily, suspending covert operations against North Vietnam.

In the South, Tonkin gave Khanh the excuse to dismiss Minh and pass a charter vesting dictatorial powers in the office of the president. This measure predictably provoked widespread protest from students, Buddhists, and minority parties. On August 25, following an all-night conference with Ambassador Taylor and Deputy Ambassador U. Alexis Johnson, an exhausted and emotional Khanh unexpectedly announced his resignation. Outside his office, 25,000 noisy protestors celebrated. Three days of scheming and maneuvering followed. The unpopular charter was ditched and an awkward triumvirate of Khanh, Minh, and Khiem was restored to power. This arrangement lasted just one day and the premiership was provisionally passed to the civilian Nguyen Xuan Oanh. One week later, Khanh was back at the helm but presiding over a government in disarray and continuing protest. On September 13, the IV Corps commander, General Lam Van Phat, staged a coup, but was then himself a victim of a counter-coup led by younger officers who would rise to prominence in the near future: Nguyen Cao Ky, Nguyen Chanh Thi, and Nguyen Van Thieu. A High National Council was formed at the end of October, fronted by a civilian, Tran Van Huong, but this barely lasted two months. In late December, the young officers struck again in another de facto coup and set up a rival Armed Forces Council with the recycled Khanh as their figurehead. Real power had long slipped from his hands.

For the Saigon Embassy (and especially the CIA) observing these shenanigans, there was a real fear the country was about to implode. South Vietnamese were giving up, deserting in droves, hedging bets, seeking accommodation, and proving unwilling to fight. The American presence was now being viewed as a block to a solution, and ultimate defeat more than likely. Hanoi had no need to escalate because Saigon was a rotten fruit waiting to fall into its hands.

The excitement caused by Tonkin eventually died down, but the question of US policy in South Vietnam had been opened wide again. NSAM 288 no longer seemed adequate for the changed set of circumstances. On September 10, following another round of divisive discussions, NSAM 314 was promulgated. Like its predecessor, the weight of rhetoric did not match the authorized actions. The latter basically restored covert programs that had been temporarily suspended but went no further. The difference between the two documents was that overt US military action which had been viewed as an unlikely, worst-case contingency was being discussed as the next, probable step. Tonkin had turned war-talk into palpable reality. Some even enjoyed it; Taylor began talking about D-Days, and Assistant Secretary John McNaughton, a secret dove, uncharacteristically proposed the deliberate provocation of Hanoi to effectively start a war, this even as the JCS was shifting bombers and strike aircraft across air bases in anticipation that the action would start soon.

The action did start and in an air base, but not as the Joint Chiefs would have wished. On November 1, the Viet Cong launched an audacious attack against Bien Hoa Airbase, 20 miles north of Saigon. Mortars started landing shortly after midnight totally destroying five B-57 fighter bombers (each worth $1.25 million) and damaging another 22. In total, 31 aircraft of all types were damaged or destroyed. The B-57s had only arrived in South Vietnam three months earlier. Four servicemen were killed and over 70 wounded. A later interrogation report revealed that the attackers were armed with just three 61mm mortars, and six machine guns which had been concealed in the banks of the nearby Dong Mai River.[96] The assault was such a surprise the insurgents were able to mortar with impunity for half an hour, or until they ran out of ammunition and slunk back into the jungle.

Air Force personnel posted to Bien Hoa were not that surprised by the attack. Most surprising was that it had taken the Viet Cong so long to exploit the obvious vulnerability of the base sitting in a district virtually controlled by the communists. Bien Hoa was surrounded by Viet Cong checkpoints on the roads. Guerrillas hid in sampans on the river taking pot shots at the pilots, occasionally striking lucky and hitting an aircraft as it was coming in to land. The 1,500-odd mainly USAF servicemen were protected by just one ARVN company. "The attack hammered home a hard message," in the words of the *Air Force Times*, "to fight in the air, the Air Force had to be able to fight on the ground." Boots on the ground were needed – American boots, not half-asleep Vietnamese guards.

The Bien Hoa raid was a huge propaganda coup delivered just two days before the presidential election. The Joint Chiefs fumed and demanded immediate and massive retaliation (had the generals won the argument, Phuc Yen airport in Hanoi would have been flattened in a night-time B-52 raid). Taylor, Westmoreland, and McNamara advised caution. All agreed that better air base protection was required, opening a door that would lead to the deployment of marines to Da Nang in the following year. Whatever the advice, the truth was that Johnson was not about to kick-start a war on the eve of polling day. Hanoi, almost certainly, had calculated as much.

Even before the voting started, Johnson ordered a comprehensive, inter-agency review of the situation in Vietnam, chaired by William Bundy at State. This would prove to be the last collective opportunity to discuss America's stake in the country before the substantial commitment of ground forces in the following year. The intelligence advice was awkward: none of the proposed military actions was likely to succeed. Bombing would not decisively end support to the Viet Cong or succeed in interdicting the supply lines in Laos; Hanoi would not hold its arms up in surrender; and the insurgency was rooted in the southern population anyway. The South Vietnamese government was fragile and "plagued by confusion, apathy and poor morale." The insurgency was gaining ground, perhaps unstoppably. All the prevailing orthodoxies were subsequently challenged in the working groups: the domino theory; the argument that American prestige and honor was on the line and had to be defended at any cost; and the presumption that China or the Soviet Union would intervene in the event of US bombers crossing the 17th parallel. As all these propositions had in one way or another been used by officials in the past to justify policy options, the challenging questions amounted to pulling the rug from under everyone's feet. Except that all the principal protagonists in the room simply picked themselves up, rearranged the chairs, collected their papers, and continued to debate their prejudices as if nothing had happened.

The working group deliberations threw up three options which were really the same option with different temperature settings. The maximalist JCS position was discounted as was the minimalist position that logically led to withdrawal (even while conceding that world opinion by the end of 1964 was expecting a US withdrawal from a hopeless situation). This only left a middle-ground of some more military pressure, some more measures to bolster the South Vietnamese government, and the possibility of negotiations at some vague, future date. There was no clear idea where all this "some more" would lead. All the participants found different reasons for "more" and some dimly saw the prospect of "ending the war on favorable terms," but there was little conviction except in the corridors of the JCS which viewed the present course as "abject humiliation."[97] The most that could be said for the selected option (Option "C") was that it would stretch out the situation, which seemed a counter-intuitive goal. The final policy proposals were so tepid they did not even warrant another NSAM. Instead, Johnson was offered a 30-day phase one option (essentially NSAM 314 with Barrel Roll armed recce missions over Laos, augmenting the Yankee Team armed escorts that had been running since the previous May); followed by a phase two option of limited air strikes against North Vietnam, if the President gave the go-ahead. As Johnson was not prepared to countenance the phase two option, another month of deliberations and staff effort had yielded more of the same. In the meantime, Saigon witnessed another mini-coup, staged in December, that resulted in the purging of all civilians from the government. When Ambassador Taylor tried to reason with the generals he almost found himself declared persona non grata.

Johnson won his election comfortably on a wave of national prosperity. GNP had risen by $112 billion in three years to $630 billion. The value of stocks on the New York Stock Exchange had risen by 34 percent in two years. While Europeans were wallowing in the fashionable, despairing philosophy of Existentialism, Americans were going on a crazy spending spree: $90 billion annually on girth-busting food alone; $20 billion on vacations, which had become a middle-class national ritual; and $43 billion on motoring, a patriotic birth right and duty (General Motors made a staggering gross profit of $16.4 billion that year, making it richer than virtually every Third World country). Americans now owned half a million swimming pools; more garages than Europe had cars; and more gadgets (American students alone were estimated to be spending $22 billion on "stuff," which inevitably ended up in the garages). American women were spending $5.5 billion on cosmetic products and procedures (more than North Vietnam's defense budget). Disposable income hit $433 billion and retail sales $262 billion. There seemed to be no end to this orgy of consumption.[98] A resounding election victory duly delivered to Johnson his mandate for "The Great Society" – what could possibly stop him now?

Chapter 6

JUPITER'S THUNDERBOLT, JANUARY–DECEMBER 1965

Saigon ended 1964 with a bang. It happened at the Brinks BOQ on Hai Ba Trung Street, a US officers' billet housing Army and Navy nurses. A 200-pound car bomb left in the underground car park shattered the front of the six-story block and sent a plume of gray smoke over the city skyline. Street vendors selling plastic nativity scenes, giant Bethlehem stars, and party hats scattered from the sidewalk in confusion. The timer had been set at 5.58pm on Christmas Eve. Two American servicemen were killed and 65 injured. Over 40 Vietnamese were also injured.

The bombing was planned and conducted by Viet Cong guerrilla Nguyen Thanh Xuan, using an accomplice to impersonate an ARVN major. In his words:

> When we arrived there the secret police saluted our impostor major. They then opened the way for him to come in. Our major, after entering the ground of the hotel and descending from his car, asked for an American colonel, saying he was coming back from the city of Da Lat and that an appointment had been made with him.

In fact, Xuan had deliberately chosen the name of a colonel who had left for the United States "because we had secret agents

inside the Saigon regime and knew about their movements."
In the confusion that followed, the guard allowed Xuan to park
the explosives-laden car and go for lunch outside. "The secret
police agreed to this, and so I left the building. I sat in a coffee
shop nearby to wait for the explosion, which came about at exactly
17:45 hours."[1]

By any reckoning it was a cynical attack, but exploding bombs
were not the only hubbub on the streets of Saigon. The city had
once again become alive with the din of Buddhist protests. This
brazen attack clearly demanded a sharp response from Washington,
but the combination of a Congressional recess, political chaos in
Saigon, and the festive season, conspired against retaliatory action.
Johnson was at home in his ranch, McNamara was out of town,
and staffs were on Christmas leave. By the time the matter was
raised with Johnson on December 29, the moment for retaliatory
action had passed.[2]

Away from the trouble in Saigon, the situation in the countryside
appeared to be deteriorating badly. A renewed Viet Cong offensive
had added another 169 American battle casualties to the lengthening
list of killed and wounded. US military advisors had little faith
in the ARVN, but when two South Vietnamese marine battalions
at Binh Gia were wiped out in a week-long battle, which began
on December 26 and ran into the New Year, alarm bells rang. If
the marines could not be trusted, where could American faith be
vested – in the ARVN battalions, now being employed as personal
militia by squabbling, venal generals? This was hardly the way to
celebrate Johnson's handsome election victory, but in Washington
the inauguration gala went ahead with 10,000 guests invited to
the National Guard Armory. Five balls were held and there was
a two-hour variety show graced by a ballet performed by Nureyev
and Fonteyn. Johnson was described as beaming and triumphant.
His supporters were ecstatic. Two days later he was admitted to
Bethesda Naval Hospital for bronchial congestion and exhaustion.
It proved an augury for the difficult year ahead.

In Vietnam, attacks against American personnel continued. On
February 7, Camp Holloway near Pleiku, HQ of 52nd Aviation

Brigade in the Central Highlands, suffered a surprise raid. "The attack ... was received at the White House as if the Germans had just broken through the Maginot Line."[3] The assailants made their stealthy approach at 2am and easily bypassed the ARVN guard force and barbed wire defenses. They then proceeded to cause mayhem at the air base. Fire engines deployed to douse burning helicopters were caught in the middle of cross fires. Three pilots managed to take off – as if taking part in a Pearl Harbor re-enactment – but one crashed almost immediately. The control tower was cut off and surrounded but managed to beat back the attackers.[4] By the time the shooting died down, seven American servicemen were dead, 104 had been wounded, and 22 destroyed or damaged aircraft littered the parking bays.

The attack on Pleiku was just one of several hundred in the now ritual, post-Tet holiday resumption of hostilities. But at this juncture, National Security Advisor McGeorge Bundy happened to be in Vietnam on a fact-finding mission. In the North, Premier Aleksey Kosygin happened to be visiting Hanoi. Following a conference with the in-country team, Bundy telephoned Deputy Secretary of Defense Cy Vance. It was evident to Bundy that Washington was angered by the incident at Pleiku and determined to authorize a reprisal attack.[5] This accorded with the mood in Saigon where it was judged the communists had "thrown down the gauntlet." Later, Bundy visited some of the victims in hospital and reportedly was affected by the experience. This led to the widely repeated charge that "cool as cucumber" Bundy became emotionally overwrought and pitched the administration into precipitate action. In his words this was "a lot of nonsense."[6] With his deliberate speaking manner, Bundy was hardly a model of emotional flamboyance. It seems more likely he reinforced the incensed mood in a Washington where Johnson had become abusive and ungrammatical, vowing to "lean on them bastards hard."[7]

This self-exculpation aside, the attack at Pleiku did briefly transform McGeorge Bundy into the administration's alarmist-in-chief. On the flight back to Washington he penned a memo to the President that suggested tiredness had overtaken cool judgment.[8]

Defeat was inevitable within the year unless Washington intervened, he warned. The stakes were "extremely high." America's investment was "very large." This was an "ideal opportunity" to seize the moment. There was time to rescue the South Vietnamese damsel "but not much" – act now, he advised Johnson, or all is lost.

When dissected, Bundy's arguments amounted to a re-hash of fears over American "international prestige" and even older anxieties of a communist takeover of Southeast Asia. This contrasted with later testimony in which Bundy maintained that his principal motivation was the honorable impulse that the United States could not simply ditch South Vietnam after a ten-year involvement in the country.[9] Whatever his private motivations, the memo was dangerous because it argued two points that would have been rejected by the previous administration. Kennedy had been scrupulous that this was a Vietnamese war that had to be fought by Vietnamese. Within one month of the start of Johnson's second term, this orthodoxy was being dispensed with. The view of South Vietnamese as helpless children was Bundy's. "There is no way of unloading the burden on the Vietnamese themselves," he advised Johnson, with the logical conclusion that Washington would have to take over the war. This was to argue that America should become Vietnam's masochistic servant, humping the great weight of intractable problems because the Vietnamese child could not possibly solve them. Setting aside the implicit cultural arrogance behind this proposition, the obvious corollary to the argument was that America not only had to take over the war, it had to go to war. This conclusion, however, was side-stepped. Instead, Bundy asserted a Rostow-style policy of gradualism, somewhat disingenuously dragging the country team with him: "The policy of graduated and continuing reprisal ... is the most promising course available, in my judgment. That judgment is shared by all who accompanied me from Washington, and I think by all members of the country team."[10]

The second deviation was outright rejection of any peace negotiations. Only surrender was acceptable: "we should not now accept the idea of negotiations of any sort except on the basis of a stand down of Viet Cong violence." These were the thoughts of someone confident he held the winning hand.

It was perhaps inescapable that Bundy would express sweeping confidence in his own rightness. This was the son of a Boston Brahmin and diplomat, top of his class, a member of Yale's elite Skull and Crossbones club, and the youngest-ever dean at Harvard – how could he possibly be mistaken? In one passage he found no difficulty in identifying the sentiments of an entire nation with his own ego (a nation about to prove him very wrong on this point): "It is our belief that the people of the United States have the necessary will to accept and execute a policy that rests upon the reality that there is no short cut to success in South Vietnam." In a second, he graciously dispensed his inherited sense of superiority to the remainder of the "first team" while dismissing critics condescendingly *de haut en bas*:

> The U.S. mission is composed of outstanding men, and U.S. policy within Vietnam is mainly right and well-directed. None of the special solutions or criticisms put forward with zeal by individual reformers in government or in the press is of major importance, and many of them are flatly wrong.

And yet, despite these shortcomings, Bundy was not blind to the hazards. Far from shrilly blowing the trumpet of war, the February 7 memo to Johnson was simultaneously making the arguments about why going to war was unlikely to resolve the situation:

> We cannot assert that a policy of sustained reprisal will succeed in changing the course of the contest in Vietnam. It may fail, and we cannot estimate the odds of success with any accuracy – they may be somewhere between 25% and 75%. What we can say is that even if it fails, the policy will be worth it. At a minimum it will damp down the charge that we did not do all that we could have done, and this charge will be important in many countries, including our own. Beyond that, a reprisal policy – to the extent that it demonstrates U.S. willingness to employ this new norm

in counter-insurgency – will set a higher price for the future upon all adventures of guerrilla warfare, and it should therefore somewhat increase our ability to deter such adventures.

These arguments plainly raised many questions. With the hindsight of half a century since Bundy wrote these words, the notion that America might deter "adventures of guerrilla warfare" as he quaintly put it, seems quixotic. More fundamentally, Bundy was advising his president to adopt a policy that might fail but simultaneously reassuring him that failure would still be worth it, as if national political leadership were an exercise in attempting virtuous failures. Paul Warnke, Secretary of Defense for International Affairs, expressed it most succinctly: "We were trying to drive the Vietnamese out of Vietnam and that's a loser."[11]

The memo highlighted many other challenges, any one of which might derail Washington's support for Saigon. The Buddhists could not be marginalized – they had to be incorporated in the government, which was not happening. South Vietnam craved change, especially the young and disadvantaged, but the present leadership was unlikely to satisfy this desire for "revolution." America's intervention to date had lost as many friends as it had won. Pacification needed a boost. The Viet Cong was a formidable enemy, demonstrating an "energy and persistence" that was "astonishing." Despite suffering "extraordinary losses," they simply "came back for more." The situation, in short, was "grim."[12]

Thus it happened that after months of provocations and prevarications, it took the National Security Council just 75 minutes to authorize retaliatory air strikes against North Vietnam. One attack in Pleiku, Bundy's memo, Johnson's ill-humor, the Joint Chiefs' champing at the bit – all contributed to the swing. The only dissent came from Senator Mansfield, "a very dramatic scene," in Bundy's memory, "and one of the few cases I can recall apart from later cases involving George Ball, where there was at the table itself explicit dissent."[13]

This sudden manifestation of political resolve – not without its tensions as nobody was certain how Russia or China might react – caught the Navy completely by surprise. Only USS *Ranger* was actually on station to carry out the air strikes (USS *Coral Sea* and *Hancock* had sailed away to avoid compromising the Kosygin visit to Hanoi). Lousy weather then intervened causing many missions to abort. Eventually, a package of 49 A-4E Skyhawks and F-8 Crusaders bombed Dong Hoi Barracks, a large complex of around 275 buildings, just across the 17th parallel. However, this was the weakest option of three possible contingencies that had been prepared for reprisals. When the Battle Damage Assessment (BDA) was tallied, it transpired that 16 buildings had been destroyed, hardly the retaliation that was going to make Hanoi blink. The raid cost one A-4E Skyhawk.[14]

The first of the so-called Flaming Dart missions also missed its political objective, which was to demonstrate that the South Vietnamese government, not America, was defending itself against Hanoi's aggression. To redress this, a second attack was staged on Chap Le Barracks, a base of around 140 buildings further south near Vinh Linh. This was mounted by a mix of VNAF A1-H Skyraiders, Farm Gate aircraft (aircraft in South Vietnamese livery but piloted by Americans), and USAF fighter bombers. The raid on Chap Le was the first use of USAF strike aircraft in the war (20 F-100 Super Sabres from 90th Tactical Fighter Squadron). Despite dropping over 30 tons of high explosives, just nine buildings were destroyed. A VNAF pilot was downed but rescued and several aircraft limped home with cannon holes in their wings. Once again, a bombing raid had disappointed.[15] "Freedom shall not perish from this earth," Johnson told a Boy Scout delegation the following day, but not that many North Vietnamese soldiers were going to perish at this rate either.

In apparent retaliation, three days later, the Viet Cong bombed a hotel in Qui Nhon on the coast, killing 23 American servicemen and injuring a further 21. The attack in Qui Nhon again provoked a bombing reprisal, targeting the Chap Le and Chanh Hoa Barracks. The latter was struck by 97 aircraft launched from *Ranger*, *Hancock*, and *Coral Sea*. Chap Le was revisited by 28 VNAF Skyraiders and 32 mostly Super Sabres. The damage again proved trivial, although the Navy pilots demonstrated greater accuracy at greater cost. Two Skyhawks and one Crusader were lost, causing some consternation.

This was not the only significance of the raid. In the subsequent press conference, the White House did not bother to emphasize the retaliatory nature of the raid (the word was dropped altogether in favor of "response" to "continued aggression"); and in Saigon, the strike was simply listed as a routine air operation.[16] Within a matter of four days, and with a subtle shift of terminology, Washington was making *the* war, *our* war. In between the bombing strikes, Johnson ordered the evacuation of all US civilian dependants from South Vietnam (1,800 women and children). In addition, all PACOM forces assumed DEFCON 2 posture, a level of military preparedness Moscow almost certainly detected. An unmistakeable signal was sent that the situation in Indochina had just taken a serious turn for the worse.

If Johnson had hoped to gain some political capital by portraying himself as a tough president, he got none. The media reaction was negative from the beginning. In the *New York Times*, Louis Paul Pojman penned an article entitled "Extension of the Vietnam War Assailed," highlighting opposition to the reprisals. Robert Donovan in *Time* magazine pondered where this military action might lead America in "Look Down That Long Road." The *St Louis Post-Dispatch*, with some sense, argued that a strike-for-strike policy was no strategy at all; and the *Kansas City Star* also failed to discern a strategy in what appeared to be more a scrambled exercise in crisis management. By the summer, the *Los Angeles Times* would be questioning the confident assertions of the politicians on the East Coast in "Many Myths and Illusions Shattered Since Pleiku." It was not that the press was against robust military action against communists. Cheerleading bombing was as natural an instinct as shooting deer in provincial American newspapers. What troubled editors was the lack of purpose, not necessarily the means.

These tit-for-tat attacks proved to be the drum roll for act one of America's Vietnam War. Washington began bombing North Vietnam because it had no ground troops in South Vietnam to challenge the Viet Cong or Hanoi. But once the bombing started, the deployment of ground troops became inevitable. Failure to achieve victory from the air served to redouble the need for a ground war, and failure in the ground war nourished the air war. The dilemma had been identified ten years previously when Eisenhower had weighed intervention, and the lesson had been entirely forgotten.

In the advice of his Assistant Secretary of Defense, Admiral Arthur C. Davis:

> If it is determined desirable to introduce air and naval forces in combat in Indochina it is difficult to understand how involvement of ground forces could be avoided. Air strength sufficient to be of worth in such an effort would require bases, in Indochina of considerable magnitude. Protection of those bases and port facilities would certainly require US ground force personnel, and the force once committed would need ground combat units to support any threatened evacuation. It must be understood that there is no cheap way to fight a war, once committed.[17]

The Flaming Dart bombing runs mounted on February 7–11 mattered because, in the words of a top secret working paper, the United States had now become a "co-belligerent."[18] Where previously the policy line had been that the US was "not really directly engaged in the war" – a line which had been responsible for most of the constraints imposed on US forces – now that position was no longer credible. Washington was a belligerent. Rejection of tougher military options lost weight, "opening the way to a wider range of politically acceptable U.S. options in dealing with the war."

However, the attacks at Pleiku and Qui Nhon, rather than uniting Washington in the manner of the Gulf of Tonkin incident, only served to revive tense arguments that had been simmering within the government between a JCS seeking maximum military effort, and a camp led by Ambassador Taylor and McGeorge Bundy that supported a more graduated response. When systematic bombing of the North was first broached following the Gulf of Tonkin incident, the JCS had offered a positive assessment. North Vietnam could be forced to sue for peace, if Hanoi is bombed to its knees, the generals advised. In Moyer's recollection, the "images of WWII kept flickering across the debates on Vietnam."[19] The USAF Chief of Staff General John McConnell, a former fighter pilot with wartime experience of the Far East, was a strong advocate of decisive bombing, and he was backed by CINCPAC Admiral Sharp who argued, "the single most important thing we can do to improve the security situation in South Vietnam is to make full use of our airpower."[20]

But McConnell's and Sharp's bullishness was horror to every other government department, and to Johnson. Both John Kenneth Galbraith and George Ball, who were familiar with the voluminous studies on the effects of bombing, conducted after the Second World War, were deeply skeptical (the total output of this survey was a staggering 308 volumes totaling millions of words).[21] McNamara later in the year openly contradicted his service chiefs: "We never believed and we don't believe today that bombing in the north will drive the North Vietnamese to the bargaining table or force them to cease their terror tactics"; the point of the bombing rather was "to prove they can't win in the south."[22] Rusk was also on side: "Now, anyone who ever expected the bombing to end the war ought to have his head examined, because bombing just doesn't do that. It makes it more difficult, but it doesn't prove to be a decisive military factor."[23] Every member of the cabinet with wartime experience was skeptical that bombing alone would do the trick.

"Gradualism" thus emerged as the unhappy compromise seized by a president who could not bring himself to play the role of ruthless warmonger. Contrarily, the very voices that argued for limited bombing to alter "the equation of advantage" in Senator Fulbright's memorable analogy, simultaneously conceded "faint hope" that this would make any difference – as tepid a defense of a policy as had ever been mounted in Washington.[24] Hovering in the background was the fear that a precipitous American move might provoke "an orgasm of decision-making" in the communist capitals and a nuclear Third World War.[25] The author of gradualism was brainy McGeorge Bundy, but the play was being booed in the hostile theater of the Joint Chiefs. The receptive audience was in the White House and it was the denizen of this residence that counted.

These arguments had been reignited, following the November election victory, in a month-long working group chaired by McGeorge's brother, Assistant Secretary of State for Far Eastern Affairs William Bundy. The Joint Chiefs clamoured for decisive military action but were countered by Taylor arguing for a "progressive squeeze." This had origins in the "Rostow Thesis," seen in the last chapter:

> By applying limited, graduated military actions reinforced by political and economic pressures on a nation providing external support for insurgency, we should be able to cause that nation to decide to reduce greatly or eliminate altogether support for the insurgency. The objective of these pressures is not necessarily to attack his ability to provide support, although economic and certain military actions would in fact do just that. Rather, the objective is to affect his calculation of interests. Therefore, the threat that is implicit in initial U.S. actions would be more important than the military effect of the actions themselves.[26]

The "gradualists" won but the options proposed were both overly finessed and based on the assumption that a limited amount of bombing would affect the will of Hanoi to continue fighting. Destroy the enemy's capability first, the Joint Chiefs argued, and the will to fight vanishes. This reasoning was buried by the realpolitik of a newly elected Johnson administration unwilling to stoke war. The gradualists expressed their persuasive arguments as logical sequential actions, all intended to send "signals" to Hanoi. These seemed far more appealing than the table-thumping options offered by the Joint Chiefs. Unfortunately, the communist leaders would resolutely ignore the Morse code.

Plainly, Hanoi's provocations could no longer be ignored. The Tonkin Gulf Resolution was secured to give an American president scope to act as he judged necessary in South Vietnam, including the wider employment of military forces. At the time, the US military effort in the region amounted to four ineffective programs: the OPLAN 34-A raids; the DESOTO patrols; various covert, undeclared air missions;[27] and special force operations.

Given the ineffectiveness of these programs, it was inevitable the baton would first be passed to the Air Force and carrier-borne aircraft of the Navy, a most natural evolution in a culture that had venerated the bomber since the Second World War. This was what the Pentagon had been planning for and anticipating; the ultimate origins of the opening bombing raids of 1965 lay in OPLAN 37-64, conceived in the previous spring following the promulgation of NSAM 288. OPLAN 37-64 generated what became known as "the 94 Target List," which in turn became the reference document for the bombing. It should have helped that McNamara had specialized in studying the effects of aerial bombing during his wartime service, but it didn't. He knew what was necessary to win but set that unpleasant scenario aside. The bombing effort over North Vietnam – the *Rolling Thunder* operations that ran from the spring of 1965 – would not be a campaign of total and unconstrained destruction. Any airman would have readily grasped the arithmetic of this form of warfare. Rather, it would be about subtle persuasion, the redressing of "the equation of advantage" and this was algebra nobody in the end could fathom. There were different shades and hues in the gradualist camp but they all ultimately rested on the conceit that warfare is a controllable experiment. On this single, fallacious strategy of graduated response – and in the meddling of a hesitant president – America's majestic bomber fleets foundered for the next seven frustrating years. It would take a new president to unleash the bombers and force Hanoi to settle, but by then, America's war was over.

The decision to expand the bombing beyond reprisals – a decision somewhat masked by Bundy now using the misleading term "sustained reprisals" – was finally taken on Sunday, February 13. In preparation, the first of 30 B-52s were flown to Guam. US in-theater air power, however, was already considerable without these behemoths. Three carriers on station already contributed around 200 aircraft. The Air Force had as many as 200 combat aircraft in South Vietnam (including 48 A-1E Skyraiders) with a further 83 aircraft in Thailand. In the immediate aftermath of the Flaming Dart missions, another four and a half squadrons had been rushed to Vietnam.[28] Hanoi by contrast relied on a fleet of around 35 MiG-15 and MiG-17 based at Phuc Yen Air Base near the capital. At the time, this was the only airfield capable of fast jet operations in the North, considerably restricting Hanoi's options. A suicidal fling against the might of the USAF was never on the cards. Instead, it made more sense to allow the enemy free passage and to take him down with antiaircraft fire, and later SAM missiles. One estimate reckoned there were almost 300 antiaircraft sites mainly clustered around Hanoi and Haiphong.[29] With this density of firepower, Hanoi had little need of its MiGs.

The first strike was planned for February 20 but further political turmoil in Saigon and a fruitless British diplomatic initiative created delays. In Washington, William Bundy worked on his ultimately unfinished memo "Where are we heading?" which reprised arguments he made to Johnson on December 1 the previous year, and again to Rusk on January 6: bomb now to force Hanoi to end its aggression in the South.

Then the weather caused problems. Finally, on March 2, Operation *Rolling Thunder V* was launched, but by then the imminence of a US bombing campaign was hardly a secret. In the preceding week, Hanoi ordered evacuations and warned its citizenry of imminent annihilation. It would have brought a smile to the face of the now-retired LeMay to know that the Central Committee in Hanoi was in complete agreement with him – only an all-out air offensive would be decisive and this is exactly what Hanoi expected.

A total of 104 aircraft struck the Xom Bang Ammo Depot in an all Air Force show. Flak suppression was provided by 16 F-105

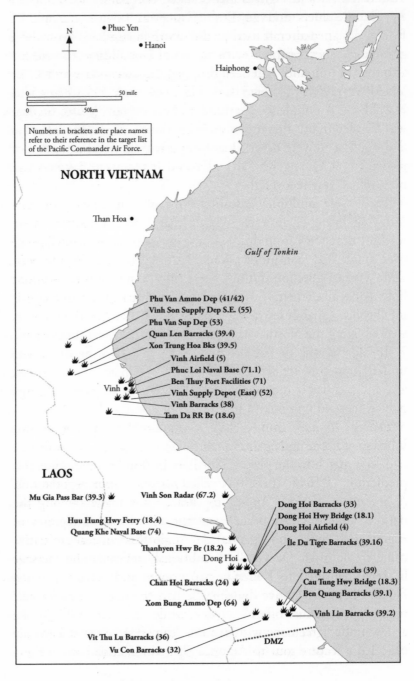

Thunderchiefs and eight Super Sabres. The bombers comprised 25 Thunderchiefs and 20 B-57 Canberras (a rare example of British-designed aircraft used by the USAF in combat). It proved a gratifyingly successful raid with 36 out of 49 buildings flattened;[30] 120 tons of ordnance had been dropped. In a secondary attack, 20 VNAF Skyraiders protected by 60 USAF escorts struck Quang Khe Naval Base. An unpleasant reminder of the cost of *Rolling Thunder* was revealed in this first mission: six aircraft were lost. Three F-105s and one F-100 were downed at Xom Bang with all but one pilot recovered; at Quang Khe an A-lH and F-100 were downed and both pilots were recovered.

There were multiple reasons for the aircraft losses, not least "growing evidence in early March that USAF intentions were reaching the enemy from the disclosure of highly sensitive intelligence over unsecured communications."[31] At this stage in the war, 2nd Aviation Division did not boast fully secure communications links across all elements in-theater. As Hanoi lacked strategic signals intelligence capabilities it may be assumed that Soviet engineers were obliging the North Vietnamese with an early warning system.

The administration had been assiduous in explaining why it was undertaking this action both to the domestic and international audience. What it did not anticipate was that even this limited operation would provoke a storm.

Rolling Thunder immediately swung public opinion against Johnson at home and against America abroad. It was as if someone had set a match to the planet. Nowhere in Bundy's memo was this prediction. U Thant at the UN called for immediate negotiations. A Seventeen Nation "Appeal for Peace" was made (among the nations appealing for peace were the blood-soaked regimes of Algeria, Iraq, Syria, and Uganda). An Anglo-Russian peace initiative came to nothing. De Gaulle lugubriously repeated the message he once delivered to Kennedy – negotiate and get out. French Foreign Minister Couve de Murville had the nerve to pay a visit to the White House offering advice, while simultaneously signing a new trade agreement with Hanoi. Jean-Paul Sartre theatrically canceled a lecture tour to America (it is difficult to conceive any sense of disappointment in the American heartlands over the non-appearance of this philosopher of depression). China stridently condemned the "imperialist" aggression. The Soviet Union was less vocal but unhesitating in exploiting the arms trade business with Hanoi, including the sale of SA-2 SAMs that would down many American aircraft in the forthcoming months. In Washington, the influential Senator Fulbright called for a halt to bombing. By the summer, Senator Russell of the Armed Services Committee – who had been broadly supportive of Johnson – was already questioning the entire rationale for the war. "I have never been able to see any strategic, political, or economic advantage by our involvement [in Vietnam]," he declared in direct contradiction to Bundy's arguments that America faced a vital struggle in Indochina.

America as cartoon villain on the world stage had already become an unpalatable fact for American missions abroad and *Rolling Thunder* made the situation worse. Between October 1964 and March 1965 there were no fewer than 25 attacks by communist rent-a-mobs and anti-American nationalists across the world. The last was in Moscow in March ("students" attacked the US Embassy). Many of the Moscow protestors were in fact hired Chinese workers. In scenes worthy of *Doctor Zhivago* the Moscow police, in black coats and fur hats, mounted on white chargers, used heavy-handed tactics to disperse the mobs. Peking then felt obliged to stage a student protest against the Soviet Embassy, just to make the point that a communist co-religionist could not bash the heads of Chinese anti-American protestors in Moscow with impunity.

Moscow and Peking were expected to act as the loudest rebroadcast transmitters of anti-American indignation. But they were not. By far the most noise was actually being made at home, ushering in the period when the peace marches began. "Hey, hey LBJ, how many kids have you killed today?" entered American consciousness, and was met by counter-marches chanting "Down with the Red traitors." When a college student set herself alight in imitation of the Buddhist monk self-immolations in Saigon, a garage posted a sign "Free gasoline for peace creeps."[32] Johnson, of course, hated the "beatniks" that he branded "a bunch of kooks."[33]

Seeing Russian interference where none existed, Johnson huffed, "the Russians have got their folk working ... they're stirring up this agitation," laying the follies of his administration at the doorstep of the innocent Ambassador Anatoly Dobrynin.[34]

Yet, for every voice shouting an anti-war slogan, there was a counter-voice, and passing by both on the sidewalk was the silent majority, as Nixon later described them, the many Americans still undecided on the expanding war. Thousands of miles away in the Gulf of Tonkin, a squadron leader aboard USS *Midway* summed up the feelings of many servicemen: "It doesn't make you feel too good when somebody gets hurt or killed to know that a bunch of our own people don't think we should be out here at all," adding, "I wouldn't bet that things are going to be a whole lot better soon but what the hell can we do?"[35]

A new type of American appeared on the street – the Vietnik – young, shaggy, and swathed in colorful attire. Or as one correspondent with a keen eye for social types described them: "hot eyed students, barefoot folk singers, pale undergraduate Ophelias, militant Oakland Negroes, bearded poets pushing baby strollers and little old ladies strewing flowers."[36] The emblem of the anti-war movement was not the British artist Gerald Holtom's peace symbol of a circle with three lines, a nuclear disarmament symbol based on the semaphore letters "N" and "D" – it was hair. The military sheared young men like sheep. The anti-war movement grew it like competitive gardeners. The more hair the better: Afro hair, hair falling off shoulders, hair under armpits, and scandalous pubic hair in the musical by the same name. How unfortunate to lose your hair young in the dawning of the Age of Aquarius. "Girls say yes to boys who say no," went the hippy slogan. In the mid-1960s, saying no to the draft became an enticing mantra for thousands of young American men indifferent to the less attractive offer being made by Uncle Sam.

The White House had anticipated a chorus of disapproval by releasing the declassified evidence of a three-year history of Hanoi's perfidy – the State Department "White Paper" on North Vietnamese aggression published on February 27 – but it made no difference on the streets. On April 7, Johnson responded to the continuing criticism by delivering a widely reported speech at Johns Hopkins University in which he suggested a conciliatory stance toward the Seventeen Nation Appeal, and offered multi-billion dollar investments in the Mekong Delta for the benefit of all Vietnamese (in fact, a recycling of an old idea suggested by a former US ambassador to Thailand, Kenneth Young). Calls for direct negotiations with Hanoi were rejected by the administration partly because all the key advisors held on to the absolutist stance, but also because it was disbelieved, with justification, that Hanoi had any interest in pursuing talks. Premier Pham Van Dong confirmed the futility of negotiations by throwing his own unacceptable Four Point Plan at the US government and denouncing Johnson's speech as a trick. As far as Hanoi was concerned, the war was waiting to be won. There was no need to negotiate. For Johnson, the canon of American prestige still held: this was not just about Vietnam; it was about every other friendly country in the region that would question the value of Washington's word. The hills were alive with the sound of music, as Julie Andrews was now joyously advising audiences in the Broadway premiere of the blockbuster film, but do-re-mi had been replaced by the crump-crump-crump of high explosive detonations in North Vietnam. Let the bombing continue.

Rolling Thunder provoked the perfect storm outside government buildings, but it also stirred turmoil inside the corridors of the Pentagon. There would be no single air war in Vietnam but rather several, often locked in internecine conflict. This was primarily a consequence of the existence of four powerful single services, each representing trenchant lobbies and each fighting to control its own resources. This conflict dated back to unresolved disputes from the Harkins era. When MACV was stood up, two separate air commands were established to control the four air forces. The USAF managed its own Farm Gate and Yankee Team aircraft, along with the VNAF; the Army controlled the larger pool of tactical US Army and USMC aircraft; and the Navy ran the carrier-borne strikes. Air Force General Anthis complained impotently over this violation of unity of command, but Harkins strongly maintained that, as there was no air war in Vietnam, the Army had primacy in what was essentially a close-support mission. In practice this meant that aircraft were assigned missions by ASOCs (Air Support Operations Centers) at field level, leaving the theater-level JAOC (Joint Air Operations Center) with little more to do than act as an air traffic controller and redistributor of aircraft.

In many respects, the USAF undermined its own position, and then fought to restore its primacy against the inertia of established headquarters structures. At the outset, both PACAFs (Pacific Command Air Force), Generals Jacob E. Smart and later Hunter Harris, deliberately constrained the USAF level of command in Vietnam to an advance echelon (2nd ADVON). This was subordinated to Thirteenth Air Force in the Philippines, which in turn reported to PACAF. In this way, they hoped to maintain the greatest control over the largest number of assets across Southeast Asia. As the Vietnam commitment grew, it became apparent that this arrangement left the USAF very much a junior partner in America's only shooting war. As a consequence, 2nd ADVON was upgraded to 2nd Air Division in October 1962. The solution was contingent and unsatisfactory as the division answered both to COMUSMACV and Thirteenth Air Force. This was the command that Major General Joseph Moore inherited, half-cocked, undermanned, and in competition with the Army and USMC air forces. Moore held a world speed record set in an F-105 Thunderchief, six years earlier. The speed of decision-making in Saigon could hardly have pleased him.

Army dominance was then confirmed in a decision taken by McNamara at an April 20, 1965 Honolulu conference, which prioritized air missions in South Vietnam over *Rolling Thunder* missions. This was partly a political decision; having opened Pandora's Box, Washington was anxious to retain control of an Air Force still arguing for total war on the North, not a campaign of ineffectual "signals." For Westmoreland, as Sharp later recalled, this decision was carte blanche to "get the absolute maximum of ordnance dropped on every objective he could find."[37] Periodically,

Westmoreland had to be fended off from appropriating Thirteenth Air Force aircraft in Thailand and Seventh Fleet aircraft. However, within his own domain in HQ MACV, Westmoreland got his way. The MACV CAOC (Combat Air Operations Center) allocated sorties through corps-level TASEs (Tactical Air Support Elements); the Combined Intelligence Center (CIC) retained first call on target nominations; and an Army-dominated MACV staff determined target selections for fighter bomber and many B-52 missions – all Air Force functions.

Naval command was equally complex. The "blue water" fleet's chain of command emanated from the Defense Secretary and CINCPAC but then diverted through the Commander-in-Chief Pacific Fleet (CINCPACFLT), the Commander of the Seventh Fleet (COMSEVENTHFLT), and finally to the carrier strike force, CTF 77. All the ships were deployed from their administrative commands in the United States to Task Force 75. These in turn were parceled out to Task Force 77, or the Carrier Task Groups (CTGs) which formed the basic tactical groupings. A typical CTG consisted of a single carrier, destroyer escorts, a handful of frigates, and occasionally a cruiser. At the height of the war there were as many as six CTGs numbered CTG 77.1 to 77.6. This commitment so eroded the serviceability of the total USN carrier fleet (then comprising 16 carriers) that it was not until the late 1970s that the fleet was fully operational again.[38]

The daily, tactical prosecution of the naval air war was the responsibility of Commander CTF 77 (who was always an aviator and Vice Admiral). His staffs were based on a carrier and these liaised with USAF counterparts both in Saigon and Thailand. Carrier attacks were all mounted from the Gulf of Tonkin. Facing no credible threat from a North Vietnamese navy or from the communist air force, the CTGs had the luxury of taking station at the same optimal launch point, known as "Yankee Station." A CTG tasked to support air strikes in South Vietnam took station at a separate point, known as "Dixie Station." The inevitable maintenance requirements of an aircraft carrier meant that every month CTF 77 had to go to port for a week. Command would then pass to a designated CTG commander (known as CTF 77.0 to avoid confusion). In practice this meant that in any six-month cycle, overall tactical command of the naval air war was being passed through the hands of several two star officers, some new to the war, others more experienced, each with his own views and personality. An Air Force officer in Thailand could never be sure, when he signaled CFT 77, whether he was reaching a sympathetic interlocutor or a grizzled matelot.

There were two modes of operation: cyclic and Alpha strikes.[39] During cyclic operations a carrier would launch between 25 and 40 aircraft every 90 minutes, for the entire duration of its 12-hour shift, and remarkably sustain this tempo over eight cycles. A pilot could be assigned to as many as three cycles in a shift and a single carrier could maintain a constant presence over a designated target area for the duration of its shift. In the case of Alpha strikes, as many as five carriers launched all available aircraft, which joined USAF bombers flying in from South Vietnam and Thailand. On these occasions, the CTGs alone were putting up more aircraft in the sky than existed in the fleets of virtually every air force in the world. The sortie rate (and destruction) demonstrated by the US Navy over the course of the war was breathtaking. General Abrams who visited a CTG returned marveling that it all resembled a "controlled crash."[40] Astonishingly, within 90 minutes of concluding an Alpha strike, an aircraft carrier was expected to resume normal cyclic operations.

Over the skies of Vietnam the air war was further functionally divided into the strategic campaign over North Vietnam, known confusingly as Special Operations (SPECOPS), almost exclusively conducted by USAF bombers based in Thailand and Seventh Fleet; the tactical campaign supporting ground troops in South Vietnam, in which all air forces contributed aircraft; and the undeclared covert air war in Laos.

A fourth air war might be added to this list; one which out-shaded the others, and which was conducted by the incumbent of the White House. No air campaign in American history has been so closely managed by the national political leadership. Lyndon Johnson would boast that the Air Force could not bomb a single Vietnamese outhouse without his permission but it was worse than that. As General Moore later recalled, Washington was instructing him how many aircraft could fly, how many bombs they could carry, and exactly when the attack had to be conducted, or aborted.[41] Johnson and the gradualists feared triggering a world war, but there was also a personal dimension. Over time, every airman casualty became "a cancer and a fungus and an explosive device inside him."[42]

At the heart of any air campaign is a targeting list – the objectives selected for attack. Political oversight of the air war meant that this responsibility – usually invested in the theater air commander and his intelligence and strike staffs – was appropriated by the White House advised by the Joint Chiefs. In effect, Washington told CINCPAC what he could and could not attack, including specific targets, and CINCPAC passed on this general and specific guidance to Commander Task Force 77 (CTF 77), and COMUSMACV. It was then up to these commanders to daily parcel out the agreed target list to their wings and squadrons, often after another round of bargaining with 2nd Air Division, or Thirteenth Air Force in Thailand.

The target list was decided, improbably, in the domestic quarters of the White House, over lunch, every Tuesday. At this select gathering, Johnson played Jupiter, chewing over both his repast and the fate of others. The regular attendees at the Tuesday lunch included McNamara, Rusk, and Rostow. As the war progressed, CIA Director Richard Helms and Chairman of the JCS General Wheeler joined this, the most powerful club of men in the world. "You can't run a war from the Oval Office," USAF pilot Cal Jewett later sentenced. "I would have loved to have had McNamara or Johnson on one of the flights with me."[43]

In-theater commanders forwarded their own target lists using the same chain of command in reverse, for consideration at the Tuesday lunch meetings. Filtered through several layers of command – each increasingly sensitive to deliberations in the White House – this list was commonly whittled down to a smaller set of uncontroversial targets. This meant that air commanders were constantly being frustrated in their efforts to attack targets based on their military judgment, rather than the political judgments of a handful of men in Washington. This went deeper than the traditional frictions between a national leadership weighing strategic considerations and military commanders wrapped in tactical perceptions. Both had a strategy – it was just not the same strategy. The military men sought to win the war. Washington sought to limit the war. Caught between these two competing strategies, air planners became the executors of nugatory planning efforts. Chief of Naval Operations Admiral David McDonald observed:

> Target lists issued by CINCPAC and JCS did not include those targets for which targeting materials had been produced [by tactical commanders]. Other [approved] targets were included that had been rejected in the scene. The lists [of approved targets] also included targets unknown to the strike force that had been developed in Washington from photography and other sources not available to fleet intelligence.[44]

Washington was commonly asking air commanders to attack targets which they themselves had rejected and for which they had no intelligence. In turn, targets which theater intelligence had carefully prepared were being rejected. The gulf of misunderstanding between the two sides could hardly have been wider.

The White House thus became a mad alchemist's laboratory with the President heating and cooling experiments in a vain attempt to discover the formula of peace, while stoking the furnace of war. This policy was best described by Taylor in a cable to Washington in late February 1965:

> We should keep our response actions controllable and optional to the maximum degree possible so that we can act or withhold action when and as we choose. This need for flexibility argues strongly for vagueness in defining criteria ... and for freedom of action to make <u>ad hoc</u> decisions in the light of our interests at the moment.[45]

Ad hoc vagueness was hardly a convincing strategy but both Johnson and McNamara seized on Taylor's view of the careful management of the air war while discounting the culmination of his argument which was that cumulative, increasing, and relentless bombing should leave Hanoi in no doubt that it faced "inevitable, ultimate destruction." Taylor later became a frustrated voice in Saigon over the management of a bombing campaign, cabling Rusk on March 8: "I fear that to date ROLLING THUNDER in their eyes has been merely a few isolated thunder claps."[46] This was contrary to his vision of increasing and inexorable destruction. The multiplicity of air wars inherently caused frictions and dissent. Resignations were threatened and inter-service rivalry grew bitter.

There were not just divisions on how the air war should be waged. There was also divergence over its message, because there were several audiences. The signal to Hanoi was that the Johnson administration was deadly serious about defending its ally in the South. The message to domestic opinion was that America used her military power in a measured and responsible manner. World opinion was also being courted by this restraint, although in this hope Washington would be frustrated. For many, the war in Vietnam was all about senseless bombing and little else. This view would rebound back and poison debate within America.

Perhaps the most important audience – at least in the eyes of Johnson, haunted by the possibility of a second Korea, or worse, a world war against the communist powers – was China. The sagging weight of the People's Republic of China was the invisible presence at every targeting meeting. It was the fear of provoking a Chinese military response that led to the prohibition of attacking any targets above the 20th parallel or within 30 nautical miles of the Sino-Vietnamese border. For the same reason, American air raids were prohibited from destroying airfields that housed the communist-supplied MiGs. This military madness effectively prevented the US air forces from achieving total dominance of the skies, which they could easily and quickly have achieved. Hanoi and Haiphong were also off limits, although this was where the richest target set lay. By 1968, unknown to MACV at the time, as many as 150,000

Chinese air defense and engineer troops had been secreted into the North, but the notion that Peking was about to re-launch a second Korean War was always fanciful.[47]

The likelihood of failure of a gradualist approach was clear from the beginning. Hanoi, far from being persuaded, became obdurate. Resolve hardened. Hatred deepened. Taylor's argument that the principal purpose of the bombing was to influence Hanoi proved naively optimistic. McGeorge Bundy's secondary argument that the objective was to turn the war in South Vietnam also proved over-hopeful. The war in the South escalated.

At first, all bombing was restricted to targets south of the 18th parallel. Each month, to ratchet the pressure, the bomb line was moved northward by one parallel. For the North Vietnamese, this methodical strategy was an invitation to evade the worst effects of the bombing. Vital supplies could be moved north ahead of the bomb line or diverted south once the bomb line had passed a particular parallel. Air defenses and interceptor aircraft could be concentrated on the next likely set of targets and air defenders elsewhere stood down. Washington might as well have been sharing its target list with Hanoi (it may be argued that it did, as in a desire to demonstrate legality, the US Government presented its target lists to the UN under the Provisions of Article 51 of the United Nations Charter). In F-105 pilot John Piowaty's later embittered recollection:

> We have since learned that our target list was shared through Switzerland with the enemy to ensure no civilians were harmed. Well, that's no way to win a war. The enemy would move out and set up somewhere else, ready to hit us on our way in and out. And, sometimes … [the] Chiefs of Staff would send us in 5 days in a row.[48]

In a very real sense the *Rolling Thunder* campaign became less a military operation and more a bargaining chip on the truce table. Mostly, the North Vietnamese were left unimpressed by this counter. If this was the worst that Washington could do, then let the thunder roll on. It was this failure that led directly to the ground war.[49] If the war could not be won from the air, then it would have to be won by boots on the ground, and plenty of them.

———————

Rolling Thunder rumbled on, but only haltingly and with sharp disagreements. One of the biggest surprises was how within two weeks of the start of the campaign, all the principal protagonists seemed to hold opposing views on the purpose and scale of the bombing runs. Taylor was especially vocal, bombarding Washington with cables and describing the air strikes as "meaningless." McNamara also ran his practiced eye over the bombing results and fretted whether the aircraft were destroying targets efficiently (he typically focused on the ratio of sorties flown to buildings destroyed and questioned whether this might be improved). Concern over own aircraft attrition was also raised. By March 2, the Navy had lost four aircraft and the Air Force five. A further seven Navy jets had sustained damage. Losses and damage among the slower VNAF Skyraiders were almost four times higher. These losses led to a quick study based on 505 missions that misleadingly concluded that attrition was no worse than that experienced in the Second World War or Korea. The study nevertheless served the purpose of encouraging McNamara into allowing more tactical latitude over the mission profiles.

After further delays, *Rolling Thunder VI* was conducted on March 14–15 against an army barracks and ammo dump. This was followed by *Rolling Thunder VIII* on March 19–25 (attacking an ammunition depot, supply depot, barracks, and three radar sites); *Rolling Thunder VIII* on March 26–April 1 (eight radar sites and one airfield); and *Rolling Thunder IX* on April 2–8 (three bridges and a radar). The eighth *Rolling Thunder* proved costly with the Navy losing nine aircraft.[50] The ninth attacked the massive Thanh Hao Bridge, dedicated to Ho Chi Minh, and the largest south of the 20th parallel with a span of 540 feet.

The difficulty of destroying a bridge in an age that lacked precision weaponry was considerable. The first raid involved dropping 254

750lb bombs and yet it still failed to destroy the bridge. The Navy scored over the Air Force on this occasion because it did succeed in destroying another bridge, and became engaged by three MiG-17s in the first instance of a North Vietnamese air-to-air interception. Frustrated, 67th Tactical Fighter Squadron returned the following day and dropped another 384 750lb bombs – again failing to destroy the bridge (there were hits, but insufficient to drop spans). To add insult, MiG-17s ambushed circling Thunderchiefs and shot down two aircraft. Thanh Hao Bridge was finally destroyed on May 14, 1972, having survived repeated attacks over the years.[51]

These last three *Rolling Thunders* barely exerted the pressure that advocates of the campaign desired. Wheeler went so far as to report that they had failed to dent Hanoi's war machine in any significant way. In response, eight- and 12-week methodical bombing programs were proposed but rejected by McNamara and Johnson who preferred a weekly reassessment of progress. In a discreet move, interdiction bombing in Laos was authorized (US aircraft were already being involved in the bombing of targets in Laos under the Barrel Roll operation). What perhaps passed unnoticed was that even this limited aerial campaign was already drawing men and aircraft west across the Pacific. To sustain *Rolling Thunder* the Joint Chiefs made a request to deploy an additional 325 aircraft to theater: one bomber squadron, nine tactical fighter squadrons, and a fourth aircraft carrier. Navy aircraft numbers rose from 200 in February to 463 by the summer. By the end of June, the 1,000 aircraft milestone would be passed, including helicopters. The number of sorties concomitantly climbed from 3,600 in April to 4,000 in May to 4,800 by June.

Verdicts continued to be mixed and contradictory. Some, like Bundy and Taylor, saw improved morale and an abatement of Viet Cong attacks. Rostow, in a memorandum entitled "Victory and Defeat in Guerrilla War: the Case of South Vietnam," offered the tempting possibility of a "clear-cut victory" based on thwarting the Viet Cong in the South and making the war too painful for the North. A Taylor April situation report went so far as to suggest that the government "may have actually turned the tide at long last" (underlining in the original).[52] The hope that one month of limited bombing had produced such an unqualified result was staggeringly wishful.

The supporters of gradualism were not the only party guilty of baseless cheerleading. At the time, RAND reporting in South Vietnam was being led by a controversial personality named Leon Goure. The RAND Viet Cong Motivation and Morale studies had already begun to attract attention. In a June 28 memo to Johnson, McGeorge Bundy noted with satisfaction, "Morale of the VC armed units has been significantly affected by air attacks within South Vietnam. Indeed, preliminary and unpublished findings [from RAND] ... indicate that morale has fallen significantly over the past few months as a result of our air harassment." This too was wishful thinking, but exactly what the White House wanted to hear.

Others remained pessimistic. Westmoreland, later so often accused of offering false hopes, failed to see any major effects. Assistant Secretary of Defense McNaughton, building on a theme of many bad options, could only see a South Vietnam that was "bad and deteriorating." McConnell persisted in warning that anything less than "an intensified application of air power" would result in failure. It fell to McNamara to summarize the effects of the bombing in a memo to Johnson on July 30:

> The bombing program now and later should be designed for its influence on the DRV at that unknown time when the DRV becomes more optimistic about what they can achieve in a settlement to us than about what they can achieve by a continuation of the war.

The logic was impeccable but he could not have imagined that the "unknown time" was seven years away, and would be secured by another president, long after McNamara had left the stage. By the summer, of course, Johnson had taken the fateful decision to commit to the ground war, described in the first chapter of the companion volume to this work. At this juncture, a single but not unimportant point may be made.

It is a singular achievement of some histories – acutely those depicting a caricature McNamara – that the embarrassing richness of evidence available in the 47 volumes of leaked top secret material – 1,000s of pages of classified government records – popularly known as "the Pentagon Papers," is bypassed. It is doubly so because the officially titled "Report of the Office of the Secretary of Defense Vietnam Task Force" was commissioned by McNamara precisely so that future generations could understand and learn from the events that led American administrations into the Vietnam imbroglio. Yet too many have detoured around all this evidence, almost as if it would ruin the story they prefer to tell.

From the end of 1964 until the summer of the following year, the overwhelming consensus – and this was the only point of agreement across a wide range of government officials and servants – was that South Vietnam was about to collapse. On nothing else could agreement be found, or as an author of the Pentagon Papers put it, "The debate over ground strategy was characterized by an almost complete lack of consensus in the first half of 1965." At one stage in the JCS, probably the most cohesive of the actors, there were at least ten different plans being championed. The same was true of the air war which as we have seen was even more divisive.

Against this awful background, escalation had its anniversary events and interventions. There was no institutionalized deceit, although there was a deliberate policy of under-playing the Vietnam commitment to the American public. Nor did officials conspire or scheme. There was intellectual and emotional anguish over how to proceed in an obviously deteriorating situation that offered only bad options.

A list of the anniversary events might include: the November 1 mortar attack on Bien Hoa Air Base; the December 24 bombing of the Brinks BOQ in Saigon; the New Year defeat of ARVN battalions in the battle of Binh Gia; the February 7 Pleiku attack and February 10 Qui Nhon bombing that killed 23 Americans; the February 19 "semi-coup" led by Colonel Thao; the March 30 bombing of the US Embassy; the decimation of two ARVN battalions at Ba Gia followed by the disastrous performance of South Vietnamese Rangers in the June battle of Dong Xoai; and the collapse of the Quat government that same month. The calamitous June battles in particular "definitely moved the whole debate in Washington to a different level."[53] Each of these events, amplified by hundreds of smaller incident and outrages, created the very "graduated pressure" that Washington was trying to impose on Hanoi.

The interventions came from all quarters: William Bundy's January 6 memo to Rusk arguing for ramping up the air campaign; his brother McGeorge Bundy's February 7 memo proposing the strategy of sustained reprisals; William Bundy's unfinished February 18 "Where are we heading?" memo repeating his bombing message; John McNaughton's March 24 "trilemma" memo, a brilliant and tortured exposition of the choices now facing Washington; Westmoreland's highly influential March 26 "Commander's Estimate of the Situation in SVN"; McGeorge Bundy's April 2 memo and subsequent NSAM 328 that repeated almost verbatim his gradualist proposals; Walt Rostow's confident May 20 "Victory and Defeat in Guerrilla Wars" memo to Rusk; and McGeorge Bundy's June 18 memo to McNamara indicating that Johnson wanted "more dramatic and effective actions in SVN." Darting between the ankles of these giants were scores of cables, telegrams, and letters arguing for one or other policy.

McNamara's inglorious and thankless task in all this was largely to respond to a tortured Johnson, mollify the ill-disciplined Joint Chiefs, and try to maintain "institutional harmony" between the different arms of government and Saigon. George Ball has sketched the beleaguered defense secretary's position best: "He was under enormous pressures from his own soldiers and sailors and airmen to escalate, and he resisted. He made his own decisions, and he kept the thing under very considerable control and under great restraint."[54] What stands out about McNamara over this period is not his espousal of any particular military strategy – he made no policy recommendations although it was well known that he strongly favored controlling any military action through a graduated response – but rather his characteristic concern with "good management." He was not in the country when Johnson decided to approve Westmoreland's famous "44 battalion request," which actually originated from the Joint Chiefs and is generally and rightly portrayed as the moment of no return. It was Taylor who was responsible for extending the radius of operation of US troops to 50 miles, and William Bundy, representing State, was responsible for informing Westmoreland in late June that he could commit combat troops anywhere in South Vietnam. A key McNamara contribution over this period was posing the questions: "Who are the Viet Cong? And what makes them tick?" (Intriguingly, the much-maligned Harkins may have been the original source of this questioning.) Seeking to answer these puzzles led to the influential and widely cited RAND Viet Cong Motivation and Morale Studies.

The facts are that Johnson brought the temple crashing down on his own head. In the frank assessment made by an anonymous Pentagon Papers author who enjoyed a privileged view of the top secret transactions between the various actors at the time when the events unfolded: "There is no question that the key figure in the early 1965 build-up was the President of the United States."

———

There was always a likelihood that Hanoi would respond to *Rolling Thunder*, not as its architects hoped, but in the same way that it responded to the first reprisal air raids. The first such response came in the form of an attack against the US Embassy. On March 30 a suicide bomber drove a car to the main entrance and detonated a large bomb. Two Americans were killed, one of them being Barbara Annette Robbins, the first CIA female employee killed in action, and 16 civilians were injured. The Deputy Ambassador U. Alexis Johnson was among the injured. Coincidentally, Ambassador Taylor was on his way to Washington when the attack took place, raising speculation that he had been summoned home for consultations because Johnson was plotting a significant escalation of the war. For his part, the President downplayed any suggestions that the "sustained reprisals" strategy was about to change as a result of this latest outrage. In Saigon, a mounting frustration had set in over the inefficacy of the bombing runs and the lack of clarity over the ground mission. Few failed to notice how a football-shaped hole had been ripped through the stars of the American flag flying over the Embassy.

Johnson's calm was disingenuous. The frustration had already spilled over in a long and detailed memorandum drafted by McNaughton in Defense the week before the Embassy bombing. The McNaughton memo was one of the foundation stones of the subsequently promulgated and crucial NSAM 328. In this respect, McNaughton had taken over the baton from the McGeorge Bundy memo at the beginning of the year.

McNaughton entitled the memo "Plan of Action for South Vietnam" but he could equally have called it, "A Justification for Going to War in South Vietnam." After 12 months of backsliding, Washington had to face the question of whether South Vietnam could be saved without massive bombing in the North or a significant reinforcement of US troops in the South, or both. The question was clearly posed rhetorically: South Vietnam would fall like a (somewhat rotten) apple into the hands of the Viet Cong and Hanoi, if Washington did not take "extreme measures." In one sense, McNaughton was saying little that was new. Many independent commentators as well as government officials were openly predicting the collapse of Saigon before the end of the year.

But why did it matter if Saigon fell? Like Bundy earlier in the year, McNaughton could offer no better reasons than the unconscionable stain to America's reputation and the hackneyed domino theory. Breaking down the matter as if it were a pie chart, he offered that 70 percent of the problem was avoiding "a humiliating US defeat," and 20 percent was keeping Vietnam, and consequently neighboring countries, "from Chinese hands." The fact that Vietnam and China were historic arch enemies and that Hanoi would resist Chinese hands as much as it was resisting American hands was ignored. A Chinese takeover of Indochina was a peddled fantasy that should have been easily demolished but it went unchallenged. It was the last ten percent of McNaughton's calculations that plainly revealed the confusion in American policy. This he allocated to permitting the South Vietnamese a "freer way of life." From the Truman presidency, spreading liberty had been trumpeted as the reason for American intervention in the Far East. And from that period, Asian regimes had shown contempt for this American export. In his memo, McNaughton was quantifying the bankruptcy of two decades of trying to coax the vexatious yellow man to embrace democracy, but seemed blind to the very outcome of his calculations.

McNaughton went further. America faced a "trilemma" of bad options. Bombing the North could fail; an infusion of US ground troops could result in a repeat of the French experience; and negotiating an early exit would amount to a "humiliation." The most hyperbolic section of the entire memo was McNaughton's alarming list of Red "flash points" – actions which he judged would carry substantial risk of a wider war. There were 11, and five related to "Chicom," or Communist China (blockading North Vietnamese ports with mines was not included in the list, although this would later be added to the long list of self-imposed restrictions on US military options). The fear of provoking China was palpable and exaggerated. Ironically, all this alarmism was broadcast by a secret dove. Like his boss McNamara, and later allies Daniel Ellsberg and Mike Forrestal, McNaughton belonged to a cabal of officials who had serious private misgivings over the direction of US policy in Indochina. Fear of blighting his career prevented him from opposing the consensus.[55]

Over April 1–2, a National Security Council meeting was held in which the McNaughton memo and a second McGeorge Bundy discussion paper acted as the key gang planks for a decision to deploy US marines to the coastal base of Da Nang. Bundy's April 1 paper was used word for word to frame the policy: *Rolling Thunder* would continue on the agreed scale and schedule, and crucially, ground troops would be authorized to conduct combat operations to defend American bases. The significance of this decision escaped no one and Johnson instructed that "all possible precautions" be taken to avoid publicity of this momentous decision. The White

House was going to war by stealth. On April 6, after Johnson assured reporters that no further actions were being considered as a result of the Embassy bombing, NSAM 328 endorsed the principle that US ground troops could engage in offensive operations against the Viet Cong.

This key decision should have settled debate, but the tensions and dissent continued to mount. The lobby for total bombing gained more converts. General Johnson, the Army Chief of Staff, had previously returned from a fact-finding mission and on March 14 he presented his findings in a 21-point plan to expand and improve the effectiveness of the campaign in the North. He could not have been more clear to the civilian leadership; "Remove self-imposed restrictions on the conduct of air strikes against North Vietnam," he argued, "which have severely reduced their effectiveness." Johnson raised the stakes further, lobbying for a "tailored division force" to defend installations and take on the Viet Cong in the Central Highlands, and recommending the deployment of a four-division force to the Demilitarized Zone (DMZ) and Laotian panhandle. Admiral Sharp followed this on March 21 with a similar plan to devastate North Vietnamese military infrastructure south of the 20th parallel. Ten days later, an indignant Sharp urged a spectacular air raid in retaliation of the US Embassy bombing, but the scheme was turned down. On April 1, even as the National Security Council deliberated over NSAM 328, Rostow waded in, urging the destruction of the North Vietnamese electricity grid in a memo to McNamara. The following day, CIA Director John McCone added to the bonfire of ideas by circulating a memo arguing that any ground intervention would prove useless without a more destructive air campaign (an argument supported by Taylor in yet another heated cable from Saigon on April 18).

Within two weeks of the publication of NSAM 328, McNamara was thus forced to call a conference to reconcile the conflicting parties. This was the Honolulu Conference held on April 20. The Joint Chiefs remained adamant: only a gloves-off bombing campaign would succeed. Taylor fell shy of this option and argued for a progressive ramping up of bombing in the North, the policy of "graduated reprisals" he had argued consistently from the beginning. McNamara was less comfortable with taking the war to Hanoi, conscious of the domestic and international reaction. A consensus agreement was reached but it satisfied few. Operation *Rolling Thunder* would remain at the same level but there would be a shift of the effort to the South to demonstrate that its purpose was the legitimate interdiction of North Vietnamese aggression.

On his return to Washington, McNamara could hardly have been reassured by an intelligence assessment waiting on his desk. This offered that anything short of a total and unrestricted bombing campaign, as the Joint Chiefs were arguing, or massive ground intervention, was unlikely to force Hanoi to sue for peace.[56] The Honolulu Conference coincided with the publication of two critical books on the war in Vietnam: *The Making of a Quagmire* by David Halberstam; and *Mission in Torment* by John Mecklin, a former public relations officer based in Saigon who candidly exposed the frustrations of trying to reform the rotten South Vietnamese state. Both men, from different perspectives, forecast the same conclusion: this was an unwinnable and corrupted war.

This was the noisy background to Honolulu. The aftermath was McCone's shock resignation on April 28, two days after a slick McNamara presented the strategy behind NSAM 328 to the press corps. In a brief memo, McCone, the first CIA director to resign over government policy, explained his decision in the starkest terms: offensive ground operations would fail because the bombing was grossly insufficient. Washington should either get serious, or liquidate its losses. The path chosen was the worst, not the best of options. His conclusion was so prophetic, it deserved a monument: "In effect, we will find ourselves mired down in combat in the jungle in a military effort that we cannot win, and from which we will have extreme difficulty in extracting ourselves."[57]

It was never the case that the Johnson administration was not warned, with passion, that the limited *Rolling Thunder* campaign was doomed to fail. What was striking about this entire period, from the Pleiku attack on February 7 to the publication of NSAM 328 on April 6, was not the warmongering, but the agonizing behind the scenes to avoid war. The White House did not drift into war. Instead, there was a series of incremental and cautious decisions, each seemingly reasonable if not logical, taken by the Johnson administration, purposely to limit conflict, the sum of which paradoxically led to a full-blown American war. Johnson in his own words famously sought to seduce rather than rape Hanoi, but ended up ravaging the country he was trying to woo. The rough fellows that bellowed loudest for smashing Hanoi were the ignored voices. The over-clever voices won the day then disastrously mismanaged the consequences of their own strategy.

Johnson's doubts over the genie that had been released revealed themselves within a matter of weeks of the Honolulu Conference. The appointment of Rear Admiral William Raborn as McCone's replacement only served to increase the uncertainty (the rushed appointment of Raborn was misjudged and he in turn would be replaced within 14 months). Then, on May 13, Johnson ordered an unannounced suspension of the bombing. Hanoi immediately exploited the pause to shift men and materials south: air reconnaissance uncovered evidence of hundreds of trucks, rail cars, and boats on the move in small packets. In the swirling institutional anarchy, Westmoreland tactlessly sent a cable to Washington the following day proposing the saturation bombing of the Viet Cong headquarters in the South by B-52s (the subsequent Arc Light missions). This was inspired by the perceived success of Operation *Black Virgin 1* in mid-April that witnessed almost 450 sorties dropping 900 tons of high explosives in an area of jungle three kilometers wide and four kilometers long, believed to be the location of the Central Office of South Vietnam (COSVN), the Viet Cong's main operational headquarters. This was followed by yet another missive from Taylor on May 16 urging a resumption of the bombing. The message was clear: neither of Johnson's two senior lieutenants in Saigon was overly impressed with the bombing suspension. In the three communist capitals – Hanoi, Moscow, and Peking – the gesture was rebuffed. "Fuck you,"

Johnson cussed; they "just spit in our face."[58] On May 18, the bombing duly resumed.

From *Rolling Thunder IX* onwards, the type and scale of mission began to evolve beyond the original "94 target set." Pre-determined point target bombing was largely replaced by interdiction. In each 24-hour cycle the combined air forces were authorized, initially, to undertake up to 24 strike sorties. These were essentially an aerial version of Westmoreland's later ground tactic of search and destroy. The basic tactical template of air operations was encapsulated by a ruthlessly short phrase: Find-Fix-Finish. Later, General Momyer coined an easily remembered acronym for this process – SLAM – which stood for Seek, Locate, Annihilate, and Monitor. It amounted to the same thing but the execution was far more difficult than the acronym suggested.

At first, the hunting ground was coastal Route 1 and its numerous lateral roads. Any military traffic along this corridor was deemed fair game. Later, the target lists expanded to include railways, bridges, and coastal infrastructure. This satisfied the USAF's desire for a more flexible campaign but not for a more intensive and decisive campaign. Nonetheless, there was belief in the beginning that through the methodical application of air power real results could be achieved, although various actors chose to see different desirable outcomes. Most critically, the capability to interdict the movement of men and materials south was grossly over-estimated. This chimera would bewitch air planners almost until the end of the war when the strategy abruptly switched to the outright destruction of important targets, a policy that personalities like McConnell had argued from the beginning (with impeccable logic, McConnell originally proposed that every target on "the 94 list" should be totally destroyed – what was the point of creating target lists otherwise?).

Just one year into the operation, a full 99 percent of all strike sorties in North Vietnam became interdiction missions, not the politically charged *Rolling Thunder* missions against pre-planned, designated targets.[59] Rather than proving the silver bullet, however, interdiction developed into an expensive and largely wasteful use of air power. Pilots were effectively being instructed to patrol routes in North Vietnam by day only and to spot targets by eye (there were no targeting pods as fitted in modern strike aircraft). This resulted in two predictable outcomes: the North Vietnamese restricted military moves to the night, and daytime travel for civilians became a lethal experience. No pilot wanted to return to base with a full bomb load (Tiger Island was used to dispense unused ordnance). The temptation to see a military target where none existed must have been irresistible for rookie pilots seeking to increase their bragging rights in the mess room. In May 1965, only 200 sorties were classified as armed reconnaissance and these were directed against just three principal roads. By the fall of that year the number had climbed to 600. By the end of the following year, there were 13,300 armed reconnaissance sorties over Laos and North Vietnam. By February 1967, the number hit a peak at 14,500 sorties.

The number of air bases also grew: seven in Thailand and 11 in South Vietnam. In Thailand, the air bases were established at Udorn, Nakhon Phanom, Takhli, Korat, Don Muang, U-Tapao, and Ubon. The principal South Vietnamese air bases were located at Binh Thuy, Tan Son Nhut, Bien Hoa, Phan Rang, Cam Ranh Bay, Nha Trang, Tuy Hoa, Qui Nhon, Pleiku, Phu Cat, Chu Lai, and Da Nang. The more the Joint Chiefs clamored for a chance to hit North Vietnam where it hurt, the more Johnson deflected their frustrations with the promise of more armed reconnaissance sorties, leaving both parties unsatisfied. Ultimately, the bombing failed Johnson's political purpose as much as it failed its military purpose.

From *Rolling Thunder XIII* to *Rolling Thunder XVIII* (April 30–June 17), 52 fixed targets were hit (less than one a day). These included six ammo dumps, five supply depots, 21 barracks, two airfields, two oil storage sites, two power plants, and one port and ferry. A Navy Phantom scored a first downing of a Chinese

MiG-17 with a Sidewinder missile on one of these missions. The crew that achieved this first hit never made it home. Downed by a fratricidal Sidewinder, they were lost in the Tonkin Gulf.[60]

The cost in aircraft and lives, inevitably, began to rise. By the end of June, the Navy and Air Force had dropped 6,850 bombs but lost 57 aircraft, with another 161 damaged (from just under 5,000 attack sorties).[61] DIA analysts (who were responsible for the Battle Damage Assessment or BDA) reckoned that by June 24, 751 buildings had been destroyed and 1,169 had been damaged. A staggering 323 bridges had been attacked. The total number of target types attacked made impressive reading: barracks (42); ammunition sites (16); POL storage sites (12); supply depots (11); power plants (17); airfields (nine); rail yards (57); ferries (five); communications sites (13); radar sites (27); and naval bases (11).[62]

The problem with this effort, as the JCS pointed out, was that the majority of the sites were now probably empty. The publicized policy not to attack any fixed site north of the 20th parallel invited the logical response of dispersing valuable assets north of this line. The North Vietnamese capacity to repair or bypass bridges was also telling: of 23 bridges successfully struck over April–May, 13 had already been repaired or bypassed.[63] It was calculated that it was taking six sorties just to destroy a single truck.[64] In late June McConnell made one last effort to persuade his "criminally responsible" masters of the inadequacy of the bombing campaign, now "more convinced than ever" of the failure of strategy.[65] Of the 94 strategic targets that really mattered, only 22 had been authorized. His plea fell on deaf ears. By now, a ground war was underway, and in McNamara's words, he did not "want one plane dropping bombs on North Vietnam if it can be used advantageously for air operations in South Vietnam."[66] In a volte-face, Taylor, now in his last month as ambassador before handing over to Lodge on a second tour, back-tracked on his hawkish stance at the beginning of *Rolling Thunder*, and similarly advised restraining the *Rolling Thunder* missions.

In the meantime, Viet Cong terrorism seemed to breed monsters. Saigon had become accustomed to the grenades and bombs. But on

June 25 there was especial revulsion when the popular, waterside My Canh Restaurant was bombed. The dynamite charges ripped through the dining room killing 27 Vietnamese, 12 Americans, a Frenchman, and a German. Diners collapsed where they sat, as if asleep, their faces buried in their plates. Viet Cong clandestine radio tactlessly described the attack as "a new glorious exploit ... dealing an appropriate blow to the U.S. aggressors." With impressive defiance, the restaurant re-opened five days after the attack.[67] The timing of this shocking and widely reported attack could not have been worse as it coincided with the period when Johnson was agonizing over entering the ground war. One month later, he took the decision.

Over July, the attacks continued with 550 armed reconnaissance missions authorized over a two-week period. Yen Son and Yen Bai depots were both struck, north of the 20th parallel, as well as military facilities at Dien Bien Phu and Son La, provoking protests from Peking. The Navy struck the Tri Dong highway bridge, and revisited the Thanh Hoa Bridge, once again failing to drop a single span. Air Force Captains Thomas Roberts and Kenneth Holcombe, with their navigators Ronald Anderson and Arthur Clark, succeeded in downing the USAF's first two MiG-17s in a cunning ambush set up by a circling EC-121 Big Eye early warning radar.[68]

The celebrations, however, were short-lived. On July 24, the North Vietnamese launched their first Russian-supplied SA-2 SAM. The missile downed a Phantom, sending the radar intercept officer, a Captain Roscoe Fobair, to his death, and the pilot, Captain Richard Keirn, to an eight-year sentence as a prisoner of war.[69] The shock provoked by the loss of an aircraft to these flying telegraph poles, as pilots nicknamed the SAMs, was profound. John McNaughton had scoffed that the SAMs were just a Russian political ploy. Hanoi thought differently.

The NATO-designated SA-2 Guideline represented crude, first generation Soviet technology, but the system deserved respect (an S-75 *Dvina*, as the Russians called the weapon, had downed Gary Powers' U-2 in 1960). These were missiles with a 350lb warhead, a range of 30 miles and a ceiling of nearly 60,000 feet. They flew at Mach 3. The spectacle and speed of a SAM launch could bewitch pilots:

> I was mesmerized, watching the soaring SAMs. It was unbelievable! The distances and speeds involved defy description. A SAM lifted leisurely off the pad at Phuc Yen, fifteen miles away, and slowly increased speed. In about ten seconds, it flashed by at twice the speed of sound.[70]

A CIA report drafted one week later confirmed, "It is now clear that at least one or more SAM sites are operational and are being controlled by Soviet personnel."

Once again, debate was reignited over McNamara's decision to prohibit attacks on SA-2 sites for fear of killing Russian technicians. The quandary, as the CIA advertised, was that the recently built SAM sites probably housed hundreds of technicians and operators: "To maintain the four sites in a ready condition for brief intervals during each day," one report assessed in the summer of 1965, "a minimum of 60–75 qualified personnel at each site (or about 250–300 personnel in all) would be necessary. Around-the-clock operation of the four sites would require at least 500–600 trained men."[71] Who wished to be responsible for the deaths of scores of Russians by an American air strike?

The debate however was short-lived. Three days later the decision was overturned and 46 Thunderchiefs, in a total force package of 102 aircraft, attacked SAM sites 6 and 7 south of Hanoi, flying at daringly low heights of 100 feet, to deliver their cargoes of napalm and CBUs (Cluster Bomb Units). As before, the audacity of the pilots came at a cost: six aircraft were downed. In a depressing revelation, it then transpired that site 7 had been empty, and site 6 had been baited with a dummy missile. The Fan Song radars had been entirely missed.[72] This should not have come as a complete suprise, as the CIA report had indicated that the SA-2 that downed Fobair and Keirn had in fact been launched from a point 42 nautical miles southwest of Hanoi, and not from SAM sites

6 and 7. The report also stated, "Photography of 28 July clearly shows site 6 to be filled with dummy equipment."[73]

In August, *Rolling Thunder* resumed once again. Another SAM site was targeted, inconclusively, and the first of the Iron Hand missions was launched (Suppression of Enemy Air Defense, or SEAD missions). The North Vietnamese air defenders replied by scoring again, downing a Navy Skyhawk. A furious response from Sharp led to the loss of a further five Navy aircraft, vainly attempting to target the elusive SAM sites. Chastened by the losses, pilots were instructed to remain outside the engagement envelopes of the lethal missiles. The pace of the air war, however, did not slacken: by the end of August, the number of authorized armed reconnaissance missions had doubled to 1,000, later increasing to a standard biweekly 1,200 sorties.[74] Before the month closed, two more Phantoms had fallen prey to Hanoi's SAMs.

The fall brought falling leaves, and even more falling aircraft as air planners grappled with the problem of North Vietnam's growing array of air defenses. Ejecting safely, never mind the prospect of capture, was challenging enough. Mike Thomas recalled:

> I caught a "Golden Beebe'" [SAM] in my engine, [and] had to eject. My wingman told me I had a trail of fire coming out of my tail pipe. Keep in mind the ejection seat is fired by a 35-millimeter shell with the lead removed … I became the projectile. When you hit the wind stream it's like getting smacked in the face with a snow shovel.[75]

Twenty-one aircraft were lost in September. One estimate suggested that Hanoi had acquired over 2,300 light and medium AA guns, ranging from 37mm to 100mm cannons capable of hitting aircraft at high altitudes.[76] "They had so many different kinds of guns," F-105 pilot Cecil Prentis remembered, "37, 57, 85, 100 mill guns. 1,700 guns in place circling Hanoi. We had briefing[s], we knew where the guns were at … but you couldn't avoid all of them. We had to go in and take our chances." Five SA-2 sites had become 18, with many more suspected. Eventually, there would be 200, serviced by 35 SAM battalions, a phenomenal expansion. The CIA, in the meantime, raised its estimate of Russian technicians: as many as 1,500 were now believed to be assisting the North Vietnamese.[77]

The answer to the missile threat lay in technology as much as tactics. The former was developed with customary, dazzling speed. The Navy began flying Big Look EC-121s equipped with APS-20 radars (a counterpart to the USAF's Big Eyes), which detected the Fan Song radars, while Skyhawks fitted with ALQ-51s were employed to break the lock of the enemy emitters. Ryan 147D drones launched from DC-130 mother ships were used to hunt out the sites. An anti-radiation missile, the AGM-45 Shrike, was introduced into service, typically launched by Navy A-4 Skyhawks or A-6 Intruders. After gaining a surprise advantage, the missile proved difficult to use effectively as North Vietnamese air defenders learned to switch off their radars, spoofing the warhead. Destroyer EB-66s (a variant of the Navy's A-3 Skywarrior) were deployed to theater, fitted with 23 jammers configured to counter the frequencies of known North Vietnamese air defense radars. Converted two-seat F-100F Super Sabres, re-designated F-105F Wild Weasels, were fitted with radar warning and homing systems. These aircraft were also later armed with Shrike. The early loss of a Wild Weasel cast doubts on their usefulness, but 6234th Tactical Fighter Squadron (TFS) that flew these machines soon recovered from the setback and began to prove their worth. Flying smaller packages and at low level to avoid detection proved a moderately successful tactic, but this was not always possible because of the terrain, and many bombs had to be "lobbed" from an altitude of 8,000 feet anyway. The other effective counter-measure was evasive maneuvering, the so-called "SAM break" – a sharp 90-degree turn, or "split-S maneuver" – but this relied on plenty of warning, pilot skill, and no small measure of luck. In pilot John B. Nichols' eloquent description, evading a SAM was "a soul-searing experience of dueling with an inanimate object that pursued its prey with almost human intelligence."[78] Moreover, an obsession with the SAM threat was somewhat distracting from the fact that the majority of aircraft were being lost to ground fire, as pilots were forced to fly low both to avoid SAM acquisition, and to deliver their ordnance with reasonable accuracy.

In the end, fewer than 200 planes were downed by SAMs from 1965 through 1972. Roughly 80 were naval aircraft, reflecting the commitment of the carriers against targets in the North. The SA-2 Guideline probability of hit ultimately proved disappointing; just one in 50 launches found a target. This statistic, however, reflected better American counter-measures over the course of the war. In the beginning, the odds were worse. One year into *Rolling Thunder*, Earle Wheeler sent a memo to McNamara advising that at least 949 SA-2 launches had been detected over North Vietnam. These had downed 32 manned aircraft.[79]

By September, the combined air forces had been hammering away at targets in North Vietnam and Laos for six months, and it was time to take stock. Ninety percent of 91 targets below the 20th parallel had been struck, many in multiple raids. Above this parallel, less than a fifth of targets had been attacked, reflecting Washington's undiminished anxieties over provoking "Chicom."[80] Over a thousand sorties were being flown every month, dumping on average more than 2,000 tons of high explosives.[81] To the mounting frustration of air staffs, the number of restrictions on the pilots – the "don'ts" – far from relaxing, seemed to augment in proportion to the number of officials in Washington trying to fine-tune the fuzes. Strike aircraft could not fly within 30 miles of Hanoi, ten miles of Haiphong, or 25 miles of the Chinese border. Pilots were not allowed to attack MiG bases, or SAM sites, within restricted areas, even if they were under attack. Calls to "put the lights out" in North Vietnam and utterly destroy its oil facilities were deflected. Targeting intelligence, however, improved immeasurably with the establishment of an Air Force-led Targeting Intelligence Directorate (TID). But what did all this effort amount to? Both PACAF and the CIA-DIA came to the rather depressing conclusion that North Vietnam's capability to wage war, infiltrate the South, and maintain the morale of its people had barely been dented.[82]

Furthermore, the cost in machines and pilots had mounted precipitously; by the end of September, 114 aircraft had been downed, equally shared between the Air Force and Navy.[83]

The average life span of F-105 pilots was fewer than 100 missions with many not even completing 50 missions before being shot down. In pilot Robert Lines' recollection:

> Looking back now, the numbers are sobering. Our tour length was 100 missions ... so that was 100 chances to get shot down. Roughly two thirds of us were downed. About half were killed or captured, and half rescued. If physically able, those rescued went back to the cockpit.[84]

The fortunes of Lieutenat Colonel James Robinson Risner reflected these odds. An ace who had recorded eight MiG kills over 110 combat sorties in Korea, he was downed on September 16, 1965 attacking the Thanh Hoa Bridge. This was his 55th mission over North Vietnam. He survived the ejection from his F-105D and endured a miserable incarceration.[85] Ed Rasimus, who later authored books on his experiences in Vietnam, recorded that over a period of intense flying his squadron lost on average one pilot a day.[86] Ted Rees mused regretfully:

> ... we soon realized there was no plan ... We were just there waiting for the Joint Chiefs of Staff to give us the target of the day. No end in sight. This was where I wanted to be, except now I was a 28-year-old Captain, with a family. Yeah, I wondered if I'd made a stupid mistake.[87]

An updated assessment now suggested that North Vietnam possessed over 4,000 air defense weapons of various calibers, a number that many pilots running the gauntlets of flak would have probably concurred with.[88]

Other pilots seemed to be protected by guardian angels. Navy Lieutenant Commander Denny Weichman began his flying career in Vietnam in 1962 flying the Farm Gate Sky Raiders. He eventually completed 625 missions and became one of the most decorated naval aviators to survive the conflict. On returning from a raid on the major SAM site at Phuc Yen in October 1967, 53 cannon and shrapnel holes were counted in his robust A-4E Skyhawk.[89]

Some were delivered by guardian angels, the audacious rescue and recovery crews. As Lieutenant Commander Tom Tucker approached Haiphong Harbor on a photo-reconnaissance mission he was hit by 37mm cannon fire and was forced to eject. He landed just 150 meters from the shore. Straightaway, junks began to converge on the "Yankee air pirate." However, within minutes, an SH-3 from USS *Kearsarge*, piloted by Commander Vermilya, arrived on the scene. Tucker's wingman, Lieutenant Commander Teague, had accompanied the vulnerable helicopter and began to strafe the junks. Ignoring the barrage of fire attempting to down the helicopter, Vermilya cooly plucked Tucker from the harbor in what was described as "one of the most dangerous rescue missions of the war."

The longest-range rescue was conducted by Captain Robert D. Furman who flew his HH-3C 105 miles northwest of Hanoi to pluck downed F-105 pilot Captain Martin H. Mahrt. On egress the helicopter was jumped by three MiG-17s. They launched missiles and missed, possibly spoofed by ground clutter. The "bogies" fled when F-4C Phantoms approached the scene.

Tom Tucker flew for Air Wing Sixteen on USS *Oriskany*. Over the course of *Rolling Thunder*:

> 3 aircrewmen from Air Wing Sixteen successfully ejected from, or bailed out of, downed aircraft and were known to be alive on the ground in enemy territory; 24 were rescued, unfortunately 19 were not. 27 others safely ejected into friendly waters around Yankee Station and were recovered. ... [In total] 70 assigned combat aircraft were hit by enemy fire 242 times during *Rolling Thunder*. 180 were damaged and 62 were knocked down. With our assigned complement of 78 combat pilots, 56 were KIA, 12 POW, and 5 MIA. Our statistical probability of surviving *Rolling Thunder* was 30 percent![90]

Others made their own luck. The first naval aviator prisoner of war was actually shot down on June 6, 1964 undertaking a covert mission over Laos. At the time, Lieutenant Charles "Chuck" Klusmann was piloting an F-8 Crusader, launched from USS *Kitty Hawk*. He partially dislocated a hip on landing and was held in a small cell, later transferred to a camp with other Laotian prisoners. Three months later he made an audacious escape bid in a rain storm accompanied by two Laotians. By this stage he had lost 40 pounds, subsisting on turnip soup. "I never did like turnips," he later commented, "I still don't." It took the escapees just three days to find friendly troops and safety.[91]

October ushered in monsoon weather complicating the task for pilots trying to find well-concealed and mobile targets. British journalist James Cameron observed, "There never was a place where such importance was attached to invisibility."[92] Hanoi's air defense planners were more than enthusiastic over co-opting Tonkin's meteorology into the invisibility cloak. Thirty percent of missions were aborted in the second half of October, and 345 Air Force raids were canceled over November.[93] Tactics improved, on both sides, but a sense of staleness had already begun to creep into the air war. Faced with so many limitations, and a limited target set, sorties were directed to re-strike targets that had been hit earlier in the year, to the ire of pilots who felt they were being asked to risk their lives to generate statistics, without real purpose. Photo-reconnaissance missions invariably showed that damaged structures – the bridges, rail lines, and roads – were repaired within a matter of days, by a ghost army of civilians (and Chinese engineers) working under the cover of darkness. In a propaganda piece, Radio Peking boasted:

> The local populations in various places have mobilized themselves to build many new roads, bridges, and culverts, in addition to repairing the damages. Militia Corps formed by workers, peasants, and students cooperate with the People's Army air defense units in safeguarding the transport lines. They stand sentinel on important bridges, ferries, and key road sections to insure that convoys and ships will pass safely.[94]

Elsewhere, the target set expanded, notably in the quadrant northeast of Hanoi where a number of important targets were attacked, including several bridges and a large ammunition depot near Long Het. Hanoi's MiGs made a late cameo appearance after a long absence from the skies, dog-fighting on November 15 and 25, but to no effect.

Dog-fighting was fast, confusing, and punctuated by a terse lexicon incomprehensible to non-pilots. This transcript of a recording of a four-ship of F-4 Phantoms offers a flavour:

> Ok, Eagle 1, pull 'em all out, keep your eyes peeled ...
> There's a MiG in front of Sunglass 1, headed right straight into the flight – he's at Sunglass 1's "9" now ...
> Tallyho, they're shooting at us alright, I've got the target in sight, Sunglass 1, 12 o'clock ...
> I've got that target, too, Arnie ...
> They're just on our wing – you gonna pop? ..
> I'm gonna roll in on the ... they're pumping away at us ... you got a bomb down there, Sunglass; let's keep it movin', move it ...
> Do you have MiGs?
> Sunglass 2, I think I lost 'em ...
> Eagle 2, that's all they had.[95]

The entire panicky encounter, for both sides, had taken a matter of seconds.

In 2016, a reunion was organized between surviving North Vietnamese MiG and *Rolling Thunder* pilots. Jack Ensch observed, "There was no feeling of hostility, animosity, ill will or any thing like that during our meeting. Forty four years ago we were just in different airplanes trying to shoot down the other one. We didn't know the person in the other cockpit. And now we sat calmly, unemotionally and discussed our air-to-air engagement of almost a half century earlier – it was almost a bit surreal."[96] Later he visited the notorious Hoa Lo prison where he was held, and was amused to be treated as a VIP.

Even as American aircraft set about attempting to dismantle the North's transport infrastructure, Viet Cong in the South were proving just as good at causing equivalent damage from the ground for a fraction of the cost and effort, the familiar paradox of counterinsurgency conflicts. On November 24, a team of two VC sappers and one guerrilla set about sabotaging the railway bridge on the Saigon-Phan Thiet railway, two kilometers south of the nearby station at Xuan Loc. They were armed with two six-kilogram mines and 400 meters of electrical cable. In the account of the subsequent interrogation report:

> The VC then taking advantage of the bubbling water running under the bridge, laid their mines and took position in a hut 300 meters away ... the train from Long Khanh stopped when it was 500 meters from the bridge ... The train started to move, and when it was on the bridge the VC set off their two mines collapsing the bridge, and one locomotive, four cars and one escort car plunged into the river. The two gds [guards] that guarded the bridge were killed ... The VC, after mingling with nearby local people, returned to their base safely.[97]

The interrogation report included a scrupulous hand-drawn sketch map of the objective, a hallmark of Viet Cong operations.

Despite the evident risks, crews continued to demonstrate the highest gallantry, and willingness to chase after targets when they could just as easily have banked away and returned to base. On October 31, Navy Commander Richard Powers, in a pathfinder A-4E Skyhawk, was guiding two flights of Thunderchiefs on a raid against a bridge northeast of Hanoi. As the attack went in, Powers detected a Fan Song radar, then visually sighted two SAM launches at a second location. Vectoring the Thunderchiefs to the radar emitter he then mounted a solo attack on the second site. He managed to drop his load of Mk-82 high-drag Snake Eye bombs but paid for his intrepidness and was shot down. Far from being deterred by the sight of the Skyhawk plummeting to earth, the Thunderchiefs then rallied, pummeled the site, spotted a third, and attacked that one as well. Navy aircraft then joined the fray attacking at low level despite the storm of ground fire and 13 more SAM launches. The attack runs succeeded in hitting all three offending SAM locations.[98] However much vacillation was shown by their political masters, America's pilots were demonstrating nothing less than full commitment to the cause.

Many came from service families with a strong, inherited sense of duty and patriotism. The eventually retired Admiral Taylor signed up because, in his words, he wondered whether all Navy pilots married girls like Grace Kelly. An uncle had served on a B-17 during the war. He completed 276 *Rolling Thunder* sorties over North Vietnam. With his two sons, grandson, and granddaughter, the family had given 83 years of active service.[99]

By December, the weather had become awful. For seven days the USAF grounded all aircraft and the Navy was forced to suspend operations for four. Even when aircraft succeeded in launching, they faced the possibility of a weather abort. This pattern culminated in one of the biggest raids to date against the Uong Bi power station, which was reckoned to supply as much as 15 percent of North Vietnam's electricity. Ninety aircraft launched on December 10 with 67 in a supporting role. Just seven Thunderchiefs were able to locate and attack the power plant, without conclusive results.[100] One aircraft was shot down, but in this case the pilot was swiftly recovered. As ever, an irritated Sharp could not let this pass. Two more Navy raids were conducted on December 19 and 22, involving, among other aircraft, A-6A Intruders equipped with night radar bombing systems. The first raid totally missed the power plant and cost one Intruder. The second dumped 25 tons of high explosives on the plant which was temporarily put out of commission. Two Skyhawks were lost along with an RA-5 Vigilante, tasked with obtaining the vital post-strike photography.[101]

What the Joint Chiefs did not know, even as they prepared more studies, refined their arguments, cajoled for better technology, and bid for more sorties, was that Johnson was about to call a bombing truce. The announcement was made just two days later on December 24, initially for 30 hours and later extended.

Behind the first of the Christmas bombing truces (there had been the brief, five-day suspension in May) was a secret diplomatic initiative, or perhaps fancy, set in motion in November, which Washington hoped might tempt Hanoi into peace negotiations. The scheme mainly involved Rusk, the US Ambassador to the UN, Arthur Goldberg, and Amatore Fanfani, the veteran Italian Foreign Minister. Ironically, Rusk voted against a bombing truce, believing it might offer him a stronger hand in negotiations, but McNamara carried the day. Regardless of these nuances, 11 months of disappointing results had failed to convince the architects of *Rolling Thunder* that the entire concept of "gradualism" had been an exercise in military tokenism. The North was stronger, not weaker, more determined, not cowed, and shovelling troops south faster than the mathematicians in the Office of Statistical Analysis could count.

By the end of the year, the official MACV Command war history recorded with some satisfaction:

> USAF jet pilots logged 10,570 strike sorties and dropped 23,610 tons of bombs over NVN in 1965. The operations which expanded over the areas authorized for strikes covered most of the country outside the Hanoi-Haiphong area. Several hundred bridges had been destroyed or damaged, thousands of primarily military type buildings smashed, [and] roads and railways interdicted.[102]

Implicit in this cheerleading was the implication: how could a powerful nation wreaking such damage on a weakling possibly lose the war?

Top secret studies produced by the Directorate of Tactical Evaluation in HQ PACAF were much less triumphant. A total of 23,194 sorties had been mounted by all air forces, resulting in 171 losses and 450 damaged aircraft. "It was evident," one study observed drily, "that the program had not achieved its objective of pressuring Hanoi into halting support in South Vietnam and Laos."[103] Morale was "not significantly shaken," and all the indicators pointed to "a prolonged struggle." Unwilling to be critical, even in a highly classified document with limited circulation, a political Sharp judged that *Rolling Thunder* had done "quite well," but added that, "Operations had not been conducted in a manner sufficient to increase the pressure on Hanoi."[104] The bottom line was that "ROLLING THUNDER had not forced Hanoi to the decision the U.S. had sought."

If Jupiter's thunderbolt could not land the sucker punch, then, with certain inevitability, Washington had to turn to her marines and soldiers. From the summer, they had begun to pour into South Vietnam in their tens of thousands. America was going to war.

NOTES

CHAPTER 1: THE SERPENT IN EDEN

1 *Life* magazine, September 3, 1945
2 The French representative was General Count Philippe "Leclerc" de Hauteclocque, later despatched to French Indochina
3 WGBH Open Vault, Interview with Douglas MacArthur, 07/02/1982
4 Harrison, Simon, "Skull Trophies of the Pacific War: Transgressive objects of remembrance," *Journal of the Royal Anthropological Institute*, 2006
5 For examination of the killing of Japanese POWs and body part trophies see Professor Richard J. Aldrich, *The Faraway War: Personal Diaries of the Second World War in Asia and the Pacific*, Corgi, 2010; Niall Ferguson, "Prisoner taking and prisoner killing in the age of total war," *War in History*, 2004; and Niall Fergusson, *The War of the World*, Penguin Books, 2007, pp544–548 for racism toward Japanese.
6 Publications du service historique de l'armée de terre consacrées a la guerre d'Indochine, *1945–1946 Le retour de la France en Indochine*, textes et documents, 19 [hereafter Service historique de l'armée de terre]
7 WGBH Open Vault, Interview with Hoang Quoc Viet, 02/18/1981
8 Roosevelt memo to Hull, January 24, 1944
9 *Life* magazine, September 1, 1967
10 Dommen, Arthur J., *The Indochinese Experience of the French and the Americans: Nationalism and Communism in Cambodia, Laos and Vietnam*, Indiana University Press, 2001, 47 [hereafter Dommen]
11 Dommen, 49
12 Dommen, 61
13 Dommen, citing an unattributed French document, LM-70, Reel 1, Frame 884, NARA
14 Currey, Cecil R., *Victory At Any Cost*, Potomac Books, Inc (formerly Brassey's, Inc), 1999, 7 [hereafter Currey]

15 See Currey for a comprehensive account of the formative years of the Viet Minh and the role of Giap

16 Currey, 84

17 Dommen, 94

18 Dommen, 63

19 Dommen, 65

20 Dommen, 75

21 Spector, Ronald H., *Advice and Support, The Early Years, The U.S. Army in Vietnam*, Center of Military History, United States Army, Washington D.C., 1983, 33 [hereafter Spector]

22 *Life* magazine, September 1, 1967

23 Patti, Archimedes L.A., *Why Vietnam?: Prelude to America's Albatross*, University of California Press, 1982, 46 [hereafter Patti]

24 WGBH Open Vault, Interview with Duong Van Thang, 02/10/1981

25 WGBH Open Vault, Interview with Archimedes L.A. Patti, 04/01/1981

26 WGBH Open Vault, Interview with Tran Duy Hung, 02/03/1981

27 WGBH Open Vault, Interview with Duong Van Khang, 02/10/1981

28 WGBH Open Vault, Interview with Archimedes L.A. Patti, 04/01/1981

29 Dommen, 96

30 Marr, David G., *Vietnam 1945: The Quest for Power*, University of California Press, 1995, 119

31 Deer Mission, summary report, September 1945

32 WGBH Open Vault, Interview with Archimedes L.A. Patti, 04/01/1981

33 Ibid

34 Deer Mission, summary report, September 1945

35 OSS newsletter, July 2005 and Spector, 67

36 Berube, Claude G., *Ho, Giap and OSS Agent Henry Prunier*, originally published on HistoryNet.com, published online May 24, 2011

37 Deer Report No. 1, July 17, 1945

38 Ibid

39 Ibid

40 Deer Mission, summary report, September 1945

41 The attack was against a POW camp in Tam Dao on July 15, 1945, Dommen, 98

42 WGBH Open Vault interview with Archimedes L.A. Patti, 04/01/1981

43 Herring, C. George, *America's Longest War*, McGraw-Hill, 1979 [hereafter Herring]

44 OSS newsletter, July 2005

45 WGBH Open Vault, Interview with Archimedes L.A. Patti, 04/01/1981

46 Patti, 156

47 Patti, 167

48 WGBH Open Vault, Interview with Archimedes L.A. Patti, 04/01/1981

49 WBGH Open Vault, Interview with Abbot Low Moffat, 01/01/1982
50 Dommen, 100
51 WGBH Open Vault, Interview with Tran Duy Hung, 02/03/1981
52 Ibid
53 Dommen, 115
54 Dommen, 109
55 Dommen, 112
56 Patti, 188
57 Dommen, 87
58 WGBH Open Vault, Interview with Frank M.White, 04/02/1981
59 WGBH Open Vault, Interview with Philip Geoffrey Malins, 07/16/1982
60 WGBH Open Vault, Interview with Doidge Estcourt Taunton, 07/16/1982
61 WGBH Open Vault, Interview with Indor Jag Mohan, 02/19/1981
62 WGBH Open Vault, Interview with Madame Nguyen Thi Binh, 02/16/1981
63 WGBH Open Vault, Interview with Philip Geoffrey Malins, 07/16/1982
64 Dommen, 125
65 Cited by Dunn, M. Peter, *The First Vietnam War*, Hurst, 1985, from 1/1 Gurkha Rifle newsletter, 218 [hereafter Dunn]
66 WGBH Open Vault, Interview with Doidge Estcourt Taunton, 07/16/1982
67 Ibid
68 Service historique de l'armée de terre, 179
69 Dunn, 203
70 Neville, Peter, *Britain in Vietnam: Prelude to Disaster, 1945–1946*, Routledge, 2007, 76 [hereafter Neville]
71 WGBH Open Vault, Interview with Doidge Estcourt Taunton, 07/16/1982
72 The verdict of Harry Brain, Gracey's political advisor, cited by Dunn, 227
73 WGBH Open Vault, Interview with John Chancellor, 10/07/1982
74 Service historique de l'armée de terre, 179
75 Neville, 80
76 Ibid, 80
77 The phrase used by Gracey, cited in Neville, 90
78 Dommen, 127–129
79 WGBH Open Vault, Interview with Herbert Bluechel, 04/23/1981
80 WGBH Open Vault, Interview with Doidge Estcourt Taunton, 07/16/1982
81 In the early 1980s, a Vietnamese refugee claimed that Dewey had in fact been mistakenly killed by a youth wing of the Viet Minh, and that his body eventually ended up in a grave near a village called An Phu Dong

(the OSS believed his body was dumped in a river near the village of Go Vap) OSS newsletter, July 2005

82 Dommen, 69

83 State Department, "Politico-Military Problems in the Far East and Initial Post-Defeat Policy Relating to Japan," June 2, 1945, 6:557–568

84 Ibid, 130

85 Pentagon Papers, Part I, A-1

86 Ibid, 171

87 Ibid, A-13

88 WGBH Open Vault, Interview with Lucien Bodard, 02/18/1981

89 WBGH Open Vault, Interview with Carleton Swift, undated

90 WBGH Open Vault, Interview with Bui Tin, 02/20/1981

91 Spector, 51–53

92 Spector, 69–72

93 Neville, 74

94 Dommen, 179

95 Pentagon Papers, Part I, A-1, A-33

96 Service historique de l'armée de terre, 128

97 WGBH Open Vault, Interview with Pham Van Dong, 02/19/1981

98 Dommen, 154

99 Service historique de l'armée de terre, 263

100 WGBH Open Vault, Interview with Vu Quoc Uy, 02/22/1981

101 Service historique de l'armée de terre, 82

102 Ibid, 284

103 Ibid, 389

104 WGBH Open Vault, Interview with Doung Van Khang, 02/10/1981

105 Time magazine, June 10, 1946, "CHINA: Bad Government"

106 Directive to Lieutenant General Wedemeyer, July 9, 1947

107 Life magazine, December 30, 1946

108 Ibid

109 Published in Life Magazine, March 18, 1946, "Getting Tough with Russia"

110 Ibid

111 NSC 68, April 14, 1950. President's Secretary's File, Truman Papers

112 Life magazine, May 19, 1947

113 Life magazine, July 17, 1950

114 Life magazine, August 7, 1950, The forcible march of 60–80,000 US and Filipino prisoners by the Imperial Japanese Army that resulted in several thousand deaths.

115 Life magazine, September 25, 1950

116 Life magazine, October 30, 1950

117 Farrar-Hockley, Anthony, Official History: The British Part in the Korean War, Vol. 1, A Distant Obligation, HMSO, 1990, 267

118 *Life* magazine, April 30, 1951
119 *Life* magazine, December 10, 1951
120 A joke told in *Life* magazine, June 27, 1960
121 Pentagon Papers, Book 7, Part V.A.
122 Allen, George W., *None So Blind*, Ivan R. Dee, 2001, 20 [hereafter Allen]
123 Spector, 112
124 Spector, 111–115
125 Spector, 114
126 Dommen, 200
127 Spector, 116
128 WGBH Open Vault, Interview with Paul C. Warnke, 08/25/1982
129 WGBH Open Vault, Interview with James Claude Thomson, 04/21/1981
130 Ibid
131 Transcript, Walt W. Rostow Oral History Interview II, 1/9/81, by Ted Gittinger, Internet Copy, LBJ Library, 18
132 Spector, 194–195
133 Spector, 196–197
134 https://www.history.com/this-day-in-history/eisenhower-gives-famous-domino-theory-speech
135 Pentagon Papers, Part II, 33
136 Spector, 174–175
137 Msg, CHHAAG Indochina to DEPTAR, Mg 2062A, 271130Z July 1954, DA-IN-74737 (TS)
138 Msg, SECSTATE to Amb (Paris), 4551, TEDUL 191, June 12, 1954 (TS)
139 Pentagon Papers, Part IV-A, 27
140 Pentagon Papers, Part II, 7
141 *Life* magazine, May 31, 1954, "French retreat to a quiet kingdom"
142 Cited in BDM Corporation, BDM Corporation Analysis Book I, Operational Analyses, Department of the Army, US Army War College, 54
143 WGBH Open Vault, Interview with Douglas MacArthur, 1982
144 Ibid
145 NSC 177
146 Pentagon Papers, Part IV-A-4, 72
147 Pentagon Papers, Part IV-A-5, 55
148 WGBH Open Vault, Interview with Douglas MacArthur, 07/02/1982
149 Ibid
150 American Friends of Vietnam, *America's Stake in Vietnam*, 8–14
151 Nixon, Richard, *No More Vietnams*, W.H. Allen, 1986, 61 [hereafter Nixon]
152 WGBH Open Vault, Interview with U. Alexis Johnson, 07/02/1982
153 Allen, 77
154 WGBH Open Vault, Interview with Everett Bumgardner, 1981

155 WGBH Open Vault, Interview with Jack Keegan, 1981

156 WGBH Open Vault, Interview with J. Lawton Collins, 1981

157 Ibid

158 Halberstam, David, *The Best and the Brightest*, Random House Publishing Group, 1992, 146 [hereafter Halberstam]

159 Gavin, James H., *Crisis Now*, Random House, 1968, 49

160 Pentagon Papers, Part-IV-A-3, 32

161 Pentagon Papers, Part-IV-A-4, 67

162 WGBH Open Vault, Interview with Everett Bumgardner, 04/29/1981

163 WGBH Open Vault, Interview with Ngo Dinh Luyen, 01/31/1979

164 WGBH Open Vault, Interview with J. Lawton Collins, 04/29/1981

165 See British Pathé footage of "The Saigon Revolt"

166 Allen, 79–83

167 WGBH Open Vault, Interview with Edward Geary Lansdale, 01/31/1979

168 Ibid

169 WGBH Open Vault, Interview with Paul M. Kattenberg, 05/07/1981

170 Ibid

171 Cited by Franklin, John K., *The Hollow Pact: Pacific Security and the Southeast Asia Treaty Organization*, ProQuest, 2006, from Sir James Cable, *The Geneva Conference of 1954 on Indochina*

172 Pentagon Papers, Part IV-A-4, 74

CHAPTER 2: KENNEDY'S FINGER IN THE DYKE

1 WGBH Open Vault, Interview with Roger Hilsman, 05/11/1981

2 Hearing before the Subcommittee to Investigate the Administration of the Internal Security Act and Internal Security Laws of the Committee on the Judiciary of the United States Senate, Eighty-Seventh Congress, First Session, Testimony of Dr Stefan T. Possony, Analysis of the Khrushchev Speech of January 6, 1961, June 10, 1961

3 *Life* magazine, June 8, 1962

4 WGBH Open Vault, Interview with Dean Rusk, 06/08/1982

5 In which the motion was passed that this house will not fight for king and country.

6 WGBH Open Vault, Interview with Dean Rusk, 06/08/1982

7 Ibid

8 Halberstam, 22–23

9 Transcript, Dean Rusk Oral History Interview I, 7/28/69, by Paige E. Mulhollan, Internet Copy, LBJ Library, 17

10 *Life* magazine, November 30, 1962

11 Transcript, McGeorge Bundy Oral History Interview I, 1/30/69, by Paige E. Mulhollan, Internet Copy, LBJ Library, 12

12 Robert S. McNamara Oral History Interview, JFK1, 4/4/64, JFKOH-RSM-01

13 JFK Library, George H. Decker Oral History Interview, JFKOH-GHD-01, 18/9/68

14 McNamara Oral History Interview, op cit

15 WGBH Open Vault, Interview with Roger Hilsman, 05/11/1981

16 Papers of John F. Kennedy. Pre-Presidential Papers. Presidential Campaign Files, 1960. Speeches and the Press. Press Secretary's Transcripts, 1960–61. Washington, D.C., with Robert McNamara, December 13, 1960

17 Robert S. McNamara Oral History Interview, JFK1, 4/4/64, JFKOH-RSM-01

18 WGBH Open Vault, Interview with David Halberstam, 01/16/1979

19 WGBH Open Vault, Interview with George W. Ball, 05/18/1981

20 Pentagon Papers Part IV-B-1, 39

21 Haynes Miller, a US aid investigator who was sacked for whistle-blowing.

22 At the time Stanley Karnow was *Time Life* bureau chief in Hong Kong

23 WGBH Open Vault, Interview with Dean Rusk, 06/08/1982

24 Pentagon Papers Part IV-A-4, 6

25 WBGH Open Vault, Interview with David Halberstam, 01/16/1979

26 WGBH Open Vault, Interview with Roger Hilsman, 05/11/1981

27 American Friends of Vietnam, *America's Stake in Vietnam*, 8–14

28 Fall, Bernard, *Ho Chi Minh on Revolution*, 339–340, cited in the Pentagon Papers Part IV-A-5, 190

29 WGBH Open Vault, Interview with Pham Van Dong, 02/19/1981

30 WGBH Open Vault, Interview with Hoang Quoc Viet, 02/18/1981

31 Service historique de l'armée de terre, 115

32 Cited in the Pentagon Papers, Part I, 207

33 Service historique de l'armée de terre, 116

34 Ibid, 202

35 WGBH Open Vault, Interview with Tuu Ky, 02/16/1981

36 Service historique de l'armée de terre, 120

37 WGBH Open Vault, Interview with Tuu Ky, 02/16/1981

38 From the *Twelve Recommendations* of Viet Minh doctrine 1947

39 State to Hanoi Tel No. 36, May 20, 1949

40 Schlesinger, Arthur, M., *A Thousand Days: John F. Kennedy in the White House*, Houghton Mifflin, 1965, 321, cited in the Pentagon Papers, Part 1, 192 [hereafter Schlesinger]

41 WGBH Open Vault, Interview with Maxwell D. (Maxwell Davenport) Taylor, 01/30/1979 [Part 1 of 4]

42 JCS memo to Sec Def, October 19, 1954

43 Lawton Collins memo to Sec State, January 20, 1955

44 Pentagon Papers, Part IV-A-4, 6
45 Spector, 225
46 The CG and SDC were formed in April 1956 and April 1957 respectively
47 Warner, Denis, *The Last Confucian*, Macmillan, 1963,107–108
48 Pentagon Papers, Part IV-A-4, 52
49 Pentagon Papers, Part IV-A-4, 8
50 Review by James Sullivan, *Culture Wars*, 1998, "Dr America: The Lives of Thomas A. Dooley by James T. Fisher; 1927–1961," Massachusetts University Press, 1997
51 Pentagon Papers, Part IV-A-5, 60
52 The overall operation was known as Operation *Passage to Freedom*
53 Pentagon Papers, Part IV-A-5, 13
54 WGBH Open Vault, Interview with Maxwell D. (Maxwell Davenport) Taylor, 01/30/1979 [Part 1 of 4]
55 Ibid
56 Pentagon Papers Part IV-A-5, 20
57 WGBH Open Vault, Interview with Frederick Nolting, 04/30/1981
58 Spector, 347
59 Bouscaran, Anthony Trawick, *The Last of the Mandarins: Diem of Vietnam*, Pittsburg Duquesne University Press,1965, 165–171, cited in the Pentagon Papers Part IV-A-5, 113
60 Ibid, 21
61 Pentagon Papers Part IV-A-5, 124
62 Honey, P.J., *The Problem of Democracy in Vietnam*, New York, Praeger, 1962, 72–73
63 Pentagon Papers Part IV-A-5, 11
64 WGBH Open Vault, Interview with Nguyen Thi Chiem, 03/11/1981
65 WGBH Open Vault, Interview with Orrin DeForest, undated
66 RAND, *RAND in Southeast Asia, A History of the Vietnam War Era*, Mai Elliott, 2010, 64
67 Ibid, 73
68 Ibid, 74
69 Edward G. Lansdale Oral History Interview, JFK1, 07/11/70
70 WGBH Open Vault, Interview with Eldridge Durbrow, 02/01/1979
71 Saigon 1151 to SecState, December 4, 1960
72 Wallace, 224–226
73 Pentagon Papers Part IV-A-5, 232
74 Hoang Van Hoan states Le Duan distorted Ho's will, 2360510020, Douglas Pike Collection: Unit 08 – Biography, The Vietnam Center and Archive, Texas Tech University
75 Pentagon Papers Part IV-A-5, 235

76 Eagle, Richard J., History 475, *The Politics of War: North Vietnam's Military Strategy 1959–1968*, December 1, 1986, 1071325008, Glenn Helm Collection, The Vietnam Center and Archive, Texas Tech University

77 This is something that has been challenged by recent scholarship (*Hanoi's War* by Lien-Hang Nguyen, and Pierre Asselin's *Hanoi's Road to the Vietnam War*)

78 Wallace, 237

79 WGBH Open Vault, Interview with Nguyen Thi Dinh, 02/16/1981

80 Pentagon Papers Part IV-A-5, 247

81 Pentagon Papers Part IV-A-5, 153

82 2311310001, Douglas Pike Collection: Unit 05 – National Liberation Front, The Vietnam Center and Archive, Texas Tech University

83 2311310013, Douglas Pike Collection: Unit 05 – National Liberation Front, The Vietnam Center and Archive, Texas Tech University

84 Spector, 338

85 Spector, 33

86 Saigon Despatch 278 to State, March 7, 1960, cited in Pentagon Papers Part IV-A-5, 242

87 Ibid, 155

88 Fall, Bernard, *Vietnam Witness*, 239 and 360–361, cited in Pentagon Papers Part IV-A-5, 156

89 Viet Cong Terrorism Documented in "White Book," 2311308015, Douglas Pike Collection: Unit 05 – National Liberation Front, The Vietnam Center and Archive, Texas Tech University

90 Pentagon Papers Part IV-A-5, 125

91 WGBH Open Vault, Interview with James Claude Thomson, 04/21/1981

92 Halberstam

93 Intelligence Memorandum: The Organization Activities and Objectives of the Communist Front in South Vietnam, 0411140001, Central Intelligence Agency Collection, The Vietnam Center and Archive, Texas Tech University

94 WBGH Open Vault, Interview with Le Minh Dao, 03/12/1981

95 WGBH Open Vault, Interview with Tran Nhat Bang, 03/03/1981

96 WGBH Open Vault, Interview with Le Van Phuc, 03/12/1981

97 Ibid

98 WGBH Open Vault, Interview with Le Minh Dao, 03/12/1981

99 WGBH Open Vault, Interview with Le Van Phuc, 03/12/1981

100 WBGH Open Vault, Interview with Jane Barton, 05/12/1981

101 WGBH Open Vault, Interview with Nguyen Huu Tho, 02/23/1981

102 WGBH Open Vault, Interview with Nguyen Thi Chiem, 03/11/1981

103 WGBH Open Vault, Interview with Nguyen Thi Nguyet Anh, 1981

104 WGBH Open Vault, Interview with Nguyen Thi Dinh, 03/02/1981

105 Ibid

106 WGBH Open Vault, Interview with Pham Thi Xuan Que, 02/28/1981
107 CIA, Intelligence Memorandum 1603/66, September 26, 1966, and Pike, Douglas, *Viet Cong*, Cambridge MIT, 1966, 115 cited in Pentagon Papers Part IV-A-5, 167
108 WGBH Open Vault, Interview with Nguyen Huu Tho, 02/23/1981
109 Hickey, Gerald, *Village in Vietnam*, Yale University Press, 1964
110 Pentagon Papers Part IV-A-5, 157
111 Pentagon Papers Part IV-A-5, 224
112 WGBH Open Vault, Interview with Tran Do, 02/17/1981
113 https://openlibrary.org/books/OL17032M/People%27s_war_ People%27s_Army
114 Study, Research and Analysis Studies – Rice in Vietnam Provinces of IV CTZ – Record of MACV Part 2, F015900260321, Vietnam Archive Collection, The Vietnam Center and Archive, Texas Tech University
115 2171306016, Douglas Pike Collection: Unit 03 – Insurgency Warfare, The Vietnam Center and Archive, Texas Tech University
116 2311702019, Douglas Pike Collection: Unit 05 – National Liberation Front, The Vietnam Center and Archive, Texas Tech University
117 Galbraith (New Delhi) to President, November 20, 1961
118 Lansdale visit January 2–14, 1961
119 Edward G. Lansdale Oral History Interview – JFK#1, 07/11/70
120 Lt-Gen Lionel C. McGarr, *Information, Guidance and Instructions to MAAG Advisory Personnel by Lt. General Lionel C. McGarr*, November 10, 1960
121 WGBH Open Vault, Interview with Roger Hilsman, 05/11/1981
122 Ibid
123 WGBH Open Vault, Interview with Dean Rusk, 06/08/1982
124 WGBH Open Vault, Interview with Nguyen Khanh, 04/29/1981
125 Cited in Pentagon Papers Part IV-A-5, 370
126 NSC 177
127 Pentagon Papers, Part IV-B-1, 57
128 Pentagon Papers, File A, Date 4-61
129 Pentagon Papers, Part IV-B-1, 69
130 Transcript, Walt W. Rostow, Oral History Interview I, 3/2/69, by Paige E. Mulhollan, 24, LBJ Library, University of Texas Archives
131 JCS DA 995131 of May 1, 1961.
132 Transcript, Walt W. Rostow Oral History Interview I, 3/21/69, by Paige E. Mulhollan, Internet Copy, LBJ Library
133 Ibid
134 Schlesinger, 337
135 Kissinger, Henry, *The White House Years*, Weidenfeld and Nicolson and Michael Joseph, 1979, 14
136 WGBH interview with Frederick Nolting, April 30, 04/30/1981

137 https://www.jfklibrary.org/asset-viewer/archives/JFKPOF/128a/JFKPOF-128a-002

138 VP memo to President May 23, 1961

139 Transcript, Walt W. Rostow Oral History Interview I, 3/21/69, by Paige E. Mulhollan, Internet Copy, LBJ Library

140 *Life* magazine, September 15, 1961

141 Pentagon Papers, Part IV-B-2, 18

142 Ibid

143 Ibid

144 Ibid, 27

145 Later Assistant Secretary of State for East Asian and Pacific Affairs

146 William Bundy to McNamara, October 10, 1961.

147 Whitcomb, Darrel, Douglas A/B-26 Invader, Operation Farmgate, online napoleon130.tripod.com

148 Ibid

149 Halberstam, 161

150 Milne, David, *America's Rasputin: Walt Rostow and the Vietnam War*, Hill and Wang, 2008

151 Pentagon Papers, Part IV-B-2, 26

152 WGBH Open Vault, Interview with Ama Hoa, 03/07/1981

153 WGBH Open Vault, Interview with Y True Nie, 03/07/1981

154 WGBH Open Vault, Interview with Y Bloc, 03/06/1981

155 WGBH Open Vault, Interview with Maxwell D. (Maxwell Davenport) Taylor, 1979 [Part 1 of 4]

156 Pentagon Papers, Part IV-B-2, 20

157 ChMAAG to McNamara, November 11, 1961

158 Pentagon Papers, 14, 11–16

159 WGBH Open Vault, Interview with Maxwell D. (Maxwell Davenport) Taylor, 01/30/1979 [Part 1 of 4]

160 Ibid

161 Pentagon Papers, Part IB-B-1, 135 in DEPTEL 618 to Nolting, November 14, 1961

162 Transcript, Walt W. Rostow Oral History Interview I, 3/21/69, by Paige E. Mulhollan, Internet Copy, LBJ Library

163 WGBH Open Vault, Interview with George W. Ball, 05/18/1981

164 Ibid

165 Pentagon Papers, Part-IV-B-1, 170

166 Galbraith (New Delhi) to President, November 20, 1961

167 Schlesinger, 547

168 Saigon telegram to Sec State, February 3, 1962, JFKNSF-195a-004-p0016

169 Transcript, Paul Harkins, Oral History Interview I, 10/11/81, by Ted Gittinger, 7, LBJ Library

170 Ibid, 2
171 Wyatt, Clarence, *Paper Soldiers: The American Press and the Vietnam War*, University of Chicago Press 1995, 100–110
172 Transcript, Paul Harkins, Oral History Interview I, 10/11/81, by Ted Gittinger, 7, LBJ Library
173 RAND, *RAND in Southeast Asia, A History of the Vietnam War Era*, Mai Elliott, 2010, 165
174 Transcript, Paul Harkins, Oral History Interview I, 10/11/81, by Ted Gittinger, 16, LBJ Library
175 Ibid, 43
176 Ibid, 15
177 Ibid, 7
178 Ibid, 15
179 See Allen for the travails caused by Colonel Winterbottom.
180 Allen, 142
181 RAND, op cit, 259
182 https://www.jfklibrary.org/asset-viewer/archives/JFKPOF/128/JFKPOF-128-010
183 WGBH Open Vault, Interview with Nguyen Cong Danh, 03/12/1981
184 Thompson, *Appreciation of Vietnam President Diem*, November 1961–April 1962
185 Thompson, Sir Robert, *Defeating Communist Insurgency: The Lessons of Malaya and Vietnam*, New York, 1966, 111
186 McGarr to Felt (CINCPAC), November 27, 1961
187 Via Roger Hilsman's "A Strategic Concept for Vietnam," February 2, 1961
188 Pentagon Papers, IV-B-2, 37
189 Ibid, 39
190 WGBH Open Vault, Interview with Earl Young, 11/06/1981
191 WGBH Open Vault, Interview with Earl Young, 11/06/1981
192 WGBH Open Vault, Interview with Everett Bumgardner, 04/29/1981
193 *Life* magazine, November 2, 1962
194 Ibid
195 Letter from Chairman Khrushchev to President Kennedy, October 26, 1962, transmitted by Department of State telegram, Moscow 7pm
196 Cited in "It's a Date: Kennedy and the Timetable for a Vietnam Troop Withdrawal" Marc J. Selverstone, *Diplomatic History*, Vol. 34, No. 3 (June 2010), 485–495
197 CINCPAC Message to MACV, 140428Z
198 Pentagon Papers, Part IV-B-4, 8
199 Ibid, 5
200 Ibid, 21

CHAPTER 3: ANNUS HORRIBILIS

1 August: 16,201; September: 16,483; October: 16,732; November: 16,456; December: 15,732, Pentagon Papers, Part IV-B-4

2 Cosmas, Graham A., *MACV: The Joint Command in the Years of Escalation, 1962–1967*, Center of Military History, United States Army, 56 [hereafter Cosmas, *1962–1967*]

3 Milton Orshefsky in *Life* magazine, January 25, 1963

4 *Life* magazine, January 25, 1963

5 Highlights of Current Situation, Honolulu Conference, May 6, 1963

6 Victor H. Krulak, Oral History Interview – JFKOH-VHK-01, 11/19/70

7 Ibid

8 Hilsman, Roger, *To Move a Nation*, Doubleday, 1967, 502

9 Victor H. Krulak, Oral History Interview, op cit

10 Memo from Robert W. Komer to President's Special Assistant for National Security Affairs Bundy, September 9, 1963

11 WGBH Open Vault, Interview with Roger Hilsman, 05/11/1981

12 Jones, Howard, *Death of a Generation: How the Assassinations of Diem and JFK Prolonged the Vietnam War*. Oxford University Press, 2003, 307

13 Jones, 375

14 Report of the McNamara-Taylor Mission to South Vietnam, October 2, 1963

15 Secretary of Defense, Memo to President: McNamara-Taylor Mission to South Vietnam, October 2, 1963

16 WGBH Open Vault, Interview with David Halberstam, 01/16/1979

17 https://www.jfklibrary.org/events-and-awards/forums/past-forums/transcripts/vietnam-and-the-presidency-keynote-by-david-halberstam

18 http://lde421.blogspot.co.uk/2012/12/george-mcarthurs-vietnam.html

19 WGBH Open Vault, Interview with David Halberstam, 01/16/1979

20 https://www.jfklibrary.org/events-and-awards/forums/past-forums/transcripts/vietnam-and-the-presidency-keynote-by-david-halberstam

21 See *Vietnam* magazine, Charles E. Kirkpatrick, "The Battle at Ap Bac Changed America's View of the Vietnam War," published online July 26, 2006, for an overview of the battle and its ramifications

22 WGBH Open Vault, Interview with David Halberstam, January 16, 01/16/1979

23 WGBH Open Vault, Interview with Dao Vien Trung, 03/12/1981

24 In fact, there were elements of 514th Regional Battalion and the 261st Main Force Battalion at this location.

25 WGBH Open Vault, Vietnam: A Television History; Interview with Nguyen Cong Danh, 03/12/1981

26 WGBH Open Vault, Interview with Dao Vien Trung, 03/12/1981
27 Moyar, Mark, *Triumph Forsaken: The Vietnam War 1954–1965,* Cambridge University Press, 2006, 194
28 WGBH Open Vault, Interview with Nguyen Cong Danh, 03/12/1981
29 Halberstam, 202–203
30 WGBH Open Vault, Interview with Roger Hilsman, 05/11/1981
31 ODCSOPS Study, DA for COS US Army, September 15, 1965
32 WGBH Open Vault, Interview with Carl F. Bernard, 07/16/1981
33 Ibid
34 WGBH Open Vault, Interview with Thich Tu Hanh, 03/16/1981
35 WGBH Open Vault, Interview with Roger Hilsman, 05/11/1981
36 WGBH Open Vault, Interview with Lucien Conein, 05/07/1981
37 WGBH Open Vault, Interview with Roger Hilsman, 05/11/1981
38 Pentagon Papers, Part IV-B-5, 93
39 WGBH Open Vault, Interview with Maxwell Taylor, 01/30/1979
40 Langguth, A.J., *Our Vietnam: The War, 1954–1975,* Simon & Schuster, 2000, 98
41 DCI Briefing "South Vietnam," July 9, 1963 (McCone for President)
42 A rich source of the official documentation that ensued can be found in the National Security Archives, George Washington University, Vietnam Project: http://nsarchive.gwu.edu/NSAEBB/NSAEBB444/
43 SNIE 53-2-63, July 10, 1963
44 WGBH Open Vault, Interview with Henry Cabot Lodge, 01/01/1979
45 WGBH Open Vault, Interview with Roger Hilsman, 05/11/1981
46 Ibid
47 Saigon Embassy to Hilsman Message 235, August 24, 1963
48 State to Lodge Message 243, August 24, 1963
49 Ibid
50 Pentagon Papers Part IV-B-5, 57
51 WGBH Open Vault, Interview with W. Averell Harriman, 01/29/1979
52 WGBH Open Vault, Interview with George W. Ball, 05/18/1981
53 Transcript, George Ball Oral History Interview I, 7/8/71, by Paige E. Mulhollan, Internet Copy, LBJ Library, 8
54 WGBH Open Vault, Interview with Roger Hilsman, 05/11/1981
55 Top Secret, Summary of Plans for Security of US Personnel in Vietnam in the event of Internal Violence, 1963
56 WGBH Open Vault, Interview with Frederick Nolting, 04/30/1981
57 Transcript, George Ball Oral History Interview I, 7/8/71, by Paige E. Mulhollan, Internet Copy, LBJ Library, 8
58 WGBH Open Vault, Interview with Averell Harriman, 01/29/1979
59 WGBH Open Vault, Interview with Roger Hilsman, 05/11/1981
60 Ibid

61 Memo of Conversation, Hilsman on Vietnam, White House, August 26, 1963

62 Memo of Conversation, State on Vietnam, White House, August 27, 1963

63 WGBH Open Vault, Interview with Henry Cabot Lodge, 01/01/1979

64 Lodge to State, Department of State, Central Files, POL 27 S VIET Top Secret, November 6, 1963

65 Embassy Saigon message 63869, August 26, 1963

66 Embassy Saigon message 364, August 27, 1963

67 Saigon Message 804, October 28, 1963

68 MACV message 1557, August 28, 1963

69 Top Secret, State to Ambassador and Gen. Harkins, 17199, August 28, 9.32pm, 63

70 Saigon to State 2050, October 29, 1963

71 State message 272, August 29, 1963

72 Memo of Conversation, Vietnam, White House, August 29, 1963

73 Top Secret, Saigon to SecState, 383, August 30, 6pm, 63; Secret, Saigon to SecState, 384, August 30, 7pm, 63

74 CBS Evening News, September 2, 1963

75 Lodge to State, November 3, 1963

76 Saigon (CAS 1445) October 5, 1965, To State from Lodge

77 CAP message 63560, October 5, 1963

78 CAS Saigon message 34026, October 5, 1963

79 CAP message 63560, October 6, 1963

80 A useful summary of this acrimonious debate is at: http://bostonreview.net/us/galbraith-exit-strategy-vietnam

81 Transcript, McGeorge Bundy Oral History Special Interview I, 3/30/93, by Robert Dallek, Internet Copy, LBJ Library, 16

82 Saigon 1896, CIA Saigon (Lodge) to State, October 23, 1963

83 Saigon 47370, CIA Saigon to CIA HQ, October 25, 1963

84 CAS Saigon message, October 25, 1963

85 WGBH Open Vault, Interview with Tran Van Don, 05/07/1981

86 Prados, John, *The White House Tapes: Eavesdropping on the President*, The New Press, 2003, October 29, 1963

87 MACV messages 2028, 2033, and 2034, October 30, 1963

88 CAS Washington message 79407, October 30, 1963

89 WGBH Open Vault, Interview with Lucien Conein, 05/07/1981

90 CIA Saigon to Sec State, Flash CRITIC, recd 2.15am, November 1, 1963

91 CIA Saigon to Sec State, Flash CRITIC, recd 2.34am, November 1, 1963

92 CIA Saigon to Sec State, Flash CRITIC, recd 2.38am, November 1, 1963

93 CIA Saigon to Sec State, Flash CRITIC, recd 2.39am, November 1, 1963

94 Lodge to State Message 860, November 1, 1963

95 Lodge to State, Z011129Z, November 1, 1963

96 CIA Saigon to Sec State, Flash, recd 4.11am, November 1, 1963
97 CIA Saigon to Sec State, Flash, recd 4.29am, November 1, 1963
98 CIA Saigon to Sec State, Flash, recd 5.57am, November 1, 1963
99 CIA Saigon to DIRNSA, 011430Z, November 1, 1963
100 CIA to White House International Situation Room, DTG unclear, possibly 22.55hrs, November 1, 1963
101 Draft outgoing to Lodge, October 29, 1963, https://www.jfklibrary.org/asset-viewer/archives/JFKNSF/317/JFKNSF-317-004
102 State Eyes Only for Lodge, 11652, October 29, 1963
103 See Moyar for a full account of the last days of Diem's life. Also see the close study: Hammer, Ellen J., *A Death in November: America in Vietnam 1963*, E.P. Dutton, 1963
104 Transcript, William E. Colby Oral History Interview I, 6/2/81, by Ted Gittinger, Internet Copy, LBJ Library, 7
105 Saigon (CAS 1445) October 5, 1965, To State from Lodge
106 CIA Saigon Station to Director NSA, November 3, 1963
107 MAC J-3 85 73, Summary Evaluation SVN, Harkins to JCD, November 2, 1963
108 Lodge to State, November 3, 1963
109 Lodge to State, November 4, 1963
110 Herring, 116
111 Memo for Moyers, Eyes Only, Discussion Concerning the Diem Regime August–October 1963, July 30, 1966
112 Memorandum for the Record of Discussion at the Daily White House Staff Meeting, November 4, 1963
113 State to Saigon Embassy, November 2, 1963
114 Memorandum for the Record of Discussion at the Daily White House Staff Meeting, November 4, 1963
115 WGBH Open Vault, Interview with George W. Ball, 05/18/1981
116 Cosmas, *1962–1967*, 121–122
117 CIA, Current Intelligence Memorandum 2703/63, August 28, 1963

CHAPTER 4: MOPPING THE FLOOR

1 *Life* magazine, August 14, 1964
2 *Life* magazine, June 19, 1964
3 WGBH Library, Interview with William Bundy, 05/06/1981
4 WGBH Open Vault, Interview with Bill D. Moyers, 05/05/1981
5 Transcript, McGeorge Bundy Oral History Interview II, 2/17/69, by Paige E. Mulhollan, Internet Copy, LBJ Library, 8
6 WGBH Open Vault, Interview with William P. Bundy, 05/06/1981
7 *New York Times*, August 15, 1963

8 Critical Analysis of Halberstam Article, Sec Def Briefing Book, August 1963
9 Pentagon Papers, Part IV-C-1, 54
10 WGBH Open Vault, Interview with Bill Moyers, 05/05/1981
11 Transcript, McGeorge Bundy Oral History Interview I, 1/30/69, by Paige E. Mulhollan, Internet Copy, LBJ Library, 22
12 WGBH Open Vault, Interview with Bill D. Moyers, 05/05/1981
13 WGBH Open Vault, Interview with George W. Ball, 05/18/1981
14 Transcript, George Ball Oral History Interview I, 7/8/71, by Paige E. Mulhollan, Internet Copy, LBJ Library, 12
15 WGBH Open Vault, Interview with Bill D. Moyers, 05/05/1981
16 Ibid
17 USOM Report on Strategic Hamlets, Long An Province, December 6, 1963
18 *Life* magazine, June 19, 1964
19 Ibid
20 Defense Secretary for President, "Trip to South Vietnam," December 21, 1963
21 Pentagon Papers, Part IV-C-2a, 5
22 CINCPAC letter to JCS, "Combined MACV-CAS Saigon Plan for Actions North Vietnam," December 19, 1963
23 "Program of Operations Against North Vietnam," January 2, 1964, 1
24 MACV Personal Assessment of 4th Quarter CY 1963, February 2, 1964; CAG Preliminary Report, February 10, 1964; SNIE 5–64, February 12, 1964; Final CAS Report, February 18, 1964
25 Bill Moyers' Journal, *Bill Moyers on LBJ's Path to War Pt 1*/PBS, excerpts from White House telephone recordings 1964 [hereafter Moyers' Journal]
26 WGBH Open Vault, Interview with Bill D. Moyers, 05/05/1981
27 Pentagon Papers, Part IV-B-1, 93
28 Moyers' Journal, February 24, 1964
29 Moyers' Journal, March 2, 1964
30 Transcript, George Ball Oral History Interview I, 7/8/71, by Paige E. Mulhollan, Internet Copy, LBJ Library, 9
31 JCSM-174-64, March 2, 1964
32 WGBH Open Vault, Interview with William P. Bundy, 05/06/1981
33 JCSM-222-64, August 14, 1964
34 Pentagon Papers, Part IV-B-3, 85
35 Allen, 121
36 Allen, 179
37 NSAM 288 [https://history.state.gov/historicaldocuments/frus1964-68vol/d87
38 Douglas Pike, Pushing On blog spot: http://lde421.blogspot.co.uk/2012/12/vincible-ignorance-doug-pikes-vietnam.html
39 Bundy to Lodge, April 4, 1964

40 WP Bundy Memo: "Discussion of Possible Extended Action in Relation to Vietnam," April 27, 1964

41 Embassy Saigon Message 1889 EXDIS for President, April 30, 1964

42 Cosmas, *1962–1967*, 443

43 Embassy Saigon Message 2112, May 4, 1964

44 Moyers' Journal, May 27 1964

45 Brian VanDeMark, *Into the Quagmire: Lyndon Johnson and the Escalation of the Vietnam War*, Oxford University Press, 1991, 178

46 Transcript, Robert S. McNamara Oral History Interview I, 1/8/75, by Walt W. Rostow, Internet Copy, LBJ Library, 27

47 Nixon, 78–79

48 Moyers' Journal

49 Lyndon Johnson and Robert McNamara on June 30, 1965, Conversation WH6506-09-8221, *PRDE*

50 https://millercenter.org/the-presidency/educational-resources/lbj-orders-some-new-haggar-pants

51 JCSM 460-64, May 30, 1964

52 JCS memo to Sec Def, "Objectives and Courses of Action – South-east Asia" (JCSM-471-64), June 2, 1964

53 House Armed Services Committee January 27–29, 1964

54 WGBH Open Vault, Interview with Bill D. Moyers, 05/05/1981

55 State Message 2095, May 26, 1964

56 JCS message 2625-64, Taylor to Felt/Harkins, May 28, 1964

57 *Life* magazine, November 27, 1964

58 Two MAAG agencies, the MAP Directorate and the Army MAP Logistics Directorate, in fact had to be retained to manage the MAP, Cosmas, 126.

59 Cosmas, *1962–1967*, 126

60 Pentagon Papers, Part IV-A-5, 226

61 Cosmas, *1962–1967*, 122

62 WGBH Open Vault, Interview with Duong Long Sang, 03/10/1981

63 Pribbenow, Merle L., *North Vietnam's Master Plan*, Vietnam, August 1999; 12, 2; ProQuest Military Collection, 30

64 Ford, Ronnie E., *Tet 1968: Understanding the Surprise*, In Cass Series – Studies in Intelligence, F. Cass, 1995, 22

65 Pentagon Papers, Part IV-A-5, 218

66 CIA memo for Sec Def, "Appraisal of the Conduct of the War in Vietnam," de Silva/Kirkpatrick, February 10, 1964

CHAPTER 5: SHOOTING AT FLYING FISH

1 *Maddox* AAR dated August 24, 1964

2 *Life* magazine, April 23, 1965

3   Hanyok, Robert J., "Skunks, Bogies, Silent Hounds and the Flying
    Fish: The Gulf of Tonkin Mystery 2–4 August," *Cryptologic Quarterly*,
    4, approved for release by the NSA on November 3, 2005 [hereafter
    Hanyok]. As a former NSA employee, Hanyok was in a unique position
    to understand the arcane world of SIGINT and he enjoyed privileged
    access to TOP SECRET COMINT material. His analysis is meticulous
    and in the author's view, unimpeachable. The author also wishes to
    acknowledge Edward J. Drea, US Army historian, who put together a
    most comprehensive account of the Gulf of Tonkin incident, from the
    perspective of the protagonists in Washington, in *MHQ*, summer 2004
    edition, "Gulf of Tonkin Incident: Reappraisal 40 years later" [hereafter
    Drea]. The subsequent paragraphs owe the detail of timings of various
    personalities to his version and research into the incident based on
    declassified materials. The third invaluable source is Edwin Moise's *Tonkin
    Gulf and the Escalation of the Vietnam War*, University of North Carolina
    Press, 1996 [hereafter Moise], also based on declassified materials, as well
    as North Vietnamese sources. In the interests of readability, the author
    has desisted from referencing every timing, movement, or message with
    a footnote. Without the sterling detective work of these three authors,
    it is re-emphasized, the account in this book could not have been pieced
    together.
4   Hanyok, 10
5   Ibid
6   Top Secret, Memorandum for the Record, *Chronology of Events of
    2–5 August 1964 in the Gulf of Tonkin*, October 14, 1964 [hereafter
    Memorandum for the Record]
7   Trần Đỗ Cẩm at: docam11@yahoo.com, 36
8   Cosmas, *1962–1967*, 160
9   Trần Đỗ Cẩm at: docam11@yahoo.com, 8
10 See http://www.mrfa.org/Operation34a.htm and Trần Đỗ Cẩm at:
    docam11@yahoo.com for details of the coastal raids
11 Sec Def to Senate Foreign Relations Committee, August 6, 1964
12 Plaster, John L., *The Secret Wars of America's Commandos in Vietnam*, Mass
    Market Paperback, 1998
13 Hanyok, 9
14 Hanyok, 10; Moise, 25
15 Hanyok, 9
16 *Maddox* AAR dated August 24, 1964
17 Secret Kimbo 011635Z ZYH FM USM 626J: Spot Report ST 220
    Probable DESOTO mission located by DRV naval entity
18 Top Secret, From DIRNSA To: NSAPAC REP VIETNAM, B26/361/64,
    WS/451, August 19, 1964

19 Secret Kimbo FM USN 27, Report 2/Q/VHN/R26-64, DRV Navy may attack DESOTO patrol, 012152Z

20 Hanyok, 13

21 *Maddox* in fact received three warning messages: USN 27 21Q/VHN/R26-64, USN 27 21Q/VHN/R27-64, and USN 414T 020640Z (unserialized DESOTO log item)

22 Cited by Hanyok: DIRNSA. "Possible Planned Attack by DRV Navy on Desoto Patrol," B205/981-64, 020302Z, August 1964

23 Hanyok, 13

24 Memorandum for the Record

25 Hanyok, 15

26 WGBH Open Vault, Interview with Phung The Tai, 02/19/1981

27 Memorandum for the Record

28 Cited by Hanyok: G11VHN/RlO-64, 040850Z August 1964

29 Memorandum for the Record, Message: F403/2 47, Subject: Desoto Patrol and 34A Operations, 262020Z

30 Hanyok, 18

31 Drea, 4

32 Memorandum for the Record

33 Hanyok, 16

34 Hanyok, 26

35 Hanyok, 28

36 There is a discrepancy of 20 nautical miles between Drea and Hanyok over *Maddox*'s position. Hanyok's estimate has been used.

37 *Life* magazine, August 14, 1964

38 Bond, James and Stockdale, Sybil, *In Love and War*, Harper & Row, 1984, 19

39 In the 2003 documentary *The Fog of War: Eleven Lessons from the Life of Robert S. McNamara*, McNamara conceded that the August 4 attack probably never happened.

40 Hanyok, 3

41 Tonkin Gulf NSA Intercepts: Declass

42 Drea, 4

43 Hanyok, 24

44 Drea, 5; Hanyok states 9.25am

45 Drea, 6

46 Hanyok, 22

47 Drea, 6

48 Ibid

49 Hanyok, 23

50 Memorandum for the Record, Tab 37

51 Hanyok, 24

52 Memorandum for the Record
53 Hanyok, 23
54 Hanyok, 27
55 Drea, 7
56 http://web2.millercenter.org/lbj/audiovisual/whrecordings/tonkin/vn_01_06.mp3
57 Hanyok, 24
58 JCS Message 7700
59 Drea, 7
60 Drea, 7
61 Ibid for all the timings in the following paragraphs
62 Hanyok, 23
63 Hanyok, 38
64 Hanyok, 25
65 DESOTO Action SITREP, 041754Z August 1964
66 Hanyok, 24
67 Hanok, 24
68 Hanyok, 25
69 Hanyok, 25
70 The author acknowledges confusion in his mind over "Report 38" quoted by Hanyok. There is a released Report Number 12 that also carries the annotation "R-38-64," timed at 041630Z (not 041650Z) which speaks of falling aircraft but not of sacrificed comrades. Report 38 has the sender redacted. Hanyok, however, confidently maintains that San Miguel forwarded the crucial messages, which the author does not doubt. The author therefore can only speculate that Hanyok viewed material not readily available, or that some re-transmission occurred. Whatever the explanation, it does not materially change Hanyok's persuasive arguments.
71 Hanyok, 3–4
72 Drea, 9
73 Telephone conversation between Johnson and McNamara, August 3, 1964, 10.30am
74 Drea, 10
75 Transcript, George Ball Oral History Interview I, 7/8/71, by Paige E. Mulhollan, Internet Copy, LBJ Library, 17
76 See Drea for a detailed synopsis of the timings
77 Ray Cline, Deputy Director of Operations, CIA
78 Transcript, George Ball Oral History Interview I, 7/8/71, by Paige E. Mulhollan, Internet Copy, LBJ Library, 18
79 https://millercenter.org/gulf-tonkin-recordings
80 WGBH Open Vault, Interview with Ray Cline, 03/09/1982

81 Transcript, Dean Rusk Oral History Interview II, 9/26/69, by Paige E. Mulhollan, Internet Copy, LBJ Library, 11

82 Hanyok, 3

83 WGBH Open Vault, Interview with Jack Valenti, 04/23/1981

84 Transcript, Dean Rusk Oral History Interview II, 9/26/69, by Paige E. Mulhollan, Internet Copy, LBJ Library, 15

85 WGBH Open Vault, Interview with Bill D. Moyers, 05/05/1981

86 Ibid

87 Ibid

88 John McNaughton diary, December 6, 1966

89 Transcript, Walt W. Rostow Oral History Interview II, 1/9/81, by Ted Gittinger, Internet Copy, LBJ Library, 31

90 The so-called "Rostow Thesis" was actually drafted in December 1963. It was not universally accepted as sound. Most notably, Henry Rowen's memo to the JCS of August 21, 1964 raised questions over its premises and doubted that it offered a path to success.

91 Analysis of the Rostow Thesis, August 21, 1964, 5

92 Kissinger, 231

93 WGBH Open Vault, Interview with George W. Ball, 05/18/1981

94 Transcript, George Ball Oral History Interview I, 7/8/71, by Paige E. Mulhollan, Internet Copy, LBJ Library, 14

95 Ibid, 16

96 Captured Documents (CDEC): Unknown Interrogation Source, Log Number 59-4667-00,, CTZ 3, Bien Hoa Province, F034600530091, Vietnam Archive Collection, The Vietnam Center and Archive, Texas Tech University

97 Admiral Mustin at the Inter-Agency Working Group

98 *Life* magazine, October 16, 1964

CHAPTER 6: JUPITER'S THUNDERBOLT

1 WGBH Open Vault, Interview with Nguyen Thanh Xuan, 03/14/1981

2 Top Secret, DOD, C.I. No. 9 Working Paper No. 4, The Flaming Dart Air Strikes Against North Vietnam, February 7–11, 1965, Part 1, 26

3 WGBH Open Vault, Interview with Bill D. Moyers, 05/05/1981

4 By coincidence, ten years later as South Vietnam collapsed, the same scene would be replayed at Pleiku, and three pilots on this occasion would also attempt to rescue their machines.

5 WGBH Open Vault, Interview with McGeorge Bundy, undated

6 Ibid

7 Allen, 184

8 Pentagon Papers IV-C-3, 31

9 WGBH Open Vault, Interview with McGeorge Bundy, undated
10 Ibid
11 WGBH Open Vault, Interview with Paul C. Warnke, 08/25/1982
12 Ibid
13 WGBH Open Vault, Interview with William Bundy, 05/06/1981
14 Staaveran, Jacob Van, *Gradual Failure: The Air War over North Vietnam: 1965–1966*, Air Force History and Museums Program, 2002, 16 [hereafter Staaveran]
15 Pentagon Papers IV-C-3, 18
16 Pentagon Papers IV-C-3, 10
17 Vice Admiral A.C. Davis cited in BDM Corporation analysis Book I, Operational Analyses, Department of the Army, US Army War College, from DOD US/VN Relations, Book 1, 11, B-6
18 Pentagon Papers IV-C-3, 8
19 WGBH Open Vault, Interview with Bill D. Moyers, 05/05/1981
20 McConnell, in passing, was very short sighted and cheated eye tests more than once, first to become a cadet, and secondly to fly. His fierce determination to succeed and perhaps not a little vanity were such that there are no official photographs of McConnell wearing glasses – but it may be presumed he wore them at the controls of an aircraft.
21 The United States Strategic Bombing Survey
22 Cited in Staaveran, 191
23 Transcript, Dean Rusk Oral History Interview II, 9/26/69, by Paige E. Mulhollan, Internet Copy, LBJ Library, 22
24 Pentagon Papers IV-C-3, ii
25 WGBH Open Vault, Interview with Dean Rusk, 06/08/1982
26 "Rostow Thesis," August 21, 1964
27 Farm Gate, Steel Tiger, Yankee Team, Barrel Roll and Blue Tree
28 Staaveran, 69
29 Staaveran, 70
30 Staaveran, 84
31 CHECO, Rolling Thunder March–June 1965 HQPACAF Tactical Evaluation Center March, 28, 1966, 25
32 *Life* magazine, December 10, 1965
33 Lyndon Johnson and Robert Spivack on April 29, 1965, Conversation WH6504-06-7378, in Beschloss, *Reaching for Glory*, Simon and Schuster, 2002, 293; Lyndon Johnson and Bill Moyers on May 13, 1965, Conversation WH6505-11-7659-7660, *PRDE*
34 Lyndon Johnson and Birch Bayh on June 15, 1965, Conversation WH6506-03-8125, *PRDE*
35 *Life* Magazine, May 14, 1965
36 Ibid

37 Cosmas, Graham A., *MACV: The Joint Command in the Years of Withdrawal 1968–73*, The United States Army in Vietnam, Center of Military History United States Army, 2007, 324 [hereafter Cosmas, *1968–73*]

38 Naval Historical Center, *Command and Control of Air Operations in the Vietnam War*, Colloquium on Contemporary History, January 23, 1991, No. 4

39 Ibid, 11

40 *Vietnam Chronicles*, 636

41 Gen Moore interview November 22, 1969 by Maj Samuel Riddlebarger and Lt-Col Valentino Castellina, cited in Staaveran, 83

42 WGBH Open Vault, Interview with Jack Valenti, 04/23/1981

43 F-105 Pilots of Vietnam Tell Their Stories: https://www.tapatalk.com/groups/theerant/over-war-f-105-pilots-of-vietnam-tell-their-storie-t97770.html

44 Jakobsen, 18

45 Pentagon Papers IV-C-3, 41

46 Saigon 2889 to SecState, March 8, 1965 SECRET NODIS

47 Cosmas, *1968–73*, 14, citing Combined Campaign Plan, 1968, an. A, p. 3, Historians files, CMH; Xiaoming Zhang, "The Vietnam War: A Chinese Perspective, 1964–1969," *Journal of Military History* 60 (October 1996): 731–762

48 F-105 Pilots of Vietnam Tell Their Stories: https://www.tapatalk.com/groups/theerant/over-war-f-105-pilots-of-vietnam-tell-their-storie-t97770.html

49 Jakobsen, 23

50 Staaveran, 95

51 Staaveran, 105

52 Pentagon Papers, IV-C-3, 81

53 WGBH Open Vault, Interview with William P. Bundy, 05/06/1981

54 Transcript, George Ball Oral History Interview I, 7/8/71, by Paige E. Mulhollan, Internet Copy, LBJ Library, 21

55 Halberstam, 366–367

56 Top Secret 185843-c cited in the Pentagon Papers IV-C-3

57 Pentagon Papers IV-C-3, 91

58 Lyndon Johnson and Birch Bayh on June 15, 1965, Conversation WH6506-03-8125, *PRDE*

59 Jakobsen, 24

60 Staaveran, 111

61 Staaveran, 141

62 Staaveran, 152

63 Staaveran, 13

64 Staaveran, 155 citing Msg, CINCPAC to AmEmb Vientiane, COMUSMACV, 260330Z Jun 65

65 Staaveran,153 citing McConnell Notebook, Item 186, June 26, 1965
66 Staaveran, 155, record of Questions and Answers at Mtg between
    Secy McNamara and His Party, Ambassador Taylor and His Staff, and
    COMUSMACV and his Staff, July 16, 1965
67 The My Chanh Bombing, 2311308023, Douglas Pike Collection: Unit
    05 – National Liberation Front, The Vietnam Center and Archive, Texas
    Tech University
68 Staaveran, 158–159
69 Staaveran,163
70 "Pak Six" cited by Steve Randolph, Arsenal, The SAM War that broke
    out in 1965 required new tactics, equipment – and just plain guts,
    1988, 2250207040, Douglas Pike Collection: Unit 03 – Technology,
    The Vietnam Center and Archive, Texas Tech University
71 Memorandum, Democratic Republic of Vietnam – Status Report on SAMs
    in North Vietnam – CIA Research Reports, F029100020482, Vietnam
    Archive Collection, The Vietnam Center and Archive, Texas Tech University
72 Staaveran,165
73 Memorandum, Democratic Republic of Vietnam – CIA Appreciation
    of SAM-2 Activity in North Vietnam During Late July – CIA Research
    Reports, F029100020487, Vietnam Archive Collection, The Vietnam
    Center and Archive, Texas Tech University
74 Staaveran, 170
75 F-105 Pilots of Vietnam Tell Their Stories: https://www.tapatalk.com/groups/
    theerant/over-war-f-105-pilots-of-vietnam-tell-their-storie-t97770.html
76 PACAF DI Report, Effects of Air Ops, SEA, 6th Edition, July 5, 1965, 9
77 CIA Intelligence Memo: Soviet Military Personnel And Air Defense
    Operations In North Vietnam, 0240306035, Larry Berman Collection
    (Presidential Archives Research), The Vietnam Center and Archive, Texas
    Tech University
78 John B. Nichols, On Yankee Station, cited by Steve Randolph, Arsenal,
    "The SAM War that broke out in 1965 required new tactics, equipment –
    and just plain guts," 1988, 2250207040, Douglas Pike Collection: Unit
    03 – Technology, The Vietnam Center and Archive, Texas Tech University
79 Memo To The Secretary Of Defense From Earle G. Wheeler: Military
    Actions Against North Vietnam, 0240515005, Larry Berman Collection
    (Presidential Archives Research), The Vietnam Center and Archive, Texas
    Tech University
80 CHECO Report, *Rolling Thunder July 1965–December 1966*, 8
81 Staaveran, 180
82 Staaveran, 185, citing CM-863, September 23, 1965 (JCS 2343/598-4),
    September 27, 1965, and PACAF DI Reports Effects of Air Os, SEA,
    September 16, 1965, 4–11, September 30, 1965, 1–14

83 Staaveran, 186

84 F-105 Pilots of Vietnam Tell Their Stories: https://www.tapatalk.com/groups/theerant/over-war-f-105-pilots-of-vietnam-tell-their-storie-t97770.html

85 Rolling Thunder Remembered: http://www.rollingthunderremembered.com/subject-rolling-thunder-remembered-24-march-1966/

86 USAF Pilot Vietnam War Experiences: https://heritageflightgeardisplays.wordpress.com/2011/01/28/usaf-pilot-vietnam-war-experiences/

87 F-105 Pilots of Vietnam Tell Their Stories: https://www.tapatalk.com/groups/theerant/over-war-f-105-pilots-of-vietnam-tell-their-storie-t97770.html

88 Staaveran, Figure 8

89 Rolling Thunder Remembered: http://www.rollingthunderremembered.com/subject-rolling-thunder-remembered-24-march-1966/

90 Ibid

91 Ibid

92 *Gravel Pentagon Papers*, Vol. IV, 622–623

93 Staaveran, 201

94 CHECO, Rolling Thunder March–June 1965 HQPACAF Tactical Evaluation Center, March 28, 1966, 68

95 Tape Recording of Radio Traffic During an AirStrike, 3671220021, George J. Veith Collection, The Vietnam Center and Archive, Texas Tech University

96 Rolling Thunder Remembered: http://www.rollingthunderremembered.com/subject-rolling-thunder-remembered-24-march-1966/

97 Captured Documents (CDEC): Unknown Interrogation Source, Log Number 08-1360-67, 05/22/1967, CTZ 3, Bien Hoa Province, Long Thanh, DistrictF034601880216, Vietnam Archive Collection, The Vietnam Center and Archive, Texas Tech University

98 Staaveran,192

99 Rolling Thunder Remembered: http://www.rollingthunderremembered.com/subject-rolling-thunder-remembered-24-march-1966/

100 Staaveran, 203

101 Staaveran, 204

102 MACV Command History 1965, 205

103 CHECO Report, *Rolling Thunder July 1965–December 1966*, 20

104 Ibid, 21

BIBLIOGRAPHY

BOOKS

Aid, Matthew M., *The Secret Sentry*, Bloomsbury Press, 2009.

Allen, George W., *None So Blind*, Ivan R. Dee, 2001.

Andradé, Dale, *Trial by Fire: The 1972 Easter Offensive, America's Last Vietnam Battle*, Hippocrene Books, 1994.

Berman, Larry, *Lyndon Johnson's War*, W.W. Norton & Company, 1989.

Blight, James G., Lang, Janet M., Welch, David A., *Virtual JFK: Vietnam If Kennedy Had Lived*, Rowman & Littlefield Publishers, 2010.

Bourke, Joanna, *An Intimate History of Killing*, Granta Books, 1999.

Bouscaran, Anthony Trawick, *The Last of the Mandarins: Diem of Vietnam*, 1965.

Brinkley, Douglas and Nichter, Luke A., *The Nixon Tapes*, Houghton Mifflin Harcourt, 2014.

Cantigny Military History Series, *Blue Spaders, The 26th Infantry Regiment, 1917–1967*, 1996.

Carland, John M., *Stemming the Tide May 1965 to October 1966*, United States Army in Vietnam, Center of Military History, United States Army, Washington D.C., 2000.

Cosmas, Graham A., *MACV: The Joint Command in the Years of Escalation, 1962–1967*, Center of Military History, United States Army, 2006.

Cosmas, Graham A., *MACV: The Joint Command in the Years of Withdrawal 1968–73*, The United States Army in Vietnam, Center of Military History United States Army, 2007.

Currey, Cecil R., *Victory at Any Cost*, Potomac Books, Inc (formerly Brassey's, Inc), 1999.

Davidson, Phillip B., *Vietnam at War: the history 1946–1975*, Oxford University Press, 1988.

Dommen, Arthur J., *The Indochinese Experience of the French and the Americans: Nationalism and Communism in Cambodia, Laos and Vietnam*, Indiana University Press, 2001.

Dunn, Peter M., *The First Vietnam War*, Hurst, 1985.

Duong Van Nguyen, *The Tragedy of the Vietnam War: A South Vietnamese Officer's Analysis*, McFarland & Company, Inc., Publishers, 2008.

Farrar-Hockley, Anthony, Official History, The British Part in the Korean War, Volume 1, *A Distant Obligation*, HMSO, 1990.

Hackworth, David H., *About Face: The Odyssey of an American Warrior*, A Touchstone Book, Simon & Schuster, 1989.

Halbertsam, David, *The Best and the Brightest*, Random House Publishing Group, 1992.

Ham, Paul, *Vietnam: the Australian War*, Harper Collins, 2007.

Hammer, Ellen J., *A Death in November, America in Vietnam 1963*, E.P. Dutton, 1963.

Helms, Richard, *A Look Over My Shoulder: A Life in the Central Intelligence Agency*, Presidio Press, 2004.

Herring, George, *America's Longest War*, 1996 (4th Edition).

Hilsman, Roger, *To Move a Nation*, Doubleday, 1967.

Jones, Howard, *Death of a Generation: how the assassinations of Diem and JFK prolonged the Vietnam War*, New York, 2003.

Kimball, Jeffrey, *The Vietnam War Files: Uncovering the Secret History of Nixon-Era Strategy*, University Press of Kansas, 2004.

Kissinger, Henry, *The White House Years*, Weidenfeld and Nicolson and Michael Joseph, 1979.

Langguth, A.J., *Our Vietnam: the war, 1954–1975*, Simon & Schuster, 2000.

Le Gro, William E., *Vietnam from Cease-Fire to Capitulation*, University Press of the Pacific, 2006.

Marr, David G., *Vietnam 1945: The Quest for Power*, University of California Press, 1995.

Miller, Edward, *Misalliance, Ngo Dinh Diem, the United States, and the Fate of South Vietnam*, Harvard University Press, 2013.

Milne, David, *America's Rasputin: Walt Rostow and the Vietnam War*, Hill and Wang, 2008.

Moyar, Mark, *Triumph Forsaken: The Vietnam War 1954–1965*. New York: Cambridge University Press, 2006.

Neville, Peter, *Britain in Vietnam: prelude to disaster, 1945–1946*, Routledge, 2007.

Nixon, Richard, *No More Vietnams*, W.H. Allen, 1986.

Pike, Douglas, *Viet Cong*, Cambridge, MIT, 1966.

Plaster L. John, *The Secret Wars of America's Commandos in Vietnam*, Mass Market Paperback, 1998.

Powers, Robert, K., *1966 The Year of the Horse*, Dog Ear Publishing, 2009.

Prados, John, *The White House Tapes: Eavesdropping on the President*, The New Press, 2003.

Prados, John and Stubbe, Ray W., *Valley of Decision, The Siege of Khe Sanh*, Houghton Mifflin, 1991.

Safer, Morley, *Flashbacks: On Returning to Vietnam*, St Martin's Press/Random House, 1991.

Schlesinger, Arthur, M., *A Thousand Days: John F. Kennedy in the White House*, Boston, 1965.

Selverstone, Marc J., *Constructing the Monolith, The United States, Great Britain, and International Comunism, 1945–1950*, Harvard University Press, 2009.

Shelby, Stanton, A., *The Rise and Fall of an American Army: U.S. Ground Forces in Vietnam, 1963–1973*, Presidio Press, first published in 1985.

Shulishmon, Jack, Marine Corps Vietnam Operational Histories Series, Department of the Navy, *US Marines in Vietnam: An Expanding War 1966*, 1982.

Sorley, Lewis, *Westmoreland: The General who lost Vietnam*, Houghton Mifflin Court Publishing Company, 2011.

Spector, Ronald H., *Advice and Support, The Early Years, The U.S. Army in Vietnam*, Centre of Military History, United States Army, Washington D.C., 1983.

Staaveran, Jacob Van, Gradual Failure: *The Air War over North Vietnam: 1965–1966*, Air Force History and Museums program, 2002.

Thompson, Sir Robert, *Defeating Communist Insurgency: The Lessons of Malaya and Vietnam*, New York, 1966.

Van Nguyen Duong, Lieutenant General, *The Tragedy of the Vietnam War: A South Vietnamese Officer's Analysis*, McFarland, 2008.

Vien, Cao Van, General, *The Final Collapse*, Indochina Monographs, Center of Military History, United States Army, Washington D.C., 1985.

Vietnam Chronicles, The Abrams Tapes 1968–1972, Transcribed and edited by Lewis Sorley, Texas Tech University Press, 2004.

Westmoreland, William C., *A Soldier Reports*, Doubleday, 1st Edition, 1976.

Willbanks, James H. Lt Col, *Thiet Giap! The Battle of An Loc April 1972*, Combat Studies Institute, US Army Command and General Staff College, Fort Leavenworth, Kansas, September 1993.

Wyatt, Clarence, *Paper Soldiers: The American Press and the Vietnam War*, University of Chicago Press, 1995.

ARTICLES, STUDIES AND REPORTS

2/503 Vietnam Newsletter No. 29, November 2012.

Benjamin T. Harrison, Christopher L. Mosher, "John T. McNaughton and Vietnam: The Early Years as Assistant Secretary of Defense, 1964–1965," University of Louisville and Arlington, Virginia, 2007.

Berube, Claude G., *Ho, Giap and OSS Agent Henry Prunier*, originally published on HistoryNet.com.

Benson, Oliver, "Wallace J. Thies, When Governments Collide; Coercion and Diplomacy in the Vietnam War 1964–1968," University of California Press Berkeley and Los Angeles, 1980.

BDM Corporation analysis Book I, *Operational Analyses*, Department of the Army, US Army War College.

Birtle, Andrew J., PROVN, "Westmoreland, and the Historians: A Reappraisal," *The Journal of Military History* 72 (October 2008).

Boian, Major Kelly Owen Carl, *Major General Melvin Zais and Hamburger Hill*, School of Advanced Military Studies United States Army Command and General Staff College Fort Leavenworth, Kansas, 2014.

Brush, Peter, "The Story Behind the McNamara Line," first published in *Vietnam* magazine, February, 1996.

Buckingham, Major William A., Jr., Office of Air Force History, *Operation Ranch Hand: The Air Force and Herbicides in Southeast Asia, 1961–1971*.

Center for Cryptologic History, National Security Agency, United States Cryptologic History, Special Series No. 5, *Essential Matters A History of the Cryptographic Branch of the People's Army of Viet-Nam, 1945–1975*, Translated and Edited by David W. Gaddy, 1994.

Coan, James, P., "The Battle for Con Thien," May 8, 1999.

Correll, John T., "Lavelle," *Air Force Magazine*, Air Force Association, November 2006.

D'amato, Anthony A. et al, "War Crimes and Vietnam: The 'Nuremberg Defence' and the Military Service Register," *California Law Review* 1055 (1969) Code A69d.

Deer Mission, summary report, September 1945.

Deer Report No. 1, July 17, 1945.

Department of the Army Vietnam Studies, *Command and Control 1950–1968*, Major General George S. Eckhardt, 1991.

Department of the Army, Vietnam Studies, *The War in the Northern Provinces 1966–68*, Lieutenant General Willard Pearson, 1991.

Drea, Edward J., "Gulf of Tonkin Incident: Reappraisal 40 years Later," *MHQ*, Summer 2004 edition.

Dyhouse, Tim, "33 Days of Violent, Sustained Combat," 2/503 Vietnam Newsletter No. 47, November 2012.

Eschwege, Henry, "The Use of Agent Orange in Vietnam," Community and Economic Development Division, Report to Republican Ralph H. Metcalfe, August 15, 1978.

Ford, Ronnie E., *Tet 1968: Understanding the Surprise*, In Cass Series – studies in Intelligence, Ilford, Essex, England: F. Cass. 1995.

Franklin, John K., *The Hollow Pact: Pacific Security and the Southeast Asia Treaty Organization*, ProQuest, 2006.

Giebel, Christoph, *Imagined Ancestries of Vietnamese Communism: Ton Duc Thang and the Politics of History and Memory*, Critical Dialogues in Southeast Asian Studies, 2004.

Hammond, William M., *Public Affairs, The Military and the Media, 1968–1973*, The United States Army in Vietnam series, US Army Center of Military History, Government Printing Office, 1988.

Hanyok, Robert J. *Cryptologic Quarterly*, "Skunks, Bogies, Silent Hounds and the Flying Fish: The Gulf of Tonkin Mystery 2–4 August," approved for release by the NSA on November 3, 2005.

Harrison, Simon, "Skull Trophies of the Pacific War: transgressive objects of remembrance," *Journal of the Royal Anthropological Institute*, 2006.

Hickey, Gerald, "Village in Vietnam," Yale University Press, 1964.

Heinl, Colonel Robert D., Jr., *Armed Forces Journal*, "The Collapse of the Armed Forces," June 7 1971.

History and Museums Division, HQ USMC, Captain Francis J. West Jr. USMCR, *Small Unit Action in Vietnam Summer 1966*.

Howard, John D., Maj, "The War We Came to Fight: A Study of the Battle of An Loc – June 1972," a student research paper written for the Student Research Report, June 1974.

HQ PACAF, "Directorate Tactical Evaluation," CHECO Division, The Cambodian Campaign April 1–June 30 1970.

Janes, Thomas W., "Rational Man – Irrational Policy (A Political Biography of John McNaughton's Involvement in the Vietnam War)," essay, March 31, 1977.

Jakobsen, Mark, "Washington's Management of the Rolling Thunder Campaign," Naval Historical Centre, Command and Control of Air Operations in the Viet Nam War, Colloquium on Contemporary History January 23, 1991, No. 4.

Jenkins, Brian M., "The Unchangeable War," RM-6278-1-ARPA, September 1972.

Johnson, Leland L., "U.S. Business Interests in Cuba and the Rise of Castro," RAND, P-2923, 1964.

JPRS Report – "East Asia, Southeast Asia, The Decisive Years: Memoirs of Vietnamese Senior General Hoang Van Thai, 19980610 109," Reproduced by U.S. Department of Commerce National Technical Information Service.

Kelly, Gail P., "Coping with America. Refugees from Vietnam, Cambodia, and Laos in the 1970s and 1980s," *Annals of the American Academy of Political and Social Science* Vol. 487 (September 1986).

Le Thi Anh, "The New Vietnam," *National Review*, April 29, 1977.

MACV Command History 1965–73.

Nalty, Bernard C., *Operation Niagara, Air Power and the Siege of Khe Sanh*, Office of Air Force History, 1991.

Naval Historical Center, *Command and Control of Air Operations in the Vietnam War*, Colloquium on Contemporary History, January 23, 1991, No. 4.

Nguyen, Lien-Hang T. "The War Politburo: North Vietnam's Diplomatic and Political Road to the Tet Offensive". *Journal of Vietnamese Studies* 1 (2006), 34.

Nguyen Van Hien, Viet Cong media *Tin Nguyen*, The Retreat from the Central Highlands.

Pollard, Robert A., *Economic Security and the Origins of the Cold War, 1945*, Columbia University Press.

Prados, John, "Operation Masher: The Boundaries of Force," *VVA Veteran Magazine*, Feb/Mar 2002.

Prados, John, "One Hell of a Fight," 2/503 Vietnam Newsletter No. 47, November 2012.

Pribbenow, Merle L. II, "General Vo Nguyen Giap and the Mysterious Evolution of the Plan for the 1968 Tet Offensive," *Journal of Vietnamese Studies*, Volume 3, Summer 2008.

Publications du service historique de l'armée de terre consacrées a la guerre d'Indochine, *1945–1946 Le retour de la France en Indochine*, textes et documents.

Report of the Department of the Army Review of the Preliminary Investigations into the My Lai Incident.

Rogers, Lieutenant General Bernard William, *Cedar Falls-Junction City: A Turning Point*, Vietnam Studies series, Department of the Army, 1989.

Sagan, Ginetta and Denney, Stephen, "Re-education in Unliberated Vietnam: Loneliness, Suffering and Death," *The Indochina Newsletter*, October–November 1982.

Sak Sutsakhan, *The Khmer Republic at War and the Final Collapse*, Monograph Program, Department of the Army, Washington DC, 1978.

Schell, Jonathan, "The Village of Ben Suc," *The New Yorker*, July 15, 1967.

Scott, LTC B., "The Battle for Hill 875, Dak To, Vietnam 1967," USAWC Military Studies Program Paper, 2/503 Vietnam Newsletter No. 47, November 2012.

Seals, Bob, MilitaryHistoryOnline.com, *Chinese Support for North Vietnam during the Vietnam War: The Decisive Edge*, 2008.

Willbanks, James, H., *The Battle for Hue, 1968*.

Wedemeyer, Albert C., *Wedemeyer Reports!*, Henry Holt & Co., New York, 1958.

AFTER ACTION REPORTS (AAR)

A comprehensive collection of AAR can be found at The US Army in Vietnam, The Bud Harton Collection at the Texas Tech Virtual Vietnam Archive
http://www.recordsofwar.com/vietnam/army/
1st Cavalry 1965 (Battle of Ia Drang)

1st Infantry Division – Lessons Learned (May 1 to July 31) Part 1
1st Infantry Division – Lessons Learned (May 1 to July 31) Part 3
1 Marines After Action Report, March 20, 1968
1/3 Marines After Action Report, Operation Utah, March 11, 1966
173 AB Bde AAR Dec 1967
1st Battalion, 26th Infantry, CEDAR FALLS operation report, January 23, 1967
II Field Force Tet Offensive, Parts 1–3
4th Inf Div, Combat Operations After Action Report (RCS:MACV J3-32)
    January 28, 1967
Combat Operations After Action Report (RCS MACV J3/32), April 28, 1966
Moore After Action Report, December 9, 1965 (Battle of Ia Drang)
Operation Junction City 1 and 2, Combat Comments 2-67, prepared by G-3,
    1st Inf Div
Operations Lessons Learned, Report 2-66, AD 502772, March 31, 1966
Op Malheur, After Action Report, 1st Bde, 101st AB Div, October 3, 1967
Op Swift After Action Report, October 5, 1967

TELEVISION, NEWSPAPERS AND JOURNALS

Armed Forces Journal
Armour
Army Times
Baltimore Sun
Bill Moyers' Journal, Bill Moyers on LBJ's Path to War /PBS
CBS Evening News
CBS News, Special Reports
Foreign Affairs
Life
Newsweek
New Republic
New York Herald Tribune
New York Post
New York Times
Stars and Stripes
The Economist
The Nation
The New Yorker
The Old Reliable (9th Infantry Division newspaper)
The Plain Dealer
Time
Vietnam magazine
Washington Evening Star

INTERNET

1st MIBARS in Vietnam
Blue Spaders: 26th Infantry Regiment Association
British Pathé archives
Gerald R. Ford Library and Museum
National Security Archives, George Washington University, Vietnam Project
Nixon Library, National Archives
Pushing On blog spot (Vietnam recollections)
The Fog of War: Eleven Lessons from the Life of Robert S. McNamara
Talking Proud (US) military website
The American Presidency Project
The Black Vault (online US Government declassified documents archive)
The Vietnam Center and Archive, Texas Tech University
This Day in History
University of Texas Archives, LBJ Library, Oral History Interviews
Vietnam magazine online
WGBH Open Vault, Vietnam Files
Wilson Center, Digital Archives

INDEX